Sh & Tell 6

D0833510

Writers on Writing

SIXTH EDITION

Excerpts & insights
from the faculty of the
Department of Creative Writing
University of North Carolina Wilmington

Cover design: Corinne Manning
Book design: Corinne Manning, Tom Dunn, and Erin Sroka

ISBN: 978-0-9823382-0-9

LIBRARY OF CONGRESS CATALOGING-IN-PUBLICATION DATA

Show and Tell: Writers on Writing: excerpts and insights from the Faculty of the Department of Creative Writing, University of North Carolina, Wilmington. — 6th ed.
    p. cm.
Includes bibliographical references.
ISBN 978-0-9823382-0-9
1. American literature—North Carolina—Wilmington. 2. American literature—21st century. 3. Wilmington (N.C.)—Literary collections. 4. Authorship. 5. Creation (Literary, artistic, etc.) I. University of North Carolina, Wilmington. Dept. of Creative Writing. II. University of North Carolina, Wilmington. Publishing Laboratory.
PS559.W55S56 2009

810.8'006—dc22

2009020978

THE
PUBLISHING
LABORATORY
UNIVERSITY OF NORTH CAROLINA **WILMINGTON**

Department of Creative Writing
University of North Carolina Wilmington
601 S. College Road
Wilmington, NC 28403-5938
www.uncw.edu/writers

TABLE OF CONTENTS

CREATIVE NONFICTION SELECTIONS

POETRY CRAFT

POETRY SELECTIONS

AS IF BY MAGIC: TOOLS & TIPS

PUBLISHER'S NOTE

SHOW & TELL FEATURES two types of writing: published creative works and essays on how to create them. The book is divided into fiction, creative nonfiction, and poetry sections, each of which presents three essays addressing a distinct element of craft in that genre. The essays reflect how their authors approach matters such as character development, setting, research, and the music of poetry in their own work. New to this edition is the appendix, "As If by Magic: Tools & Tips," including essays on grammar, revision, and the art of editing. At the behest of teachers and readers, we've also added a glossary of essential terms.

In preparing the sixth edition, we have sought to diversify and expand the model creative selections by welcoming ten new contributors: Emma Bolden, Nina de Gramont, Ben George, Eli Hastings, Sebastian Matthews, Jason Mott, George Singleton, Sharan Strange, Daniel Nathan Terry, and Peter Trachtenberg. Many of our longtime contributors have graciously granted us reprint rights to recent, award-winning work. If you're using this book in the creative writing program at the University of North Carolina Wilmington, you will enjoy the rare opportunity to ask questions of each author.

Show & Tell has come a long way since its first impression, published in 2001 under the visionary guidance of Stanley Colbert. Wrapped in a simple two-color cover, that first edition gathered the work of eleven faculty members. Now featuring more than thirty contributors, *Show & Tell* reflects a thriving creative community, collecting side by side the work of faculty, visiting writers, and alumni. A team of student editors shepherded the sixth edition into what constitutes virtually a new book. For their vital role, the Department of Creative Writing and The Publishing Laboratory are indebted to Tom Dunn, Erin Sroka, and Jennifer Weathers.

In another important regard this edition much improves upon its predecessors. Convenient tabs along the book's fore edge quickly denote the fiction, creative nonfiction, and poetry sections, and each section opens with a full list of its contents. For a design as functional as it is good-looking, we are especially grateful to Publishing Laboratory graduate assistant Corinne Manning.

Editions two through five benefitted from the editorial insights and contributions of many, including former Publishing Laboratory director Barbara Brannon. Her efforts set a high standard that we have sought to emulate in this edition. Special thanks also go to department chair Philip Gerard, who at every step championed this revision. Lavonne Adams, Wendy Brenner, Mark Cox, Sarah Messer, Robert Anthony Siegel, and Michael White, all veteran instructors of UNCW's introductory creative writing course, offered invaluable advice and helped us solicit and answer the growing needs of our department's apprentice teachers. Also, we owe thanks to the students who participated in the proofreading of the fourth, fifth, and sixth editions: Ranjan Adiga, James Dempsey, Alison Harney, Kiki Vera Johnson, Judi Kolenda, Kerry Molessa, Bryan Sandala, Mallory Tarses, and Kate Walsh.

Finally, we express our heartfelt thanks to the writers included in these pages. Many wrote original craft essays specifically for this edition, and all contributed without remuneration as an act of dedication to their craft and solidarity with this community of writers. We have benefitted greatly from their wisdom and generosity and trust that a new generation of writers will too.

On behalf of The Publishing Laboratory
Emily Louise Smith
Summer 2009

ROBERT ANTHONY SIEGEL

ART IN A WORLD
OF ENTERTAINMENT

YOU SIGNED UP FOR A CREATIVE WRITING CLASS thinking that you'd read some cool stuff and finally write that alien abduction story you've been telling your friends about. But then the professor assigns all these long, boring things that don't seem to have a story in them, and he spends the class talking about "character" and "emotion." You sense that a story about aliens may not go over all that well with this dude, but you don't want to write about feelings just to please him. Feelings suck; you deal with them all day—they're what you want to *stop* thinking about.

What are you going to do?

The problem is bigger than your writing teacher. Though you didn't know it when you signed up, creative writing class is ground zero for a fundamental division in our culture, the split between art and entertainment. Because this split is now central to your semester—not to mention your future as a consumer of cultural products—we need to stop for a moment and consider it. The "art" story, what we call *literature*, is meant to illuminate life as we actually experience it. For that reason, it tends to focus on the human experience, emphasizing character and emotion. In contrast, the "entertainment" story is designed to help us forget about our problems—to take us on vacation. The entertainment story serves as a thrilling or scary escape, rather than revealing an honest or true reflection of life. It therefore tends to focus on situation and plot and deemphasizes the messy and confusing aspects of experience. That your creative writing teacher keeps encouraging you toward art and away from entertainment doesn't imply a value judgment. Nobody is saying that art is good and entertainment is bad. The two are simply different; they fulfill different needs, and there should be room for both.

Our culture is drowning in entertainment—TV, film, video games, the Internet—but has very little room left for art. It's easy to get to college without having had much exposure to art as a living, breathing thing, rather than as a relic to be dissected (reluctantly) in high school English class. Nobody tells us that stories, poems, and essays can be deep and more compelling—not till we get to a creative writing class. Literature can offer us a vacation from our lives, of course, but something in it returns us to human experience. We recognize our own flaws, failures, and desires on the page. Wait, you say, let's stick with vacation. Isn't distraction better than sorrow? Who wants to sit around thinking about serious stuff and feeling depressed?

Well, imagine you have some kind of job that you hate. Maybe it's flipping burgers at McDonald's, or maybe it's working checkout at Costco. But for now, let's assume it's mucking out sewers. When a sewer gets clogged and threatens to burst and send truly awful, unmentionable stuff washing over the streets, they zip you into some coveralls and lower you down the manhole, and then, when your feet hit bottom, they hand you a stick to break up the clog.

Now imagine one particularly difficult afternoon down in the sewers. The clog is half a mile from the nearest manhole, so you have to wade through the—I'll call it sludge. And while you do that, following the narrow beam of light from the lamp on your helmet, you find yourself obsessively running over the fight you had with your parents the night before. You called your father a loser and your mother a moron, and through their tears they vowed to stop paying for college. How did it start? How did it get so bad? And why does it keep happening every time you go over there to do your laundry?

You can't figure out the answer, not even after unclogging the clog and climbing out of the manhole to stand beneath an impossibly early, blue-black evening sky. You feel the wind cut through your coveralls, and you realize what people have been realizing for thousands of years: that in a universe vast enough to contain stars, and planets, and suburban streets like this one, without a single person outside, or a light in any of the houses—that in such a universe, you are nothing more than an infinitesimally tiny, unimportant creature.

So you do the sensible thing: you go to the movies. You don't even bother to take off your sludge-stained overalls, you just drive straight to the mall and buy your ticket and the tub of popcorn with a super-sized cola the size of a propane canister, and you sit in the soothingly impersonal dark, mainlining salt and sugar and watching *Doomsday 15: Killing Is for Everyone.*

And you know what? Watching *D15* is pretty awesome. The screen is about two-stories high, and the sound system vibrates the seat. The giant robots fly, topple buildings, crush cars, and hurl the freeway overpass like a football. For the space of two hours, you remember nothing of that terrible moment beneath the evening sky, of your hatred for sewers, or of your sorrow and hopelessness when it comes to your family. For two hours, you are nothing but a pair of eyeballs and a pounding heart.

The problem comes later, back at your apartment. By the time you get into bed, *D15* is gone; the icy silence has returned. You can't relax, can't sleep, so you do the only sensible thing: you get up and turn on the TV.

No, wait. Imagine instead that you grab the book you're supposed to read for your creative writing class and take in the first line: "As Gregor Samsa awoke one morning from uneasy dreams he found himself transformed into a gigantic insect."

It's a little obvious, perhaps, but intriguing enough to get you going. You push through the long sentences that follow, the scenes charting minute shifts in feeling—the strange, shameful feeling you might expect in a family where the son and primary breadwinner is now a bug.

You stop at the point where Gregor's mother glimpses him in his new form and backs away in horror, yelling, "Help, for God's sake, help!" But a minute later you're reading again, when you reach the place where Gregor's father smashes him with an apple and almost kills him. Suddenly, you realize that you haven't been avoiding the story because it's boring—it's not boring. It reminds you of your family, and of yourself.

And what you realize, as dawn breaks outside your window, is that you don't find that depressing, because living through feelings is a lot better than suppressing them, just as asking questions feels a lot better than avoiding them, even if you never come up with a single answer. Art doesn't solve our problems—good art usually resists neat or easy solutions—but it reminds us of who we are and what we feel and enables us to live with those emotions, to live more richly and fully than if we spend our time ignoring them. Art encourages us to look at our lives and selves in the present moment, which turns out to be the only true place to be. ◉

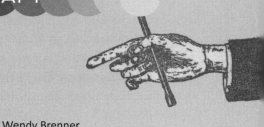

FICTION CRAFT

WENDY BRENNER

ON CHOOSING
A SUBJECT

I WOULD AMEND THE OLD DIRECTIVE to "write about what you know" to: "Write about what you only half-remember," or "Write about the subject which—for some reason that's a mystery to all your friends, who are sick of hearing about it—obsesses you." In my view, the most important rule for student fiction writers is to not know the whole story before you try to write it. You should write fiction not only to show and tell what you know, what you've seen and experienced (and if you've lived seventeen years on earth, my creative writing professor in college used to say, you've already seen enough to provide you with material for a lifetime of fiction writing), but to discover what you don't know, what you long to know, about those subjects—people, places, events, images—which most intrigue and excite and trouble you.

These subjects need not involve complete plots (not when you start writing them, anyway) or even large ideas; they should probably not be ideas at all, but rather, tangible things: a sad old house you stayed in one summer as a child, an odd conversation you overheard in a doctor's waiting room, a girl you knew for years but never really understood, an inexplicable billboard you passed on a road trip. If you want to write about a concept (e.g., good versus evil, symbolized by two rival racecar drivers, eventually the good driver wins), you should probably consider writing an essay or philosophical treatise rather than a story. Fiction is not meant to moralize, to teach lessons, but to give the reader an experience which cannot be gotten in any other way, or easily paraphrased, summed up. A good story or novel leaves you with new questions about the mystery of life, our lives, what it is to be human—not with easy answers. The tangible, sensory details are necessary to the story because they are the story.

Most writers use some form of journal to collect and keep track of these details, possible subjects and material for their fiction. A writer's journal is often more of a scrapbook than a diary; rather than recording everything important that happens to you, in a writer's journal you are interested in saving items you suspect you can use in your fiction (or poetry), though you don't necessarily have the slightest idea how. For example, you might clip police blotter stories from the local newspaper that you find especially compelling, or national or international news shorts that make you ask, "What kind of person would . . . ?" A sampling from my journal: Woman Jailed for Feeding Pigeons (she put out a hundred loaves of bread in her yard each week), Boys Hold Up Drugstore for Valentines (an eight-year-old and a ten-year-old, who planned to give the valentines to their classmates), Cannonball Smashes into Side of House (no one saw it happen, and the cannonball was of the type used in World War II). The great thing about these stories is that, like good fiction, they inevitably raise many more questions than they answer about the human experience.

You might then use one of them as a starting place for a story you write by assuming the point of view of one of the people involved, or a character you invent yourself who has some relation to the story, such as a neighbor or family member. However, it is very important if you try this exercise to resist the urge to solve why the story happened. You don't want to explain everything away, sum it all up, because then there is no story. Rather, your job as a fiction writer is to spend some time with a person who has nothing and everything in common with the rest of us, take us somewhere we might otherwise never go.

Other items for your journal might include lines of overheard dialogue and descriptions of particularly vivid people, objects, and locations you observe in your day-to-day life, in your travels, or on television. I especially like talk shows and the local news for people speaking candidly and un-coached about subjects of importance to them, and I like locally produced commercials for their often Zen-like absurdity and artlessness. You might also use your journal as a place to keep track of ideas for plots, conflicts, and characters, and memories from your childhood that you hadn't thought about for years until you started taking creative writing classes.

I like the following exercise for generating subject material because it not only helps you access sensory experiences from your childhood but also helps you create or rekindle a sense of longing and inner conflict, something that's present in all successful fiction. Recall a toy or object you always wanted but never got, something you coveted for weeks or months or just momentarily. Perhaps a friend of yours had one, or perhaps you only saw the item on TV, or in a catalog. Perhaps it was something around the house. One student in my class wrote about his mother's flour sifter, which was kept on a high shelf away from him after he'd gotten his hands on it once when he was three and put dirt, soap, cookies, and water through it. He remembered and was devoted to the powerful, weapon-like feel of it in his hand, the sound it made— *schwit, schwit*. Write a page of fiction describing your toy or object in full sensory detail, focusing as much as possible on the object. (Don't worry about characterizing yourself or anyone in your family.) Make your readers see the toy or object as you did at the time. What did it look like, remind you of, feel like, smell like, sound like? What would you do with it if you got it? Avoid summarizing from the point of view of an adult looking back from a distance: "Boy, was I a greedy kid." Instead, immerse yourself in the past, so your concrete description comes from that place of purest, most intense desire. This exercise can be developed into a scene or a complete story in itself. (As an example of a story that could have come from such an exercise, you might check out Andrew Alexander's "Little Bitty Pretty One" in Algonquin's *New Stories From the South*, 1999.)

Finally, you will discover when you present your work in creative writing workshop that the material you thought the least about or consider boringly personal is often the stuff your classmates find most original and exciting; do not fail to trust that your own predilections, aversions, and loves will shine through on the page, illuminating and transforming what you fear is mundane. Poet Adrienne Rich says that "students learn to write by discovering the variety and validity of their own experience." ❧

REBECCA LEE

HOW TO TALK A CHARACTER INTO YOUR STORY

A FRIEND OF MINE ONCE HAD A DATE with a guy named Ross (this is true), and prior to going out to dinner, she showed him around her apartment. Right before they left, he asked to use her bathroom. "Yes, of course," she said, gesturing, and then a few minutes later he emerged, with her makeup on his face. Some blush, a little eyeliner, glossy lipstick. It wasn't particularly garish, and he wasn't smiling as if it were a joke. It was just tastefully applied. And off they went.

I mention this only to make this distinction—this is not necessarily an especially good thing for a date to do, but it is an excellent move for a character in a short story. Which leads me to suspect that maybe all good stories resemble, in some ways, bad dates; that is, both are concerned with the rifts that open suddenly and subtly between people as they try to communicate, both involve people usually carefully scrutinizing faces and situations for small but crucial clues, both teeter precariously always on the edge of disaster, comic or otherwise. Most significantly, and this is the point I really want to make, both involve surprise, psychological surprise, a surprise that springs out of the complicated, unpredictable nature of human emotion. My feeling is that the surprise of a story, the moment when it turns and reveals a different face than predicted, should be internally motivated, not externally. For instance, if a boulder suddenly falls on a character, that's not so interesting dramatically, but if a character suddenly turns to another and realizes the other is actually plotting against him, even as she's declaring her love, then that's a dramatic moment. Again—bad date, good story.

One of the real pleasures of writing (and thank god there are a few, since it is so difficult) is that a character, if you give it time, will always be larger, or wiser, or stranger, or more eccentric than you could ever dream at the outset of the story. The best thing you can do for your characters is release them slowly and carefully from your initial idea of who they are and let the deep and fertile powers of your concentration and imagination produce changing, and therefore living, characters. Graham Greene wrote, "The moment comes when a character does or says something you hadn't thought about. At that moment he's alive and you leave it to him."

How does the writer allow for this? This is the great mystery, but I believe it involves patience and intensity, simultaneously. I think that writing often feels less like construction, less like you are building characters, and more like you are finding them, waiting on them, taking care of them, being nice to them, giving them a home in your imagination for long enough that eventually they tell you who they are. "Be very patient," Katherine Mansfield wrote, "until she steps slowly into the light."

Once I asked Bob Reiss what to do when a character you are trying to write into a story continues to elude you, and he gave me this simple but extremely useful piece of advice, which was to ask the characters what they desire, and also what they are afraid of. A character's desire leads them to action, and their fear throws up boundaries, and suggests limits. And it is this tension that runs quietly under every story. It seems that to know a character's desire is the starting point of any story—it sets the machinery spinning. Somebody wants something, and from that flows plot as they set about to get it, failing or succeeding along the way. It's impossible to find a story that doesn't embrace this idea in some way. I suspect that if the writer spends a few days dreaming on paper about what the character truly wants from the world—love or money or another person or a second chance or forgiveness or to set foot on their native land—then this desire will ripen and spill over into action, and there will follow the whole beautiful skein of consequence and decision and heartbreak that we call fiction.

A footnote: My friend didn't date that guy Ross again, but they became friends, not fast friends really, but long-distance, dinner-once-every-few-months-friends, and years later, she found herself visiting with him around his tiny, kinda dingy kitchen table in his apartment in the East Village. He'd had a brief career as a comic, and had been in a few commercials, and then abruptly had fallen on some hard times; now he was unemployed, kind of alcoholic, generally a little depressed. But this night, he was in a nostalgic mood. "Remember that time," he said to her, "when we put on makeup together?"

"No," she said. "I don't remember it quite that way." But she smiled. It was a nice moment, the strung lights of the Village twinkling into the small dark room, and she saw suddenly how he had seen that occasion long ago, as if it had been really sweet and companionable, a lovely memory. He had surprised her again, and cast a somewhat different light on the past, made her think twice, which is sometimes what stories can do. ❧

PHILIP GERARD

STORY, SETTING, *and* SCENE

ONE DEFINITION of a *story* is simple: a character we care about acts out of desire or fear to achieve a goal and either wins, loses, or draws. Somebody or something tries to interfere with the fulfillment of that desire. It may be another character, a force of nature or technology, or the inherent flaws of the main character himself. This is all we mean by *conflict*. Until the character acts on a desire or a fear, nothing much is happening. Characters who sit around and think aren't very interesting to watch. And if the character gets what she wants too easily, there's not much of a story.

And what a character wants may not be obvious at first. It may not be what she thinks she wants. Or he may turn out to want something else after all, and reach this understanding through the events of the story.

For its movement, a story, like a film, relies on a kind of *persistence of vision*. In film, the term simply means that in between frames of light are frames of darkness, so that a conventional film is built on an optical illusion of continuity. In a story, the writer presents a relatively small number of complete scenes—stepping stones of action—connected by narration and exposition, creating the illusion that every minute of the characters' lives is accounted for, that the reader is getting the whole story. In fact we are seeing only selected moments in the characters' lives: the parts when something interesting happens. The rest—most of what happens in their lives, which we aren't interested in—is summarized or implied.

Stories are built on *scenes*: completed dramatic actions that further the plot, the themes, and the emotions of the story, moving it forward. A scene is a mini-drama set in a specific location and time and lasting for a specified duration.

For example, a couple boards a Ferris wheel car. What she has desired since the story opened is certainty about their future together. What she has feared is that she may lose him and be left alone. He is aware that they are fast approaching that point in a relationship when they must commit themselves to the next, deeper level of involvement, or part ways. This tension makes him cross, though he doesn't mean to be. He says something offhand but thoughtless, and they begin to quarrel.

The scene will probably last only as long as the ride, a few minutes. It begins when they step into the car and ends the moment when they step out again. What happens in between is the scene. What happens will consist of talk (dialogue) and action. Like most couples, they will probably not speak directly about the thing that they're really quarreling about. This *indirection* will make their dialogue oblique and dramatically interesting, giving the reader the pleasure of interpretation, or reading between the lines. And the unspoken tension will crackle through their dialogue.

For example, they argue about money (she thinks he's cheap), but what they are really arguing about is his unwillingness to share bigger things with her: his deeper feelings, the future. She thinks he is about to enlist in the Army and has kept it a secret from her, and the idea terrifies her.

What she wants: intimacy, reassurance, security.

What he wants: purpose, the end of grief and guilt.

As you can see, the location of the scene provides not just *setting* but a stage for action. That is, just as in a play, there's a dramatic reason the scene happens where it does. Confined in the little rocking car of the Ferris wheel, they cannot escape each other. If the scene happened on a different stage—in a coffee shop, say—one or the other could simply walk out at any point, robbing the quarrel of the intensity of no escape. If the setting is not crucial to the scene, find a setting that is. It's often useful to play against expectations. That is, set the scene in a place no one would ordinarily expect it to happen, one that adds inherent interest and even comments on the action.

Each character carries into the scene his or her *backstory*, the life events that have formed them. He lost an older brother, whom he idolized, in Iraq. He is in fact thinking of enlisting but is also afraid—afraid to do it, and afraid to tell her. She never finished college and feels insecure about her future. She grew up as a Quaker and doesn't believe in the war. And so on.

Underlying the visible setting (time and place) are the circumstances of the scene. The argument between the couple on the Ferris wheel will be heightened by the rocking of the car, the stomach-lifting motion of the wheel. A good setting provides props for the characters, vivid reminders of where they are. Maybe one of them is prone to motion sickness or afraid of heights. Since fear is part of the issue between them, this resonates with the larger themes of the scene and story. Maybe they get stuck at the top and the precariousness of their romance is mirrored by the car swaying in the wind. The action may be subtle: he presses into the corner of the car, she attempts to touch him, they kiss awkwardly. Maybe the wind blows off his cap and it startles them. As he watches the cap fall to the ground far below, we glimpse an intimation of death. The emotion of a scene escalates as the scene plays. More and more is at stake.

The characters define themselves by what they say and do, by how they react to each other. Often the movement of a scene includes a significant change in the relationships between characters. A scene usually culminates in a moment of truth when some issue is decided, ending this particular mini-drama and setting up the next one. Each decision causes a new, more interesting conflict.

For the scene to matter—and it must matter, or else be cut from the final draft—it must advance the story. Usually this means that at the end of a scene we know the character better than before, either because the action has revealed new information about him, or because we have now seen the character act in stressful circumstances and understand her better. Or, in a good scene, both. The conflict is simply the thing that causes the stress, the unfinished business between them that must be settled, or at least addressed, in the story.

Thus, by revealing character, the scene moves the plot along: every action causes a consequence requiring new action, which causes further consequences in a firecracker chain of causality that accumulates more and more meaning.

In our little amusement park scene, the setting itself can provide part of the stress. It traps the two characters together for a little while. It swings high above the earth—thrilling but also a little frightening. The action has been quiet and intimate: he shrinks from her touch, they kiss awkwardly, his hat flutters to the ground far below.

Yet, if the writer has written the scene with vivid clarity and a deft hand, we now know them both better, and we also watch the consequences unreel: She steps off the Ferris wheel. He turned away from her touch and now she knows in her heart that she must move on with her life without him. When he goes to war, she will not wait for him. What will she do next?

Perhaps in the next scene we will be inside the drugstore with him as he pays cash for a one-way bus ticket to report for induction into the Army. She will walk by outside, a white shopping bag on her arm, and see him through the window. The distance between them will have grown. A silver convertible will pull up at the curb and she will get in. Or maybe all that would be a cliché of a scene and tell us no more than we already surmise. You write the next scene.

Several scenes building upon one another—a *suite* of scenes—have a collective impact greater than any individual scene. As the scenes progress, emotion runs higher, the stakes are raised, and the decisive moment is more and more important.

At last we reach the decisive moment of the story itself, the scene that resolves the main conflict of the story.

Or maybe there is no next scene after the Ferris wheel ride. She loves him but must leave him, and he knows this. Maybe this, after all, is the main conflict of the whole story, which is always likely to be, in the words of William Faulkner, "the human heart in conflict with itself." ❧

CLYDE EDGERTON

HOW EFFICIENT IS YOUR WHEELBARROW?:
Carrying Story through Voice

ELEMENTS OF VOICE

If you were asked to pick your mother's voice from several other voices you could probably do it. Likewise, identifying a page of writing from a favorite author among pages from other authors would probably be an easy task. Some teachers suggest that as a writer you should try to remove yourself from your writing. Well, no. Don't do that. Do try to remove distractions from your writing, but don't try to remove the "you," because you can't. My favorite writers: Hemingway, Crane, Twain, Faulkner, Welty, O'Connor, McCarthy, Brown, Nordan are—on the printed page—usually immediately identifiable to me. Their storytelling voices are as different as their faces. It's supposed to be that way. The teller cannot be separated from the tale (see *The Teller In the Tale* by Louis Rubin).

The writer's voice carries the story's plot (what happens), and voice and plot get all mixed together when we feel the effect of a story. The plot helps create the impact of the story, its final effect and meaning.

And the voice—the wheelbarrow that carries that plot—also makes a difference in the story's impact.

So if we assume for a moment that we can separate voice and plot (we can't, of course), we may ask: what are several elements of voice (the wheelbarrow) that determine the voice's efficiency in carrying a certain plot? There are many elements of writerly voice and these elements may vary between writers—but also among stories of a specific writer.

In the process of discussing elements of voice below, I am in a sense asking: "What—regardless of plot—makes one story different from another story?"

You must make choices about how to create voice in a particular story. Those choices include 1) point of view, 2) use of time, 3) scene and exposition interplay, 4) atmosphere and setting, and 5) tone.

At the end of this essay I will propose a process to help you think through these elements during revision. It's called the revision checklist method. But first, here are some elements of voice.

POINT OF VIEW
A single point of view is usually, but not always, maintained throughout a story.

First Person: Reliable (or Unreliable) (or in-between)
This point of view allows the reader to see the story through the eyes of a single narrator, "I."

> *I wanted to watch television last night, but instead I drove to the store and bought groceries.*

The character who narrates the story may present personal insights, feelings, or emotions but can only speculate about the inner life of others. A reader cannot know for certain what another character is feeling unless that character truthfully describes aloud his or her feelings. A reliable narrator is one that can be trusted by the reader. Unreliable narrators give accounts that may be unusually partial, ill-informed, or otherwise misleading. One joy of reading unreliable narrators comes from the irony in the difference between what they say and what is probably true.

Second Person

This point of view usually stems from a first person reliable narrator addressing the reader, "you."

You arrive and there on the couch is your enemy, Clarence.

Third Person Scenic

In third-person scenic point of view, we have no entry to anyone's thoughts or feelings beyond what they say or do.

Bob walked into the room. "Hello," he said.
"Hi," said Mary. "Where have you been?"

This point of view can be powerful precisely because it invites the reader to supply the inner emotion of the characters. (Read "Hills Like White Elephants" by Ernest Hemingway. If the story doesn't make sense, read it again, very carefully.)

Third Person Limited

Third person pronouns (he, she) are used as the main point of reference.

She sat in a chair by the window and looked at her neighbor's house.
She wondered where her brother might be.

The reader is limited to the inner thoughts or feelings of one specific character and is unable to directly access the inner workings of other characters. This point of view can be similar to first person—a significant difference is the use of "he" or "she" rather than "I."

Third Person Comprehensive

This point of view allows the reader to be inside the heads of two or more characters. This point of view is like third person limited but it applies to more than one character.

Mary felt lonely as she ate the ice cream.
Bob, sitting beside her, was thinking about Sally.
Sally walked in. "Hi, Mary," she said. Sally decided not to speak
to Bob.

Omniscient

Omniscient is similar to third person comprehensive, with this addition: the narrator reveals facts or sentiments from the present, future, or past that no character in the story can know.

There are many ways of classifying point of view. The whole business of POV can become complicated, and you may find classifications that are more helpful than others. For example, multiple first person points of view, not listed above, come through the eyes of one character only—for one novel chapter, for example—and then through the eyes of another character in the next chapter (see *As I Lay Dying* by William Faulkner). This perspective is more likely found in a novel than in a short story.

As you write, you will begin to come up with your own classifications of point of view. Study your favorite writers to see how they use point of view. Keep in mind that a point of view usually remains consistent within the framework of a story or novel.

TIME

The plot of a story can follow at least one of three basic time directions (or may use a combination).

Linear

The events of a linear story progress in chronological order. This type of plot is usually the simplest and most straightforward of the three.

Non-linear Story

Events are not in the sequence of chronological time. An example is *Slaughterhouse-Five* by Kurt Vonnegut.

Linear with flashbacks

Flashbacks break away from the main story and cut to scenes of significant, spelled-out memories of the past.

Flashbacks may enrich a linear story by adding layers to the plot. But be careful: a flashback can also break up an important and vibrant scene, thus frustrating the reader. The information contained in a flashback may be brought into the story not through a flashback but instead through dialogue, or memory, or the writer may find during revision that a flashback can simply be deleted. Effective flashbacks are often short and dove-tailed into what comes just before and just after them. (See *My People's Waltz* by Dale Ray Phillips.)

SCENIC/EXPOSITORY SHIFTING

A scene presents a story event in what appears to be real time. Usually two or more characters are talking to each other and the reader "sees" things happening. What the reader sees seems to happen in about the same time it takes to read it. The following would be a very short scene or part of a longer scene:

> Bill bent over the injured dog. He looked up at Sue. "What happened?" he said.

The following would not be a scene:

> Bill had lived in many cold places over the years. Often he became lonesome and depressed in winter. One evening he drove the six-hour drive from Cashborough to Dills Hollow.

Action and dialogue are the lifeblood of scenes, whereas exposition depends on the author telling in some detail—or perhaps summarizing—an event or action or phenomenon.

Here's a simple trick that may be helpful in categorizing scenic and expository writing: count the lines in the story which are in scenes and the lines which are not. If there are more lines in scenes, then consider the story scenic, otherwise it is expository. This is a rough guide and may not be useful for all stories.

ATMOSPHERE AND SETTING: REAL/UNREAL

Atmosphere differs from tone. Atmosphere is a quality normally provided by the psychological and/or physical setting of the story whereas tone is more of an attitude expressed by the author. Atmosphere is "inside" the story; tone originates "outside" the story—in the author. The atmosphere may be spooky, while the tone is dry and journalistic.

Real atmosphere is grounded in ordinary, everyday life. The unreal pushes our imagination to accept things that cannot be real in everyday life. For example, the setting (a park bench) may be real but if a character in the story sits there for thirty years then the atmosphere (the passage of time, for example) is not. Thus we may consider the story unreal. Conversely, the atmosphere may be logical but the setting is on another planet, thus the story is considered, again, unreal. If either atmosphere or setting is unreal then we declare the atmosphere unreal. In some stories ambiguity may prevail. Juxtaposing real and unreal elements is a characteristic of a kind of fiction writing called magical-realism.

TONE

A light tone may be created by a humorous approach—even to a serious subject. For example, a children's story may approach the serious subjects of friendship and loyalty lightly.

A heavy tone is often related to somber meanings.

The key here is in how the story's theme, or meaning, seems to be seen or felt by the author (as opposed to the narrator). Friendship and loyalty in the imagined story above may be treated with a light tone by the author even while the first person narrator is quite serious.

In order to understand tone, we must consider more than just the basic plot of the story. We must understand the intentions of the author.

Possible story tones besides heavy and light include the following: cold, warm, sensual, surreal, sarcastic, dry, dreary, intimate, ironic, satirical, sardonic, angry, sad, gothic, morbid, grotesque, demonic, silly, or combinations of these.

Remember that tone refers not to action, scene, character, plot, or subject matter, but to the apparent attitude of the author—to your attitude toward the story you are writing.

THE REVISION CHECKLIST METHOD

We've looked at elements of voice, the wheelbarrow. Now let's consider the content of the wheelbarrow—your story's plot, and importantly, its intended meaning (what it's about).

In using our checklist we relate the elements we have discussed to the meaning of the story you are revising—that is, relate form to meaning—in ways that help you understand how the story is working. This understanding can lead to a better story in its next revision.

Often the first draft of a story simply comes to you—complete with its own elements—and you don't have to think about point of view options, or time options, etc.

But by the start of the second draft, you've probably asked yourself an important and central question: what is this story about?

Let's think about the meaning of a story on three levels, each more specific than the one before it. For example, you've written a story about loss. More specifically, about the feelings of loss experienced by a young girl. And more specifically than that, about how Mary, given the death of her goldfish, feels lonely and deserted when she comes to believe that her mother does not understand her feelings.

At this point in the revision process let's say your story is

1) in first person, from Mary's point of view (POINT OF VIEW)
2) chronological (TIME)
3) expository (SCENIC/EXPOSITORY)
4) real (ATMOSPHERE AND SETTING)
5) and heavy (TONE).

You go to the checklist and you examine different points of view up against what your story is about. Would third person scenic give a better view of the mother's perspective than your present draft does?

As to "time": do you need one flashback to the time the father purchased the goldfish for Mary?

And could you use more scenes to get at the meaning of your story? (After all, meaning in fiction often lies in scene.)

What if your atmosphere changed in the middle of the story and Mary imagines herself swimming with her goldfish in a magic pond?

What about tone? What if you, the author, treated the whole story as light and insignificant while allowing the reader to glimpse Mary's sense of profound loss? Perhaps in that way the intended meaning of your story could be felt most strongly by a reader.

Go through the checklist more than once during revision, asking yourself about potential shifts in voice.

CONCLUSION

I've discussed several ways that stories—regardless of what they are about—are different in voice. Understanding these different elements of voice and systematically using a checklist can help you revise effectively, making the voice of the story a better match for what the story is about, thus giving your creative effort more heft and authority. ✎

FICTION SELECTIONS

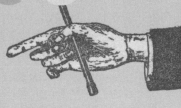

CLYDE EDGERTON

SEND ME TO THE ELECTRIC CHAIR

TWO OTHER EVENTS happened that same summer Mrs. Toomey killed her son Paul's kitty, Inky, with a baseball bat to put him out of his misery. One of the other two big events started a few weeks later, when Mrs. Toomey was putting on lipstick, getting ready to take Paul up to see the electric chair for the first time. She thought about Terry Daniels. Terry was about Paul's age—six. She would take him along too. The Danielses lived two houses down, and Mrs. Daniels had started going to church some. They were poorer than the Toomeys, but Mrs. Toomey told herself that shouldn't make a difference.

When Mrs. Toomey and Paul stopped by to get Terry, Terry's mother squinted through the door screen like she might be afraid, but as Mrs. Toomey explained the purpose of the trip, Mrs. Daniels considered the dress Mrs. Toomey was wearing, a white dress with big blue flowers. And Mrs. Toomey's hair had nice waves in it, and little Paul was so neat, his hair pushed back in front with what, water? or maybe some of that gel that pushed up a crew cut in front. As Mrs. Toomey talked, Mrs. Daniels began to take it in, to understand, that what Mrs. Toomey was about to do was exactly right for Terry at that time in his life. She said, "Terry, go get on some pants and shoes."

"We'll just wait out here in the swing," said Mrs. Toomey.

In the swing, Paul held his mother's hand. His legs didn't reach the porch floor. He looked over at the gas station across the road. There was a man drinking a beer, turning up a dark bottle with a long swelled neck. He knew to take his eyes away. If he kept looking, his mother might ask him what he was looking at. Inside the Danielses' house—through the window screen near his elbow—he saw the foot of a bed, a rumpled sheet. He'd never seen an unmade bed in the daytime. It made the room seem wild.

Inside, Mrs. Daniels, following Terry into the room, said, "Where's 'at other sock?"

"I 'on' know."

"Didn't you have it on yesterday?"

"No."

"Do you want me to whip you?"

"No."

"You say no ma'am."

"No ma'am."

"You say no ma'am to Mrs. Toomey, you hear?"

"Yes ma'am."

"She's taking you to see the electric chair, and if you don't behave, when you grow up that's where you'll end up. Just like she said."

Mrs. Toomey let Paul and Terry sit in the back seat together. That way they could kind of talk and she could kind of hear what they talked about.

"Did you know Mr. Riggs has a electric paddle?" Terry asked Paul.

Mrs. Toomey said, "Honey, I don't think that's true about a electric paddle. I think somebody made that up."

"That's what Leland said. Said he had one in his office."

"Well, I know, but I don't believe that's true. That's a rumor."

Paul rolled a little red metal car up and down his leg.

"Can I play with that?" asked Terry.

Mrs. Toomey stretched her neck, looked in the rearview mirror. The strong, acrid odor from the fertilizer factory came in through the open windows.

"Paul. Let Terry play with the car." Paul handed the car to Terry and said, "I got about five more."

"I got a wood one that's bigger."

They drove past the Dairy DeeLight, where Mrs. Odum, the Toomeys' next-door neighbor, worked part time. Mrs. Toomey decided they might stop by on the way back from the prison for a little reward if Paul and Terry behaved. She wasn't above getting a little reward for herself, either. "Now, the reason we're doing this," she said, "is so you-all can see what will happen if you ever let the devil lead you into a bad sin. If you commit a bad crime they'll put you in the electric chair and electrocute you. And little crimes can lead up to big crimes."

"Leland said it burns your tongue out," said Terry. "He said he knew a man went to the electric chair."

"I don't know about that," said Mrs. Toomey. "I think somebody made that up."

They drove past red clay roadbanks, past green pastures with cows, wood outbuildings, fishing ponds, some pastures holding a line or two of thick, dark cedar trees.

When they parked, Mrs. Toomey said, "See how big the building is? That's because there's so many prisoners."

Along the walkway, Paul reached for his mother's hand.

"See up there?" said Mrs. Toomey. "If they try to escape, that guard will shoot them. That's a shotgun he's got."

The guard at the gate said, "Yes ma'am. What can I do for you? Hey boys."

"I called ahead to see about showing these boys the electric chair."

"Oh, yeah. We got a note about that." He opened one gate, then another. "There's a door buzzer at that second door over there. Just push it and they'll let you in." As the boys walked by, the guard said, "How old are you boys?"

"Seven," said Terry.

"Six," said Paul.

"This one's mine," said Mrs. Toomey.

A man in a gray guard outfit let them in the building.

"What'd she say?" the guard on the tower asked the gate guard.

"Show them boys the electric chair." He shook a Lucky Strike up out of a pack, lit it with a flip-top lighter that had a rising sun on the side. "They won't but six and se'em year old."

"I wish I'd brought Buck up here once a year or so from the time he was six or seven. Maybe he'd a stayed in school and made something out of hisself."

"You can't ever tell. When did he drop out?"

"Eleventh . . . tenth. Somewhere in there."

Inside, a guard led Mrs. Toomey and the boys through a jail door, several other doors, and finally to a small room with a large metal door. The door had an eye-level window about the size of a saltine cracker box.

"You boys come over here and I'll show you the switch first. My name's Floyd. Here it is. There's the white, which is off. The green means ready. And the red is zap. You see, the executioner can't see the prisoner. Here, let me get you boys a stool. Mrs. Toomey, you can look through that little window there, if you want to, to see it."

Mrs. Toomey looked. Paul went next. He saw a chair made of dark shiny wood, not as big as he thought it would be, on a low platform. Straps hung to the chair arms and legs, and a light-colored canvas bag hung from the top of the chair back.

"What's that bag?"

"That's what you put over his head so you don't see his face when the charge hits him. That's something you don't want to see."

"Let me see," said Terry.

"Let's let Terry see," said Mrs. Toomey. She placed her hands under her son's arms, lifted him and set him on the floor. Terry stepped up.

"Where's the paddle?" said Terry. "The electric paddle."

"Oh, they just got them at school," said Floyd. He looked at Mrs. Toomey and winked. "Now, this chair though. Our bad people up here use this chair twiced—first time and last time." He winked at Mrs. Toomey again.

"I don't think you can teach them too soon," said Mrs. Toomey.

Mrs. Odum stood waiting behind the small open serving window at the Dairy DeeLight. It seemed to Paul as if her large, sad, moon-shaped face with the dark eye circles filled up the entire little window. "Hi y'all," Mrs. Odum said, very slowly. Her whole body seemed sloped downward somehow—lines out from her eyes, her mouth, her shoulders, all sloped downward.

"Just fine, Mrs. Odum, how you doing today?" Mrs. Toomey placed her purse on the counter.

"Oh, I'm doing all right, I reckon."

"We want to order three banana splits. These boys have been real good today."

Mrs. Odum pulled three bananas from a bunch in a fruit bowl and turned to begin her work. She picked up her lit Pall Mall from a Miami, Florida, ashtray and took a deep draw. The cigarette tip was orange, then gray. She moved slowly, as if she were underwater. "Where y'all been?"

"We been up to see the electric chair."

"Oh?"

"I don't think you can start teaching them too young."

"About . . . electricity?"

"Right and wrong. About right and wrong."

"Oh yes. Well, one thing is for sure—you just can't beat the electric chair for putting a mean man to death."

"I guess that's right."

The boys seated themselves at a table. Terry watched Paul roll his car up his arm. Mrs. Toomey stood at the order window, waiting, talking to Mrs. Odum.

Mrs. Odum smoked and worked, and in a few minutes she placed three banana splits on the counter at the window.

"Oh, my," said Mrs. Toomey.

At the table, Paul asked his mother, "What do prisoners get to eat?" A glob of whipped cream stuck to his lower lip. Mrs. Toomey wiped it off with her napkin.

"They eat bread and water. Maybe a few vegetables."

The last big event that summer started when Paul stood holding a grocery sack of loaf bread and a quart of milk, watching Terry Daniels and Leland Pendergrass dig for fishing worms out behind Mr. Pendergrass's auto shop. Leland dug up a hunk of black dirt and Terry shook it apart for worms.

Paul understood something, he wasn't sure what, about the difference between Terry and Leland. Leland was mean and Terry was mostly scared. Terry was back in there somewhere. When you looked at him or when he talked, it seemed like the real him was back in there somewhere, usually not saying what he was thinking. Leland, on the other hand, was always outside himself, doing something bad, saying exactly what he wanted to say, doing something to a dog or cat or somebody littler than him.

The hoe blade was sharpened until it shined—sharp as a razor. Leland hoed up a clump of black dirt, Terry picked it up and shook it, checked it for worms. Paul was just standing there watching. Leland and Terry were working well together—hoe up dirt, can the worm, hoe up dirt, no worm, hoe up dirt, no worm, hoe up dirt, can the worm, hoe up dirt—when half a worm dropped out of a clump of dirt and landed wriggling. Paul saw it and Terry must have seen it because he reached for it. Leland didn't see. The hoe commenced its powerful arc downward, razor edge glinting in the sun, the blade cutting down so fast it made a swish sound, a sound like a burning rag through the air, and the angle of strike was a full ninety degrees at the meeting place of the hoe blade and the thumb—just on the outside of the thumb's big joint. Terry drew his hand back as if he'd touched fire, as if he could get the hand back to his breast quickly enough to undo the violence, as if he could save it—as he drew it back he realized something was horribly wrong. He stopped his hand in midair and the thumb swung back and forth, dangling, and Paul's refusing-to-believe eyes saw hanging there, not a severed thumb, but instead a greatly enlarged worm, bunched into a little sausage, running blood all over itself. A bloodworm. And the news that Terry's thumb was cut off came to the boys in a terrible silent two seconds—thousand one, thousand two.

Terry's scream, threaded with hysteria, got the attention of all people within hearing distance. He started running toward his house, toward his mama and daddy. It was a Saturday, the day his daddy would be home drinking because it was by God the end of the week and he deserved a little relaxation and relief from his business of bringing in money to support a wife and daughter and a boy who got on his nerves awful because he couldn't learn things as quick as—my God Almighty, what the hell was that God-awful screaming about? Gotdamn.

Paul and Leland, walking, followed Terry. Paul looked at the hoe propped on Leland's shoulder, like a soldier carries a rifle. Leland stopped, held out the hoe and looked at it himself, dropped it. "I got to go to the bathroom," he said.

Terry, holding his thumb to his shirt, had disappeared around the back corner of the auto shop.

Paul wondered if maybe he had to go to the bathroom, too. But the lure of the chopped thumb drew him toward the Danielses' house, and as he rounded the corner he saw Mr. Daniels walk unsteadily to meet Terry, ask him something, and before Terry could answer, hit him with his open hand on the butt hard enough to propel Terry forward toward the house. Terry had placed the thumb back and was holding it there, thinking it would maybe stick back and hold, that the blood would work like the glue in school, and dry, and in so doing fasten the thumb back the way it had been—with nothing to show but a thin red line.

Inside the house, Mr. Daniels hollered something, and Mrs. Daniels screamed.

Paul thought of Terry's presence, his being, the way he was—always far back inside himself, looking out as if he were afraid. And in a sweat, in a heat that suddenly covered his head and ears, Paul wanted somebody to rescue Terry, somebody to go in there and get him out and take him to the hospital. He would run tell his mother.

A man over at the service station called out, "What happened, son?"

"Terry cut his thumb just about off. It's just hanging by a little piece of skin."

And with that, two men sitting on the bench over there stood. Paul felt compelled to stand there and watch as the first man crossed the road, walked up the steps, and knocked on the Danielses' door.

Cheryl, Terry's sister, rode up on her bicycle, leaned it against the steps, and walked into the house, past the man waiting on the porch.

Paul stood there in the narrow front yard of the Danielses' house, the porch pretty high up off the ground, as Mr. Reddings, the man who owned the service station, drove his black '39 Ford sedan into that little yard, and the two or three men from the gas station bench now stood by the porch to get a better look at the thumb as the Daniels family came down the steps. Terry had stopped crying, and his right hand was wrapped in a pillowcase, bloodied. He looked a little pale.

Around the side of the house came the entire Pendergrass family— Leland and his mama and daddy. Mrs. Pendergrass had gotten the word and sort of put two and two together and figured she needed to do the right thing by getting on over there with Leland. She'd asked her husband to come along in case Mr. Daniels was drunk.

Mr. Daniels held Terry's elbow as they came down the high front-porch steps. When Mr. Daniels saw Leland he stopped, still holding to Terry. "What happened, Leland?" he said. He stared at Leland with hard eyes.

"I didn't do nothing," said Leland. He pointed—pointed past every-body—at Paul. "Paul done it," he said.

Heads turned. The service-station man nearest Paul stepped back a step to give the world room enough to look on him, and then the atten-tion of all the people swung back to Terry, standing with his free hand holding the bloody pillowcase wrapped around his other hand.

Paul felt something collapsing, imploding in his chest like those old buildings that blow up from the inside, collapsing into themselves. He knew, in spite of his scant experience in the world, what was coming.

Terry raised both hands, one holding the other, and pointed his index finger. "Paul done it," he said.

The electric chair floated up into Paul's view, the shiny wood, the straps, the white, green, and red paint beneath the switch.

He turned, ran home, and in the kitchen told his mother what had happened, all of it, as fast as he could, crying, trying to get his breath. She led him to the front door, knelt down, put her hands on his shoul-ders, and told him that there were times in life when you had to do the right thing. He had to go back down there by himself and tell those people the truth. All those people. Jesus would go with him. She stood and pushed him on out the door.

In the yard he slowed down, stopped, looked back. Mrs. Toomey walked out to him, knelt down again, placed her hands on his shoulders. "You got to do the right thing," she said. "You can't let people lie and you not do nothing. Jesus will be with you. And God, too. Now, go on like I told you."

Paul felt as if he were walking toward a firestorm. When he passed the hedgerow and saw the Danielses' porch and yard empty except for Cheryl sitting on the steps, he decided with lifted spirits to go on down and tell Cheryl the truth.

As they sat on the steps together, Cheryl listened, nodding her head, agreeing, understanding, believing him. Then they talked about her bicycle, about the difference between a girl's bike and a boy's bike, and then for a while she talked about the atomic bomb, about all the people it killed, and how America had called Japan on the telephone before they dropped it, so they could get all the little children out of town. ●

AFTER WORDS

In the mid-nineties, I started remembering images from my life before I was six years old. A couple included my mother taking me to see the electric chair, and a neighbor friend almost losing his thumb. Once I'd generated a list of images I started writing a novel about a boy and a small rural community. As I wrote, I realized the two above mentioned images might form the backbone of a short story. Guilt, fear, and religion made up a sizable part of my early "life of the mind," so I used those elements as well as the two images—electric chair and thumb—and made up the rest. I tried to make the two big remembered events serve the relationships between people that are established in the story, rather than having those events be the focus of the story.

WENDY BRENNER

I AM THE BEAR

I SAID: OH, FOR GOD'S SAKE, I'm not some pervert—you think I'm like that hockey puck in New Jersey, the mascot who got arrested for grabbing girls' breasts with his big leather mitt at home games? I'm a polar bear! I molest no one, I give out ice cream cones in the freezer aisle, I make six dollars an hour, I majored in Humanities, I'm a girl.

I was talking to the Winn-Dixie manager in his office. Like every grocery-store manager, he had a pudgy face, small mustache, and worried expression, and he was trying very hard, in his red vest and string tie, to appear open-minded. He had just showed me the model's letter of complaint, which sat, now, between us, on his desk. *The polar bear gave me a funny feeling,* the model had written; *I was under the mistaken impression that the bear was male but much to my surprise it turned out that I was wrong. The bear was silent the whole time and never bothered to correct me.*

It was part of my *job* not to talk, I explained to the manager. I read to him from my Xeroxed rules sheet: *Animal representatives must not speak in a human manner but should maintain animal behavior and gestures at all times while in costume. Neither encourage nor dispel assumptions made regarding gender.* I said, See? I was holding my heavy white head like a motorcycle helmet in the folds of my lap, my own head sticking out of the bureau-sized shoulders, my bangs stuck to my forehead, a small, cross-shaped imprint on the tip of my nose from the painted wire screen nostril of the bear. I can't help my large stature, I said. That's why they made me a bear and not one of those squirrels who gives away cereal. I was doing exactly what I was supposed to do. I was doing what I was *designed* to do.

She would like an apology, the manager said.

You say one becomes evil when one leaves the herd; I say that depends entirely on what the herd is doing, I told him.

Look, the manager said, his eyes shifting. Would you be willing to apologize, yes or no. He reminded me of a guy I knew in high school— there was one in every high school—who made his own chain mail. They were both pale and rigidly hunch-shouldered even as young men, as though they had constantly to guard the small territory they had been allotted in life.

Did you notice how in the letter she keeps referring to me as "the bear"? I said. No wonder she didn't know I was a girl, she doesn't even know I'm *human*! And incidentally, I added, when the manager said nothing, you would think she'd be more understanding of the requirements of my position—we are, after all, both performers.

The manager seemed offended that I would compare myself, a sweating, hulking bear, to a clean, famously fresh-faced girl, our local celebrity, and I was let go. This wasn't dinner theater, he said, and at headquarters, where he sent me, I was told I could continue to be a polar bear but not solo or in a contact setting. This meant I could work corporate shows, which in our area occurred never. I saw myself telling my story on *People's Court*, on *Hard Copy*, but I was a big, unphotogenic girl and I knew people would not feel sympathy for me. Plus, in the few years since college I had been fired from every job I'd had, for actual transgressions—rifling aimlessly through a boss's desk drawers when she was out of the office, sweeping piles of hair into the space behind a refrigerator in the back room of a salon, stopping in my school bus, after dropping off the last of the children, for a cold Mr. Pibb at Suwannee Swifty—and I believed absolutely in retribution, the accrual of cosmic debt, the granting and revoking of amnesty. I was, simply, no longer innocent. I was not innocent even as I protested my innocence.

No, I hadn't molested the girl, but even as I sat in the manager's office I could still smell the clean spice of her perfume, feel the light weight of her hands on either side of my head, a steady, intoxicating pressure even through plaster and fake fur. I could not fully believe myself, sitting there, to be an outraged, overeducated young woman in a bear suit. Beneath the heavy costume, I was the beast the manager suspected me of being, I was the bear.

The girl had been shopping with her mother, a bell-shaped generic older woman in a long lavender raincoat. The moment they rolled their cart around the corner into my aisle, still forty feet away, the model screamed. She was only eighteen, but still I was surprised—I would have thought Florida natives would be accustomed to seeing large animals in everyday life. She screamed: Oh my god, he's so cute! She ran for me, and I made some ambiguous bear gesture of acknowledgement and surprise. Hey there, sweetie, she said, pursing her lips and talking up into my face as though I were her pet kitten. I scooped a cone of chocolate chip for her but she didn't even notice. Mom, look, she yelled.

The lavender-coated mother approached without hurry or grace. Her face, up close, was like the Buddha's, and she took the ice cream from my paw automatically, as though we had an understanding. The model was rubbing my bicep with both her narrow tanned hands. He's so soft, she said. I faced her, making large simpering movements, and noticed the small dark shapes of her nipples, visible through her white lacy bodysuit. I blushed, then remembered I needn't blush, and that was when she reached for me, pulling my hot, oversized head down to her perfect, heart-shaped face. The kiss lasted only a moment, but in that moment I could feel how much she loved me, feel it surging through my large and powerful limbs. I am the bear, I thought. And then it was over, and I remembered to make the silly gestures of a human in a bear suit pretending to be embarrassed. The model's mother had produced a small, expensive-looking camera from some hidden pocket of her raincoat and matter-of-factly snapped a photo of me, a bear pretending to be a friendly human, with my arm around the model's skinny shoulders, my paw entangled in her silky, stick-straight golden hair.

They left then, the mother never speaking a word, and they were all the way down the aisle, almost to the other end, when the produce manager stuck his head around the corner right in front of them and yelled my name, I had a phone call. The model looked back once before they disappeared, and though she never saw my face—I wasn't allowed to take off my head in public—it was obvious from her expression that she understood. It was an expression of disturbed concern, the way she might look if she were trying to remember someone's name or the words to a song she once knew well, but there was something else, too, a kind of abashed sadness that looked out of place on her young, milky face.

I could imagine how she must have felt, having once fallen in love with an animal myself in the same swift, irrevocable way I imagined she had. The Good-Night Horse, he'd been called—that heading had appeared beside his picture on the wallpaper in our cottage's bathroom at the Sleepy Hollow resort, and the words stayed in my head for years, like a prayer. The wallpaper featured reprints of antique circus posters and flyers, the same six or seven over and over, but the good-night horse was the only one I paid attention to: he was a powerful black shape that seemed to move and change form like a pile of iron shavings under a magnet, quivering slightly. He was muscular, a stallion. I was six. "Katie is masturbating," my mother said, in her weary, matter-of-fact voice.

I would lie on the floor on my side under the toilet-paper dispenser, my face a few inches from the wall. The good-night horse was shown in a series of four different postures. In the first two pictures he was wearing boots and trousers on his hind legs, but in the wild third picture, my favorite, he was tearing the trousers off dramatically. Clothes were flung on the ground all around him, his tail swished in the air, and the trousers waved wildly from his mouth. In the last picture he was, with his teeth, pulling back the covers of a single bed with a headboard, like my bed at home. "The World's Greatest Triumph of Animal Training," the poster said.

There was no problem with my masturbating, because my parents were intellectuals; they had given me a booklet called "A Doctor Talks to Five- to Eight-Year-Olds" that included, as an example of the male genitalia, a photograph of Michelangelo's statue of David. The photo was small and black-and-white, so you couldn't really get a good look at what was between his legs, but it appeared lumpy and strange, like mashed potatoes, and I found it unsettling. The book had already given me a clear picture of sexual intercourse: it was a complicated, vaguely medical procedure in which you were hooked up to an adult man and microscopic transactions then occurred. And though my parents had said, "You're probably too young to picture it, but someday you'll understand," I *could* picture it—I saw an aerial view of me, naked, and the statue of David lying side by side on a white-sheeted operating table, me in braids and of course only half his height. But this vision was the furthest thing from my mind when I looked at the good-night horse.

I wasn't stupid, I knew people didn't marry horses, or any other animal. I just wasn't convinced that the good-night horse was necessarily an animal—the more I looked at his picture, the more he seemed to be a man in some important sense. It was not his clothes, or the tricks he did, but something both more mysterious and more obvious than that. He reminded me a little of Batman—and, like Batman, he might have a way of getting out of certain things, I thought. He was sensitive, certainly—his forelock hung boyishly, appealingly, over his eyes, and his ears stood up straight, pointing forward in a receptive manner (except in the trouser-flinging picture, where they lay flat back against his head)—but you could tell that he was in no way vulnerable, at least not to the schemes and assaults of ordinary men. He was actually more a man than ordinary men, and something began to swell in my chest unbearably after a few days, weighing me down so that I could not possibly get up off the floor, and my father finally had to carry me, sobbing, from the bathroom—I was sobbing not only because the good-night horse and I could never meet, but because I understood with terrible certainty, terrible finality, that I would never be happy with anything else, anything less.

And it was true that no man had yet lived up. I had been engaged once to a social theorist who was my age but refused to own a TV and said things like "perused" in regular conversation and expected to be liberated by what he called my "joyous nature," but it ended when I discovered while he was writing his thesis that he had not gotten around to

treating his three cats for tapeworm and had been living with them—
the cats and the worms—contentedly for weeks. And now, at twenty-
eight, I only dated, each man seeming a degree more aberrant than the
last. The last had been a stockbroker who was hyperactive (rare in adults,
he said) and deaf in one ear—he yelled and slurred and spit when he
talked and shot grackles with an AK-47 from his apartment window
but was wildly energetic even late at night, boyish and exuberant and
dangerous all at once, a little like the horse. On our second and last date,
however, he took me to an Irish pub to meet his old college roommate,
and the roommate engaged me in an exchange of stomach-punching
to show off how tightly he could clench his abs, only when it was his
turn to punch mine he grabbed my breasts instead, causing the stockbroker to go crazy. He dragged the roommate out onto the sidewalk and
pushed him around like a piece of furniture he could not find the right
place for, and I kept yelling that it was only a joke, I didn't mind, but in
the scuffle the stockbroker's visor—the kind with the flashing colored
lights going across the forehead band—got torn off and flung into the
gutter, its battery ripped out, and when the fight was over he sat on the
curb trying in vain to get it to light up again and saying, "He broke my
fucking visor, man," until I told him I was taking a cab home, at which
point he spit, on purpose, in my face.

So I could understand how the model might feel. I could see how,
from looking at me, the miserable, small-minded Winn-Dixie manager
would believe I had no business comparing myself to her, but, not being
a bear himself, he did not understand that appearances meant nothing.
I was a beast, yes, but I also had something like X-ray vision; I was able,
as a bear, to see through beauty and ugliness to the true, desperate and
disillusioned hearts of all men.

It was not difficult to figure out where she lived. She had been profiled
earlier that month on *Entertainment Tonight* along with her sister, who
at twelve was also a model, and the two girls were shown rollerblading
around their cul-de-sac, and I knew all the cul-de-sacs in town from
having driven the bus. So, a few days after I was fired, I drove to her
house. To be a bear was to be impulsive.

It had been a record-hot, record-dry July, and the joke topic of the radio call-in show I listened to as I drove was "What have we done to antagonize God?" Callers were citing recent sad and farcical events from around the world in excited, tentative voices, as though the DJ might really give them the answer, or as though they might win something. Only a few callers took the question personally, confessing small acts of betrayal and deception, but the DJ cut these people off. "Well, heh heh, we all do the best we can," he said, fading their voices out so it would not sound as though he were hanging up on them mid-sentence. Asshole, I thought, and I made a mental note to stop at the radio station sometime and do something about him.

The model's house was made of a special, straw-colored kind of brick, rare in the South, or so *ET* had said. As I drove up, I saw the model's mother step out onto the front steps, holding a canister of Love My Carpet, but when she saw my car she stepped quickly back inside. The model's sister answered the door. She was a double of the model, only reduced in size by a third and missing the model's poignance. Her face was beautiful but entirely devoid of expression or history; her small smooth features did not look capable of being shaped by loss or longing, not even the honest longing of children. This would be an asset for a model, I imagined, and I could see where the mother's Buddha-nature had been translated, in her younger daughter, into perfection: desire had not just been eliminated, but seemed never to have existed in the first place.

"I am a fan," I said, and, perhaps because I was a girl, showered and combed and smiling, I was let in. I had also brought, as props, a couple of magazines which I held in front of me like a shield, but I was not nervous at all. I understood that I had nothing to lose, that none of us, in fact, had as much to lose as we believed. I sensed other bears out there, too—my fierce brothers, stalking through woods and villages, puddles and parking lots, sometimes upright and sometimes on all fours, looking straight ahead and feeling the world pass beneath their heavy, sensitive paws.

The model's sister led me past ascending carpeted stairs and a wall of framed photos to the back of the house, where the model's bright bedroom overlooked a patio crowded by palmetto and bougainvillea, visible through sliding glass doors. A tiny motion sensor stuck to the wall above the glass blinked its red light as I entered. The model was bent over her single bed, taking small towels of all colors and patterns from a laundry basket, folding them, and placing them in piles. "Fan," the little sister said, and the model straightened and smiled and came forward, her perfume surrounding me and sending a surge of bear power through me, a boiling sheet of red up before my eyes. For just a moment as we shook hands I was sure she would know, would remember the feel of my paw. But then she stepped back, and my face cooled back down.

"I'm a huge fan," I said.

"Well, thanks, that's so sweet," she said. She had taken the magazines from me automatically, just as her mother had taken the ice cream at the store, and was already scribbling across the shiny likeness of her face. "Should I make it out to anyone?" she said.

"My boyfriend," I said, and I told her the stockbroker's name.

"You're so lucky you're so tall," she said, handing the magazines back. "That's my biggest liability, I can't do runway. Well, thanks for coming by."

I looked around at the white dressers, the mirrored vanity, not ready to leave, and was shocked by a short row of stuffed bears set up on a shelf on the wall behind me. They were just regular brown teddy bears with ribbon bows at their necks, no pandas or polar bears, but they stared back at me with identical shocked expressions, another motion sensor glowing on the wall over their heads, unblinking. "Nice bears," I said. I had to force myself to turn away from them.

"Oh, I've had those forever," she said. "See that one in the middle, that looks so sad? I found him in the street when I was six years old! Doesn't he look sad?"

"Yeah, he really does," I said. The bear was smaller and more lumpish than the other bears, with black felt crescents glued on for eyebrows.

"I used to make them take turns sleeping in my bed with me," the model said. "But even if it wasn't his turn I let him, just 'cause he looked so sad. Isn't that funny? I used to kiss him thirty-two times, every night, right after I said my prayers."

"Thirty-two," I said.

"My lucky number," she said brightly.

"But you don't kiss him anymore," I said.

She stared at me, frowning. "No," she said. She stared at me some more and I stood, my arms hanging, as a bear would stand, waiting. "Well, I better get back to work," she said.

"On your towels," I said.

She put her hands on her hips and gazed helplessly at the towels, as though they had betrayed her. "They're dish towels, isn't that queer?" she said. "I got them from a chain letter. My cousin started it, and I was second on the list, so I got like seventy-two of them sent from, like, everywhere. Isn't that pathetic—she's, like, twenty-two, and that's her hobby. You can have one, you want one?"

"Seriously?" I said.

"God, take your pick," she said. "I guess I have to remind myself sometimes that not everyone's as lucky as me, but, like, dishtowels, I'm sorry."

I had to brush past her to get to the bed, the snap on the hip pocket of my jeans rubbing her arm. I took the top towel from the nearest stack, a simple white terrycloth one with an applique of a pair of orange and yellow squash. "Thanks, I'll think of you every time I use it," I said. I held the towel, stroking it. It was not enough, I was thinking.

"Well, thanks for coming by," she said. She had moved to the doorway and stood looking at me in the same way she had looked at the towels. The row of bears watched from over her shoulder, the slumped, sad one seeming braced by its brethren. I imagined the model and her soulless sister laughing at me after I'd gone, at my terrible size, my obvious lie about a boyfriend.

"I really have to get back to what I was doing . . ." she said.

"I'm sorry, I was just so nervous about finally meeting you," I said, and I could see her relax slightly. "I almost forgot to ask, isn't that funny? I hate to ask, but do you by any chance give out photos?"

"No, you'd have to contact the fan club for that," she said. Her face was final, and I turned, finally, to go. "But actually, wait," she said. "I do have something, if you want it."

What happened next was certainly not believable in the real world, but in the just, super-real world of the bear it only confirmed what I had known. She slid an envelope out from beneath the blotter on her white desk, picked through it with her slim graceful fingers, and pulled out a photograph which she passed to me hurriedly, as though it were contaminated. "Here, isn't that cute?" she said.

There we were, her and me, her small, radiant face beside my large, furry, inscrutable one, my paw visible, squeezing her small shoulders together slightly, the flash reflected in the freezer cases behind us, making a white halo around both of our heads. Something seemed to pop, then, noiselessly, as though the flash had just gone off around us again in the bedroom. Like a witch or spirit who could be destroyed by having her photo taken, I felt I was no longer the bear. "He's so cute," I murmured.

She snorted, but it had no heart to it, it sounded like she was imitating someone. Then, for a moment she no longer saw me; she just stood there looking at nothing, her dark blue eyes narrowed, the faintest suggestion of creases visible around her mouth.

I had to take a step back, such was the power of her face at that moment. Then she too became herself again, and we were just two sad girls standing there, one of them beautiful and one of them something else. "Well, goodbye," I said, and she looked relieved that I was leaving—but also, I thought, that it was only me deserting her and not, as before, the heartbreaking, duplicitous bear.

On the way out I encountered her mother, who had materialized again beside the front door. It was the simple gravity, the solid, matter-of-fact weight of the woman, I decided, that made her silent appearances and disappearances so disconcerting, so breathtaking—wasn't it more impressive to see a magician produce from the depths of his bag a large, floppy rabbit, to see the ungraceful weight of the animal dragged up into the light, than to watch him release doves or canaries, already creatures of the air, flashy but in their element? "Goodbye," I said. "Sorry."

She smiled and did not step but rather shifted several inches so that I could get past her, and then stood in the open doorway, round and lavender, smiling and watching my retreat. Only when I was halfway down the walk to my car did she say goodbye, and then her voice was so deep and strange and serene that I was not sure if I had really heard it, or, if I had, if it had really come from her.

I did use the towel and sometimes thought of the model when I used it. The photo I didn't frame or hide or treat with any ceremony, but I did look at it often, trying to experience again that moment of transformation, that rush of power that had gone through me in the seconds before it was snapped.

But after a few months even the memory of it became weak. I was after all no longer the bear and could no longer remember well what it felt like to be the bear. The animal in the picture appeared only to be a big, awkwardly constructed sham, nothing you could call human. When I looked at it I felt only confusion and shame. How had I become that shaggy, oversized, hollow thing? Once I had been an honest little girl, a girl who had to be dragged away from the object of her love, but somehow, somewhere, everything had changed. How had it happened, I wondered. I studied the photo as though the bear could answer me, but it only stared back with its black fiberglass eyes, its grip on the real human beside it relentless. ❧

AFTER WORDS

This story is 100 percent fictional; I have never worked as a polar bear or any other kind of mascot. I got the idea from watching a famous supermodel interview a man in a polar bear suit on TV, promoting the 1992 Winter Olympics. I noticed that the model was treating the bear as if he were a real bear (a friendly, cute bear). She even kissed him on the nose. I started wondering about the man inside the bear suit, how he must feel. I find it somewhat embarrassing to read this story aloud, because the first-person narrator says and does things I personally would not say or do. However, I hope this creates tension in the story; the reader is unsure how far this narrator will go, what she will do next.

GEORGE SINGLETON

SHOW-AND-TELL

I WASN'T OLD ENOUGH to know that my father couldn't have obtained a long-lost letter from the famed lovers Héloïse and Peter Abelard, and since European history wasn't part of my third-grade curriculum, I really felt no remorse at the time for bringing the handwritten document—on lined and hole-punched Blue Horse filler paper—announcing its value, and reading it to the class on Friday show-and-tell. My classmates—who would all later grow up to be idiots, in my opinion, since they feared anything outside of South Carolina in general and my hometown of Forty-Five in particular, thus making them settle down exactly where they got trained, thus shrinking the gene pool even more—brought the usual: starfishes and conch shells bought in Myrtle Beach gift shops, though claimed to have been found personally during summer vacation; Indian-head pennies given as birthday gifts by grandfathers; the occasional pet gerbil, corn snake, or tropical fish. My father instructed me how to read the letter, what words to stress, when to pause. I, of course, protested directly after the first dry run. Some of the words and phrases reached beyond my vocabulary. The general tone of the letter, I knew, would only get me playground-taunted by boys and

45

girls alike. My father told me to pipe down and read louder. He told me to use my hands better and got out a metronome.

I didn't know that my father—"a widower" is what he instructed me to call him, although everyone knew how Mom ran off to Nashville and hadn't died—had once dated Ms. Suber, my teacher. My parents' pasts never came up in conversation, even after my mother ended up tending bar at a place called the Merchant's Lunch on Lower Broad more often than she sang on various honky-tonk stages, waiting for representation by a man who would call her the next Patsy Cline. No, the prom night and homecoming of my father's senior year in high school with Ms. Suber never leaked out in our talks, whether we ate supper in front of the television screaming at Walter Cronkite or played pinball down at the Sunken Gardens Lounge.

I got up in front of the class. I knew that a personal, caring, loving, benevolent God didn't exist, seeing as I had prayed that my classmates would spill over their allotted time, et cetera, et cetera, and then we'd go to recess, lunch, and then sit through one of the mandatory filmstrips each South Carolina elementary-school student watched weekly on topics as tragic and diverse as Friendship, Fire Safety, Personal Hygiene, and Bee Stings. "I have a famous letter written from one famous person to another famous person," I said.

Ms. Suber held her mouth in a tiny O. Nowadays I realize that she was a beauty, but at the time she was just another very old woman in front of an elementary-school class, her corkboard filled with exclamation marks. She wasn't but thirty-five, really. Ms. Suber motioned for me to edge closer to the music stand she normally used on Recorder Day. "And what are these famous people's names, Mendal?"

Ricky Hutton, who'd already shown off a ship in a bottle that he didn't make but said he did, yelled out, "My father has a letter from President Johnson's wife thanking him for picking up litter."

"My grandma sent me a birthday card with a two-dollar bill inside," said Libby Belcher, the dumbest girl in the class, who later went on to get a doctorate in education and then became superintendent of the school district.

I stood there with my folded document. Ms. Suber said, "Go on."

"I forget who wrote this letter. I mean, they were French people."

"Might it be Napoleon and Josephine?" Ms. Suber wore a smirk that I would see often in my life, from women who immediately recognized any untruth I chose to tell.

I said, "My father told me, but I forget. It's not signed or anything," which was true.

Ms. Suber pointed at Bill Gilliland and told him to quit throwing his baseball in the air, a baseball supposedly signed by Shoeless Joe Jackson that none of us believed in, seeing as the signature was printed, at best. We never relented on Gilliland, and later on he plain used the ball in pickup games until the cover wore off.

I unfolded the letter and read, "'My dearest.'"

"These were French people writing in English, I suppose," Ms. Suber said.

I nodded. I said, "They were smart, I believe. 'I want to tell you that if I live to be a hundred I won't meet another man like you. If I live to be a hundred there shall be no love to match ours.'"

The entire class began laughing, of course. My face reddened. I looked at Ms. Suber, but she concentrated on her shoe. "'That guy who wrote that "How Do I Love Thee" poem has nothing on us, my sugar-booger-baby.'"

"That's enough," Ms. Suber belted out. "You can sit down, Mendal."

I pointed at the letter. I had another dozen paragraphs to go, some of which rhymed. I hadn't gotten to the word "throbbing," which showed up fourteen times. "I'm not making any of this up," I said. I walked two steps toward my third-grade teacher, but she stood up and told everyone to go outside except me.

Glenn Flack walked by and said, "You're in trouble, Mendal Dawes." Carol Anderson, who was my third-grade girlfriend, looked as if she was going to cry, as if I'd written the letter to Ms. Suber myself.

Ms. Suber said, "You've done nothing wrong, Mendal. Please tell your daddy that I got it. When he asks what happened today, just say Ms. Suber got it, okay?"

I put the letter in my front pants pocket. I said, "My father's a widower."

●●●

My father was waiting for me when I got home. Like everyone else, he started off in textiles, then gave it up. I never really knew what he did for a living, outside of driving around within a hundred-mile radius of Forty-five buying up land and then reselling it when the time was right. He had a knack. That was his word. For a time I thought it was the make of his car. "I drive around all day and buy land," he said more than once, before and after my mother took off to replace Patsy Cline. "I have a Knack."

I came home wearing my book bag, filled with a math book and an abacus. I said, "Hey, Dad."

He held his arms wide open, as if I were a returning P.O.W. "Did your teacher send back a note?"

I reached in my pocket and pulled out the letter from Héloïse to Abelard. I handed it to him and said, "She made me quit reading."

"She made you quit reading? How far along did you get?"

I told him how I only got to the part about sugar-booger-baby. I said, "Is this one of those lessons in life you keep telling me about, like when we went camping?" My father taught me early on how to tell the difference between regular leaves and poison ivy, when we camped out beside the Saluda River, far from any commode, waiting for him to gain a vision on which tract would be most salable later.

"Goddamn it to hell. She didn't say anything else after you read the letter?"

My father wore a seersucker suit. He wore a string tie. I said, "She called recess pretty much in the middle of me reading the thing. This is some kind of practical joke, isn't it?"

My father looked at me as if I'd peed on his wingtips. He said, "Now why would I do something like that to the only human being I love in this world?"

I couldn't imagine why. Why would a man who—as he liked to tell me often—before my birth played baseball for the Yankees in the summer, football for the Packers in the winter, and had competed in the Olympics, ever revert to playing jokes on a nine-year-old son of his? "Ms. Suber seemed kind of mad."

"Did she cry? Did she start crying? Did she turn her head away from y'all and blow her nose into a handkerchief? Don't hold back, Mendal.

Don't think that you're embarrassing your teacher or anything for telling the truth. Ms. Suber would want you to tell the truth, wouldn't she?"

I said, "Uh-huh. Probably."

"Uh-huh probably she cried, or uh-huh probably she'd want you to tell the truth?" My father walked to the kitchen backwards, pulled a bottle of bourbon from a shelf, and drank from it straight. Twenty years later on I would do the same thing, but over a dog that needed to be put to sleep.

I said, "Uh-huh. I told her you were a widower and everything. We got to go to recess early."

My father kept walking backwards. He took a glass from the cabinet, then cracked open an ice tray. He put cubes in the glass, poured bourbon into it, and stood staring at me as if I had told secrets to the enemy. "Did she say that she's thinking about getting married?"

I said, "She didn't say anything."

I wondered if my mother stood before a group of men and women drinking house beer, if she sang "I Fall to Pieces" or "Crazy" or any of those other country songs. It wasn't but three-thirty in my father's house. There was a one-hour time change, at least, in Nashville.

"I've gotten ahold of a genuine Cherokee Indian bracelet and ring," my father said the next Thursday night. "I ain't shitting you on this one. Your mother's father gave them to us a long time ago as a wedding present. He got them when he was traveling through Cherokee County up in the Cherokee country. Your grandfather used to sell cotton, you know. Sometimes those Indians needed cotton. They traded things for cotton. That's the way things go."

I said, "I was thinking about taking some pinecones I found." I had gathered up some pinecones that were so perfect it wasn't funny. They looked like Christmas trees built to scale. "I was going to take a rock and say it was a meteorite."

"No, no. Take some of my Cherokee Indian jewelry, son. I don't mind. I don't care! Hot damn I didn't even remember having the things, so it won't matter none if they get broken or stolen," he said. "This is the real thing, Bubba."

What could I do? I wasn't but nine years old, and early on I'd been taught to do whatever my elders said, outside of drinking whiskey and smoking cigarettes when they got drunk and made the offer, usually at Sunken Gardens Lounge. I thought, Maybe I can pretend to take my father's weird jewelry and stick it in my desktop. Maybe I can stick a pinecone inside my lunch box. "Yessir."

"I won't have it any other way," he said. "Wait here."

My father went back to what used to be my mother's and his bedroom. He opened up a wooden box he'd fashioned in high school shop, and pulled out a thin silver bracelet, plus a one-pearl ring. I didn't know that these trinkets once adorned the left arm of my third-grade teacher, right before she broke up with my father in order to go to college, and long before she graduated, taught in some other school system for ten years, and then came back to her hometown.

I took the trinkets in a small cotton sack. My father told me that he'd come get me for lunch if I wanted him to, that I didn't need to pack a bologna sandwich and banana as always. I went to the refrigerator and made my own and then left through the back door.

Glenn Flack started off show-and-tell with an X-ray of his mother's ankle. She'd fallen off the front porch trying to run from bees—something the rest of us knew not to do, seeing as we'd learned how to act in one of the weekly filmstrips. I got called next and said, "I have some priceless Cherokee Indian artifacts to show y'all. The Cherokee Indians had a way with hammering and chiseling." My father had made me memorize this speech.

I showed my classmates what ended up being something bought at Rey's Jewelers. Ms. Suber said, "Let me take a look at that," and got up to take the bracelet from my hand. She peered at it and then held it at arm's length and said, "This looks like it says 'sterling' on the inside, Mendal. I believe you might've picked up the wrong Indian jewelry to bring to school."

"Indian giver, Indian giver, Indian giver!" Melissa Beasley yelled out. It wasn't a taboo term back then. This was a time, understand, before we all had to say Native American-head penny.

I said, "I just know what my dad told me. That's all I know." I took the bracelet from Ms. Suber, pulled out the ring, and stood there as if offering a Milk-Bone to a stray and skittish dog.

Ms. Suber said, "I've had enough of this" and told me to return to my desk. I put the pearl ring on my thumb and stuck the bracelet around the toe of my tennis shoe. Ms. Suber said, "Has your father gone insane lately, Mendal?"

It embarrassed me, certainly, and if she had said it twenty or thirty years later, I could've sued her for harassment, slander, and making me potentially agoraphobic. My desk was in the last row. Every student turned toward me except Shirley Ebo, the only black girl in the entire school, four years prior to lawful integration. She looked forward, as always, ready to approach the music stand and explain her show-and-tell object, a face jug made by an old, old relative of hers named Dave the Slave.

I said, "My father has a Knack." Maybe I said nothing, really, but I thought about my father's Knack. I waited.

Ms. Suber sat back down. She looked at the ceiling and said, "I'm sorry, Mendal. I didn't mean to yell at you. Everyone go on to recess."

And so it continued for six weeks. I finally told my father that I couldn't undergo any more humiliation, that I would play hooky, that I would show up at school and say I had forgotten to bring my show-and-tell gimcrack. I said, "I'm only going to take these stupid things you keep telling me stories about if it brings in some money, Dad."

Not that I was ever a capitalist or anything, but I figured early on that show-and-tell would end up somehow hurting my penmanship or spelling grade, and that maybe I needed to start saving money in order to get a head start in life should I not get into college. My father said, "That sounds fair enough. How much will you charge me to take this old, dried Mayan wrist corsage and matching boutonniere?"

I said, "Five bucks each."

My father handed them over. If the goddamn school system had ever shown a worthwhile Friday filmstrip concerning inductive logic, I would've figured out back then that when Ms. Suber and my father had had their horrific and execrable high school breakup, my father had gone over to her house and gathered up everything he'd ever bestowed on her, from birthday to Valentine's Day to special three-month anniversary and so on. He had gifts she'd given him too, I supposed much later, though I doubted they were worthy of monogamy.

But I didn't know logic. I thought only that my father hated the school system, had no trust whatsoever in public education, and wanted to drive my teacher to a nervous breakdown in order to get her to quit. Or, I thought, it was his way of flirting—that since my mother had "died," he wanted to show a prospective second wife some of the more spectacular possessions he could offer a needful woman.

He said, "I can handle ten dollars a show-and-tell session, for two items. Remind me not to give you an hourglass. I don't want you charging me per grain of sand."

This was all by the first of October. By Christmas break I'd brought in cuff links worn by Louis Quatorze, a fountain pen used by the fifty-six signers of the Declaration of Independence (my father tutored me on stressing "Independence" when I announced my cherished object to the class), a locket once owned by Elmer the glue inventor, thus explaining why the thing couldn't be opened, a pack of stale Viceroys that once belonged to the men who raised the American flag on Iwo Jima. I brought in more famous love letters, all on lined Blue Horse paper: from Ginger Rogers to Fred Astaire, from Anne Hathaway to Shakespeare, from all of Henry VIII's wives to him. One letter, according to my dad, was from Plato to Socrates, though he said it wasn't the original, and that he'd gone to the trouble of learning Greek in order to translate the thing.

Ms. Suber became exasperated with each new disclosure. She moved from picking names at random or in alphabetical order to always choosing me last. My classmates voted me Most Popular, Most Likely to Succeed, and Third Grade President, essentially because I got us ten more minutes of recess every Friday.

I walked down to the County Bank every Friday after school and deposited the money my father had forked over in a regular savings account. This was a time before IRAs. It was a time before stock portfolios, mutual funds, and the like. They gave me a toaster for starting the account and a dinner plate every time I walked in with ten dollars or more. After a few months I could've hosted a dinner party for twelve.

●●○

On Saturday mornings, more often than not, I drove with my father from place to place, looking over land he had bought or planned to buy. He had acquired a few acres of woodland before my birth, and soon thereafter the Army Corps of Engineers came in, flooded the Savannah River, and made my father's property near lakefront. He sold that parcel, took that money, and bought more land in an area that bordered what would become I-95. He couldn't go wrong. My father was not unlike the fool who threw darts at a map and went with his gut instinct. He would buy useless swampland, and someone else would soon insist on buying that land at twice to ten times his cost in order to build a golf course, a subdivision, or a nuclear-power facility. I had no idea what he did between these ventures, outside of reading and wondering. How else would he know about Abelard and Hélöise, or even Socrates and Plato? He hadn't gone to college. He hadn't taken some kind of correspondence course.

We drove, and I stuck my head out the window like the dog I had owned before my mother took him to Nashville. We'd get to some land, pull down a dirt road usually, and my father would stare hard for ten or fifteen minutes. He barely turned his head from side to side, and he never turned off the engine. Sometimes he'd say at the end, "I think I got a fouled spark plug," or "You can tell that that gas additive's working properly."

He never mentioned people from history, or the jewelry of the dead. I took along Hardy Boys mysteries but never opened the covers. Finally, one afternoon, I said, "Ms. Suber wants to know if you're planning on coming to the PTA meeting. I forgot to tell you."

My father turned off the ignition. He reached beneath his seat and pulled out a can of beer and a church key. We sat parked between two gullies, somewhere in Greenwood County. "Hot damn, boy, you need to tell me these things. When is it?"

I said, "I forgot. I got in so much trouble Friday that I forgot." I'd taken a tortoise to show-and-tell and said his name was John the Baptist. At first Ms. Suber seemed delighted. When she asked why I had named him John the Baptist, I said, "Watch this." I screamed, "John the Baptist!" When he retreated into his shell and lost his head, I nodded. She had me sit back down. None of my classmates got the joke.

"The PTA meeting's on Tuesday. It's on Tuesday." I wore a pair of cut-off blue jeans with the bottoms cut into one-inch strips. My mother used to make them for me when I'd grown taller but hadn't gained weight around the middle. I had on my light-blue Little League T-shirt, with Sunken Gardens on the front and 69 for my number on the back. My father had insisted that I get that number, and that I would thank him one day.

"Hell, yes. Do I need to bring anything? I mean, is this one of those meetings where parents need to bring food? I can make potato salad and cole slaw, you know."

"She just asked me to ask if you'd show up. That's all she said, I swear."

My father looked out at what I understood to be another wasteland. Empty beer cans were scattered in front of us, and the remains of a haphazard bonfire someone had made right in the middle of a path. "Maybe I should call her up and ask if she needs anything."

Although I didn't understand the depth of my father's obsession, I said, "Ms. Suber won't be in town until that night. We have a substitute on Monday, 'cause she has to go to a funeral somewhere."

My father drank from his beer. He handed the can over and told me to take little sips at first. I said, "Mom wouldn't want you to give me beer."

He nodded. "Mom wouldn't want you to do a lot of things, just like she didn't want me to do a lot of things. But she's not here, is she? Your momma's spending all her time praying that she never gets laryngitis, while the rest of us hope she does."

I didn't know that my father had been taking Fridays off in order to see the school secretary, feign needing to leave me a bag lunch, and then stand looking through the vertical window of my classroom door while I expounded the rarity of a letter sweater once worn by General Custer, or whatever. When the PTA meeting came around, I went with my father, though no other students attended. Pretty much it was only parents, teachers, and a couple of the lunch ladies, who had volunteered to serve a punch of ginger ale and grape juice. My father entered Ms. Suber's classroom and approached her as if she were a newspaper boy he'd forgotten to pay. He said, "I thought you'd eventually send a letter home asking for a conference. I thought you'd finally buckle under." He said, "Go look at the goldfish, Mendal. You've always liked aquariums. Maybe I'll get you one."

I looked at the corner of the room. My classmates' parents were sitting at tiny desks, their knees bobbing like the shells of surfaced turtles. My third-grade teacher said, "I know you think this is cute, but it's not. I don't know why you think you can recount me however many years later after what you did to me back then."

My father pushed me in the direction of the aquarium. Ms. Suber waved and smiled at Glenn Flack's parents, who were walking in. I said, "Can I go sit in the car?"

Ms. Suber said, "You stay right here, Mendal."

"I might not have been able to go to college like you did, Lola, but I've done good for myself," my father said. I thought one thing only: *Lola?*

"I know you have, Lee. I know you've done well. And let me be the first to say how proud I am of you, and how I'm sorry if I hurt you, and that I've seen you looking in the window when Mendal does his bogus show-and-tells." She pointed at the window in the door. Mr. and Mrs. Anderson walked in. "I need to start this thing up."

My father said to me, "If you want to go sit in the car, go ahead." He handed me the keys, leaned down, and said, "There's a beer in the glove compartment, son."

Let me say that this was South Carolina in 1968. Although my memory's not perfect, I think that at the time, neither drinking nor driving was against the law for minors, nor was smoking cigarettes before the age of twelve. Five years later I would drive my mini-bike to the Sunken Gardens, meet one of the black boys twirling trays out in the parking lot, order my eight-pack of Miller ponies, and have it delivered to me without conscience or threat of law.

I pretended to go into the parking lot but circled around to the outside of Ms. Suber's classroom. I stood beneath one of the six jalousies, crouched, and listened. Ms. Suber welcomed the parents and said that it was an exciting year. She said something about how all of us would have to take a national test later on to see how we compared with the rest of the nation. She said something about a school play.

Ms. Suber warned parents of a looming head-lice epidemic. She paced back and forth and asked everyone to introduce himself or herself. Someone asked if the school would ever sponsor another cake-and-pie sale in order to buy new recorders. My father said he'd be glad to have a potato-salad-and-cole-slaw sale. I didn't hear the teacher's answer. From where I crouched I could only look up at the sky and notice how some stars twinkled madly while others shone hard and fast like mica afire.

By the time I reached high school, my mother had moved from Nashville to New Orleans and then from New Orleans to Las Vegas. She never made it as a country singer or a blues singer, but she seemed to thrive as a hostess of sorts. As I crouched there beneath a window jutting out above boxwoods, I thought of my mother and imagined what she might be doing at the moment my father was experiencing his first PTA meeting. Was she crooning to conventioneers? Was she sitting in a back room worrying over panty hose? That's what I thought, I swear to God. Everyone in Ms. Suber's classroom seemed to be talking with cookies in their mouths. I heard my father laugh hard twice—once when Ms. Suber said she knew that her students saw her as a witch, and another time when she said she knew that her students went home complaining that she didn't spank exactly the way their parents spanked.

Again, this was in the middle of the Vietnam War. Spanking made for good soldiers.

My third-grade teacher said that she didn't have anything else to say, and told her students' parents to feel free to call her up should they have questions concerning grades, expectations, or field trips. She said she appreciated anyone who wanted to help chaperon kids or to work after school in a tutoring capacity. I stood up and watched my friends' parents leave single file, my father last in line.

Fifteen minutes after sitting in the car, five minutes after everyone else had driven out of the parking lot, I climbed out the passenger side and crept back to Ms. Suber's window. I expected my father to have Lola Suber in a headlock, or backed up against the Famous Christians of the World corkboard display. I didn't foresee their having moved desks against the walls in order to make a better dance floor.

My father held my third-grade teacher in a way I'd seen him hold a woman only once before: one Fourth of July he had danced with my mother in the backyard while the neighbors shot bottle rockets straight up. My mother had placed her head on his shoulder and smiled, her eyes raised to the sky. Lola Suber didn't look upward. She didn't smile either. My father seemed to be humming, or talking low. I couldn't hear exactly what went on, but years later he confessed that he had set forth everything he meant to say and do, everything he hoped she taught the other students and me when it came to matters of passion.

I did hear Lola Suber remind him that they had broken up because she had decided to have a serious and exclusive relationship with Jesus Christ.

There amid the boxwoods I hunkered down and thought only about the troubles I might have during future show-and-tells. I stood back up, saw them dancing, and returned to the car. I would let my father open the glove compartment later. ●

AFTER WORDS

I wrote "Show-and-Tell" when I wanted to have an adult narrator looking back at all the quirky, irrational things his parent(s) might've done. I'm a slow learner, and I didn't realize how much fun it could be to look at all the mysteries and outright weirdness that surrounds us all between the ages of, say, three and fourteen. My only memory of a show-and-tell experience occurred when I brought in a perfect seashell I'd found over summer vacation, and this one loudmouthed kid named Tony said he thought I'd bought it at a store, that it looked like it read "Made in China" or something on the inside of the shell, and so on. Everyone—at least I thought so at the time—believed this kid Tony's story. I went on to college and became a writer. That kid flunked out of college, and last I heard, he worked at Lowe's. I win, unless I want a deal on some lumber.

After I wrote the story, I went on to write a slew of Mendal-Dawes-looks-back-at-growing-up-with-an-insane-father stories that appear in The Half-Mammals of Dixie *and* Why Dogs Chase Cars, *for better or worse.*

PHILIP GERARD

A FLEXIBLE FLYER

TO WISH FOR A SLED for Christmas was to wish for two nearly impossible things to come true at once: an expensive gift at a time in our family's life when my parents were barely holding their own, and snow. Where we lived, it almost never snowed.

We studied pictures in our geography books of snowdrifts that buried automobiles in Buffalo, blizzards that swept across the Great Plains, heaping snow against fences and barns, New England snows that turned farm lanes into postcard trails for horse-drawn sleighs.

But in Delaware, our home, we never got real snow. A dozen flurries a year. Once or twice, a couple of inches that would turn to slush or get sluiced away when the weather turned warm and rainy the following day.

My little brother Nick wanted a sled.

He'd found a picture of one in *Boy's Life* magazine: two happy scouts screaming down a snow-covered hill on a gleaming sled with shiny steel runners. The logo streaming across the bottom of the advertisement read FLEXIBLE FLYER RACER.

"That's the ticket," Nick said. We were sitting side by side on the couch in the basement rec room watching *Sergeant Preston of the Yukon* on TV. Sergeant Preston's giant malamute Yukon King was chasing some bad guys through the snow, breasting through the drifts with his powerful chest, spraying surfy clouds of spindrift.

"You're too young for a sled," I told him. "You're only six." I was ten. Between us we had a sister, Molly, who was eight.

"Seven, almost," he said. And he was right. His birthday fell on the day after Christmas, a really lousy time for a kid to have a birthday. I mean, he was practically sharing it with Jesus. And no matter what our parents did, even Molly and I had to agree that Nick always got cheated out of a real birthday with a party and cake and amazing presents.

"There aren't any hills around here, Nick," I said. "Where you going to ride it?"

"On the church hill," he said.

Again, he was right. St. Stephen's, our Catholic church, stood at the pinnacle of a long, gentle slope outside of town in what was still considered the country. The road ran several miles up the hill past cornfields and pastures to a cleared lot tucked into the side of the woods where the old church had been built of pasture oak and fieldstone half a century earlier.

"Okay, so there's one hill, Nick. But there's no snow."

On TV, Yukon King had captured the bad guys and dunked them headfirst into a snowbank and stood grinning for his master. Every episode ended the same way, and Sergeant Preston always got his man.

"It might snow."

"What makes you think it's going to snow?"

"But it might. It has to snow sometime."

"Okay, okay. It *might* snow."

"So I want one. A Flexible Flyer." He sat there with the magazine in his lap, his legs splayed, and stared at me, his pale freckled cheeks reddening, blinking his green eyes fast the way he always did when he was getting ready to cry. He took after our mother in looks and had her stubborn streak, too.

"Okay, Nick," I said. I didn't have the heart to say anything else. I grabbed his legs and squeezed them just above the braces and he giggled like he always did. He liked for me to rub his legs because they cramped up and went all spastic if he sat too long. My mother used to sit for hours every night and rub his legs while Nick bit his lip and grinned with pain or with how good it felt, I could never tell which.

That was the real reason it was crazy for Nick to want a sled: he was a cripple. My mother forbade us to use that word, "cripple," but that's what Nick called himself. One day last summer, Nick came back from the YMCA swimming pool and lay down for his nap. When he got up, he couldn't walk.

Polio, Doctor Everhart pronounced.

This was the time of polio, and that was the summer it came to our town. Doctor Everhart whispered the word, shaking his head, looking around to make sure it didn't escape from the upstairs bedroom Nick and I shared. Polio was an evil spell—invisible and deadly. It could seep through walls and closed doors and strike without warning, and it always struck kids.

Nobody seemed to know what caused it, or how to cure it. It came out of nowhere, struck at random, lurked in the shadows of kids' bedrooms like the bogeyman. People treated it like the Black Plague—it was believed you caught it in crowds from bodily contact with other people. From breathing their bad poisoned air, or brushing against their clothes, or swimming in the same water. Some people claimed that it only struck down the bad kids, but that was crazy. Being good was no defense. When somebody in your family caught it, the neighbors' kids stopped coming over to play. People avoided you at the supermarket. "Polio," they said knowingly, and pointed. The other person would nod and frown and duck down the produce aisle.

We wanted to grow up fast, to outrun polio.

Doctor Everhart couldn't predict if Nick would ever walk again. There was no miracle cure, no magic operation. At least Nick wasn't forced to live in an iron lung, like the boy in our fifth-grade reader.

Nick's legs were strapped into metal braces—he called them his "Frankenstein legs"— and he propped himself up stiff-legged between little kid-sized crutches that made his shoulders hunch up and his red crew-cut head bob forward. He fell a lot, and we got used to the sound of his clattering braces and his crutches rattling against the slick linoleum floor of the kitchen and Nick hooting with pain and laughter. He was always bruised and sore, but he didn't complain much. He just sort of banged his way through the world and hoped for the best.

Nick wasn't the only kid strapped into steel leg braces.

In our small town that summer, people stopped going to the movies. The YMCA pool closed, as did all the public pools. Nobody gave birthday parties, and the church day camps shut down for lack of attendance. Brides postponed their weddings indefinitely. When school started, half the kids stayed home and nobody got in trouble.

People even stopped going to church. Not our family, though. My mother, who was second-generation immigrant Irish, said, "We won't turn away from the Good Lord now, just because he's given us a trial."

But Sunday after Sunday, the pews were mostly empty, and Father Cruikshank's ringing sermons echoed in the empty space. At the early Mass, there were always a few old crones in the back row, dressed in shapeless black smocks, their heads swathed in black veils so that they were indistinguishable from one another, faceless and bent, clicking on their Rosary beads and silent except for their mumbled chant of Latin responses to the priest. By now I was one of only a handful of altar boys who would still serve Mass.

The Sunday after Nick told me he wanted a Flexible Flyer, two weeks before Christmas, I kneeled on the hard stone at the foot of the altar answering Father Cruikshank's cues: he would say, *Introíbo ad altáre Dei*, I will go in to the altar of God, and I would respond, *Ad Deum qui laetíficat juventútem meam*, The God of my gladness and joy.

But I didn't feel very glad—I felt mad at God for what he had done to Nick and scared stiff it would happen to me. I shared a room with him, I rubbed his legs every day, I breathed his air. I rattled off the Latin by heart, thinking of Nick and his lousy braces and how he wanted a sled, the stupidest thing in the world for a cripple to want in a place without hills or snow.

I didn't have to turn around and look to see Nick in the front pew, where our family always sat because my father would have it no other way—"If I'm going to church, I want to see and hear everything that's going on," he always said. Nick's red buzz cut would be shining like a lightbulb. His crutches would be stacked against the front rail of the pew and Molly would fidget beside him, her brown curls bouncing each time she wagged her head. On one side sat my mother, small and wiry, red hair pulled back tightly into a bun, a small dark green hat pinned to her head; then my father in his charcoal suit, only a little taller, motionless, completely absorbed in the liturgy, watching it transfixed the way he watched a baseball game or the six o'clock news—as if he were seeing it for the first time, and at any moment something wonderful might happen and he didn't want to miss it.

I was so distracted, I missed my first cue for ringing the bell and later almost dropped the wine cruet. Tall, heroic Father Cruickshank leaned down to me and squinted and said, "You all right, son?" Like I might have suddenly been stricken with polio too, and I wondered for a cold split second if I had, and that was why I was so clumsy. I nodded yes.

After Mass, Molly and I held a pow-wow and decided we would all ask for the sled together. "It's what Nick wants," she said blithely.

"It's a stupid idea," I warned her. "It means you won't get a bike."

"I don't think I'm getting a bike anyway," she said, flipping her curls. Molly was always blasé about herself, like she would get along fine in the world and why did the rest of us worry so much about every little thing? We didn't know much about money in those days—I have no idea even now what salary my father earned from the clothing store he and my mother ran. As bookkeeper, she took no salary, I do know that. And business had fallen off; people just weren't going out anywhere, even shopping, unless they had to. They were hunkered down in their homes, doors and windows shut tight, trying to keep out polio.

Molly and I went to our parents together, as a kind of delegation, and told them: "We want a sled."

My father said, "Do you have special information I don't? Because, Buster, the last time it snowed enough for sledding, you weren't even born yet."

"Just in case," Molly said with an offhand logic. "Sooner or later, it's got to snow, and when it does, we'll be ready."

"I thought you wanted a new bike," my mother said. "Something you can use every day."

"No, we want a sled," she said, as if it had been so obviously true for years that only a moron would think different. "A Flexible Flyer." She held out the picture, scissored out of *Boy's Life*.

That night, I could hear our parents downstairs in the kitchen. Sometimes they'd sit up after we had all gone to bed and sip coffee at the Formica table and talk about the store, or the news, or things they remembered from when they were first married. I used to like listening to them talk like that, private and low, but sometimes too it reminded me that they had once lived in a world that didn't include us, and I would lie awake scared of something I couldn't even name.

"I don't know if we can even get one this late," my father's voice said.

"I called Western Auto—they can have it by Christmas Eve."

"What in God's name are they thinking? The radio is calling for rain all week. They'll be so disappointed—"

My mother's voice said, "Oh, for the love of Jesus, just buy them the adjectival sled. It's Nicky who wants the thing."

"Nicky? What use will it ever be to him."

On Christmas Eve it was tradition that we all went to midnight Mass. We piled into the old green Buick and drove up the hill to St. Stephen's in a cold drizzle. I don't remember a gloomier ride than that Christmas Eve ride in the caravan of headlights and taillights crawling up the long hill in the rain, the fields on either side of us dark, nobody talking, not even the radio on to play Christmas carols.

I was serving the Mass with Tommy D'Onofrio, so as soon as we hit the parking lot I scooted out and scrambled into the sacristy by the back way and buttoned on my starched cassock and slipped the bleach-white surplice over my shoulders. Tommy let me light the candles, which I always enjoyed. I genuflected at the foot of the altar and lit the two golden candelabras and then the special candles next to the Nativity scene on the left side altar, under the statue of the Virgin Mary. In front of the Nativity scene burned a whole rack of votive candles, flickering red—one of them, I knew, my mother had kept burning for Nick ever since July.

At special masses, Father Cruickshank liked to enter from the front door rather than the sacristy and march up the aisle. So when he was all robed in his vestments, we slipped out the back and walked outdoors to the front of the church and I felt the rain turning to sleet on my cheeks and dabbing my hair, and my surplice was spotted with dark blotches in the floodlights. The lights reached down beyond the parking lot to the edge of the meadow that sloped down alongside the road toward town.

As we entered the front door, the congregation turned to watch us process up the aisle. For the first time since summer the church was full. And in every pew, it seemed, there were kids in steel leg braces. Crutches—dozens of pairs—leaned against the backs of the wooden benches in front. Other children were laid across the benches, swaddled in blankets and car coats, unable even to sit up.

As he passed each pew, parents stared at Father Cruikshank accusingly for some answer he didn't have, their faces white and their eyes dark with fatigue. There was none of the usual shuffling and coughing and throat-clearing. There was something frozen about the way they looked, all those grown-ups with the damaged children they could not protect.

We sang "O Come All Ye Faithful," even the Latin verses, and Tommy and I served the Mass without a hitch. We sang the other carols, but there was no choir—they had stopped rehearsing in the summer for fear of polio—and the singing was ragged and off-key with the organ. Father Cruikshank read the St. Luke Gospel of the Bethlehem story. He did not read the Matthew Gospel, which tells of Herod seeking out the young children of the region and putting them to the sword. I don't even remember his sermon. Only about half the congregation dared take communion, and by the end of Mass everybody was itching to leave.

I looked out across the congregation—they had all sat too long in a crowded place, a place of danger. Now they did shuffle and cough and clear their throats. They didn't look at their neighbors. They huddled their own children between them. When Father Cruikshank pronounced the final blessing, they sprang up like pop-up dolls. We processed back down the aisle, feeling them crowd along behind us. And when Tommy D'Onofrio and I flung open the big double doors, outside was a howling blizzard.

The air was wild with snow, blowing so thick you could hardly see the cars in the parking lot, all layered with white. Already the parking lot was covered with drifting snow.

The earlier rain had frozen under the snow, which made it impossible to walk on the pavement without falling down. Men wearing street shoes with slick soles and women in high heels lost their footing and grabbed each other's coat sleeves for support.

The D'Onofrios herded their five kids into their new Ford and tried to make it down the hill ahead of the rush, but only a couple of hundred yards down, the big car slid sideways into a ditch and Mrs. D'Onofrio fell hard while getting out. Mr. D'Onofrio sent Tommy back for help—he ran through the corn-stubble drifts and reached us, out of breath.

My father said, "Come with me."

Slipping and sliding, somehow carrying Nick between us, we followed him to our Buick and he opened the trunk with a brass key. He reached in and pulled out a long flat package wrapped in red paper. "Go ahead and open it, Buster," he said.

"Let Nicky," Molly said, and Nick hooted and clawed at the paper while we held him upright. In the floodlights, the banner was bright red against the varnished blond wood, the letters glossy black: FLEXIBLE FLYER.

"I need it to help Mrs. D'Onofrio, all right?" my father said.

Nick nodded, smiling big.

"For now, everybody go back inside," my father said. "Nobody's going anywhere until the plow comes."

So it was that my father and a few of the other fathers trudged through the snow across the road to the D'Onofrios' car and laid Mrs. D'Onofrio on the sled and hauled her up the hill and back into the church. Her ankle was broken clean, Doctor Everhart said. They laid her in a pew on a pile of coats and everybody else made themselves comfortable back in the church. They tried to call into town, but the phone line was already down.

Soon after, the power went out, too, so we had only candlelight that played on rows of grim faces. A few people whispered—a muffled complaint, a quick biting hiss to hush a cranky child. Then Father Cruikshank announced it was all right to talk if we did it respectfully. Father Cruikshank sent me and Tommy D'Onofrio to get more candles, and we lit them all along the main aisle and by the front doors and around the sanctuary, and the dancing shadows they made were like a whole world of other people, not us, dark humped figures afraid to stand straight and face each other.

The air smelled like wet wool and beeswax. A man in the next pew over said to his wife, "I told you we shouldn't have come tonight."

She said, "Don't even start."

Another man said, "Get over it, pal."

A woman started crying softly and her husband cursed and then tried to put his arms around her but she pulled away. Other voices complained now, murmuring in that low ugly way of people getting ready to do something stupid that they'll regret. It was the first time I felt ashamed of being in church.

Father Cruikshank stood at the foot of the altar and raised his hands. I stood close enough to touch him. He was lean and darkly handsome and his voice had an anger in it, just barely. "Stop it, please. It's not the snow. You know what's wrong." He paused. "The thing we never dared speak about."

Somebody in the back called out, "Let it be, Father."

Father Cruikshank faltered—no one had ever dared talk back to him in church—then started again. "I know this is not the kind of Christmas you wished for. Prayed for." He glanced toward the Nativity scene and then looked back at the sullen congregation. He waited for their murmuring to die down and it took a long time. "What has happened here, this has never happened before. Sometimes—sometimes we're at a loss."

He stopped talking and everybody waited now, quiet. Usually he could speak for an hour without stumbling but now he groped for the words. His voice went soft, but everybody was listening now and so it didn't have to be loud. He looked at me, as if I could tell him what to say next, but I didn't have a clue. All I had running through my head were those memorized Latin responses, so I said stupidly, "*Ad Deum qui laetíficat juventútem meam.*"

Father Cruikshank frowned, puzzled, then took a slow step toward them. "We are forgetting—we are forgetting the *joy.*"

A man in the front pew put his face in his hands and his shoulders shook like something was wrong with him.

"We're not sure. Not sure if we still believe. How can I say this?" He scanned their faces, looking from one to the other and seeing just blank, unforgiving stares. His neck was crimson with anger above the pure-white alb. "Today we celebrate the birth of a child. When a child is born, that's the miracle. Always. Then, later—it's true—the child suffers. That's the world."

He lifted both of his big hands and ran them over his face, like he was washing it. "But the suffering is not all there is." He shone his eyes over them like trying to light up a dark place with a small flashlight, like he wanted to find one face in which he recognized faith, and he settled on my mother. She stared back at him hard and I could not read what was in her heart. "There is also—there is always the joy."

There was utter silence then, like they were waiting for him to say more, but he had no more to say. Some of the parents looked down at their laps. One man got up and clomped loudly down the aisle and out into the snow and I wondered if others would follow him, but nobody did. They hunkered down in the pews just as they had in their homes, not brave or burning with faith but just tired and wanting to go home, and maybe ashamed.

Father Cruikshank walked slowly back to the sacristy to change out of his vestments. He held his head up, as he always did, but I could tell it was a struggle, that this night had cost him something.

He did not have the power to fix what was wrong, but he had broken the spell. The silence lasted till he was out of sight and for a minute or so longer. Then my mother started whispering to another, asking what she had been doing since summer, and after a few minutes some of the other women gathered timidly in a little knot near the side confessionals and talked first in halting whispers and then in regular voices about what the doctor had told them or what they had read in a magazine or what they planned to resolve for the New Year. And somebody started crying and somebody else reached across and patted her arm and said, "There, there."

A couple of men excused themselves to use the restroom in the sacristy and even with the heat off it was warm enough to take off our heavy coats.

To pass the time, Mr. D'Onofrio suggested we sing Christmas carols, and he started off the first verse of "It Came Upon a Midnight Clear" in a fine tenor voice. At first people sang softly and a little embarrassed, then a few started to sing loud and even smiled at the old familiar words. It was not very good singing—half-hearted and a little off-key—but I heard my mother's soft, melodious trill and my father's flat baritone. We sang only the one carol, as if that was all we had in us.

All the while the snow came down outside, thick and hard, and the wind rattled the windows and drafted in every crack in the old church, flickering the candles.

And soon enough people started sacking out on the pews, cuddling up with their kids and babies and loved ones and closing their eyes, snoring, breathing the deep peacefulness of sleeping in a blessed place. Molly said, "It's like pioneers, and we're all gathered in the fort so the Apaches can't get us."

Nick giggled and said, "Or the Devil."

Father Cruikshank in his long flowing cassock patrolled the aisles like a real father, watching over their sleep. The fluttering candles made shadows across the walls and lit up eerie slivers of blue and red and gold in the stained-glass windows.

Outside the snow came down like the blazes all night long. Father Cruikshank went out in back of the sacristy to smoke a cigarette, which he always did after Mass. When we were sure our parents were asleep, Molly and I gently nudged Nick awake and I rubbed his spastic legs for a few minutes and then between us we carried him outside, where our Flexible Flyer stood propped against the stone side of the church.

At the far end of the building, we could see Father Cruikshank standing in a corner out of the wind, smoking his cigarette. He looked our way, nodded, and let us be.

I shook the snow off it, laid it down on its shiny runners, and set Nick aboard with his feet stuck out in front. Molly squeezed on in front of Nick so he could lean against her shoulders. Slipping and sliding, I hauled them across the parking lot to the edge of the meadow, where it sloped down along the road pure white. The sky glowed from the snow light. I climbed on behind and tucked my feet into the steering paddles.

The rest of our lives opened out ahead of us full of trouble and heartbreak, we knew that, even as kids we knew that. Tomorrow and for years to come, Nick would wake up with legs iron-stiff with pain, and there would be no Christmas visits and my mother would cry herself to sleep again.

But this night, a field of unbroken snow spread out before us. Far below, we could see the bright headlights of the snowplow grinding up the hill to rescue everybody.

"How did you know, Nick?" I said and he just giggled and caught the falling snowflakes on his tongue. Then I pushed off with my hands, hugged Nick hard, and we went flying down the snowy hill. ✹

AFTER WORDS

I grew up on the tail end of the time of polio, when our grammar school readers were full of pictures of kids in iron lungs, kids on crutches, kids struck down mysteriously; and I never forgot what it felt like. Once when I was an altar boy, we had an amazing snow storm on Christmas Eve, one of the only times that ever happened in my childhood. It was the only year we received sleds for Christmas. I like mystery, coincidence, kids, and sledding; and faith is something I wrestled with for years. They all came together in a hilltop church with a bunch of scared, sullen people, a funny kid who happened to be suffering the crippling effects of polio. The kid is not necessarily brave—I didn't want a Tiny Tim—but he is funny and likable and honest. He deserved a sled ride at the end of the story.

ALL NITE VIDEO

HERE'S THE TRUTH: our biggest money came from porn. Most of our rental library was Hollywood legit, but the hottest items were in the adult video closet and on the mag rack behind the counter. One dude in spandex and a crash helmet lugged his bike in on his shoulders and lectured me on physical fitness while he bought reams of printed smut. But most men bought that stuff with their eyes cast down. Shame lingered in that place like cigarette smoke, and yes, some of it was mine.

A guy named Eric Ambler was our most loyal porn fiend. He jotted notes on a notepad while he scoured the adult closet with the door wide open. He'd duck his bowl-cut head of hair through every doorframe, nodding his Roman Polanski nose. He'd glance at me like maybe he also expected any minute a drama would unfold in the pitiful quiet of the store—a surprise twist, a sudden jolt into the second act.

All Nite Video had a few seemly patrons, like the albino Bailey Dannon whose hair was like dreadlocked cotton puff. She had unraveled Q-tips for eyebrows, fingernails shining tender pink without polish. Probably nineteen or twenty like me, she wore kid's sneakers with fading Super Grover decals. I kept a private inventory of her rentals on an index card—Woody Allen, David Lynch, John Cassavetes, Ingmar Bergman. In case we ever ended up talking.

She'd thrust through the entrance and march toward a shelf with her fists curled tight. Kneeling in the aisle, she focused video boxes inches from her convex glasses. She slapped the tapes back in place and groaned like she was always settling for less than she expected. Me—I'd already hatched this nutcase dream that one of my six unfinished screenplays would someday be the exact film she was hunting for.

One night both Bailey Dannon and Eric Ambler showed up around the same time. Bailey's over here squinting at the artsy films in the foreign section while Ambler's over there slouched inside the porn closet, stacking a pile of tapes on the floor, amending his notes and crunching numbers into a pocket calculator.

Ambler spotted Bailey the second he ducked out of the closet with three tapes in his grip. He paused, soaked up her image, cocked his head like that scene in *Frankenstein* with Karloff and that little girl tossing flowers into the pond. I could only guess at his sick thoughts when he saw a girl half his age, an exotic girl like Bailey.

Even during checkout, he kept pitching glances at her, and I wished something in my power could stop him. He trudged away eyeing her until he shoved the door open and an arctic blast struck him. Then he lurched outside and loomed there by the display window, fished a wrinkled cigarette pack from his jacket. Still he watched her through the smoke and steam he exhaled.

"Hi," Bailey said. I caught a waft of coconut suntan lotion from her direction, but it couldn't douse my nerves. I fretted through her payment, slid the bagged video into her hands, and only when she turned toward the door did I manage to say, "Wait. I don't trust that guy out there."

She pinched the frames of her glasses and winced.

"Over there," I said.

Bailey strutted to the storefront window and rapped her knuckles against the glass. She waved at Ambler with both arms like some manic groupie at a rock concert. He sidestepped away into the dark between the dim streetlamps.

"Do you know that guy?" I asked.

"Never seen him before in my life."

"His name's Eric Ambler. He's a pervert. You should stay here at least until we're sure he's gone."

She twirled the video bag beside her hip like a lasso. "And why should I trust you instead of him?"

"Because you know me—or at least you've seen me enough times. I know that's not logical, but I'm an employee here, and he's some scary dude lurking in the dark."

"Fair enough," she said. Bailey had silver irises that gathered light like solar receptors. I don't know why but I asked if she'd take off her glasses.

She looked at them on her face, cross-eyed. "Why?"

"I'd like to see your eyes better."

"Aren't you afraid I'm pathetically self-conscious—that I might feel like, what, some freak show attraction?"

"I'm sorry," I said.

She tipped the glasses down the slop of her nose and folded them into her fist.

"Albinos get a shitty rap in the movies," she said. "They were all vampires in *Omega Man*. They were homicidal kids in *Village of the Damned*. An albino stalked Goldie Hawn in *Foul Play*."

I said, "Some pagan cultures celebrated the birth of an albino female. They thought she was their moon goddess reincarnated."

"Yeah," she said. "Nothing magical happens anymore."

We popped popcorn in the microwave and played the video Bailey rented, something called *Ice Castles* about figure skaters falling in love and going blind. When Bailey got bored she grabbed a shrinkwrapped package of dirty magazines from the rack behind us. "Three for the price of one," she read. "What a steal. *Dirty bitches get nekkid together*. Hmm. *Cocksucking princesses*? Such colorful detail."

"Let's microwave this crap video," I suggested.

"Win a pair of Jenna Jameson's panties? Who's that?" Bailey shoved a cluster of popcorn into her mouth and snickered at the gravity of smut.

"I want to be a filmmaker," I said. "But not adult videos, and not Hollywood blockbusters, either. More like regional filmmaking. You know, independent movies."

Still chewing, Bailey flapped the popcorn bag at me, spilling kernels into my lap. I told her that I wanted to film our little village of Hammersport, New York, in black-and-white silence, lingering on the grit and workaday rust and freeze. Bailey listened until an hour before dawn when she tugged her pom-pommed toque over her head and trudged away through the snow.

At sunrise my boss Josephine came to read the nightly profit reports. She hobbled through the rear office on a forearm crutch, holding her kindergartner Bobby by the hand. This boy, according to Josephine, had been born dead. "But," she'd say, "just look at him now." Bobby sprang into dizzying laps around the previewed video bins, squealing.

"Just found out my ex-husband's out on parole," Josephine said. "He called us four times last night. This is the guy who stands in our driveway with a rifle and shoots out all our windows. And they go letting him out of jail?"

"Did you call the police?" I asked.

"Just if he shows up here, don't go giving him our address. We had to move the trailer because of him. Did I tell you this? Tell him I said leave us alone."

"What if he brings that rifle?" I asked.

"Don't worry. He's just a stupid ass."

Three nights passed before Bailey came back. She rushed in with a coffee from Java Queen's saying, "Figured you'd probably need caffeine." All evening I'd been eyeing the door for Bailey or Ambler or Josephine's gun-toting ex. I was worried that the blinking fluorescent overhead wasn't enough light to stage either a showdown or a love affair.

"My father gets pissed at me for being up all night," Bailey said. "He claims he can't sleep with me pacing around. I don't pace. We both can't sleep—that's the thing. So I leave him alone and rent my movies."

"I sleep all day," I said. "In the winter I hardly ever see the sun. Makes one gloomy after a while."

"Yeah, well, zero sleep makes one hallucinogenic," Bailey said, and that's right when Eric Ambler lurched through the doorway, snow dusting his shoulders like dandruff. He reached deep inside his jacket lapel and produced what, it turns out, was just a videotape. "Return," he said. Bailey stood back, warming her hands with the coffee she'd bought me.

"He's been following me," she said when he was gone. "Java Queen's, now here. He asked me if I wanted to 'grab' breakfast."

"You should call the cops," I said.

"Why? A man has a right to ask. He's harmless."

"He's a pervert. A middle-aged, married one."

"I can handle myself."

"But I can't believe his nerve."

"You want me to come back later when you're done working yourself up?" In her pale smirk, I saw she meant only a minor sting, but hours later when I was drifting asleep in my third-floor studio apartment, I wondered how much these months of nothing but moon glow had corroded my passions. I stared at my vintage posters of *A Clockwork Orange* and *Taxi Driver*, thinking that maybe too many years of prowling in the dark had ruined Eric Ambler, and now it was eating away at me. I wanted Ambler punished for that. I wanted maybe just a little sunlight, but I was dozing, breaking up like a TV signal going static.

Around midnight my next shift I found Ambler's phone number in the membership files and called. If he answered I'd just disconnect, but the voice was groggy and female, asking, "Who is this? What's wrong?"

"This is All Nite Video calling to remind you that you have a rental three nights overdue."

"All night—a video? Rental? What time is it?"

"The video was rented by Mr. Eric Ambler. *The Devil in Miss Jones: Part 6.*"

"The devil what?"

"It's an adult title, ma'am. An X-rated movie."

The dead air between us chilled like frost. "My husband doesn't rent those. He's never even been to—what's it called?"

"You might want to check with him."

"I don't know," she said. She lilted her voice like she hoped this was a mistake, but she knew. I was almost nauseous with triumph because I wanted to think Ambler had nothing but dust and desire in his heart. Our OPEN sign glowed, inviting his revenge.

Instead, Bailey arrived, but not until five hours later, lugging a vinyl satchel. "I come bearing gifts—well, a loaner," she whispered. "JVC camcorder. It's got one of those nifty little pop-out screens, but you can still stick your eye in it too. I'm letting you borrow it."

"I can't just start taping—"

"It's my dad's," she said, "but he doesn't use it. He bought it to film my mom when she was a stage actress at the community theater in Rochester, but she wanted bigger gigs in New York, so she split. Last year."

"I'm sorry," I said.

Bailey shrugged and passed the satchel. "You wanted to make a movie, so let's go. Improvisation."

"I only have a half-hour lunch break."

"We'll probably need an hour—tops," she said.

So twenty minutes later I sat dangling my legs through the canal bridge railing with the grates freeze-branding their shape into my ass. Through the camera lens I taped Bailey, fifteen feet below me in the canal basin, drained almost empty for the season. She slid on ice and arched her arms like a figure skater, twirling in her Super Grover sneakers. Her body caught the glimmer of the downtown streetlights like a living constellation spinning through a black galaxy.

"I wanted to be a skater," she said to me or the camera, "but my mother was afraid my vision would cause some trouble, that I would fall and bleed and never clot. So I didn't—no success story, no defying the odds." She seemed unreal, like a clockwork ballerina in a music box.

"I called Eric Ambler's wife," I said. "I got him back for what he did."

Bailey stopped. "What'd he do?"

"You know, stalking you. Trying to pick you up."

"I was just joking. He didn't say shit." She began to slide again, disinterested. The picture streaked as I tracked her elusive routine.

"I told his wife he had an overdue porno," I said.

"That's crude. Now she'll go ballistic, kick him out. He'll torch the store out of spite."

I lost sight of her, then I heard scrambling on the sandstone canal bed. I tried but I couldn't target her location with the viewfinder. I said, "At least my boss will get the insurance."

"Done filming, Hitchcock?" She stood beside me with a dust of snow flickering around her. Through the camera it looked like tiny bits of her face falling away.

"Ambler deserved it," I said. "He was a pervert."

"And you're a saint?" She leaned closer until her features blurred into whiteout.

I stopped filming and lowered the camera against my chest. The subzero wind tried to beat us, but Bailey grasped my face with her frozen hands.

Somehow, a footrace ensued. My shoes crunched over hardened sidewalk slush, and I lost her through the village shopping district, caught her distant shadow leaking across the vacant Superette parking lot. I found her heaving for breath beside the entrance to All Nite Video. "Kicked your skinny ass," she gasped.

Inside the store we warmed ourselves with the heat blasting from behind a missing plywood panel. Bailey's glasses fogged and then cleared while I filmed her browsing through comedies, horror, musicals.

"Have you ever considered acting, like your mother?"

"She didn't even say goodbye, you know. My mother. I remember the night she and my dad were dancing to 'Total Eclipse of the Heart' in the living room. Mom sang along and Dad did the 'turn around bright eyes' part. Candles lit all over the place—pretty sticky stuff. I went to bed, and then later mom peeked in and said goodnight. Not goodbye. Just goodnight. Then the next morning she was gone, like nothing." With both hands she flattened her white hair, but it plumed back outward again.

I peered through the camera and cradled its gentle whirling body in my hands and felt a kind of security I never knew before. My movie eye followed her through a doorway into orange light and a wall of cover boxes drenched with smut. The porn closet.

"There's a whole lot of fucking in here," Bailey said.

"I should have warned you," I said.

"Chill out," she said. "Can you imagine? Albino porn? I'd make a killing. You know there's a thirsty market for it."

"You'd have to be another kind of person," I said.

"You're right," she said.

The video image must have jittered while she spoke. I thought of

Ambler, how I'd indicted him for less than I was considering now.

"No customers around," Bailey said, and she wiggled the army jacket from her shoulders. Below she wore a silk tropical button-down; I noticed with that careful attention any guy pays to a girl's clothes when they're about to be removed. She unclasped buttons, exposing white skin.

She shoved past me, back into view of the storefront window as big as a Cineplex screen. I shivered and tensed and several times stumbled while I trained the camera on her bare shoulders as they drifted down another aisle. The microphone captured her chilly laughter. The camera tracked her as she peeled away her clothes—through the open video racks that flickered her image like vintage film. She screeched, laughing, and dashed for the checkout station wearing nothing but sneakers. Her body was like the outline of a woman carefully snipped from each frame, white as projector light itself.

She ran again, toward the office, and she splayed herself across the futon there. I zoomed inward, revealing just beneath her skin all the veins that spilled over her shoulders and arms, collecting in blue currents at her wrists. I gawked, allowed by the camera to gawk, and wondered why I should be granted this gift over anyone else, over Eric Ambler. For a second I might've even imagined myself more handsome or smarter or worthier, but please—

The image went blue and the battery icon flashed.

"Uh-oh," I said.

"No, no—damn it," said Bailey. She lunged and snatched away the camera. "It's dead, isn't it? The battery?" She punched buttons like her panic might spark a backup.

"We got plenty of footage."

"Why don't they make eight hour batteries?"

"People don't have the patience," I said. Subtle chimes jingled with my words. This sound was not magic but, rather, the entrance bell. Bailey hugged her knees, balled herself up to hide the nudity. I threw myself around the office in search of coverings. Nothing but empty boxes and packaging.

"Just go," she whispered.

I pulled the office door shut behind me. On the floor below the sci-fi section Bailey's army jacket lay discarded. A little further down was her tropical shirt. I scooped these up on my way toward the checkout, where my customer waited with his pants seat leaned against the countertop. A scruffy guy maybe forty in a flannel shirt and dusty hiking boots. Eyes concealed by his Mets baseball cap. He loafed like the place belonged to him. That's how I knew he was Josephine's felon ex-husband.

"Where's Jo?" he asked.

I froze beside a Christmas-themed endcap. Bailey's boxer shorts—yes, with smiley faces—lay crumpled on the counter near the ex's elbow. "She's not here."

Dull dawn had washed over the widescreen backdrop, lighting the grime and the gray-crusted snow. Now was the hour of Josephine's arrival, but a rush of loyalty forbade me from telling him. Plus she always came through the back, where Bailey now hid in the buff.

"Bullshit. She ain't at home, so she's here."

"But she's not," I said.

I considered his dry, ruddy knuckles and the larger bulges in his jacket where a weapon might be stuffed. He nudged the boxer shorts with his thumb to check if they were really dead. "What's going on around here, Chief? What's this all about?"

Boldfaced honesty seemed appropriate—admirable even. "My girl—"

"Jo's in the back room, ain't she?" Ex unzipped his jacket.

Mortal danger, panic—these disarmed my aptitude for clever banter, so instead I said "Don't you have a restraining order?"

"How the fuck you even know who I am? Who're you?"

"I work here," I said.

A car veered into the parking lot and its headlights tracked upon us through the window. Eric Ambler exited the shotgun seat with a cardboard box in his hands. I saw nothing of the driver except her permed ball of hair, but she had to be his wife. Ambler nudged his hip against the entrance. His box was overflowing with more than a dozen porn tapes, all in their original lurid boxes.

Ex-husband reached into a jacket pocket. I squinted, feeling woozy.

Oblivious, Ambler came to the counter and dropped his collection. I couldn't budge from where I obstructed the aisle that might lead these men toward Bailey.

"I need to return these," Ambler said.

My senses revved, ready to capture every beat of what I witnessed. I'd remember it all for Bailey.

From his pocket, ex-husband produced a tissue and blew his nose into it. He studied his emissions like they were his fortune, then he shoved the tissue away. "Son of a bitch," he muttered.

I told Ambler: "We don't really accept purchase returns that have been opened unless they're damaged."

"Damaged," the ex-husband said with a snort.

Ambler cleared his throat. "I don't need a refund. I just need you to take this merchandise because I can't keep it. You can resell it for profit."

His wife honked her horn and startled all three of us. With that jolt, we were diffused. The Amblers, our saviors. The ex nodded his cap brim at Bailey's clothes, at the office door behind me, at Ambler's smut stash on the counter. "You know who I am, then you tell her I was here, right?"

The Amblers' car had rumbled away by the time I collected Bailey's clothes—one sock draped over a copy of *Rear Window* on the Hitchcock shelf. Where Josephine's ex-husband had gone I didn't know. Out of sight, off screen, he didn't exist.

Bailey had succumbed to a fetal sleep on the office futon. She'd cloaked herself with sheets of bubble wrap packaging, and her skin magnified in the domed cells as if they were infused with milk. Over her hazy nakedness I laid her pants, her shirt, her jacket. I knelt beside the couch, listening to her breath, tapping the effects buttons on her camera. Somehow the videotape ejected with the clatter and whirl of robotics, but Bailey didn't wake.

Back at my station I chose a screwdriver from Josephine's miniature toolbox. I set the videotape lengthwise on the countertop and shimmied the screwdriver through its midsection until the cassette broke and spilled its two white spools and celluloid reams like the entrails of a gutted animal. Now those images it had captured were forever mine alone. No one else would ever see them like I had. No one else could judge whether or not I deserved them.

I lifted a handful of videotape, held it like a loose pom-pom. Just then Josephine limped through the office door, and her son Bobby burst out from behind her and barreled toward the gumball machine. He strangled it with both hands, throttled it so the gumballs jostled inside the glass.

My boss didn't seem to have noticed Bailey on the couch back there, but I wasn't surprised. Apparitions are not meant for everyone's eyes. And now: here's Bobby in his berserker glee filching my video ribbon and jogging a marathon of circles, hands aloft, fluttering the ribbon through his fingers like a banner for some sort of cause. Bailey and I are riding inside of those twisted reels. We are staging an overnight dream-play that will sleep now for always. ◉

AFTER WORDS

"All Nite Video" followed me through eleven years of my fiction apprenticeship, revised more than anything else I've written. In many ways it's a typical undergrad story, similar to narratives I see from my own students and in too many independent films: ambitious but disaffected-for-no-good-reason narrator meets sarcastic girl of his dreams. But it came from plenty of truth that's been deleted, twisted, and reexamined throughout the story's evolution. Plus it was the first story that my mentor Wendy Brenner was truly excited about. It was staged at SUNY Brockport, my undergraduate institution, and later as a single-showing play at UNCW, but it didn't really spark to life until I started working in a seedy video store (now defunct) in Wilmington, NC. It was freakishly like the place I imagined years earlier, except with better details to steal. Still, the revisions and rejections went on until 2006 when the Pedestal Magazine *mercifully helped me put it to rest. I still get a kick out of it because it's a tall tale version of how my wife and I met, so different from my other fiction, so weirdly optimistic.*

TIM BASS

YOU WANT FRIES WITH THAT?

HE SITS ACROSS FROM ME with a pink face and pillow hair, looking as if he has just dragged out of bed. A ridge of wrinkles crunches up one leg of his slacks and one arm of his T-shirt. He has slept on his left side, maybe on a couch. His eyes sag half-closed. His neck shifts to keep his head upright, as if at any second he might fall away in sleep. It is two thirty in the afternoon.

I position my pen on a clean copy of the Student Advising and Midterm Academic Progress Report.

"Thomas," I say, "let's talk about how your semester is going."

He nods.

"All right," I say. "How many absences do you have in your biology class?"

He puts a hand to his chin and appears to ponder the question. But he doesn't answer.

"How many absences do you have in biology?" I ask again.

"Hmmm," he says. "I'm going to need to think about that one."

He draws in a deep breath and makes an air balloon in his mouth. He rolls it from cheek to cheek. Then he puffs out the air and sits staring at the carpet, the filing cabinet, the books on my shelves. Anything to avoid eye contact.

●

He wants to know how many times I've missed biology. Biology? Man, I barely remember going there at all. Maybe when the semester started. I think that was the big class, the one with the professor with the pointy ears. He wore a necktie, too. All these guys wear neckties. Even this advisor guy. He's wearing one. Blue.

I don't wear ties. I can't tie them. I tried, but I couldn't get the hang of it. Over, under, through the loop. It all ran together. My dad, he said, "Son, go to college and major in business. You'll get a good job, and maybe somebody will teach you how to tie a tie." Any job that needs a necktie is not a job for Thomas R. Jenkins. That's what I wanted to tell Dad. But I came to college anyway, and the first professor I saw had pointy ears and a necktie. I told myself, "That's about all the biology I think I'm going to need."

Now this guy here wants to know about biology. All I know about it is my body needs rest. I didn't go to bed last night until noon today, when I crashed on Snarfo's couch. I'd still be there now, except Snarfo and his girlfriend came in and started going at it, right on the spot. I had to get out of there before I saw parts of Snarfo that I didn't want to see. I guess I could tell this advisor guy about that. I mean, it's biology.

●

I look down at the file titled JENKINS, THOMAS R. First-semester freshman. Mostly Cs on his high-school transcript. A D-minus in Phys. Ed. He's not even close to U of A material, or UT, or Tech—the other schools where his buddies probably ended up. Excellent SATs, though. At a place like this, these numbers will get your application a second look. I glance over at Jenkins, who is scratching his head. I'm glad to know *something* is going on in there. But what? How much of his brain is he using? Not much, I suspect, judging from the looks of his face and his file. I'm suspect one good morning in an SAT exam room might be the only reason Jenkins, Thomas R. is on this campus today, seated in my advising office now, about to discuss his early progress toward a college degree. To be of any help to him at all, I have to know whether he goes to class. That's the minimum. I will run down the whole list with him: bio, then English, French, psych, and trig.

"How many absences in biology?" I ask him again.

"I'm still thinking," he says.

●

I'm thinking about going back to bed, but my room is clear across campus. Snarfo's place is a lot closer. Maybe he's got his girlfriend out of there now, and I can go back to the couch.

I could sleep, like, twenty-five hours a day. It's just the way God made me. If this place had a major in sleeping, I'd graduate with honors. But they don't. I checked on it. The closest thing is philosophy.

That biology class he's asking about, it's at eight in the morning. *Eight.* That's just not convenient. If these people want me to go to biology, they ought to make the pointy-eared guy teach it at one in the morning. I'm awake then.

●

Along with 199 other students, Thomas R. Jenkins is my charge—an advisee assigned to me when he showed up for summer orientation and indicated somewhere on some form that he had some interest in some area of fine arts, humanities, or the social sciences. These are my areas. Maybe he wrote down theatre or history. I get a lot of those, plus the occasional anthropology. It doesn't matter. For the first three semesters everybody takes general studies anyway—a lit class, a math, foreign language, western civ, one here one there, until they climb into a major. I help them negotiate the maze. I push the intro courses, try to keep them from getting in over their heads. A lot of mine say they want to major in cinema studies or forensic psychology, but our school doesn't offer cinema studies or forensic psychology. I suggest communications and criminal justice.

"Absences," I say to Thomas R. Jenkins. "Biology."

He scrunches up his face and pooches out his lips. He looks like a goldfish.

●

You know, if you stick your lips out far enough, you can see them. But it's not so easy with your chin.

●

Jenkins is working his lower jaw like a dinosaur. He appears to be studying something.

I dig deeper into his file. On his orientation form he first said he wanted to major in business, but he scratched through that and put photography. We don't have a photography major. But I don't care about that right now. What I care about is getting Thomas R. Jenkins to give me his class attendance so I can read him the riot act if he needs it or pat him on the back if he deserves it. Then I can do my paperwork and get him out the door so I can bring in the next advisee on my list.

I will spend three weeks rounding these people up. I have never met most of them. They are names on file folders and greenbar printouts. The great majority—I'd say 94 percent—will be doing fine in their classes: A few are on their way to the dean's list, most are on solid ground, some are hitting rough spots but will hang in there. They're OK.

The rest, that final 6 percent, are crashing and burning. Drinking, parties, up all night. They can't imagine learning as fun. They see fun as fun. They never get closer to the library than the smoking area by the front doors. For them, college would be great if classes didn't interrupt their free time. At the end of the semester, they will sell their textbooks in brand-new condition for pennies on the dollar.

I suspect Thomas R. Jenkins is among the 6 percenters. Maybe he thinks if he comes clean—if he tells me that he does not go to class regularly, or seldom, or ever—I will call the dean or his parents or some college-level truant officer. The truth is, I won't call anyone. But I don't tell him I won't.

●

My dad, he says if I don't get on the stick, he's sending me to the Army. I told him, "Nah, man, you can't just *send* somebody to the Army. It's not like mailing a package." He told me, "Son, with thinking like that, you better stay in college." Mom took his side. They'd freak if they knew how I'm doing here. But grades don't come out until the end of the semester. I'll shape things up by then. Get my ducks in a row, bull by the horn, monkey off my back. All that animal stuff. But this guy here, he wants to know about biology. He's waving his pen at me.

"I need to put down a number," he says to me.

"OK," I say to him.

He comes right back at me.

"So," he says, "how many absences do you have in your biology class?"

●

Jenkins bites his tongue and makes a squishing noise.

"Absences?" he says to me.

"Right," I say.

"In which class?"

"Biology."

"Biology?" he asks.

"Biology," I say.

"Absences in biology class?" he asks.

"Yes," I say.

It occurs to me that maybe Jenkins does not know the word *absences*. Or maybe he has aural difficulties and hears some other word, like *abscesses*. In that case he hears me asking, "How many abscesses do you have in your biology class?" I give him the benefit of the doubt, even though he has used the right word himself—*absences*—at least twice so far.

"Absences," I say. "Missed classes. Cuts."

●

This guy thinks I'm either hard of hearing or hard of thinking. What I want to tell him is, "Dude, can you just hang on about biology for a second? Because I need to tell you something. What I need to tell you is, that's about the bluest necktie I've ever seen in my life. I didn't know they made neckties that blue. I've never seen *anything* that blue. I've got a block of cheese that's been in my refrigerator since August, and it's pretty blue, but not *that* blue. That's bluer than blue. Isn't that a song? True blue. *Too* blue."

But I don't say all that. I can't come in here to this man's office and insult his taste in neckties. At least he doesn't have pointy ears.

●

No response. I glance at Jenkins's file and see nothing about aural difficulties. I decide to work with him, maybe draw him out bit by bit.

"Do me a favor," I say.

"You got it," he says.

"Close your eyes."

•

This is turning weird. Maybe he's going to hypnotize me.

"Let's say your biology professor gets the class together," the advisor guy says to me.

"All right," I say to him.

"There's a room. With desks. Maybe a blackboard."

"Yeah," I say. "I see that." And I really *do* see that. This man doesn't know neckties, but he can sure paint a picture.

"OK, good," he says. "Now, everybody gets together—the whole biology class."

"The whole biology class," I say.

"Except you," he says. "You're *not* there."

"I'm *not* there."

"Right," he says. "Everybody's there but you. Has that ever happened?"

"It might have," I tell him.

"Excellent!" he says, like he's getting all excited. "Now, how many times?"

•

Jenkins cranks his neck until it pops. Then he opens his eyes.

"Are you sure I'm in biology?" he asks.

"It says so on your registration," I say.

•

"I don't remember signing up for biology," I say, which is the truth. "I don't even like biology." That's the truth, too. "I'd have never signed up for biology if anybody had given me the chance to take something else. *Any*thing else. So maybe there's been some kind of mistake." I tell the guy all of this.

"You have to take a life science," he tells me back. "It's required."

"What about photography?" I ask. "Can't I take that?"

I decide not to break the news about photography.

"You have to take a life science," I say. "Biology is a life science. Photography is not a life science."

"Roger that," Jenkins says.

"Good," I say. "Now, how many times have you missed that class?"

"Photography? I'm not in photography."

I have learned not to get worked up during these sessions. I see dozens of students each week, hundreds each semester, so I pace myself. I help them pick their courses. I suggest professors to take and professors to avoid. I say go to class, schedule your study hours, get tutoring, spend time in the library. I say you need to choose a major. I hear their roommate problems, their parent problems, their credit card problems. I listen to their excuses and their lies. But no matter who the students are, from the highest achievers to the slackest slackers, when I ask how many times they have missed a class, they always, always come up with a number—*some* number—and we move on.

"*Biology*," I say to Thomas R. Jenkins. "How many times have you missed *biology*?"

"Wow," he says, looking surprised all of a sudden. "That's a tough one."

"What's tough about it?" I ask.

"The professor doesn't take attendance," he says.

My impulse is to follow up on that. I want to tell Thomas R. Jenkins it doesn't matter that the professor doesn't take attendance, but what does matter is that he, Jenkins, *must* go to class. Especially biology class, because he doesn't like biology, and the only thing worse than taking a class you don't like is *re*taking a class you don't like.

That is exactly what I would tell my 199 other advisees. But I don't say it to Jenkins. I let him go without the speech. I simply say goodbye and release him from the seat where he has twisted and grimaced for the past ten minutes. He has spent more energy not answering my one simple question than he would in a whole complicated semester of biology lectures and labs. He looks exhausted.

I'm exhausted. But he says we're done, so I'm out of here. Once I told him about the professor not taking attendance, he seemed to get where I was coming from. For a guy in a necktie like that, he's not so bad.

•

After Jenkins plods off, I look at his Student Advising and Mid-term Academic Progress Report. It is a clean form, empty of all information about how this young man is making his way in this university. I have no idea how he is making it. I have no idea who he is, whether he will ever attend another biology class—or *any* class, for that matter—no idea whether he will join the 6 percenters and end up washing out and back home wearing a paper hat and asking, "You want fries with that?" Or whether he will wake up one day and turn things around, grab his chance and make it here as his SATs indicate he can do, if he wants to. I can't predict what he will do. I have no idea if he will even find his way out of the building.

I put my pen to the form and write *Jenkins, Thomas R.* And in every box, I draw a big, bold question mark. ☙

AFTER WORDS

This story came to me after an advising session I had with a student. Getting him to answer a simple question—"How many times have you missed your biology class?"—was more challenging than doing surgery on a caffeinated ferret. I first wrote the story from the narrator's perspective only but later added the student's voice for balance. I wanted to avoid the tired tendency to create a wise-guy narrator who takes cheap, easy shots at the expense of a clueless character. This forced me to see the situation from the student's perspective in addition to the advisor's. Through writing and rewriting, I moved deeper into fiction and further from the scene that happened in real life. All that's left are that original question, along with the student's eventual answer: "The professor doesn't take attendance." I want my fiction to resemble real people and real events. But I make the stuff up.

REBECCA LEE

THE BANKS OF THE VISTULA

IT WAS DARK; the campus had turned to velvet. I walked the brick path to Humanities, which loomed there and seemed to incline towards me, as God does the sinner in the Book of Psalms. It was late on a Friday afternoon, when the air is fertile, about to split and reveal its warm fruit, that gold nucleus of time, the weekend.

Inside, up the stairs, Professor Stasselova's door was open, and he lifted his head. "Oh," he said. "Yes." He coughed, deep in his lungs, which I found stirring, and motioned me in. He had requested this visit earlier in the day, following class. His course was titled Speaking in Tongues: Introductory Linguistics. Stasselova was about fifty-five, and a big man, his torso an almost perfect square. Behind his balding head the blonde architecture of St. Olaf College rose into the cobalt sky. It looked like a rendition of thought itself, rising out of the head in intricate, heartbreaking cornices that become more abstract and complicated as they rise.

I was in my third week of college. I loved every moment of it, every footfall. The students were the same students as in high school, Scandinavian midwesterners like myself, whose fathers were all pastors or some declension thereof—but it was the professors who thrilled me.

Most had come from the East Coast, and those ones seemed so fragile and miserable to be in the Midwest. Occasionally during class, you could see hope rising in them for us, and then they would look like great birds in a difficult landscape, pale and overextended, asking mysterious questions, trying to lead us someplace we could not yet go.

At any rate, I wanted to be noticed by them, to distinguish myself from the ordinary mass of students, and to this end, I had plagiarized my first paper for Stasselova's class. And this was why, I presumed, he had called me to his office.

The paper, which was titled "The Common Harvest," was on the desk between us. I had found it in the basement of the Kierkegaard Library. It was a chapter in an old green cloth book that was so small I could palm it. The book had been written in 1945, by a man named Delores Tretsky, and not signed out since 1956. I began to leaf through it, and then crouched down to read. I read for a full hour; I thought it beautiful. I had not once in all my life stopped for even a moment to consider grammar, to wonder how it rose out of history like a wing unfurling.

I had intended to write my own paper, to synthesize, as Stasselova had suggested, my own ideas with the author's, but I simply had nothing to contribute. It seemed even rude to combine this work with my own pale, unemotional ideas. So, I lifted a chapter, only occasionally dimming some passages that were too fine, too blinding.

"This is an extraordinary paper," he said. He was holding his coffee cup over it, and I saw some had already spilled on the page in the form of a small, murky pond.

"Thank you," I said.

"It seemed quite sophisticated. You must not be straight out of high school."

"I am," I said.

"Oh. Well, good for you."

"Thanks."

"You seem fully immersed in a study of oppression. Any reason for this?"

"Well, I do live in the world."

"Yes, that's right. And you say here, a shocking line, that a language must sometimes be repressed, and replaced for the larger good. You believe this?"

"Yes."

"You think that the East Bloc countries should be forced to speak, as you say here, the Mother Tongue?"

Some parts of the paper I had just copied down verbatim, without really understanding, and now I was stuck with them. Now they were my opinions. "Yes," I said.

"You know I am from this region."

"Is that right?"

"From Poland."

"Whereabouts in Poland?" I asked, conversationally.

"The edge of it, the Black Forest, before Russia took it over completely. As a child, we were forced to speak Russian, even in our homes, even when we said goodnight to our mothers as we fell off to sleep."

"Oh my."

"When did you write this?" he asked.

"Last week."

"It reads like it was written fifty years ago. It reads like Soviet propaganda."

"Oh," I said. "I didn't mean it that way."

"Did somebody help you?"

"Actually, yes. Certainly that's all right?"

"Of course, if done properly. Who was it that helped you, a book or a person?"

"My roommate helped me," I said.

"Your roommate. What is her name?"

"Solveig."

"Solveig what?"

"Solveig Juliusson."

"Is she a linguistics scholar?"

"No, just very bright."

"Maybe I can talk to Solveig myself?"

"Unfortunately, you can't."

"Why not?"

"It's complicated."

"In what way?"

"Well, she's stopped eating. She's very thin; her parents were worried so they took her home."

"Where does she live?"

"I don't know."

We both sat silently. Luckily, I had experience lying to my pastor father, and knew it was possible to win even though both parties were aware of the lie. The whole exercise was not a search for truth at all, but rather a test of exterior reserve.

"I'm sure she'll be returning soon," I said. "I'll have her call you."

Stasselova smiled. "Tell her to eat up," he said, his sarcasm curled inside his concern.

"Okay," I said, and got up, hoisted my bag over my shoulder. As I stood I could see the upper edge of the sun, as it fell down off the hill on which St. Olaf was built. I'd never really seen the sun from this angle before, from above as it fell, as it so obviously lit up another part of the world, perhaps even flaming up the sights of Stasselova's precious, oppressed Poland, its black forests and onion-dome churches, its dreamy and violent borders.

My roommate Solveig was permanently tan. She went twice a week to the booth and bleached her hair frequently, so that it looked like radioactive foliage growing out of dark moody sands. Despite all of this, she was very sensible.

"Margaret," she said, when I came in that evening. "The library telephoned to recall a book. They said it was urgent."

I had thought he might check the library. "Okay," I said. As I rifled through the clothes on my closet floor, I decided it would have to be burned. I would finish the book and then I would burn it. But first there was tonight, and I had, that rare thing, a date.

My date was from Stasselova's class. His name was Rolf; he was a junior whose father was a diplomat. He had almost auburn hair that fell to his neckline. He wore, always, long white shirts whose sleeves were just slightly, almost imperceptibly puffed at the shoulders, like a little elegant joke, and then very long so they hung over his hands. I thought he was articulate, kind. I had, in an astonished moment, asked him out.

The night was soft, warm. We walked through the tiny town, wandered its thin river. We ate burgers. He spoke of Moscow, where he had lived that summer. I had spent my childhood with a vision of Russia in the distance, an anti-America, a sort of fairy-tale, intellectual prison, but this was 1986, the beginning of perestroika, of glasnost, and all that was changing. The televisions were showing a country of rain and difficulty and great humility, and long shots of Gorbachev, who was always bowing to sign something or other, whose head bore the mysterious stain of a continent one could almost name, but not quite. I said to Rolf I wanted to go there myself, though it had never occurred to me before that moment. He said, you can if you want. We were in his small iridescent apartment by now. "Or perhaps to Poland," I said, thinking of Stasselova.

"Poland," Rolf said, "Yes. What is left of it, after men like Stasselova."

"What do you mean, men like Stasselova?"

"Soviet puppets."

"Yet he is clearly anti-Soviet," I said.

"Now, yes. Everybody is anti-Soviet now." The sign for the one Japanese restaurant in town cast an orange worldly light into the room, carving Rolf's body into geometric shapes. He took my hand, and it seemed then the whole world had entered his apartment. I found him intelligent, deliberate, high-hearted. "Now," he said, "is the time to be anti-Soviet."

On Monday afternoon, in class, Rolf sat across from me. We were all sitting around a conference table, waiting for Stasselova. Rolf smiled. I gave him the peace sign across the table. When I looked back at him, moments later, Rolf's hands were casually laid out on the table, palms down. I saw then, for the first time, that his left hand tapered into only three fingers, which were all fused together to the top knuckle. It looked delicate, surprising. I had not noticed this on our date, and now I wondered if he had purposefully kept me from seeing it, or if I had just somehow missed it. I even, for a brief, confused moment, wondered if it had happened between then and now. Rolf looked me squarely in the eye. I smiled back.

Stasselova then entered the room. In light of my date with Rolf I had almost forgotten my visit with him on Friday afternoon. I'd meant to burn the book over the weekend in the darkness at the ravine, though I dreaded this. My own mother was a librarian, and I knew the vision of her daughter burning a book would have been like a sledgehammer to her kind and literate heart.

That class, it seemed to me that Stasselova was speaking directly to me, still chastising me. His eyes kept resting on me, disapprovingly. "The reason for the sentence is to express the verb—a change, a desire. But the verb cannot stand alone; it needs to be supported, to be realized by a body, and thus the noun. Just as the soul in its trajectory through life needs to be comforted by the body."

The sun's rays slanted in on him, bisecting his own soulful body into clean shafts, as Stasselova veered into very interesting territory; "All things in revolution," he said, "in this way, need protection. For instance, when I was your age, my country Poland was annexed by the Soviet Union. We had the choice of joining what was called Berling's Army, or the Polish Wing of the Russian Army. Many considered it anti-Polish to join the Russian Army, but I believed, as did my comrades, that more could be done through the system, within the support of the system, than without."

He looked at me. I nodded. I was one of those students who nod a lot. His eyes were like brown velvet, under glass. "This is the power of the sentence," he said. "It acts out this drama of control and subversion. The noun always stands for what is, the status quo, and the verb for what might be, the ideal."

Across the table Rolf's damaged hand, spindly and nervy, drummed impatiently on the table top. I could tell he wanted to speak up. Stasselova turned to him. "That was the decision I made," he said, "twenty years ago. Right or wrong, I thought it best at the time. I thought we could do more work for the Polish cause from within the Red Army than from outside it."

Rolf's face was impassive. He looked years older suddenly—austere, cold, priestly. Stasselova turned then to look at me. This was obviously an issue for him, I thought to myself, and I nodded as he continued to speak. I really did feel supportive. Whatever army he thought was best at the time, that was fine with me.

In the evening I went to the ravine in the elm forest, which lay curled around the hill on which the campus was built. This forest seemed deeply peaceful to me, almost conscious. I didn't know the reason for this at the time, that elms in a forest all spring from a single elm, unlike the wild, proliferating forests of my adolescence, which bred indiscriminately. Rather, this was in fact a single elm, which had divided herself into a forest. It was an individual, with a continuous DNA, in whose midst one could stand and be held.

The ravine cut through like an old emotional wound. I crouched on its banks, glanced through the book one last time. I flicked open my lighter. The book caught instantly. As the flame approached my hand, I arced the book into the murky water. It looked spectacular, a high wing of flame rising from it. Inside, in one of its luminous chapters, I had read that the ability to use language, and the ability to tame fire arose from the same warm, shimmering pool of genes, since in nature they did not appear, one without the other.

As I made my way out of the woods, into the long, silver ditch that lined the highway, I heard about a thousand birds cry, and I craned my neck to see them lighting from the tips of the elms. They looked like ideas would, if released suddenly from the page and given bodies, shocked at how blood actually felt as it ran through the veins, as it sent one wheeling into the west, wings raking, straining against the requirements of such a physical world.

I returned and found Solveig turning in the lamplight. Her hair was piled on her head, so unnaturally blond it looked ablaze and her face was bronze. She looked one thousand years old. "Some guy called," she said, "Stasselova or something."

He called again that night, at nearly midnight. I thought this unseemly.

"So," he said, "Solveig's back."

"Yes," I said, glancing at her. She was at her mirror, performing some ablution on her face. "She's much better."

"Perhaps the three of us can now meet."

"Oh," I said, "it's too early."

"Too early in what?"

"In her recovery." Solveig wheeled her head around to look at me. I smiled, shrugged.

"I think she'll be okay."

"I'm not so sure."

"Listen," he said, "I'll give you a choice; you can either rewrite the paper in my office, bringing in whatever materials you need, or the three of us can meet together, and clear this up."

"Fine, we'll meet you."

"You know my hours."

"I do," I hung up, and explained to Solveig what had happened—Stasselova's obsession with language and oppression, my plagiarism, the invocation of her name. Solveig nodded and said of course, whatever she could do she would.

When we arrived that Wednesday, the light had already left his office, but was still lingering outside the windows, like the light in fairy tales, rich and creepy.

Solveig was brilliant. Just her posture, as she sat in the spiny chair was enough to initially chasten Stasselova. In her presence, men were driven to politeness, to sincerity, to a kind of deep, internal apology. He thanked her, bowing a little in his desk. "Your work has interested me," he said.

"It is not my work, sir. It's Margaret's. We just discussed together some of the ideas."

"Such as?"

"Well, the necessity of a collective language, a mutual tongue."

"And why's that necessary?" Stasselova leaned back and folded his hands across his vast torso.

"To maintain order," she said. And then the sun fell completely, blowing one last blast of light across the Americas before it settled into what was left of the Soviet Union, and some of that light, a glittery, barely perceptible dust, settled around Solveig's head. She looked like a dominatrix, an intellectual dominatrix, delivering this brutal news.

"And your history in psycholinguistics?" he said.

"I have only my personal history," she said, "The things that have happened to me." I would not have been surprised, at that declaration, if the whole university had folded up, turned to liquid, and flowed away. "Besides," she said, "All the research and work was Margaret's. I saw her working on it, night after night."

"Then Margaret," he turned his gaze on me. "I see you are intimately connected with evolutionary history, as well as Soviet ideology. As well, it appears you've been steeped in a lifetime's study of linguistic psycho-social theory."

"Is it because she's female," Solveig asked, "that she's made to account for every scrap of knowledge?"

"Look," he said, after a long, brutal silence, "I simply want to know from what cesspool these ideas arose. If you got them from a book, I will be relieved, but if these ideas are still floating around in your blood-lines, in your wretched little towns, I want to know."

I was about to cave in. Better a plagiarizer than a fascist from a tainted bloodline.

"I don't really think you should be talking about our bloodlines," Solveig said, "It's probably not appropriate." She enunciated the word appropriate in such a way that Stasselova flinched, just slightly. Both he and I stared at her. She really was extraordinarily thin. In a certain light she could look shockingly beautiful, but in another, such as the dying one in Stasselova's office, she could look rather threatening. Her contact lenses were the color of a night sky when it is split by lightning. Her genetic information was almost entirely hidden—the color of her hair and eyes and skin, the shape of her body, and this gave her a psychological advantage, of sorts.

Stasselova's lecture on Thursday afternoon was another strange little affair, given as long autumn rays of sun, embroidered by leaves, covered his face and body. He was onto his main obsession again, the verb, specifically the work of the verb in the sentence, and how it relates to the work of a man in the world.

"The revolution takes place from a position of stability, always. The true revolutionary will find his place within the status quo."

"And this is why you joined the Russian Army in attacking your own country?" This was Rolf, startling us all.

"I did not attack my own country," Stasselova said, "Never."

"But you watched as the Nazis attacked it in June of 1941, yes? And used that attack to your own purposes?"

"This night I was there, it's true," he said. "On the banks of the Vistula, and I saw Warsaw burn. And I was wearing the fur hat of Russia, yes. But when I attempted to cross the Vistula, in order to help across those of my countrymen who were escaping, I was brought down, clubbed with a rifle to the back of the head by my general, a Russian."

"That's interesting, because in accounts of the time, you are referred to as a general yourself, General Stasselova, of course."

"Yes, I was a Polish general, though. Certainly you can infer the hierarchy involved?"

"What I can infer," Rolf's voice rose, and then Stasselova's joined in, contrapuntally, "What you can infer," and for a moment it reminded me of those rounds of songs we sang at summer camp. "What you can infer," Stasselova drowned out Rolf, "is that this was an ambiguous time for those of us who were Polish. There is not a way to judge after the fact. Perhaps you think that I should be dead on those banks, making the willows to grow." Stasselova's eyes were shot with the fading light; he squinted at us and looked out the window momentarily. "You will stand there and think maybe certain men in certain times should not choose their own lives, should not want to live." And then he turned away from Rolf. I myself scowled at Rolf. So rude!

"And so I did live," Stasselova said finally, "mostly because I was wearing my Russian hat, made of the fur of ten foxes. It was always Russia that dealt us blows, and it was always Russia that saved us. You see?"

The next day I was with Rolf, in the woods. We were on our stomachs in a clearing, looking to the east, where the rain was stalking us through the trees.

"What I want to know," Rolf was saying, "is why's he always asking for you to see him?"

"Oh," I said. "He thinks I plagiarized that first paper."

"Did you?"

"Not really."

"Why does he think so?"

"Says it smacks of Soviet propaganda."

"Really? Well, he should know."

"I agree with him, that you're judging him from an irrelevant stance." "He was found guilty of treason by his own people, not me, by the Committee for Constitutional Responsibility. Why else would he be here, teaching at some Lutheran college in Minnesota? This is a guy who brought down martial law on his own people, and then we sit here in the afternoon and watch him stalk around in front of us, relating everything he speaks of, *comma splices* for Christ's sake, to his own innocence."

"Yet all sorts of people were found guilty of all sorts of meaningless things by that committee."

"I bet he thinks you're a real dream, this woman willing to absolve the old exterminator of his sins."

"That's insulting," I said. But it was interesting to me, how fond I'd grown of him in his little office, drinking his bitter coffee, night descending into the musky heart of Humanities.

And then the rain was upon us. We could hear it on the tiny ledges of leaves above us, more than feel it. "Let's go," Rolf said, grabbing my hand with his left, damaged hand. The way his hand held mine was alluring; his hand had the nimbus of an idea about it, as if the gene that had sprung this hand had a different world in mind, a better world, where hands had more torque when they grasped each other and people held things differently, as hooks held things, a world where all objects were shaped something like lanterns, and passed on and on.

The next morning was gray, with long, silver streaks of rain. I dragged myself out of the warmth of bed, and put on my rain slicker. It was nine forty-five as I headed toward Stasselova's office.

"Hello," I said, knocking on the open door. "I'm sorry to disturb you outside your office hours." I was shivering; I felt pathetic.

"Margaret," he said, "Hello. Come in." As I sat down, he said, "You've brought with you the smell of rain."

He poured me a cup of coffee in a Styrofoam cup. During our last class I had been so moved by his description of that night on the Vistula that I'd decided to confess. But now I was hesitating. "Could I have some of this cream?" I asked, pointing to a little tin cup of it on his windowsill.

"There it is again," he said, as he reached for the cream.

"There is what again?"

"That little verbal tic of yours."

"I didn't know I had one," I said.

"Oh you do," he said. "Using definite articles where the indefinite would be more expected. It's quite moving."

I had no idea what he was talking about, so stayed silent.

"I noticed it first in class," he said. "You say 'this' instead of 'that'; 'this cream', not 'that cream'. The line a person draws between the things they consider this, and the things they consider that is the perimeter of their sphere of intimacy. You see. Everything inside is 'this', everything inside is close, is intimate. Since you pointed at the cream, and it is farther from you than I am, this suggests that I am inside the things you consider close to you. I'm flattered," he said and handed me the creamer, which was, like him, sweating. What an idea, that one could, by a few words, catch another person in a little grammatical clutch, arrange the objects of the world such that they border the two of you.

"At any rate," he said, "it's fortunate you showed up."

"It is?"

"Yes. I've wanted to ask you something."

"Yes?"

"This spring, the college will hold its annual symposium on language and politics. I thought you might present your paper. Usually one of the upperclassmen does this, but I thought your paper might be the more appropriate."

"I thought you hated my paper."

"I do."

"Oh."

"So you'll do it."

"I'll think about it," I said. He nodded and smiled, as if it were settled. The rain was suddenly coming down very hard. It was loud, and we were silent for a few moments, listening. I stared out the window beyond his head, which was blurry with water, so that the turrets of campus looked like a hallucination, like some shadow world looming back there, in his unconscious.

"This rain," he said then, in a quiet, astonished voice, and this word, this, entered me as it was meant to—quietly, with a sharp tip, but then, like an arrowhead, widening and widening, until it included the whole landscape around us.

The rain turned to snow, and winter settled on our campus. The face of nature turned away—beautiful and distracted. After Christmas at home (where I received my report card, a tiny slip of paper that seemed to have flown across the snows to deliver me my A in Stasselova's class), I hunkered down in my dorm for the month of January, and barely emerged. The dorm in which most of us freshman girls lived was the elaborate, dark Agnes Mellby Hall, named after the formidable virgin whose picture hung over the fireplace in our lounge.

As winter crept over us, the sun falling by three thirty on the darkest afternoons, we retired earlier and earlier to Mellby. Every night in that winter, in which most of us were nineteen, was a slumber party in the main sitting room, amongst its ornate furnishings, which all had the paws of beasts where they touched the floor. There, nightly, we ate like Romans, but childish foods—popcorn and pizza and ice cream—most of us spiraling downstairs now and then to throw up in the one private bathroom.

On one of those nights, I was reading a book in the lounge when I received a phone call from Solveig, who was down at a house party in town, and wanted me to come help her home. She wasn't completely drunk, but calculated that she would be in about forty-five minutes. Her body was like a tract of nature that she understood perfectly—a constellation whose movement across the night sky she could predict, or a gathering storm, or maybe, more accurately, a sparkling stream of elements into which she introduced alcohol with such careful calibration that her blood flowed exactly as she desired, uphill and down, intersecting precisely, chemically, with time and fertility. Solveig did not stay at the dorm with us much, but rather ran with an older pack of girls, feminists mostly, who that winter happened to be involved in a series of protests, romantic insurrections, against the president of the college, who was clearly terrified of them.

About ten minutes before I was to leave, Stasselova appeared in the doorway of the sitting room. I had not seen him in over a month, since the last day of class, but he had called a few times. I had not returned his calls, in the hopes that he would forget me for the symposium. But here he was, wearing a long gray coat over his bulkiness. His head looked huge, the bones so widely spaced, like the architecture of some grand civic building.

The look in his eyes caused me to look out across the room and try to see what he was seeing—perhaps some debauched canvas of absolute female repose—girls lying everywhere in various modes of pajamas and sweats, surrounded by vast quantities of food and books. Some girls, and even I found this a bit creepy, had stuffed animals that they carried with them to the sitting room at night. I happened to be sitting above the fray, straddling a piano bench, with a book spread in front of me, but almost everybody else was lying about, on their backs with their feet propped on the couch, or stretched up in the air in weird hyper-extended angles, with extremities cast about. We were Lutherans, after all, and unlike the more promiscuous Catholic girls across the river, at Carleton College, we were losing our innocence right here, amongst ourselves. It was being taken from us physically, and we were just relaxing until it fell away completely.

Stasselova, in spite of all he'd seen in his life, which I'd gleaned from what he said in class—the corpulent Goerring marching through his forest, marking off Nazi territory, and later Stalin's horses, breaking through the same woods, heralding the swath that would now be Soviet—still managed to look a little scared as he peered into our sitting room, eventually lifting a hand to wave at me.

I got up, approached him. "Hey," I said.

"Hello, how are you, Margaret?"

"It's good to see you. Thanks for the A."

"You deserved it. Listen, I have something for you," he said, mildly gesturing for us to leave the doorway, since everybody was looking at us.

"Great," I said, "But you know, right now, I need to walk downtown to pick up Solveig at a house party."

"Excellent," he said, "I'll walk you."

"Oh. Okay."

I got my jacket and the two of us stepped into the night. The snow had arranged itself in curling waves on the Mellby lawn, and stuck in it were hundreds of silver forks which the freshman boys had, in a flood of early evening testosterone, placed in the earth, a gesture appropriate to their sexual frustration, and also their faith in the future. As Stasselova and I stepped through them, they looked spooky and lovely, like tiny silver grave sites in the snow. As we tread across campus, Stasselova produced a golden brochure from his pocket and handed it to me. On the front it said, in emerald green letters, 9TH ANNUAL SYMPOSIUM ON LANGUAGE AND POLITICS. Inside, there was my name under keynote student speaker. It said, Margaret Weatherford, "The Common Harvest." I stopped walking. We paused there, at the top of the stairs which floated down, off the campus, into the town. I felt extremely, inordinately proud. Some winter lightning, a couple of great wings of it, flashed in the north. Stasselova looked paternal, grand.

The air at the party was beery and wildish and the house itself seemed the product of a drunken, adolescent mind—its many random rooms, and slanting floors. We could not spot Solveig at first, so Stasselova and I waited quietly in the hallway until a guy in a baseball cap came lurching toward us, shouting in a friendly way, over the music, that we could buy a plastic glass for the keg for two dollars apiece. Stasselova paid him and then threaded through the crowd, gracefully for such a large man, to stand in the keg line. I watched him as he patiently stood there, the snowflakes melting on his dark shoulders.

And then Rolf was on my arm. "What on earth?" he said. "Why are you here? I thought you hated these parties." He'd been dancing, it seemed. He was soaked in sweat, his hair curling up at his neck.

I pointed to Stasselova.

"No kidding," Rolf said.

"He showed up at my dorm as I was leaving to get Solveig."

"He came to Mellby?"

"Yes."

"God, look at him. I bet they had a nickname for him, like the Circus-man or something. All those old fascists had cheery nicknames."

Stasselova was now walking toward us. Behind him the picture window revealed a nearly black sky, with pretty crystalline stars around. He looked like a dream one might have in childhood. "He is not a fascist," I said, quietly.

"Professor!" Rolf raised his glass.

"Rolf, yes, how are you?"

"This is a wonderful party," Stasselova said, and it actually was. Sometimes these parties could seem deeply cozy, their wildness and noise a reeling affirmation against the formless, white midwestern winter surrounding us.

He handed me a beer. "So," he said, rather formally, lifting his glass. "To youth."

"To experience," Rolf smiled, lifted his cup.

"To the party," Stasselova looked pleased, his eyes shining from the soft lamplight.

"The Party?" Rolf raised an eyebrow.

"This party," Stasselova said forcefully, cheerfully.

"And to the Committee," Rolf said.

"The Committee?"

"The Committee for Constitutional Responsibility."

In one of Stasselova's lectures he had taken great pains to explain to us that language did not describe events, it handled them, as a hand handles an object, and that in this way, language made the world happen under its supervision. And I could see Rolf had taken this to heart, and was making lurching attempts in this direction.

Mercifully, Solveig appeared. Her drunkenness and her dignity had synergized into something quite spectacular, an inner recklessness accompanied by great external restraint. Her hair looked the color of heat, bright white. She was wearing newly cut-off jeans and was holding the disassociated pant legs in her hand, absently.

"The professor," she said, when she saw Stasselova. "The professor of oppression."

"Hello, Solveig."

"So you came," she said, as if this had been the plan all along.

"Yes. It's nice to see you again."

"You as well," she said, "Why are you here?"

The whole scene looked deeply romantic to me. "To take you home," he said.

"Home?" she said, as if this were the most elegant and promising word in the language. "Yours or mine?"

"Yours, of course. Yours and Margaret's."

"Where is your home again?" she asked. Her eyes were glimmering with complexity, like something that is given the human after evolution, as a gift.

"I live downtown," he said.

"No, your real home. Your homeland."

He paused. "I am from Poland," he said finally.

"Then there. Let's go there. I have always wanted to go to Poland."

Stasselova smiled. "Perhaps you would like it there."

"I have always wanted to see Wenseslaus Square."

"Well, that is nearby."

"Excellent, let us go." And Solveig swung open the front door, walked into the snow, in her shorts and T-shirt. I kissed Rolf goodbye, and Stasselova and I followed her.

Once outside, Stasselova took off his coat and hung it around Solveig. Underneath his coat he was wearing a dark jacket and tie. It looked sweet, made me think you could keep undressing him, finding darker and darker suits underneath.

Solveig was walking before us on the narrow sidewalk. Above her on the hill hovered Humanities—great, intelligent, alight. She reached in her pocket and pulled out, to my astonishment, a fur hat. The hat! The kopek. The wind lifted, and the trees shook off a little of their silver snow, to get a better look. Humanities leaned over us, interested in its loving but secular way. I felt as sure as those archeologists who discover a single bone, and can then hypothesize the entire animal. Solveig placed it on her head, and turned to vamp for a moment, opening and closing the coat, then raising her arms in an exaggerated gesture of beauty above her head. She looked like some stirring, turning simulacrum of communist and capitalist ideas. As she was doing this, we passed by the president's house. It was an old-fashioned house, with high turrets, and then a bizarre modern wing hanging off one end of it. Solveig studied it for a moment as she walked, and then suddenly shouted into the cold night, "Motherfucker."

Stasselova looked as if he'd been clubbed again in the back of the head, but kept walking. He pretended nothing had happened, didn't even turn his head to look at the house, but when I turned to him I saw his eyes water, and his face stiffen with shock. I said, "Oh," quietly, and grabbed his hand for one moment to comfort him, to let him know everything was under control, that this was Minnesota and there would be no implications. Look, the president's house is still dark as death, the moon is still high, the snow sparkling everywhere.

His hand was extraordinarily big. After holding Rolf's hand for the last few months, Stasselova's more ordinary hand felt strange, almost mutant, its five splayed and independent fingers.

The next night in the cafeteria, over a grizzly and neon dish called Festival Rice, I told Rolf about the hat. "I saw the hat," I said.

A freshman across the cafeteria stood just then and shouted, in what was a St. Olaf tradition, "I want a standing ovation." The entire room stood and erupted into wild applause and hooting. Rolf and I stood as well, and as we clapped I leaned over to yell, "He's been telling the truth, about that night overlooking Warsaw; I saw the hat he was wearing."

"What does that mean? That means nothing. I have a fur hat."

"No," I said. "It was this big Russian hat. You should have seen it. This big beautiful Russian hat. Solveig put it on. It saved his life."

Rolf didn't even try to object, just kind of gasped, as if it hurt the great gears of logic in his brain to even pass this syllogism through. We were still standing, applauding. I couldn't help but think of something Stasselova had said in class, that in rallies for Stalin, when he spoke to crowds over loudspeakers, one could be shot for being the first to stop clapping.

●●●

I avoided my paper for the next month or so, until spring crashed in huge warm waves and I finally sought it out, sunk in its darkened drawer. It was a horrible surprise. I was not any more of a scholar, of course, than five months earlier, when I'd plagiarized it, but my eyes had now passed over Marx and a biography of Stalin (microphones lodged in eyeglasses, streams of censors on their way to work, the bloody corpses radiating out of Moscow) as well as the gentle Bonhoeffer. Almost miraculously, I had passed over that invisible line, beyond which people turn into actual readers, when they start to hear the voice of the writer as clearly as in a conversation. "Language," Tretsky had written, "is essentially a coercive act, and in the case of Eastern Europe must be used as a tool to garden collective hopes and aspirations."

As I read it, with Solveig napping at the other end of the couch, I felt a thick dread forming. Tretsky, with his suggestions of annexations and worse, of solutions, seemed to be reaching right off the page; his long, thin hand grasping me by the shirt. And I could almost hear the wild mazurka, as Stasselova had described it, fading, the cabarets closing down, the music turning into a chant, the boot heels falling, the language fortifying itself, becoming a stronghold—a fixed, unchanging system, as the paper said, a moral framework.

Almost immediately I was on my way to Stasselova's office, but not before my mother could call. The golden brochures had gotten out in the mail. "Sweetie!" she said, "what's this? Keynote speaker? Your father and I are beside ourselves. Good night!" She always exclaimed "good night" at times of great happiness, one of those lovely misfirings in the brain left over from childhood, a moment from deep in it when she had experienced great joy, perhaps, as somebody shouted good night from a far window, a sweet rag of long ago waving in the brain. I could not dissuade her from coming, and as I fled the dorm, into the rare, hybrid air of early April, I was wishing for those bad, indifferent parents who had no real interest in their children's lives.

The earth under my feet as I went to him was very sticky, almost lugubrious, like the earth one sometimes encounters in dreams. Stasselova was there, as always. He seemed pleased to see me. I sat down, and said, "You know, I was thinking that maybe somebody else could take my place at the symposium. As I reread my paper I realized it isn't really what I meant to say, at all."

"Oh," he said, "Of course you can deliver it. I would not abandon you at a moment like this."

"Really, I wouldn't take it as abandonment."

"I would not leave you in the lurch," he said, "I promise."

I felt myself being carried, mysteriously, into the doomed symposium, despite my resolve on the way over to back out at all costs. It is almost impossible to win an argument against somebody with an early training in propaganda. I had to resort finally to the truth, that rinky-dink little boat in the great sea of persuasion. "See, I didn't really write the paper myself."

"Well, every thinker builds an idea on the backs of those before him, or her, in your case," he smiled at this. His teeth were very square, and humble, with small gaps in between each one. I could see that Stasselova was no longer after a confession. I was more valuable if I contained these ideas. Probably he'd been looking, subconsciously, for me ever since he'd lain on the muddy banks of the Vistula, Warsaw flaming across the waters. He could see within me all of his failed ideals, the ugliness of his former beliefs contained in a benign vessel, a girl, high on a religious hill in the Midwest. Somebody he might oppose, and in this way absolve himself. He smiled. I could feel myself as indispensable in the organization of his psyche. Behind his head, in the winter sunset, the sun wasn't falling, only receding further and further.

The days before the symposium unfurled as the days before a wedding one dreads—both endless and accelerated, the sky filling with her springtime events—ravishing sun, great winds, and eccentric, green storms that lifted everybody's attention. And then the weekend of the symposium was upon us, the Saturday of my speech rising in the east. I awoke early, and fled the dorm to practice my paper on the red steps of Humanities, in whose auditorium my talk was to occur. Solveig was still sleeping, hung over from the night before. I'd been with her for the first part of it, watched her pursue a man she'd discovered—a graduate student, actually, in town for the symposium. I had thought him a bit of a bore, but I trusted Solveig's judgment on the affair. She approached men with stealth and insight, her vision driving into those truer, more isolated stretches of personality.

I had practiced the paper countless times, and revised it, attempting to excise the most offensive lines without gutting the paper entirely, and thus disappointing Stasselova. I was still, that morning, debating over the line, *If there could be a common language, a single human tongue, perhaps then a single flag may unfurl over the excellent earth, one nation of like and companion souls.* Reading it now I had a faint memory of my earlier enthusiasm for this paper, its surface promise, its murderous innocence. Remembering this, I looked out, over the excellent earth, at the town down the hill. And there, as in every view, was a tiny, gothic graveyard which looked so peaceful, everything still and settled finally under the gnarled, knotty, nearly human arms of apple trees. There were not apples yet, of course: they were making their way down the bough, still liquid or whatever they are before birth. At the sight of graves I couldn't help but think of Tretsky, my ghost writer, in his dark suit under the earth, delighted and preparing, thanks to me, for his one last gasp.

By noon, the auditorium had filled with a crowd of about two hundred, mostly graduate students and professors from around the Midwest, as well as Rolf and Solveig, who sat together, and two rows behind them, my long-suffering parents, flushed with pride. I sat on a slight stage at the front of the room alone, staring out at the auditorium, which was named Luther. It had wooden walls and was extremely tall; it seemed humble and a little awkward in that way the tall can seem. The windows stretched its full height, so that one could see the swell of earth on which Humanities was built, and then above all manner of weather, which this afternoon was running to rain. In front of these windows stood the reformed genius of martial law himself, the master of ceremonies, Stasselova. Behind him were maple trees, with small green leaves waving. He had always insisted in class that language, as it rises in the mind, looks like a tree branching. From finity to infinity. *Let every voice cry out!* He'd once said this, kind of absently, and water had come to his eyes, not exactly tears, just a rising of the body's water into one's line of sight.

After he introduced me, I stood in front of the crowd, my larynx rising quite against my will, and delivered my paper. I tried to speak each word as a discrete item, in order to persuade the audience not to synthesize them into meaning. But when I lifted my head to look out at the audience, I could see they were doing just that. When I got to the part where I said the individual did not exist—*merely shafts of light lost, redemptively, in the greater light of the state*—I saw Rolf bow his head, and rake his otherwordly hand through his hair . . . *And if force is required to forge a singular and mutual grammar, then it is our sacred duty to hasten the birthpangs.* I could hear, even from this distance, Stasselova breathing, and the sound of blood running through him, like a quiet but rushing stream.

And then my parents. As the speech wore on—harmony, force, flowering, blood—I could see that the very elegant parental machinery they had designed over the years, which sought always to translate my deeds into something lovely, light-bearing, full of promise—was spinning a little on its wheels. Only Solveig, that *apparatchik* of friendship, maintained her confidence in me. Even hung over, her posture suggested a perfect alignment between heaven and earth. She kept nodding, encouraging me.

I waited the entire speech for Stasselova to leap forward and confront me, to reassert his innocence in opposition to me, but he did not, even when I reached the end. He stood and watched as everybody clapped in bewilderment, and a flushed floral insignia rose on his cheeks. I had come to love his wide, excited face, the old Circusman. He smiled at me. He was my teacher, and he had wrapped himself, his elaborate historical self into this package, and stood in front of the high windows, to teach me my little lesson, which turned out not to be about Poland, or fascism, or war, borderlines, passion, or loyalty, but just about the sentence; the importance of; the sweetness of. And I did long for it, to say one true sentence of my own, to leap into the subject, that sturdy vessel travelling upstream through the axonal predicate, into what is possible, into the object which is all possibility, into what little we know of the future, of eternity, the light of which, incidentally, was streaming in on us just then through the high windows. Above Stasselova's head the storm clouds were dispersing, as if frightened by some impending goodwill, and I could see the birds were out again, forming into that familiar pointy hieroglyph, as they're told to do from deep within. ❧

AFTER WORDS

This story is not autobiographical, exactly, but its setting is the college I attended as an undergraduate. The characters are all sort of bizarre versions of people I actually know, and the event that kicks off the story—a girl plagiarizing a paper and then re-fusing to admit to it— really did happen, though not to me. Over the course of the few years (!) it took me to write this story, I literally crammed into it everything I possibly could—my study of language, an interest in fascist political thought, the total beauty of the seasons passing through the Midwest, and, of course, tormented love.

BY HIS WILD LONE

I. MIA

MY LITTLE SISTER grew up to be a tall, broad woman. But as a child, before adolescence, she was the tiniest, most fragile fairy creature you can imagine. Mia's bones were made of finer stuff than the rest of ours—hollow, like imported ivory. When you picked her up, it felt like she measured in ounces rather than pounds. She walked with a skip that originated in her slender knees, so springy that her feet barely touched the ground. It seemed a miracle that she'd even cast a shadow.

I usually don't have faith in my childhood memories. "Oh, Natalie," my mother always said, if I mentioned an event she didn't recall, "you must have dreamed it." But I do know that once on a Cape Cod beach the wind lifted Mia up off the sand. My brother Mark corroborates this: he was twelve, I was ten, Mia was six. The three of us stood on the beach late in the day, heading toward sunset, watching a stormy evening roll its way to shore. Dramatic, swirling winds and a thick, persistent mist. Heat lightning above our heads and across the melting horizon. Gust after gust assaulted us, but one felt like it came from below rather than above—like it had traveled across the waves horizontally, hugging the water and then the sand, to rise up inches from our feet in a full-force gale. And it lifted little Mia as if she were a sail or a parachute, her blond hair floating like a mermaid's, her body folding into a U and billowing upward into the air so that Mark and I each had to grab one hand and pull her back to the ground.

For a long time afterward, that storm seemed to live inside Mia. Before, she had been manageable and eager to please. Not exactly docile, but certainly not at all wild—which is what she became after the wind took her. She could no longer be trusted or controlled. Anything lost or broken, anything gone amiss, could always be traced to Mia. At the same time, when my parents attempted to punish her, she would turn up startlingly attractive, flashing an electric and remorseless grin several times bigger than herself, her tiny, blue-eyed form surrounded by a mischievous, glittering patina.

Before the storm, when Mia was well behaved, I loved her in the patronizing way of older sisters—remembering her mittens and tying her shoes, cultivating my own importance through small, tending tasks. After the storm, I stopped holding her hand when we crossed the street, or correcting her when she recited misinformation. Even Mark—twice her size and age—admitted to feeling a little nervous around Mia. But in a funny kind of way, we loved her more. In this particular phase, she possessed an intimidating sort of glamour: not the kind you see on the cover of magazines, but the kind witches use, to change form or to dazzle.

But Mia's store of electricity seemed to run out as she grew, and her personality returned to its original quiet. By fourteen she stood five foot eight with a substantial body mass index. She wore bras. She menstruated. She deferred to boys, to our parents, and to her teachers, eventually distinguishing herself by being the only girl in history to go away to college and stay faithful to her high-school sweetheart. Everybody loved Clay, and Mia returned home to marry him almost immediately after graduation. Their three children arrived in quick succession. Mia was a disorganized mother, but a loving one. Compassionate, selfless, always juggling everyone else's needs—running a house full of cats and children with a scattered, lenient sensibility. A likable woman, even an admirable one. The first person you'd call if you came down with the flu and needed soup or extra blankets. But still—and a little sadly if you'd known her as a child: surrounded with the dull light of day like the rest of us.

As an adult, Mia retained a taste for the odd and romantic: she loved stories with tragic endings. She loved myths and fairy tales about characters—especially cats—who transformed because of events, nightfall, or weather. But in her daily life, we never saw so much as a spark from that original storm until years later: the autumn Walter Engel lost control of his car at the corner of Sea Street and Vine, careening into the old post oak and catapulting Mia facefirst through his windshield.

At the time of Mia's accident, she and I both lived in the Cape Cod town where we'd spent our summers as children. I'd moved there from Vermont two and a half years before, wanting to be close to my sister on the heels of my thirtieth birthday and a humiliating divorce. Our old summer home had originally belonged to my mother's family, and she'd kept it after her own divorce from our father. She loaned it to Mia and Clay when Oscar, their first child, was born—temporarily, so they'd have a free place to live until they got on their feet financially. Which never happened. Clay worked as a teller at the local bank, and Mia wanted to stay at home with the children—who drained what little money Clay managed to earn. My mother attempted a few summers living with Mia, Clay, and their multiplying brood, but couldn't stand Mia's method of running a household, which was no method at all. Mia was the kind of mother who paid more attention to tears and tantrums than to dust and clutter. Mom finally threw up her hands and relinquished the place altogether. A year later she remarried and moved to Florida.

I lived footsteps down the road from Mia and Clay, in a weathered old Cape that sat above the beach where we used to play. At home I had no one but my Border collie Scout for company. Thanks to our family's local connections, I had landed a cushy job working from home, editing a column called "Special Memories" for a Cape-based magazine. The job was supposedly full-time, and paid me accordingly, but it rarely took more than one day a week. The magazine expected me to read each of the hundreds of letters sent in by readers, detailing life's particularly precious events, and choose one or two to run each week. Instead I'd wait until the end of the week and spend one morning reading twenty or thirty of the submissions. If this smaller pool didn't yield anything, I'd borrow a cute anecdote from one of Mia's children and attach a pseudonym. It was very easy, and left me plenty of time to spend with Mia and her family.

My mother's old house overlooked the marina, a picturesque but bustling view: I found the ocean sights and acoustics of my new place much more soothing. And when the shoreside winds knocked out my power, I could walk down the road and camp out at Mia's. Oscar, Juliette, and Deirdre (Mia's children) provided me with hugs and unconditional love whenever I needed them, and helping Mia made me feel useful and productive—especially when it came to six-year-old Oscar. Deirdre was barely two, naturally attracting plenty of lavish attention, and at three Juliette was a pretty and confident goody-goody, constantly correcting her siblings and asserting her own superiority. But Oscar had always been a sensitive, needy child—colicky as an infant, and so precocious as a toddler that you had to watch what you said around him before he was a year old. I loved Oscar—that particularly strong and poignant love inspired by awkward children. Whenever I picked him up at the Waldorf school, the sight of him made my heart constrict: Oscar blinking through thick glasses, an empty backpack strapped to his shoulders while he clutched an unwieldy stack of books and loose papers in his arms. Mia had named him after Oscar Wilde, and even before his classmates had a chance to torture him ("Oscar the Grouch," "os-SCAR"), he seemed burdened with angst worthy of his persecuted namesake.

When anything went wrong for my sister or myself—when Juliette was stung by a bee, when Mia ran out of milk, when I heard news of my ex-husband, Geoffrey, and Lacey, his new girlfriend, or when I stepped on a rusty nail and had to be rushed to the Med Stop for a tetanus shot—we were in shouting distance of each other. At the same time, I always had my own home for escape, away from the chaos of children and the fluff and swirl of Mia's cats, whose names she had chosen with her usual romantic pessimism—Heloise, Abelard, Icarus, Persephone, and Ophelia.

The Friday night Walter Engel crashed his car, I was at Mia's house in seconds. I pulled into the driveway to find Oscar pressed against the front bay window, sobbing hysterically through his myopic squint, two cats winding themselves around his ankles.

My dog Scout reached him first. She leapt up onto the windowsill, sent the cats leaping for safety, and covered Oscar's swollen face with rapid dog kisses. In my own agitated state, not knowing how bad Mia's accident was, I felt relieved to have Oscar to comfort. I scooped him out of Scout's clutches and rocked him, his tears gathering in the hollow of my collarbone.

Oscar and I sat up for hours before Clay called from the hospital in Hyannis, his throat chafed with shock, his deep voice reduced to a shaky whisper. Mia hadn't worn a seat belt, and shot through Walter's windshield like a cannon salute.

"She's in a coma," Clay told me. "The doctor rates it as a seven on a scale from one to ten."

I called my mother in Coral Gables, my brother Mark in Boston, my father in Jackson Hole. They all arrived the next day. Since I couldn't leave Mia's kids or bring them to the hospital, I was the last one to visit her. On Monday afternoon I finally made it to the hospital, my arms full of books from Mia's shelves. Considering her trip through the windshield, Mia looked remarkably all right. It was an eerie relief to see her lying there, looking peaceful and unbloody despite her broken cheekbone and the wires in her jaw.

Every day that week, while my mother, father, Clay, and Mark rotated watching the children, I sat by Mia's bedside and read her books aloud. I read her Japanese myths where vampires took the form of cats, and Chinese myths about cats warding off evil spirits in the night. I read a fairy tale called "The King of the Cats," where the family pet disappears up the chimney, and four different versions of "Puss 'n Boots."

I read her "The Cat That Walked by Himself," the Just So Story where a cat tricks a cavewoman into giving him the benefits of fire, hearth, and milk, but never really allows himself to be tamed. I'd bought this particular book for Mia several years before, when I was still married. Sitting by her bedside, I found myself reaching for it more often than any of the others. Not that it helped: Mia seemed to wither away by the hour, appearing more dependent on life-sustaining machinery with every passing day. "I am the Cat who walks by himself," I read, hoping the words might impress her subconscious with their autonomy, "and all places are alike to me."

● ● ●

The person who put in the most consistent bedside hours, aside from me, was Walter Engel. Clay, after all, had the kids, and occasional trips to check in with the bank. My parents had to rotate their shifts in order to avoid each other, and Mark had to travel back and forth from Boston. Walter had been given time off from his job at a resort hotel, and in the midst of familial comings and goings he paced Mia's room—his eyes watery and bloodshot, his curly blond hair in anguished disarray, his tall, bent figure filling up the room more often than I would have liked. Such a sad and broken emergency ought to be private, I thought. I assumed Walter's vigilance sprang from guilt—his being the driver, the owner of the car, and the relatively unscathed fellow victim. Walter's injuries were glaringly non-life-threatening: a broken wrist and a nasty cut over his eye. But he'd worn a seat belt, and compared to Mia was in great shape—and deep trouble, his blood having registered an alcohol level of .13.

None of us suspected anything scandalous between Mia and Walter. They'd known each other since their first swimming lessons at Squire's Pool. And while Mia generally spent evenings with her children, it wasn't unheard-of for her to go to an occasional party, or out for a drink, while Clay stayed home and watched the kids.

Also, everybody thought Walter was gay. He liked to wear outfits: matching socks and T-shirts, his gorgeous hair combed specifically—tousled or slicked—to jibe with jeans or chinos. More than once I'd heard him refer to a sweater or coat of Mia's as "a beautiful piece." True, he often spoke of girlfriends and conquests in a contrived, overly boyish manner, but we ignored this as so much closeted bluster. There was no real reason to think of him and Mia as anything but old childhood friends.

When Mia started to wake, ten days after the crash, her behavior seemed more or less as one would expect: groggy, vague, drifting in and out of consciousness. The doctor promised a full recovery, and we all felt enormous relief. I went home and slept for the first full night since the accident, then got up and put my column together. When I arrived at the hospital that afternoon, my mother pulled me aside. "Mia's been saying strange things," she told me.

"How do you mean?" I asked.

"She's been saying things that seem terribly odd to me."

"What kind of things?"

Mom rolled her eyes, unwilling to elaborate. I shrugged and took a seat beside my sister.

"Hi," Mia said. She waved from her elbow, a forlorn gesture. I was struck by how spindly she'd become after ten days of feeding tubes. She looked pale and very thin, her blue eyes strangely colorless. Even her freckles looked gray. Somehow, her hair had grown at an accelerated rate during her coma. It looked much longer and wilder than two weeks before.

"Hi," I said. "How do you feel?"

"Not so good," Mia said, as clearly as she could with her broken jaw. She jerked her head delicately toward Mom, who stood by the window arranging Walter's gladiolas in a cobalt blue vase. I thought they looked beautiful, but my mother frowned and muttered, "Who brought these funeral flowers?"

"She's driving me insane," Mia whispered, which seemed normal enough. I noticed that she didn't ask about Oscar, Juliette, and Deirdre. But she'd just emerged from a two-hundred-and-forty-hour coma, so I didn't question her parental devotion.

Mia smiled in a pleased, dreamy way. Then she turned her head and looked directly at me, her long, unwashed hair clinging to her scalp.

"Natalie," Mia said, clicking her syllables through the wires fusing her jaw. "Would you please ask the nurse to bring me some mouthwash? I need to give Walter another blow job."

"Excuse me?" I glanced back toward the doorway, where Clay stood chatting with a doctor.

Mia sighed with faint exasperation and laid her head back down on the pillow. "I need to give Walter another blow job," she muttered, and turned her dreamy stare out the window.

The doctor assured us this was not unusual. Lots of patients who'd suffered head injuries went through a stage of sexual fixation. Of saying wildly inappropriate things. It would pass, he promised. We should all try to gloss over it.

But it was hard to ignore Mia's placidly graphic remarks. In the middle of a perfectly normal hospital conversation—about the food, or Mia's luck in getting a private room—she'd interject in the same slightly garbled tone she'd used to complain about the Jell-O. "That reminds me of the time Walter took me from behind," she said to Mark, my father, and me. "Out in the parking lot by Nauset Beach. Do you remember?"

"Sorry," Mark said. "I don't think we were there." I jammed my elbow into his ribs. My father looked like he might cry.

Sometimes Mia described innocuous impersonal acts. She made a comment about monkeys and parakeets in pear trees that might have been poetic if only she'd omitted the phrase "sucking off." Mostly, her comments involved detailed sexual acts executed by Walter and herself. An occasional doctor or celebrity would enter the scenario, but—we all noted—never her own handsome husband. One morning in the cafeteria Clay said, "It would be nice if I could get in on this action occasionally. I'm starting to feel neglected." Mark and I laughed in a burst of relief that Clay's general confidence afforded him a sense of humor about even this.

Because we still didn't suspect anything between Mia and Walter. Despite the fact that he'd blush furiously if he happened to be in the room—which he often was—when she made these comments. We attributed it all to some subconscious connection between the accident and the sexual act. When they finally unwired Mia's jaw and pronounced her fit to go home, none of us had any right to be shocked when she announced she'd be moving in with Walter. But we all were.

Like the rest of my family, I'd always been fond of Clay. He was a sweet man, an attractive guy, a great father. Still, if Mia had left him for any other reason, my allegiance would have naturally fallen with her. She was my sister, after all.

But in this circumstance, I couldn't help but sympathize with Clay. In my own marriage, I'd been equally unsuspecting. It took Geoffrey four months to tell me about his affair with Lacey, one of his graduate students at Bennington. Mia told me I should have seen it coming—an insight I understood much more clearly after her accident. And I had known that Geoffrey and Lacey were close. I even knew the two of them had gone camping together. They went for a six-day hike on the Appalachian Trail, with my clueless blessing.

Like Clay's misguided naïveté, the reason I never suspected anything between Geoffrey and Lacey had more to do with prejudice than trust. Her fondness for long walks notwithstanding, Lacey weighed more than two hundred pounds. She had a quick wit and extensive knowledge in her (and Geoffrey's) field, especially impressive for a student. She dressed surprisingly well, and I forever found myself complimenting her outfits. I understood why Geoffrey liked her. But love her? I never for a moment believed my husband capable of attraction toward someone so simply huge. When Geoffrey first told me, I thought he was joking. I honestly laughed. And when the conversation took that surreal turn—in the moment I began to believe him—I felt a level of anger I don't think would have been present had it been one of his many nymphet or homecoming queen protégées. "Are you kidding me?" I'd screamed at Geoffrey. "*Lacey?* The woman is enormous."

Enormous or not, Lacey lifted my husband quite handily.

Now, I couldn't help but compare my original attitude toward Lacey to Clay's toward Walter. Clay had been so nice to him, despite his role in Mia's condition: he welcomed Walter by his wife's bedside, and never questioned his overly distraught, grief-ridden demeanor. I myself had included Lacey in party plans and dinner invitations. How she must have laughed at me—offering her leftovers, loaning her books and scarves and CDs—while she disguised her salacious relationship with all those extra pounds of flesh.

By the time they discharged Mia from the hospital, more than a month after the accident, Mom and Dad had already returned to their respective homes. Mia gave me a list of things she wanted from her house. I felt a sisterly duty to help her, regardless of my disapproval, but I was astonished by her list.

"Mia," I said. "There's no kid stuff here."

"I don't need any," Mia said. "Clay's taking the kids."

"For now?"

"Probably forever," she said breezily. "I think they'll be happier with him. Don't you?"

I stared at her. With the wire removed from her jaw, Mia looked approximately like herself in a spooky way—her left cheekbone just slightly higher than the right. No scars at all, but she had lost an enormous amount of weight. As she folded pajamas that were now several sizes too big into an overnight bag, it was impossible to look at her without being conscious of her bones—pointing through the skin of her elbows, wrists, and knees. Her old jeans, which had been snug, hung off her hips like something borrowed from a burly boyfriend.

"What about your cats?" I asked her.

"Walter doesn't like cats," Mia said. I took a mental inventory of Mia's cats and children—as if her assignment of all those ill-fated namesakes had foreshadowed this appalling abandonment. "Mia," I said. "Are you telling me that you're just deserting your husband, your pets, and your *three beautiful children* for a man who's obviously gay?"

"What do you mean?" She zipped up her bag and sat on the bed, drained from the effort of folding and packing.

I raised my eyebrows, and Mia laughed. "Believe me," she said. "Walter is not gay."

I raised my hand in a please-don't-tell-me gesture. "He's a man, Mia," I said. "A gender famous for having sex with sheep. Plastic blow-up dolls. He doesn't have to be heterosexual to have sex with you."

"Look, Natalie," Mia said. "If you're not going to help, then just don't. I can get the stuff myself."

"Sure," I said. "It will give you a chance to see your children." I had a vision of my sweet sister when I'd stepped on that rusty nail. She'd rushed over with all three children, carrying Deirdre in a Snugli at her chest. She'd assigned Oscar and Juliette age-appropriate tasks to keep them busy; and she'd washed out my foot with touching gentleness, wrapping it cleanly and expertly, moving with such grace that her baby in tow seemed just an extension of her body.

"Mia," I pleaded. "Think about what you're doing. This is not you."

She didn't reply, just closed her suitcase and snapped it shut. I tossed her list onto the bed and tried to leave the hospital room, but bumped into Walter in the doorway. I took a second to glare at him, and noticed that his clothes—baggy corduroys, faded Rockports, and a handsomely frayed Shetland sweater—were exactly right for collecting an illicit lover from the hospital.

"Don't worry," Walter said to me, as I tried to storm by him. "I'll take good care of her."

Mia stared at Walter with that dreamy, emotionless gaze. Like someone who'd been hypnotized. I had to remind myself that their relationship had started before her trip through the windshield, that it was not purely the result of trauma and lost brain cells.

"Look at her," Walter said, a similarly vacant film glazing his eyes. "Isn't she beautiful?"

I looked back at my sister. A funny stardust light gathered under the fluorescent ceiling bulbs, illuminating the uncombed frizz of her hair like a halo. She looked strangely electric, and I had to agree with Walter.

But not aloud. I elbowed past him and marched myself down the sterile, muted hospital corridor.

II. ABELARD

Of course it astounded me most that Mia would abandon her children—one of whom, Deirdre, was in that best developing phase, just starting to talk and be her own unique self. But I also couldn't believe Mia would desert her cats. It was one thing when she thought Clay would be at the house taking care of everybody. But two weeks into their separation—when it became clear that this was not coma-induced dementia but the new structure of their lives—Clay announced he would not stay in our family's home. When he said that he would of course take his children but the cats were Mia's problem, she employed her new approach to all responsibility: she shrugged it off.

"Remember the Just So Story?" she said to me. "It doesn't matter where the cats go, really. One house is as good as another."

"Mia," I said, annoyed that she would use that story to justify herself. "These are your pets."

"How much of a pet can a cat really be?" Mia replied. "Remember how the cat walks? 'Through the Wet Wild Woods, waving his wild tale, and walking by his wild lone.' That's the thing. Cats will accept what comfort they can get, but when it comes down to it, they'll always take care of themselves."

I wasn't about to let my mother's house be overrun with Mia's confused, abandoned cats. And I couldn't entreat Clay, who had more than his share to deal with. So I collected them myself. I gave Persephone to the astrologer at my magazine. I brought Icarus and Ophelia to Boston, to Mark's, and he gave them to coworkers. Icarus, I heard, settled in nicely with a family in Newton. But Ophelia escaped from her North End apartment, never to be found. After Cape Cod, the city must have felt like another planet, and I had the saddest image of her wandering through foreign streets, rummaging in the dumpsters of Italian restaurants, trying to find her way back to Mia, who, she had no way of knowing, had for all feline purposes ceased to exist.

I took Heloise and Abelard—not that they were the pair their names would imply. Both neutered in this instance, Heloise had no use for Abelard, and vice versa. They kept to opposite ends of the house, not disliking each other but showing a decidedly unromantic indifference. Heloise had been Mia's first cat, predating all the children. Fat and docile, Heloise made the move to my house splendidly, not even bothered by my dog Scout. Having no interest in going outside, Heloise tamped a permanent nest for herself in my down comforter, where she'd spend the day, staring out to sea as if waiting for some lost sailor to return. And the night, purring loudly at the pleasure of my company.

Abelard was another story altogether, both in his transition to my house and his mysterious origins. A stray who one day just appeared, Abelard started out half-feral, and remained so with everyone except for Mia. No matter how many years he lived in the same house with Clay, he still fled at sudden movements, and he never went near strangers, or any of the children.

But Abelard loved Mia. He shadowed her on and off during the day, jumping in and out of the window she left open for the cats, always watching for the rare moment when Mia's lap would be free. Then he'd leap into it, suddenly completely tame, purring with rapt, creaky ecstasy. He would rub his face against hers with the most obvious adoration—particularly sweet because he'd lavish it on her alone. I couldn't believe Mia would leave him behind.

Neither, apparently, could Abelard. He paced my house like a caged panther, yowling intermittently throughout the day and night, waking me at intervals like a newborn infant. When Abelard first found Mia, he'd been sleek and rangy. Now, although he still moved with that stealthy, jungle-cat grace, years of ready access to food had given him a gently swaying paunch. In daylight his coat looked washed with a sooty brown tint. But at night Abelard looked deeply black—so dark, the only discernible features on his face were his startlingly round eyes, which generally registered frantic distrust when turned on me. Once, long before leaving her children and cats, Mia told me that ancient Egyptians believed cats stored sunlight in their eyes. "That's why they see so well at night," she said, pointing out Abelard's unearthly iridescent eyes.

"Just give him some time," Mia said now, when I told her of her once beloved cat's misery. "He'll get used to you."

If I pleaded, Mia would dispense terse caretaking instructions for cats over the phone—but she never came by, to visit me or them. There really wasn't much advice Mia could give to help Abelard, whom I didn't want to let outside. "That's ridiculous," Mia said. "The cat was a stray. Who knows how long he survived on his own? What do you think's going to happen?"

I ignored her and kept him in. Abelard was so obviously waiting to bolt to parts unknown. As long as he was inside, I at least knew that he was safe.

Clay carried his new burdens with stoic forgiveness. He rarely said a negative word about Mia, was in fact more inclined to make derogatory comments about himself as a husband. "I guess I was kind of boring," Clay told me one evening, when he picked up the kids from my house. "Mia missed out on a lot of romance. I guess Walter gives that to her."

Before Mia and Walter became a couple, Clay had thought, like all of us, that Walter was gay. But afterward, he never breathed a single aspersion toward Walter's preferences. This impressed me immensely, particularly given my own experience with cuckoldry and divorce. When Geoffrey left me, I had spewed and railed against him endlessly. And "obese" was the least of the words I'd assigned to Lacey.

But Clay wouldn't allow himself to descend to that level. Instead he organized his life. He moved into a small house on a busy street in Scargo—less expensive than our cloistered neighborhood, which was so seldom traveled, I could leave Scout outside, untethered. Clay consolidated his hours at the bank to four days a week. He put Juliette and Deirdre in the same morning preschool, and he pulled Oscar out of his private Waldorf school and enrolled him midterm in public first grade. Before making this switch, he changed Oscar's name to Jake.

"The poor kid's had enough to bear," Clay said. "He's going to start a new school with a clean slate and a normal name."

With Clay as primary caretaker, the fanciful chaos that had ruled the children's life seemed to vanish. He had specific and unbending rules, which the children would recite with novel glee. "No sugar before dinner," Juliette told me, faintly incredulous, turning her little nose up at a Popsicle. Clay's new house was clean and orderly. "It's so much easier to find things," Juliette said. "Mommy's house was always such a mess."

Mia and I each took care of the kids two afternoons a week, dividing up the days Clay worked. I was amazed by the change in Oscar—or Jake, as he himself was quick to remind me. "It's Jake now," he'd say, with palpable relief. When he arrived at my house Jake would scoop Heloise into his lap, his cheeks rosy with the glow of normality. "Nobody teases me at this school," he told me, pushing his glasses up on his nose. "It's really working out." He'd throw his backpack—full of appropriate school material—into a corner, then play with his little sisters, or curl himself on the couch with Heloise and a book several times above his expected reading level. Sometimes he'd help me with my column, either by choosing a letter or recalling something sweet Juliette or Deirdre had done. I'd never imagined a child could so obviously flourish in the voluntary absence of his mother. It was almost as if with Mia, the children had absorbed and emulated her chaotic, emotional style. With her gone, there was no reward for misery and gushing tears. They could heave aside romantic disorder in favor of neat rooms, tightly run schedules, and general contentment. Everything exactly where it belonged—with the seeming exception of Mia.

Living in Walter's one-bedroom apartment over the Scargo ice cream parlor, which was closed for the off-season, Mia seemed a ghost of her former self—but a happy ghost. Initially her new life confounded me. It seemed to revolve exclusively around Walter. He had lost his driver's license in his post-accident plea bargain; Mia decided not to get a job so she'd be free to drive him to and from work. Because she couldn't afford new clothes ("I'll probably just gain the weight back, anyway"), she wore her old ones cinched and belted—hanging and draping off her bony figure in a strangely flattering way.

She used Walter as a blanket excuse for all her actions. When I implored her to take Abelard, she shrugged helplessly and said, "Walter doesn't think cats belong in the house."

"But he's pining for you," I begged.

"It's the whole litter box issue," she sighed. "Walter says they're crawling with disease."

When Clay asked Mia to give Juliette's fourth birthday party, she said that ever since the accident, groups of children gave Walter headaches. "Walter's tired of taking care of things," Mia explained to me later.

"What has Walter ever taken care of?" I asked.

"Oh, you know," she answered, waving her hand vaguely. "Things."

Slowly I realized: "Walter" was her new code word for "Mia." At first I assumed Mia had decided to leave Clay and the children because she imagined herself overtaken with a new and greater love. But on speculation, I realized I'd never heard her say this. In fact, Mia didn't see a whole lot of Walter, who worked long hours at the hotel. The drive back and forth to his work amounted to the bulk of their time together. Other than the two afternoons with her children and occasional visits from me, Mia—after years of immersion among living things—spent most of her time alone.

One chilly morning, heading out of autumn and toward winter, Mia and I took Scout for a walk along Scargo Beach. While Scout joyfully herded shorebirds and waves, Mia admitted that if it hadn't been for the accident, she probably would not have left Clay.

"I think the thing with Walter would have just come and gone," she said. She huddled in her winter coat, more affected by the cold now that she'd lost her body fat. "No one would have known, and when it ended life would have just gone back the way it was. Before, I don't think I could have stood leaving Clay, because of what people would say. What people would think of a mother leaving her children." She pushed her hair behind her ears and squinted toward the ocean. "It's funny," she said. "Things don't really bother me since the accident. I think about the sexual things I said in the hospital, and I don't mind at all. The old me, before the accident, would have been mortified.

"We climbed up on the jetty. Scout jumped down and splashed through the water. A little way out on a cluster of rocks, three fat seals rolled off their lazy perch and into the water. Their dark, big-eyed heads bobbed, observing curiously, waiting for us to leave.

"I've been feeling like a child lately," Mia said. "For instance right now. I'm completely enjoying this moment. I'm not worrying about Oscar at school, or whether Deirdre's getting toilet trained fast enough, or whether some cat has peed in a corner. I'm just thinking about how beautiful it is out here, how quiet. I feel the same way when I'm with my kids. I can just enjoy them, and understand them. I think it makes me a better mother."

"You think living in a different home and spending two afternoons a week with your children makes you a better mother?"

"Well," she said. "I'm happier spending time with them. It's not out of obligation anymore. Now I really feel joy when I see them. And they seem happier. Don't they?"

I had to admit they did. Mia smiled, languorously serene. In her huge clothes, with her lank hair and makeup-less face, she should have looked wan and unbeautiful. But she didn't, any more than the eel grass—faded to wheat after its summertime green, but catching the sunlight just the same.

●●●

That night the wind kicked up fiercely. These were the times I still hated Geoffrey: alone in the dark on my wind-battered bluff, everything extraordinary about my house suddenly frightening. Last winter, on a night like this I would have walked down the road to Mia's. Now I cursed both my sister and my ex-husband as the lights flickered.

I walked into the kitchen to search for candles. The room went black for almost a full minute while I reached into the silverware drawer and fumbled for wax amidst the metal. When the lights came back on I turned, facing the window, and let out a startled gasp. Abelard sat on the sill, as utterly dark as the room had been. Against the blackened window, his outline was barely visible except for his round green eyes, which seemed to hang in the air like the Cheshire cat's smile.

Abelard thumped down and floated to the kitchen door, letting out a yowl so plaintive and mournful, it turned my spine to velvet.

I never would have let Heloise out on a night like this. But Abelard in that moment seemed perfectly suited to winds and ravages. Darkness and wildness: his origins, his homeland. So I opened the door. Watching his tail poof and disappear into the night, I felt a strange amalgam of admiration and dread.

The lights restored themselves uneventfully, but my sleep was restless. I kept waking to listen for Abelard. Several times I went downstairs, opened the door, and called his name. The wind howled reproachfully, like a moving force field the cat couldn't possibly cross.

"You give the cat too much credit," Mia said the next morning, when I called to report his disappearance. "And then you sell him short. There's nothing emotional about him wandering off. It's territorial. Meanwhile, he's perfectly capable of catching mice and so forth. If he gets hungry—if he has half a brain—he'll find his way back to your house."

"So in the meantime, what am I supposed to do?"

"Just don't worry about it."

But I did. I worried throughout the day, so much that I tried to distract myself by starting my column early. As I read insipid letters about first teeth, Santa Claus, and thirty-fifth wedding anniversaries, I kept an ear cocked toward the door. But no sound.

In the afternoon, when the children arrived, Jake—formerly Oscar—suggested walking by the old house to look for Abelard. "Don't worry," Jake reassured me as I loaded Deirdre into her stroller. "Abelard is one tough cat."

Juliette took my hand, and Jake led the way. He walked ahead of us, calling for Abelard and making meow sounds. He looked like a little man, very confident and in charge. I felt a small, involuntary pang. Sometimes it seemed like Jake was a completely different person— assertively taking the place of dear, neurotic little Oscar.

When we rounded the bend, Deirdre gave a little whoop of joy at the sight of her old house. There sat Abelard, comfortably settled in a patch of sunlight near the fence. He stood at the sight of us—this little army from his past—and hesitated, deciding whether he felt pleased or displeased by the reunion.

Abelard bristled, in the same lazy, obligatory way the seals had rolled off their rocks. By the time I parked Deirdre's stroller away from the street, he'd bolted into the bushes.

"There," Jake said in his clipped, precocious way. "You see, Natalie? He's perfectly all right."

We walked back through the marina so the kids could look at the boats. Jake identified various fishing boats for me and the girls, but I only half listened. The sight of Abelard, whole and healthy but wild and alone, had filled me with an odd combination of consternation and relief.

Back at my house, Jake and I made coq au vin. "Yuk," Juliette admonished, pointing at our block of salt pork. We ignored her, and at six o'clock, when Clay came to collect the kids, we had just lowered it to a fatty simmer. Deirdre lay asleep on the couch, Juliette watched a video. Clay poured himself a scotch and sank down next to Deirdre, stroking the soft perfection of her two-year-old cheek.

At dinner, Clay and I drank half a bottle of wine. Over the children's heads, we spoke in broken code about our respective divorces. "Sometimes," Clay said, "I still feel B–L–A–M–E, and self-righteousness. Other times, 1 feel like I've been given this gift, to start from the beginning, to . . . I don't know, to be a person who . . . " He glanced around the table cautiously. Jake listened to every word with alarming intensity. "You know what I mean," Clay said.

I did. I felt it too sometimes, that strange happiness, though I'd have been loath to admit it when my divorce was new. The feeling at night, suddenly stretching diagonally across a queen-sized bed; or just before leaving the house, automatically searching for pen and paper to jot down my whereabouts, and realizing with great liberation that I didn't need to.

But other times—like that night, after Clay left: the small bits of freedom paled in comparison to the emptiness of a house—an emptiness whose surface even the jingle of Scout's collar and the hum of Heloise's purr couldn't scratch. I kept thinking of Abelard, picking himself out of the sunshine to escape from me and the children, his own family. The image of loneliness, of misguided independence, made me too antsy to sleep. I pulled on my coat and walked in my slippers down the road.

Stepping outside, I felt embraced by crisp, frigid air and the sound of the fulminating ocean. The low-tide stench of salt and skate egg thinned to a vague perfume against the dry-leafed chill. I remembered one of Mia's stories: a black cat saves a woman by telling her that late-night hours belong to fairy people, who become angry when mortals invade their time. But I felt strangely protected. Heading to my childhood home, passing the other locked and vacated summer houses, my steps were buoyant with melancholy freedom.

The spot where Abelard had been that afternoon now stood empty of both cat and sunlight. Calling him, I circled the house twice, peering under the porch and into the bushes—as if I could possibly have seen that sooty black cat against the night's cover.

From the marina, boat masts chimed their haunting, wind-driven music. As I walked by, I saw a feline specter saunter across the dimly lit parking lot. I matched my footsteps to his, and slunk to the edge of the lot, where I whispered his name.

He stopped, curious, visibly assessing the situation and weighing his options. I sat down on a stack of old pilings, and Abelard came to me—a gesture of courtesy, fulfilling his obligation toward an acquaintance on a dark night. He climbed up beside me to sit, alert and companionable.

Then I pounced on him. I scooped him into my arms, pinned him against my chest, and gathered the scruff of his neck into my fist. Surprisingly, he didn't make any noticeable protest—no noise, not even much of a squirm. I started the walk toward home.

Every yard or so, Abelard tried to twist himself out of my arms and I would tighten my grip, my breath quickening. I walked with an irrational sense of urgency, determined not to let go, no matter how much he wriggled. By the time I got him inside my house and dropped him to the floor, my arms were so tight I could barely unfold my elbows. I shook them vigorously and heard Abelard from the kitchen, alighting to his bowl on the counter and crunching into his food. I felt great relief that he didn't seem traumatized to be back. And I felt heroic—for having captured and carried him in my arms all the way home.

Later, in bed, I awoke to a brush of fur and bone against my face. I thought at first it was Heloise. But when I opened my eyes I could tell—by the fact that I could hardly see him in the dark, and by the unaccustomed rotor of his purr—that it was Abelard.

"You know," Mia said a few days later, when we took the kids to an exhibition at the Model Train Club. "I always left a window open for my cats. Even in the winter, I let them come and go as they pleased. A cat's nature is nocturnal and independent. There's something violent about what you do. Locking them in the house at night, always keeping track of where they are."

"I'm trying to be responsible," I said. "Taking care of *your* cats."

"They're your cats now," Mia said. "I'm only trying to help." She ran a finger across a miniature crack as an engine approached, and shivered. "Ooh. A little shock." She drew her finger back and shook it. "Jake," she called, decidedly non-maternal. "Check this out."

On the drive home, the kids crowded in back, an alert Jake perched between Juliette and Deirdre, who slept in their car seats. Mia rolled down her window, letting in a cold, salty gust. Jake yelped in protest. "Sorry," she said. "But I'm going to miss the clean ocean air. I always think this is the best time of year here."

"Miss it?" I said. "Why would you miss it?"

"Didn't I tell you? Walter and I are moving to New York."

If it hadn't been for the kids, I would have pulled over. I would have grabbed her by her collar and shaken her so that her skinny bones rattled in her billowy clothes.

"Mia," I said instead, forcing calm into my voice. "How can you possibly move to New York?"

"Walter got a job at a hotel in Gramercy Park," she told me. "I'm really excited about it."

I cast a desperate glance toward the backseat.

"Oh, it's all right," Mia said. "They already know."

I turned into the parking lot of Millstone Liquors and turned off the ignition, my hands trembling. "What are you doing?" Mia asked. "Do you need to pick something up?"

"What am I doing? What am *I* doing?" I could hear my voice rise to a hysteria reminiscent of Geoffrey's and my breakup. "You can't go to New York," I said, feeling like I might cry, but battling against it in deference to the children. Mia just sat, her face blank as usual, crossing her arms heartlessly in front of her chest. From the backseat, Jake leaned forward and put his little hand on my shoulder. "It's all right, Natalie," he said. "She'll come to visit. New York's not that far away."

"Four and a half hours by car," Mia sang cheerfully. "Do you want me to drive home?"

"You have three little children," I whispered. "You have a husband."

"*Had* a husband," Mia corrected me. "And the children will be fine."

"We will," Jake reassured me. Behind his glasses, his eyes were wide—not with anxiety, but with pleasure at his role as consoler. "We'll be just fine, Natalie. Walter's going to show us the Statue of Liberty. You can walk all the way to the top."

I started the engine and pulled back onto the road. Mia dug a sodden lump of Kleenex out of her pocket and offered it to me—a pale echo of her old, motherly gestures. "No thank you," I said. And then added, in a vicious whisper, "I don't see how you can do this."

"I don't see why you care so much," Mia said. She rolled down the window again, the gust making all of us—even Deirdre and Juliette, in their sleep—shiver with the sudden chill.

"To tell you the truth, it's kind of a relief," Clay said over our next dinner. Jake and I had made eggplant Parmesan. "This way, everything will be more cut-and-dried. I won't have to see her all the time. Not to mention W-A-L-T-E-R."

"Well," I said. "If it's any consolation, every time I see him, I think she must be . . . you know . . . to have done this whole thing."

"Thanks," Clay said. "I always thought the same of Geoffrey." We clinked wineglasses. Clay looked older these days, like someone who knew the world a little better. And I felt a deep kinship with him—deeper, really, than anything I'd felt toward Mia in the last few months. So much so that I didn't say a word when, as Jake and I cleared the table, Clay opened the door and let Abelard out into the night.

"Daddy," Juliette scolded. "Natalie doesn't let Abelard outside."

"That's all right," I said quickly. "I'm sure he'll be fine." I reached out and touched Clay's hand, absolving him.

Abelard did not return that night, or the next, or the night after that.

"You've got it all wrong," Mia said, in response to my frantic phone call. "You think the cat *needs* you. But to him, you're just a luxury. The warm house, the canned food, the kibble. It's all nice, but it's all expendable."

Mia's coldhearted comfort did nothing to convince me. In the next week I spent a lot of time walking—from my house to Mom's, through the marina, into the backyards of surrounding homes. Every squirrel or rabbit's rustle infused me with hope. All night long I listened for the sound of a cat begging entry.

Meanwhile, there was Heloise: perfectly nonproblematic, lounging comfortably, staring out to sea, accepting affection and food whenever it was offered. And Scout, who would bound out the door but stick close to the house, completely reliable, delighted to be a pet in that pure dog way, brimming with love. Both these animals profoundly tame. Despite their presence, Abelard somehow occupied me more: my odd sense of culpability for his fate—combined with an exquisite vision of his nocturnal travels, and his effortless passage through the night.

●●●

After ten days I gave up my walks; but periodically I would drive by the house, slowing in case I glimpsed him emerging from the bushes. And one afternoon, there he sat—in his old patch of sunlight, his tail twitching. His household paunch vanished, he looked like the same rangy self he'd been the day he first appeared to Mia.

I pulled into the driveway and got out of the car stealthily, leaving the door open, not making any loud noises or sudden movements. Abelard stared, unblinking. As I approached, he stood and stretched. I bent to pet him and he arched into my palm—happy to see me, not protesting as I collected him in my arms, carried him down the hill, and deposited him inside my car. Driving home, I felt the same triumphant euphoria of his last capture.

Scout greeted us as we pulled into the driveway. I picked up Abelard and stepped out of the car, kicking the door shut behind me. At the sight of the dog, Abelard became an electric package of fur, bristling and squirming out from my grasp.

I should have grabbed him by the scruff of the neck. Better yet, I should have just let go—Scout wouldn't have hurt him, and Abelard might have dashed into the house for safety's sake. But instead I tried to cling, with the same senseless clutch I'd used carrying him home from the marina. The cat transformed into a near-liquid being, slithering up toward my shoulder, trying to give himself leverage for a leap out of my arms, which I tightened around his shrunken middle.

Abelard struggled his upper body free just enough to turn on me. In the instant it became clear to him that I would not release my grip, he sunk his teeth and both front claws into the back of my skull. I heard his hind claws ripping my jacket—thankfully thick enough to protect my chest. I let him go.

An odd film rolled in my head, an outward vision of the incident—how chaotic and preposterous it must have looked, the cat turning so suddenly vicious, employing its every weapon against me. Scout jumped up to lick my face, but I pushed her away and ran toward the house. When I opened the door, Abelard scooted over the threshold and disappeared underneath a chair.

I left Scout barking outside and fled to the bathroom. My face looked stucco-white, and I felt an odd sense of shock—alternating between nausea and dizziness. As if my body were composed of pixels rather than flesh and blood. I couldn't see the wound no matter how I tilted my head toward the mirror, but when I pressed my palm to the curve of my skull, it came down wet with blood.

"Jesus Christ," Mia said. We stood together in the bathroom, me leaning over the sink, Mia parting my hair so she could assess the damage. She'd arrived within minutes of my phone call, and when she walked through the door, I realized it was the first time since her accident I'd seen my sister's new self in an old place. My mind flooded with visions of other times she'd been in my house: the former, larger Mia, surrounded by children. I wanted to sit her down, to feed her, to keep her.

"Does it hurt?" she asked. And though it did hurt—in an achy, puncturing way—the worst part was feeling assaulted. By the cat, whom I'd been trying to help. By this woman, this girlish slip of a woman, who'd taken over my dear and predictable sister.

Mia rinsed out a washcloth and pressed it against my head. "You should really see a doctor," she said.

"Just clean it out," I said impatiently. "My tetanus shot is up-to-date. We know he doesn't have rabies. Let's just clean it out and try to forget about it."

"I wish you could see it," Mia said. "Remember that myth about Japanese vampires and cats? That's exactly what this looks like. Two deep little puncture wounds—a vampire bite. And all these scratches. He really savaged you."

"To tell you the truth," I told her, "I feel savaged more on an emotional level."

Mia laughed. "You would," she said.

I watched her at work in the mirror, cleaning out my injury with her old expertise, using hydrogen peroxide and Neosporin, gently affixing a gauze bandage and then covering it all up by pulling my hair back into a ponytail. "We should clean this out again tomorrow," Mia said. She handed me three Tylenol tablets and a glass of water, and we walked into the living room. Abelard's tail twitched on the rug from underneath the chair.

"What am I going to do with that cat?" I asked my sister.

She shrugged. "Forget about him. Or keep him anyway. What else can you do?"

Then Mia did something she hadn't done in the longest time: she held out her arms. I collapsed, my head pressed into her bony neck, her slender arms wrapped around me. And I cried like a girl from one of Mia's fairy tales. As though my heart would break.

Later, after Mia had gone and dusk had fallen, Scout had resigned herself to the back stoop, and Heloise lay curled up in the easiest easy chair. The wind raged outside—the kind of night when indoors felt especially in: safe and warm and sealed. Abelard emerged from his hiding place and slunk to the front door. He didn't make a vocal request, just placed himself at the threshold and looked back to me.

If I didn't open the door, but insisted on confining him, the cat would eventually find some way out. Up through the chimney, like the King of the Cats. Or maybe he would transform into a different sort of creature—a vampire, walking out on human legs. While I wreaked the havoc owed someone who battles against what's best left to fate and nature.

I lifted myself, still feeling battered, and walked obediently to the door. Abelard slipped outside, noiseless, his form black as coal, black as ebony, black as black can be. I watched him disappear into the bleak, gusty, salt-scented night. Not believing, really, in any force beyond the tangible, the detectable, the visible.

But still. I couldn't help but notice, despite the glow from my porch light, and all the silhouettes cast by surrounding trees: the cat proceeding into the wild, without even the company of his shadow. ●

AFTER WORDS

The narrative in "By His Wild Lone" threads together a series of images and moments from disparate places. That opening scene—of the little girl rising into the air during a windstorm on the beach—is taken from a story my husband tells about his youngest sister. Mia's car accident is based on something that happened to a close friend of mine who went through a windshield then woke up from a coma making bizarre, graphically sexual comments. And of course the image of the black cat in the darkened window, only his eyes visible before he slinks off into the night, is for me the defining moment in the story. I had been reading a lot of mythology about cats, and because of this overload, the story was nearly cut from my collection. Just before the book went to press my agent called to say he didn't think it worked, there was too much going on. "You've even got vampires in there," he said. I could see what he meant, but for all of its image overload, I felt too attached to the story to let it go. Strangely enough, this coincides with its themes of excess and wildness, and their victory over the practical.

KAREN BENDER

THE FOURTH PRUSSIAN DYNASTY: AN ERA OF ROMANCE AND ROYALTY

ELLA BELIEVED THAT SHE HAD BEGUN the journey toward her husband, Lou, long before she met him, when she took a salesmanship class at George Washington High School. Seventeen girls and three boys were enrolled in the course. They were all immigrants or the children of immigrants, and they were all sixteen years old. On the first day of school, the teacher, Mr. Reilly, asked them to come back the following morning in their best clothes—or, rather, their best selling clothes—so that he could examine them. He was going to tell them if they had the skills to become salespeople; he was going to tell them who they were.

Ella had grown up in Dorchester, in a four-room tenement apartment, with five other people: her parents and her three older sisters. The ceiling was tin, and the air in the rooms seemed always to be the color of dusk. The hallway smelled of unclean breath and sour urine from the toilet they shared with their neighbors. The apartment itself couldn't contain the relentless sound of six personalities trying to assert themselves in a small space, and Ella was never sure how to make her own voice distinct.

Ella was the only one of the sisters who had been born in America. Her father had emigrated from Russia alone, and it had taken him six years to make enough money to bring the others over to Boston. She was the product of her parents' reunion. At the dinner table, she sometimes went hungry, because in Russia her sisters had learned early how to grab. Sometimes she suspected that they secretly wanted to starve her. They were big, anxious girls with thick accents, and they seemed less like sisters than a force of weather.

What had her parents been like before their lives here? The rest of the family knew this history, and thus inhabited a world of feelings that was forever denied to her. It was hard to believe that her parents could have been different from who they were now. Her mother was shy and tousled and smelled of boiled meat. She poured herself so completely into her tasks that, at times, she seemed to disappear. Ella's father was too tall for the apartment and was often restless, eager to get away. Sometimes she came upon her parents in a kiss that looked stronger than love; in its rage it reached toward an innocence. It was only in such moments that they really seemed married.

From the time she was young, Ella had wanted to be loved, and she needed that love to be immense, ferocious. After her sisters married and moved away, she often sat alone in the bedroom she had shared with them, wondering whom she would love. And who would love her? The streets outside her window at night were empty, silvered by the moon. She longed to be able to walk down them joined wholly with someone else.

A job led you to the man you would marry, but in 1920 only a few jobs were available to unmarried girls in Boston. Ella watched her sisters to see what they chose. Their jobs shaped them in basic ways. Every day, Esther, the oldest, limped home after ten hours of shouldering huge plates of food at Bloom's Kosher Restaurant, barely able to make it up the stairs. She got married first, to one of her customers, a large, moonfaced man who frequently ordered omelettes; they met when he let her sit in his booth to rest her feet. Ruth worked the graveyard operator shift at New England Telephone and turned into a pale, ghostly person who rarely spoke. She married late, in part because she spent her time packed in a room with fifty other female operators, and few people bothered to flirt with a voice on the telephone.

Deborah had the best job. She worked at the women's hat counter in Filene's, where there were silver mirrors at the jewelry counters and the aisles were sweet with fragrance. Ella felt as though she knew a famous person—her sister, Filene's hat girl—and she enjoyed watching Deborah smoothly tell a well-dressed woman, someone who would not even nod to her on the street, "I know this hat would be perfect for you."

On the second day of Salesmanship, Mr. Reilly moved around the classroom, examining the students as they stood by their desks in their best clothes. He told them that not only had he been born in this country but his parents had been, too—and he, therefore, knew what was what. "Look at this jacket," he said to Jacob Katzman. "It's red. You look like a clown. From a circus. Do you want the world to laugh at you? Do you want a red nose to go with it?" Trish O'Donnell, a slight girl, stood shivering in a mealy black sweater. "You," he said, "are a scaredy-cat. Why would anyone want to buy anything from you?" To Rosie Delano, done up in wrinkly, baby-pink chiffon, he said, "You think you're a princess? You're coming out of the castle for us?"

Mr. Reilly complimented only three students, and not on what they were wearing. He praised John Delaney for his impressive height—six feet one—"like an oak tree." He approved of Pearl Johnson's melodious voice and told her to say "Pleasure to meet you" several times; and then he admired Ella's smile. "Look at this," he said, turning her head, like a doll's, for the other students to see. "Is this a smile you would buy a hat from? A dress? A vase?" He paused and answered, "Yes!"

He gave them rules, and Ella wrote down every one. When a woman walks into the store, watch her closely to see which piece of her clothing she wears most proudly, then compliment it. Make sure your hands are perfectly clean. Nod one full second after someone asks you a question, not before. When a customer walks in, count to ten before you say, "May I help you?"

The students practiced looking into each other's eyes with confidence. "Pretend you see a flower inside your customer's head,"

Mr. Reilly said. Face to face with her classmate Pearl, Ella tried to find roses, lilies, marigolds blooming behind her nervous eyes.

"This time, look interested," said Mr. Reilly. "The flower is shrinking. Keep watching it until it goes away." Rosie Delano was better at looking interested than anyone, but John Delaney had the most confident look. When the others asked him what flower he saw, he answered, "A very big, blue rose."

"There's no such flower as a blue rose!" they shouted, and he shrugged.

"That's what I saw," he said.

During the semester, they had to sell numerous absurd items that Mr. Reilly brought into class: an ugly rag doll, a satin shoe without a heel, a cracked marble, a banana peel. At first, almost everyone stuttered and spoke in a wispy voice. Mr. Reilly stood at the back of the room and yelled, "What? I can't hear you! Americans speak loud." He pounded his chest. "Loud! Are you an American? Or do you want to go back?"

Some of the items were impossible to sell. It took three students to get rid of the banana peel. (By that time, it had dried up.) Of course, no one actually bought anything, but Mr. Reilly knew when a customer was ready to buy. It was a specific moment, and Ella learned to detect a subtle change in the room, a longing that hadn't been there. When Anna Stragowski held up the black banana peel and said, "You need this. You must buy. Why? Because it is a duster!" and then whirled around the room, whisking the stiff peel against desks and windows, the students were quiet with amazement, breathing softly: there really was one more thing that they could want.

Mr. Reilly was hard on Ella for the whole term. She did not live up to the unintended promise of that first smile. So she wanted to do well when he handed her the final object to sell—a tiny, broken child's tooth. Ella cupped it in her hand. She could not think of what to say.

"Hello," she whispered. "I am Ella and I have something—"

"Louder!" Mr. Reilly yelled. "Who's talking? I can't hear you!"

"I am Ella—"

Mr. Reilly was shaking his head. She felt as though she were yelling, too.

"Do you have trouble chewing?" she asked. "This is what you need!"

The field of faces blinked and yawned. A few students laughed. "With this extra tooth you can have a better smile!"

"They already have teeth," Mr. Reilly said. Ella's panic was rising. She popped the tooth in her mouth and swallowed it. She and the other students stared at each other, stunned.

"Where'd it go?"

"She ate it!"

Ella put her hand on her stomach. She had swallowed a stranger's tooth. Whose mouth had it come from? Why had she swallowed it? Would it harm her insides? Would Mr. Reilly want it back?

Mr. Reilly stood up. The class was in an uproar. "Mr. Reilly! Now we can't buy the tooth!"

"Ella, where is the tooth?" asked Mr. Reilly. Ella gently patted her stomach.

"Tell me, class. Do you want that tooth?" Mr. Reilly said.

Nineteen pairs of eyes looked at her. "Yes!" the students shouted.

"Then I have to say that you pass," Mr. Reilly said.

Ella stood in front of the class for one more moment before she sat down, feeling those rapt, hungry eyes on her. She knew that the others wanted the tooth only because it could not be had.

Ella's tooth-swallowing trick so impressed Mr. Reilly that when she graduated from high school two years later he referred her to his friend Marvin, a floorwalker at Johnson Massey Treasure Trove. It was a plum job, even more prestigious than being a hat girl at Filene's.

The Treasure Trove was situated on the fifth floor of the elegant department store. On the directory posted in each elevator, the shop was indicated by a scrolled gold plaque. The moment Ella walked into the Treasure Trove, she knew that she did not belong. It was full of the things she imagined finding only in rich people's homes—vases and lamps and china figurines. The door was flanked by two black Grecian columns, and inside were jade dogs and horses and rabbits and domed chests encrusted with purple stones. There were gentlemen customers with bowlers and ladies in silk dresses and feathered hats. Above, a teardrop chandelier sparkled like frozen raindrops. Ella kept her hands out of her pockets to show everyone that she was not a thief.

"Reilly sent you?" asked Marvin. He had a strange accent, almost English. His face was thin, with fine cheekbones that made him appear sophisticated. Ella nodded.

"Let's get a look at you," he said.

She turned around, arms held out, and tried to smile. He looked her over. "What do you think of all this?" he asked her, gesturing at the room.

"It's beautiful," she said. Her voice was thick with feeling.

"Fine," he said. His accent slid a little. "We'll fit you up in a uniform. Be here tomorrow at nine."

And, that quickly, Marvin had hired her. She came in every morning and dusted off the figures made of jade or ivory or gold. She wore a uniform, a forest-green cap-sleeved blouse with a calf-length skirt. On her collar, she had a sparkling rhinestone lapel pin with the initials "JM," for Johnson Massey. Ella did not think that the pin's jewels were real, but she also did not want anyone to tell her they weren't.

She memorized everything Marvin told her about the objects; the information seemed culled from an encyclopedia. "Jade is much prized in the Orient. Different methods for carving it are used in China and Japan." Sometimes, when she was tired, she made up her own facts. "This fine chest stored dishes in the castle of King Howard the Fourth," she said. She loved how the customers nodded as they listened, vulnerable with fragile objects in their careful hands.

Ella and Lou had met when Lou wandered into the Treasure Trove by chance. She came up behind him and asked, "May I help you?" Lou turned around and saw her. He lowered his hat.

"I'm just a salesgirl," she said. "You can put your hat—"

"You're Ella," he said, reading her name tag. "A pleasure to meet you. I'm Lou." He gazed at her. "I'm searching for a gift from"—he looked around—"the Fourth Prussian Dynasty," he announced.

"Yes," she said.

"From 1834 to 1857. A great era in history. A time of riches. Beautiful queens." His voice echoed strangely. She could not recall anything about the Fourth Prussian Dynasty.

"Ella," he said. "Show me what you have."

They strolled past the delicate, glimmering objects. There were no other customers or salesgirls in the store just then. He followed her, his shoulders hunched, assuming a protective posture.

"Prussia," she said, hoping for more help from him.

"I'd say the year 1852," he said.

She gazed around the room. A feeling of boldness came over her. "This!" she tried, pointing to a gold-filigree grandfather clock. "This is from that time."

He went up to the clock, rapped it with his knuckles. His face went soft with approval. "It is," he said.

Ella stepped back, surprised. The clock was certainly not from the Fourth Prussian Dynasty, whatever that was.

Each understood that the other was lying. The light in the room seemed to brighten.

"It chimed to call them to dinner," he said.

"I think so," she said, smiling. A puff of glee burst in her chest.

They walked around the room. Almost all the objects in it, they decided, must be from the Fourth Prussian Dynasty. "This," Lou said, gripping a vase dangerously by its neck, "held the bracelets that belonged to Edwina, the Prussian princess."

"No," she said. "That was for her earrings. Her bracelets"—she tapped a long, curved ivory tusk—"hung on this."

Ella began to feel a little dizzy. Lou walked close to her, so close that it was as if they were already intimate, and when she took her place behind the counter again he looked lost. He bought the least expensive item in the room—a tiny jade rabbit—and seemed stunned that he had purchased anything.

"Thank you very much, Ella," he said in a puzzled way, clutching the store bag. "Thank you for helping me today." And then, as though afraid of what he might say next, he dashed out of the store.

A few days later, as she came out through the glass doors of Johnson Massey, she saw Lou standing by the store windows. He was moving his hat restlessly from hand to hand; when he saw her, he quickly put it on. "Ella," he said, his face stern, "I'm Lou."

It was a fall day, and the sky was pale with cold. His hands seemed clumsy and large in brown mittens. His breath curled in the chill air. "What a lovely pin," he said, looking at the sparkling "JM" on her lapel.

"I think they're diamonds," she said, and then stopped, embarrassed.

He smiled, so that she knew that he knew the stones could not be diamonds. They began walking together, toward nowhere. The afternoon seemed to part before them.

"If you're still looking for presents," she said, knowing he wasn't, "Sophie can help—"

"I have something for you," he blurted. They stopped. He held out a package, badly wrapped. It was easy to accept the present; she was curious. She unwound the tissue. It was the rabbit she had sold him.

"There was no Fourth Prussian Dynasty," she said. She had looked it up in an encyclopedia.

"No?" He laughed. He knew. His face was as open as a child's. "But you were so . . . helpful. I wanted to give it to you."

She touched the rabbit's glossy ears. She had never owned anything from the Treasure Trove.

"Have dinner with me," he said. The words seemed to come from a tender place inside him. He stepped back a little. There was a brisk gust of wind, and his coat flapped around him.

Ella began to look forward to seeing Lou come through the Grecian columns of the Treasure Trove. Soon he was visiting her several times a week. She was cautious, but she liked him, partly because the other girls did. They hovered beside him, laughing at his jokes, the way he made fun of the gaudiest, most grotesque objects. "What fool would buy this?" he said, lifting a huge gilt ashtray with cupids balancing on the edges. The girls shrieked with laughter. Ella watched them change lipsticks, looking for the one color that would make him love them. They acted like men when they flirted, slapping him playfully, calling him "mister" or "kid," as though this gave them new rights to him. They smiled coldly at Ella. She did not understand her claim on Lou, but she tried to love him almost to appease them.

After work, Ella and Lou took walks together. He was full of opinions, and he seemed so happy to be with her that she wanted to listen. He told her about the classes he had taken in college; how he helped manage his mother's suit store; how he had read about California and wanted to live in a place that was always warm. Lou was full of jokes when he visited the store, but when they were alone he had an earnest quality that told her that he took her seriously. His admiration seemed to be part of him, like bone.

He had money. That gave him confidence; he entered restaurants, stores with none of her trepidation. She began to love the careful, greased slickness of his hair, which gleamed like black licorice, and the way he shook his coat on, commanding and sharp. He was educated; he read all the sections of a newspaper. He walked through the world knowing he belonged in it.

One night, she was eating dinner with Lou in a bright-red booth in a diner in Brookline. She sat, anxious, straightening the fork on her napkin. She had ordered brisket, but it wasn't a fancy place and when her meal arrived the meat was too tough to cut. Her knife skidded from her hand to the floor.

"They should take it back," Lou said. "It should be more tender." Ella felt embarrassed, responsible somehow.

"No, I like it this way," she said. He looked at her.

"Then let me try," he said.

Lou slid her plate over to his side, pressed his fork deeply into the meat, and carefully cut off a small piece. He held it up as though it were a jewel.

"How's this?" he asked.

She stared at him. "Fine," she said. He cut the meat into bite-sized pieces for her. Then he set the plate back in front of her. "That should be better," he said.

She could not look at him. It was wonderful, the way he cut her meat for her. Lou chewed his green beans. For a moment, Ella stopped eating her brisket. She was so certain of her future, she did not feel she needed to do anything—pick up her fork, drink her water. An odd happiness filled her. Life would carry her to the next good place.

The wedding was a rush of images: the rabbi's gray, acne-marked face, her boned, ivory-satin dress, paid for by Lou's family, and the juicy red roast beef they had also provided. At one point, she was held up in a slight wooden chair, dozens of hands reaching for her, as though she were floating on a wild sea. She barely saw Lou during the party, until, emerging from a flurry of rice, they disappeared into a taxi that took them to the Hotel Essex. Lou registered them as Mr. and Mrs. Lou Rose. It was that easy; this was who she was.

She had never been inside a hotel. Their room was creamy-walled, with a ruby-red carpet. There were dark-blue linen drapes, and a big, tidy bed. A bottle of champagne sat in a silver bucket. The room smelled clean, antiseptic. Ella wanted to touch everything. She moved around, examining the night table, opening and closing the drawers.

Lou followed her. "Let me introduce my wife to the dresser," he said. His voice was hoarse. "Let me introduce my wife to the lamp—"

The word "wife" startled her, as if an intruder had entered the room. In the bathroom she found fragrant squares of soap, and picked one up. "It's our first soap," she said to Lou. "Hold out your hands." He did; his palms were exquisite and pale pink. Gently she washed their hands together. He dried his with the plush hotel towel. They went back into the bedroom, and Lou leaned toward her face and kissed her.

It was all very fast. She wanted to be a good bride, to be still as Lou unzipped her dress and pushed it down her shoulders, but she also wanted to kiss back. She stepped out of her dress in one quick, determined motion. He unhooked her bra and took her breasts in his hands. It was an astounding sight, her breasts, pale and soft, in his hands. It seemed too easy, too calm.

Lou gently guided her down to the bed. The gold bands on their fingers gleamed, ghostly in the darkness, as though they belonged to the same club. His fingers had a rubbery quality, and she felt the edge of his fingernail inside her. There was a loneliness that she had not expected. "Ella," he whispered. Suddenly frightened, she wrapped her arms around him; she was aware of the cotton sheet and the clock ticking on the wall and his breath, so fast, doglike. She pressed her forehead into his shoulder, wanting to touch more than his body.

Then he stopped, and rolled off her, pushing his face into a pillow. His ear was so close to her lips she wanted to shout into it, but she did not know what she would say.

"Well, my love," Lou said. "We're married."

They blinked into the brackish, honeyed smell of each other's breath.

Lou fell asleep, and Ella watched him as he slept. Suddenly, she understood that no one completely owned anyone else in the world. Even together in their wedding bed, they would separate into two different people in their dreams. As her eyes adjusted to the darkness, she saw her wedding dress, stiff and opalescent in the deep-blue light. It looked as if it had fallen and were trying, very delicately, to stand up.

It took nothing to send them to California: a cramped attic apartment; a newspaper article that said homes in Los Angeles were cheap. It was 1924. They moved West, a new bride and groom, in a used Ford. Gripping hands, Ella and Lou watched as each state fell away behind them, revealing the vast country, alternately brown or verdant beneath the springtime sun. ◉

AFTER WORDS

My grandmother, who grew up in a situation similar to Ella's in Boston at the turn of the century, once told me that she worked at a store like the Treasure Trove. Her apartment, when she was older, was basically like living in the Treasure Trove; it was a compendium of every porcelain/jade/china chachka one could imagine. She also told me that she took a class in salesmanship in high school, and I wondered what a class of recent immigrants and children of immigrants would be like, as they all attempted to "sell" themselves to this new world.

ROBERT ANTHONY SIEGEL

MY REFUGEE

1.

I STOOD IN THE FOYER of my little apartment, the napkin still tucked into my shirt, the soup spoon still in my hand, as I listened to the urgent tapping on my front door. "Let me in," said a woman's voice. "They want to kill me."

It was just a whisper, the voice, but so rich and strange, so full of the suffering of real life. I put my hand to the door and felt—I'm not making this up—the beating of her heart, and then the pounding of my own in rhythm with hers.

This wasn't at all like me; my habits are cautious and frugal. I find the newspaper on the subway; I reuse paper bags. "It's dinnertime," I said, hoping that she would understand: I am too civilized to unhook the chain and turn all six locks for anyone but the delivery guy.

"They're coming," she said.

Indeed, I could hear the elevator door opening at the far end of the hall, the blunt thud of many boots on the carpet. I put my eye to the peephole and caught a glimpse of a black lock of hair, an ear.

If I opened the door for her now the killers would push inside too. They would make me watch as they murdered her, and then they would kill me for good measure, probably using a straight razor or a meat hook, something bloody that would ensure maximum suffering. One of them would hold a video camera so they could put the footage on their website.

"Please," she shrieked.

"I'm sorry, I have company," I said, though in fact no one was there but me, and then I backed up slowly, into the living room.

2.

No, that's not what happened. What happened is that I let her in. The killers banged on the door till I thought the hinges would rip from the wall, and then disappeared to the bar downstairs, to drink and fight among themselves. Hours later I saw them from the window, stumbling toward the bus stop on the corner, their uniforms torn and disheveled.

She sat for a while at the table, shaking—a woman of thirty in dirty jeans, with the myopic look of somebody who had lost her glasses along the way. I gave her my soup and she ate with the efficiency of the habitually hungry, wiping the bowl dry with a piece of bread. If she'd been a movie I would have called her *grittily realistic*, but she was in fact real, and so I couldn't call her anything at all. "I've always had great sympathy for the underdog," I told her. "I've been a Cubs fan for many years."

She looked at me as if she'd never heard the word *baseball* or *fan* or known the agonies of misplaced loyalty. "The men of our village were ordered to dig a ditch and climb inside and then they were shot," she said. "The women were ordered to fill it up."

"At least you made it out."

"My husband was in that ditch."

"Well, you can't blame yourself for that." It was a piece of advice that I had used very successfully in my own life any number of times. "Just the other day, we had a major filing error at work, and it turned out—"

Perhaps she got the point, because she stood up and moved very close, looking me up and down. "We have a lot to do," she said.

The smell of the forest rose off her, the scent of wet earth and leaves. A heavy lock turned inside my chest. That one word, *we*: it was like I had been waiting my entire life to feel it shoot through my veins and warm my toes. I sat with her at the table, watching her lips as she outlined complicated plans for rescuing aunts, cousins, neighbors. The details were hard to grasp, involving bank robberies to fund the purchase of plane tickets, but I liked the way her plans spread out like two strong arms, grasping me close. No more of that nightly vertigo, as if I were falling straight through the world into nothingness.

Wasn't life wonderful? One moment eating soup alone, the next on a sort of impromptu first date with a woman who had seen her husband dig his own grave.

3.

No, that's not what happened, either. What happened is that I backed away from the door and, as they beat her in the hall, went to the window overlooking the bus stop—threw it open and leaned outside, drawing in great gulps of air. It was dark out, and a group of people stood in the lit glass enclosure, looking like exhibits in a museum diorama titled *Urban Anomie*. There was a man in raincoat, smoking a cigarette, and a woman with many packages, and two little girls wearing silver tiaras and pink backpacks, all of them staring out like birds on a power line. And none of them knew what a close call I'd had. ❧

AFTER WORDS

I was asked to write something about the Holocaust and found myself completely intimidated, so I did what any reasonably thoughtful person would do: procrastinated, while getting more and more nervous about it. Finally, I remembered that wonderful, horrible cliché about writing what you know, and I realized I would be all right if I just stuck to the boundaries of my own life experience. And so, while nothing in my life has prepared me to understand what it would be like to be transported to a death camp, or to do the transporting or gassing or cleaning up, I had to admit that I know a lot about being a bystander. Anyone who opens up a newspaper or watches the news on TV is a bystander to terrible things—implicated up to the eyeballs by knowledge and inaction. So there was the story I could tell: the bystander's story. Once I understood that, my obligation was just to tell that story as simply and honestly as possible.

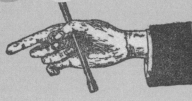

CREATIVE NONFICTION CRAFT

PHILIP GERARD

●●●●●●●●●◌◌

WHAT *IS* CREATIVE NONFICTION ANYHOW?

IT WAS LATE AFTERNOON, the day before the close of the Bread Loaf Writers' Conference in Vermont, when Bob Reiss approached the lectern of the Little Theatre to give the final reading of an eleven-day marathon of readings. A warm, breezy day, with just a hint of fall in the lengthening mountain shadows. The Little Theatre was crowded. Writers and would-be writers craned forward in their folding wooden chairs. At the open screens of French doors along the rustic clapboard walls, other conferees leaned in as if watching a summer stock production of some new Eugene O'Neill play.

Behind Reiss clustered all the literary ghosts of Bread Loaf, the celebrities who had stood where he was standing now and read from their genius: among them Saul Bellow, John P. Marquand, Theodore Roethke, A.B. Guthrie, Jr., Richard Wright, May Sarton, Maxine Kumin, Toni Morrison and the patron saint of the mountain, snowy-haired Robert Frost. This was a place of repose, a place of poetry, a literary rendezvous.

Reiss was thin and drawn, just returned from the war zone known as the Sudan, where he had spent weeks behind rebel lines and survived mortar attacks, a harrowing unauthorized plane trip at the mercy of a malaria-ridden pilot, and being trampled to death by a famine-crazed mob of refugees.

In his open chambray shirt over black T-shirt, with his sunburned cheeks and raw lanky wrists, fighting off stomach parasites and the accumulated fatigue of weeks in the field, he didn't look like a guy who creates literature. He said amiably, "I'm not going to read fiction or poetry. I'm going to read some *non*-fiction for all you *non*-men and *non*-women."

The crowd laughed easily and then listened, intrigued.

He read, indeed, nonfiction: a tale of suffering and heartbreak and idealism. The arc of the story was simple: Altruistic men and women try to deliver food to the starving multitude of refugees in the Horn of Africa. The protagonists were idealistic young people, foreign service officers with a humane sense of duty, and bureaucrats doing the unglamorous fund-raising and paperwork of rescue. The antagonists were distance, red tape, bad roads, the rainy season, armed and irrational political factions, time running out, and the dark side of human nature.

The rebels made deals about food. Ordinarily peaceful people rioted over food. People stole food, shared food, killed for food, suffered without food. The conflict was compelling: food was the prize, there were precious few winners, and it was a true story.

Creative nonfiction: timely, but also timeless. His story didn't come out of a quiet country house or a private reverie. He'd gone out there into the dangerous world to find it, to recover it, to make it, and he had brought it back to us.

People listened hard, some of them holding their breath. In every line, there was an implicit courage, a moral and physical stand against what was wrong with the world. Not polemic, not prescription, not opinion or editorial, just clean, accurate description; real characters who leapt to life in a few quick strokes; an overwhelming and unsettling sense of a far-off, perilous place; deft connections between CIA analysts in Washington, sacks of grain tumbling out of the blue African sky, an airplane bogged down in a muddy cow pasture being hauled out by four hundred laboring Dinkas, malnourished babies being weighed to determine if they qualified for extra rations, food thieves prowling the deadly bush after nightfall, a few choice statistics, and a bunch of American kids in concert T-shirts trying to do the right thing far from home in the middle of a shooting war.

Nonfiction.

Creative nonfiction.

Literature.

THE RENAISSANCE IN NONFICTION:
A HUNGER FOR THE REAL

These days creative nonfiction is enjoying an astonishing renaissance. Many of the finest writers in our literature, including eminent poets and novelists, are writing it. Even the National Endowment for the Arts recognizes the genre in its fellowship awards, and many state arts agencies are following suit.

"I think it is invariably a response to crisis. Nonfiction flourishes in times of great upheaval," theorizes William Howarth, who teaches nonfiction at Princeton University and whose articles and essays have appeared regularly in *National Geographic* and the *New York Times*.

David Bain, author of *Sitting in Darkness: Americans in the Philippines*, compares the present resurgence with the enormous popularity of reportage, factual stories, during the tumultuous days of the Second World War. "People needed something concrete that they could use to measure what was going on in the world," he explains. "Since we are again in a period of serious flux, without people knowing what's really going on or what they should believe in, that could call for it."

It's always seemed odd to me that *nonfiction* is defined, not by what it *is*, but by what it is *not*. It is *not* fiction. But then again, it is also *not* poetry, or technical writing or libretto. It's like defining classical music as *nonjazz*. Or sculpture as *nonpainting*. As Reiss himself says in his wry New York accent, "I feel like the Rodney Dangerfield of literature—nonfiction don't get no respect."

Historically, nonfiction was around long before fiction—at least in the form of the short story and the novel—ever came on the scene. But nobody called it that. Farther back still, nobody seems to have made much distinction between the two. Aristotle divided the literary world into History and Poetry, and, much to everybody's surprise, Poetry seems to have included literary nonfiction. *The Iliad* of Homer was long considered to be "only" myth by those who cared about such distinctions, until one reader, Heinrich Schliemann, used it as a nonfictional document to discover the actual remains of Troy. A real place, after all, even if it was fought over by mythical gods and goddesses. Poetry and History together.

Ron Powers, contributing editor of *GQ* magazine and winner of the Pulitzer Prize for media criticism, says, "The novel is a way of creating a mythic truth from your own personal mythos. And the contract with the reader is that the reader is sharing your myth, and that's powerful simply because we're a storytelling species. We like stories. The nonfiction act is similar to that, except that it satisfies our hunger for the real and our need to make sense, make order, out of chaos."

TELLING STORIES, TELLING LIVES

On the face of it, the term *nonfiction* doesn't make much sense. No other genre suffers under this metaphysical definition by negation.

The term is doubly odd when you realize that we're defining the factual, the actual, the things that really happened, with an explicit disclaimer that assures the reader we didn't make it up—as if *making it up* were the primary way to communicate the events of our world. As if, were any reader to come across a narrative of people, events and ideas—a *story*—he or she would assume, unless assured otherwise, that the story was fiction.

Well, it turns out that's not such a bad assumption. Our natural tendency in real life seems to be to tell stories: the story of what we did at the office all day, the story of how we met our husband or wife, the story of what happened at the party last night. And, in telling stories, we invariably surrender to the delicious temptation to make fiction—or, less politely, to lie. When we're kids, being accused by our parents of "telling a story" means being caught in a lie.

The nonfiction writer must always rein in that impulse to lie, in all the subtle ways we can shade the truth into something less than—or more than—the truth. The nonfiction writer must be more truthful than we usually require of ourselves or of each other.

We lie a lot. We don't mean to—not always, at any rate—but no matter how clear-cut or simple the events we're trying to relate, the minute we open our mouth or take up our pen we are delivering fiction. We embellish. We misremember. We inadvertently change what somebody actually said because we didn't happen to have our tape recorder handy. Or worse, we paraphrase their words, giving them a different emphasis, a sharper tone. We conveniently leave out details that make ourselves look bad and leave out other information because it seems irrelevant and leave out still more details because we just plain didn't see or hear them.

And what's left out can change the story of what happened—a lot.

We're limited by our point of view—from where we stand, we can see only so much of the action. Our vision is blocked, or crucial things happen in several places at once and we can be in only one place at a time. Or we assume a God-like objective omniscience that equally distorts pure fact. We make judgments about which character (we've already turned real people into characters) is important, which event deserves emphasis, which detail best conveys the feeling of the moment.

And we tell it all out of order—we want to establish suspense, after all. Give it a dramatic punch. But telling events out of order can be a kind of lying, of fictionalizing. Or it can be a better way of being truthful. It's a tricky business, but it's made less so if we remember always that our first obligation is to tell the truth. Every strategy, every dramatic convention, every selective choice must be employed in the service of making the story *more* not *less* truthful.

So when we label a piece of writing *nonfiction*, we are announcing our determination to rein in our impulse to lie. To test our memory more carefully, do a little research to fill in the holes in what we witnessed, draw dear lines around what we are offering as objective fact (as if such a thing exists—more on that later) and what we are offering as opinion, meditation, analysis, judgment, fancy, interpretation.

In the past few years, the lines between all the genres have blurred: poetry and stories merge into the prose-poem, fact and fiction into "faction," the so-called nonfiction novels of Truman Capote or Norman Mailer. But there is a meaningful distinction between fiction and non-fiction, Powers says: "It's interesting to me that people who otherwise would say that it's *all* fiction, that there's no such thing as nonfiction, because truth is infinitely elusive—I happen to agree with that last part—they're the same people who would get very exercised when George Bush says that the wetlands aren't wetlands after all. They don't say, "What a marvelous act of deconstruction or reexamination of the 'text.' They say, Let's impeach that so-and-so."

Expletive, of course, deleted.

YOU CAN'T MAKE IT UP

The hardest part of writing creative nonfiction is that you're stuck with what really happened—you can't make it up. You can be as artful as you want in the presentation, draw profound meanings out of your subject matter, but you are still stuck with real people and real events. You're stuck with stories that don't always turn out the way you wish they had turned out.

I once sent a piece to a producer at National Public Radio's *All Things Considered* who had used a couple of my radio essays in the past. The piece was a reflection on our American obsession with *things* from the point of view of a long-haul moving man, which I was for a summer. Most of what we trucked back and forth across the interstates of America was pure junk.

But one woman's belongings were all antiques, beautiful and probably priceless: lovely furniture, original paintings, heirloom crystal. We picked up the load at a warehouse in Florida, where we knew the crates had been damaged but had no idea how badly. When we unpacked them in Las Vegas, everything was destroyed. Completely, utterly smashed.

It wasn't our fault. A careless forklift operator back at the warehouse had probably dropped the container full of her crated belongings onto a concrete floor.

As we unpacked piece after broken piece, the woman cried, and I didn't blame her. We spent several hours taking inventory of the damage, filling out forms for the insurance company, and I sat with the woman while the driver made all the necessary phone calls. After awhile, somewhat embarrassed, the woman regained her composure, stopped crying, and told me, "It's not right to cry over things." As a parting gift, she gave me a paperback novel to read on our way west to Beverly Hills, our next stop.

The book was William Styron's *Sophie's Choice.*

The NPR producer liked the piece a lot, but she thought *Sophie's Choice*—a novel about a woman caught up in the Holocaust—was a pretty heavy book to drop into a piece about losing everything. Couldn't it be a different book?

Well, no, I told her. It happened to be that book. The woman was real, and when she was done crying she was a little embarrassed and oddly grateful to us, and she gave me a real book, and that book was *Sophie's Choice.* Not only that, but I read it on the way to Beverly Hills, and, reading it, I understood her remark about not crying over things: Styron's novel is about a woman who loses everything—and everyone—to the Nazi Final Solution. Reading it in the context of what I had just witnessed moved me beyond words. By the time I had finished reading it, I had developed a profound respect for that woman in Las Vegas and a deep curiosity about what—whom—she'd really been crying about as we uncrated the broken souvenirs of her life.

Too bad, the producer said. They didn't use the piece.

I really wanted them to use the piece. It had every natural irony real life ever offers—including Las Vegas *and* Beverly Hills in a piece about materialism. The problem was, the truth seemed as if I had contrived it. The ironies were too neat to be believed in real life. I could not fault the producer—she wanted the story to *sound* true as well as *be* true, and it may be that, in her experience, other writers took greater liberties with the form. Radio commentaries frequently tend toward memoir, which the reader or listener recognizes as inherently looser and less objectively reliable than other kinds of nonfiction.

But to me, such a change would have broken my contract with the listener. It was *non*fiction. That's the first good reason for the term *nonfiction*: to announce that, while every story tends toward fiction, *this* one at least owes an allegiance to the truth of events.

The second reason is simpler. Nobody has yet come up with a better term. Lee Gutkind, a writer and long-time faculty member at the University of Pittsburgh who founded and edits the journal

Creative Nonfiction, explains why he avoided other terms, such as "literary journalism," in coining the name: "Because I thought the word 'journalism' would frighten away those in the creative writing program and the word 'literary' would frighten away those in the journalism department."

FIVE HALLMARKS

But what in the world makes nonfiction *creative*?

Five characteristics: First, it has an apparent subject and a deeper subject. The apparent subject may be spectacular or mundane. Unlike in a feature article, it is only part of what we are interested in.

John Steinbeck's *The Log From the Sea of Cortez,* for instance, is the chronicle of a voyage of exploration in the Gulf of California. But it is also a meditation on the creative process, especially for the writer using the facts of the world meticulously observed and recorded: "The design of a book is the pattern of a reality controlled and shaped by the mind of the writer," he confides to us in his introduction. "This is completely understood about poetry or fiction, but it is too seldom realized about books of fact." Again and again he returns to this implicit comparison between a voyage of discovery and a book of nonfiction.

But the apparent subject must itself be made fascinating—as Steinbeck makes fascinating the tidal pools and ports-of-call and beer-drunk companions of his maritime expedition. Gutkind says that the best nonfiction always teaches the reader something: "One important distinguishing factor is this teaching element—a reader reads on to learn something. It's not just personal experience."

Second, and partly because of the duality of subject, such nonfiction is released from the usual journalistic requirement of *timeliness*: long after the apparent subject ceases to be topical, the deeper subject and the art that expresses it remain vital. That doesn't mean it isn't triggered by today's headlines—in fact, every great piece of creative nonfiction I've ever read seems driven by the writer's felt urgency to tackle that subject right now, not tomorrow.

But what captures the writer's attention is not just what everybody else sees—the current crisis. In today's headlines, the writer recognizes larger trends, deeper truths about the way human beings behave.

The particular event offers an epiphany, a way of getting at the deeper subject. This ironic tension between the *urgency of the event* and the *timelessness of its meaning* keeps the writer firmly planted in particulars, in the concrete detail that will make the larger abstract truth come to life on the page.

Writers are passionate about different subjects at different times in their lives. They are attentive to the world and alert to the hinges of history—those great and terrible moments of promise, crisis, impending salvation or doom—and they are drawn to write about them in an effort to affect the outcome. Thus Bob Reiss writes about famine relief in the Sudan ostensibly because it is an urgent practical and political problem *right now*. We—our country, the world, private citizens—have some hard choices to make, and it's the nonfiction writer's job to make us face our choices.

And, to be practical, that's the moment when editors and readers are most likely to care about the subject. To assign the piece and publish it. To read it with at least a shadow of the writer's urgency. The writer must not only write about what he or she cares about but must do so *at the time* he or she is most passionate about it. That sense of passion, of personal urgency, cannot be faked. And it endures.

All art seems grounded in paradox, and nonfiction is no exception. Triggered by the timely meeting of writer and subject, a piece may stand outside of time. Beyond the particulars of present-day politics, Reiss's story about famine relief is almost biblical in its archetype: Do you give the starving man fish, or do you teach him to fish? And what does he eat while he's learning to fish?

Third, creative nonfiction is narrative; it always tells a good story. "So often, it ends thirty minutes after it begins—something is happening in time," Gutkind says. It takes advantage of such fictional devices as character, plot and dialogue. "It moves," Gutkind explains. "It is action-oriented. Most good creative nonfiction is constructed in scenes." And, he says, just as in a good short story or novel, "There is always a magic moment. Your readers are waiting for that magic moment to occur, waiting for a change to occur, a lightbulb to flash, something to happen."

In Ted Conover's journal of riding the rails, *Rolling Nowhere*, the entire journey—and thus the whole story—moves toward that moment when Conover, a clean-cut college boy, will at last be initiated as a true hobo. And like the best magic moments, when it happens it brings surprising and dramatic consequences—once he has truly entered the world of the railroad tramp, he is terrified that he will never find his way back to the world he knew, the person he was.

The moment comes in the hobo jungle in Everett, Washington, as Conover watches his bickering alcoholic companions binge on cheap wine and sees one possible future for himself reflected in their violence, their incoherent babble, their broken teeth and ruined bodies. He searches out a gas station washroom, where he scrubs his teeth and washes his long hair, and then calls long distance to a college roommate. "In a complete turnabout from my earlier concerns, I wanted a guarantee that, while I could get close to tramps I could never really become one, and they would never permanently 'rub off' on me," he tells the reader. But of course there is no such guarantee. The roommate ironically congratulates him on having proved himself a true hobo—for Conover, at this stage in his travels, a truly frightening insight.

We anticipate that magic moment, we expect it, but some part of it is always unexpected.

Fourth, creative nonfiction contains a sense of *reflection* on the part of the author. The underlying subject has been percolating through the writer's imagination for some time, waiting for the right outlet. It is *finished* thought.

The purported subject of the piece, though it may seem like a target of opportunity, is actually one that has preoccupied the writer for some time. He has written about it before, in other ways and in exploring apparently unrelated topics. He has brooded about it, asked questions all his life about it, trying to make up his mind. He is building on what he has already learned, what he has already written, coming to ever more sophisticated insights with each pass.

Terry Tempest Williams, author of *Refuge: An Unnatural History of Family and Place*, says that it takes time for an experience to sink in, that the writer must meditate on what she has done and observed to discover what it means, how to write about it. "There's such a pressure to write fast, to get it done," she says. "But one of the most important things in writing nonfiction is to have patience."

In such a reflective piece, you'll see the writer making connections between the subject at hand and books he has read, between history and philosophy and a remark his fifth-grade teacher once made. So Conover invokes Jack London. In *Arctic Dreams: Imagination and Desire in a Northern Landscape,* Barry Lopez talks about early Arctic explorers. Steinbeck ruminates on a political stance he has been cultivating for years. Even in the context of a boat trip on the Sea of Cortez, he finds insight about the relationship between government and people in a democracy, one of his chief preoccupations as a writer in both his fiction and his nonfiction.

In other words, the piece reflects not only whatever immediate research was necessary to get the facts straight on the page, but also the more profound "research" of a lifetime.

"I tend to write about subjects I was born to," observes Anne Matthews, whose book about the landscape inhabited by eight generations of her family, *Where the Buffalo Roam: The Storm Over the Restoration of America's Great Plains,* was a finalist for the 1993 Pulitzer Prize in nonfiction. "It takes a lifetime to know a subject."

When I set out for Paris to track down the haunts of Ernest Hemingway for a piece on the twenty-fifth anniversary of the publication of *A Moveable Feast,* the memoir of his formative years in Paris as a young writer learning his craft, my journey was steeped in fifteen years of reading Hemingway's books and wondering about his marvelous, troubled life. We had shared an editor at Scribner's. Hemingway's Nick Adams stories had given me my first inspiration to try writing stories of my own. I wanted to go to Paris to find out what had been so special about that city to him—did the Paris he knew still exist, and could it still inspire a young writer to greatness? So that journey back to the city of *his* first inspiration was one I had been preparing to make for a very long time.

Fifth, such nonfiction shows serious attention to the craft of writing. It goes far beyond the journalistic "inverted pyramid" style—with interesting turns of phrase, fresh metaphors, lively and often scenic presentation, a shunning of clichés and obvious endings, a sense of control over nuance, accurate use of words, and a governing aesthetic sensibility.

Finding the writing is as important as finding the subject. Good writing is elegant—cleanly arresting rather than gaudy or merely decorative. It carries itself gracefully and falls rhythmically on the ear. It is artistic, and often informed by other art. "There's a certain voice, where the voice doesn't get in the way," explains Lisa Bain, senior editor at *Glamour* who learned her trade at *Esquire*. "Which is one thing with a lot of heavy stylists—you get caught up in the language, rather than having the language forward the story." Editors have a phrase for wonderful writing, she explains: they say it *sings*. "Good writing has a lyricism and a rhythm to it," she says. "It's very hard to put into words."

Look closely at this brief passage from Lopez' *Arctic Dreams*: "Winter darkness shuts off the far view. The cold drives you deep into your clothing, muscles you back into your home. Even the mind retreats into itself."

Listen to it. Hear the writing *sing*?

Or this sentence from *White Town Drowsing,* Powers's book about Hannibal, Missouri, a hometown he shared with Mark Twain: "I grew up in a town that seemed less a town to me than a kingdom."

The simple, unadorned writing opens an elegant metaphor.

THE ART LIES IN THE CRAFT

A good way to approach writing creative nonfiction, paradoxically, is to forget about the *creative*—the literary—part and concentrate on the *nonfiction* part. Pay enough attention to the craft of learning the story and telling it clearly, accurately and economically, and the art will happen when you're not looking.

Writing nonfiction is simple. You find out some facts, you figure out how to arrange them in light of a larger idea, then you do something artful with the arrangement. Simple, but hard. Like climbing a mountain—all you have to do is keep going up. The most important step is always the next one. That's the craft of it—paying attention to what's under your feet, what your hands are grabbing hold of, working against the gravity of all your bad habits.

"I consider myself a storyteller," says Reiss, author of seven novels and two books of nonfiction and a correspondent for *Outside* magazine. "And I distinguish between stories I make up and stories I find out." Creative nonfiction is the stories you find out, captured with a clear eye and an alert imagination, filtered through a mind passionate to know and tell, told accurately and with compelling grace. ❧

PETER TRACHTENBERG

A CAGE OF ONE'S OWN:
CREATIVE NONFICTION
AND ITS GENRES

EVERY WRITER WORKS INSIDE A CAGE. By cage, I mean a genre and its requirements. In nonfiction, the bars of the cage are facts. They are irremovable and irreplaceable. They give your work its impetus and focus. I once wrote a book because I'd read about the tattoos of the Dayaks, the indigenous people of Borneo, and was so taken by the designs and the stories behind them that I went to Borneo myself. When I got there, I found that traditional tattooing had almost died out, surviving only as some smudged vein-like patterns on the hands and forearms of old people who were mortified by them because they marked them, in the eyes of their more sophisticated neighbors, as "primitive." My story might have been more exciting if I'd reported that Dayaks were still getting tattooed (maybe, as in the old days, to commemorate a successful headhunting expedition), but that would have been blatantly untrue, and so instead I wrote, among other things, about the vanishing of tradition and the way that people come to feel ashamed—are *taught* to feel ashamed—of things they once valued. Those were the facts.

The strictest forms of nonfiction are telephone directories and train timetables. They are nothing *but* fact. In their case, the bars of the cage are set so close together that the writer is unable to see anything beyond them, nor is he discernible to the curious reader who may wish to peer inside. Nobody talks about the literary style of the Yellow Pages. Traditional journalism puts a little space between the bars, but not very much. The reporter may observe that the president answers questions with what sounds like exasperation. He may note the tears in the eyes of the laid-off auto worker. He may seek the possible reasons for this. But he won't venture far beyond those facts, won't tell us what he thinks about the president's temper or the worker's grief. The moment he did that he would stop being a reporter and become a columnist.

The writer of creative nonfiction inhabits the same sort of cage as the reporter, but its bars are set farther apart. There are many types, or subgenres, of creative nonfiction, from biography to travel writing, immersion journalism to memoir and lyric essay. In some of these forms, the cage bars of fact are spaced so widely that the writer can slip between them and out into the world. In other subgenres, the bars are as flexible as taffy. In still others they are rigid, but the writer is allowed to paint them vibrant colors or braid them with ivy. Of course the facts are still crucial, and depending on which subgenre he's working in, the writer may need to know more of them, more thoroughly, than most journalists do. Yet at times the nonfiction writer is tacitly permitted to depart from those facts, or move beyond them.

The subgenre of biography requires the writer to include all the significant facts about her subject, with the stress on *significant*. A study of the life of Ulysses S. Grant may say nothing about his favorite foods or his skills as a marksman but is obliged to touch on the notorious scandals of his presidency. Yet a biographer isn't just a collector and relater of facts, but their interpreter. One biographer of the unfortunate eighteenth president may paint him as a political innocent who failed to recognize his associates' self-dealing, while another finds a more cynical, compromised figure who tacitly gave the people around him permission to peddle offices and collect bribes. The two writers may have combed through the same archives and come up with more or less the same pertinent facts, but they've interpreted those facts differently. Of course, if either of them has cherry-picked facts in the service of a particular interpretation—if, say, she's left out letters which suggest that Grant knew perfectly well that his underlings were raiding the national till—the resulting biography will be worthless as anything but posthumous PR.

You can explore this process for yourself by choosing someone you know as the subject of a hypothetical biography or biographical sketch. For your purposes, an acquaintance is preferable to an intimate. It might be a teacher you had in high school, or a distant cousin, or one of your roommates' friends, the one with the great hair who laughs hysterically at her own jokes. Collect every fact you can find about that person (you may want to make sure your subject's okay with this rather than risk getting accused of stalking!): the schools she attended and her grades, her favorite chip, the make of her first car, the nicknames of her pets. Don't worry about organizing the facts, just write them down in random order. Then see what sorts of different—and even conflicting—narratives you can derive from those facts. The same excellent grades may suggest that your subject is a natural scholar or an anxious grind. She may play all those video games because of pent-up aggression or to keep her boyfriend company. Your tenth-grade calculus teacher was mean; your tenth-grade calculus teacher had no patience for fools. Remember: you have to take *all* the facts into account, and you can't write a biography that's faithful to some facts while riding roughshod over others.

Just how closely or widely the bars of fact are spaced is largely determined by the extent to which a literary subgenre is concerned with the objective world. Or, as some people like to say, the *real* world. Just what constitutes the real world is better left to philosophy. For the purposes of writing, though, your obligation to the facts increases in direct proportion to the factual density of your subject matter, its weight in documentation, witness, and memory. Any presidency leaves its factual evidence in the form of official records, memos, newspaper stories, legislation, transcripts, the journals and diaries of the men and women who labored in it, not to mention the secondary works of historians and political scientists. Those pieces of paper and the acts enshrined in them will make up the bars of the biographer's cage. A writer of immersion journalism depends less on documents than on the testimony of the living inhabitants of the world in which he immerses himself, like the charismatic and oddly innocent gang-bangers and teenage mothers of Adrian Nicole LeBlanc's *Random Family*, the prison guards of Ted Conover's *Newjack*, the struggling low-wage workers of Barbara Ehrenreich's *Nickel and Dimed*. These people are both the writer's informants and his characters. Because the world he's writing about is *their* world, they can explain codes that might take him years to decipher, tell him stories he might otherwise never learn. But they're also witnesses. If the writer portrays their reality falsely they will know it, and he should fear their judgment: not because of what they might do to him but because they are the owners of the truth that he betrayed.

Among the reasons so many writers are drawn to memoir is the freedom it seems to offer, especially the freedom from facts. No need to spool through smeared microfilms or do interviews in the old-folks' home. Why research your own story? And it *is* your story, in the sense that a memoir is not the account of a life but of the *memory* of a life, and who owns memory if not the rememberer? But memory is still caged by fact. The facts are what you remember. The living room rug with the wine stain on it that as a child you mistook for blood. The wild neighbor kids who terrorized you and your sisters. The time your family moved and the truck, which was overloaded, got one flat after another. Maybe your memories are hazy or distorted. That rug may not have been in your house but your grandmother's, and those neighbor kids didn't dump your cat in the wood-chipper; they just threatened to. But beyond a certain point of distortion, memory is no longer memory: it's imagination or hallucination or invention. It's fully conceivable that a writer may remember the three hours he spent in a police holding tank following his arrest on a DWI as having lasted all night, but it defies belief that he will remember those three hours as being three months, or his DWI as a railroad accident that happened to kill his high school sweetheart.

Tobias Wolff, who has written both memoir and fiction, compares the truth of memoir to the truth that gets told at a family Thanksgiving dinner. Your uncle's version of an incident that happened fifteen years ago seems totally, laughably, incorrect. "So, you say, no, no, no, it wasn't like that, and you go on, and you give your version of events. But, later

NONFICTION CRAFT

171

TRACHTENBERG

that night, you go home, and you're stretched out digesting this meal, and you sit there, and you think back to what you've said and you insisted, so ferociously, this is the case.

"There isn't a doubt being . . . maybe."

The most open cage in creative nonfiction is the one housing writers of the lyric essay, a form that uses the techniques of nonfiction to accomplish the ends of poetry. Among the lyric essays I've taught is one that jumps back and forth between an account of a marathon game of Monopoly and a tour of the scabrous ghetto of Atlantic City, the town on which the game was based. Another piece takes the form of an impossibly difficult recipe for a traditional French dish, "roast boned rolled stuffed shoulder of lamb," that has more in common with Marcel Duchamp than with Julia Child. Still another may or may not be the transcript of a session in a psychiatrist's office but is certainly a meditation on the way we imagine—which is to say make up—not just other people, but ourselves. The author of that last piece, Thalia Field, in an interview with the Seneca Review, describes herself as being, "among those writers who say 'I think through writing' and in the practice of keeping an open mind, the writing comprises an *essai*. [French for essay.] Sometimes the thinking is more argumentative than other times, sometimes more playful and without purpose. Sometimes the questions I'm thinking through require a lot of outside voices, languages, testimony imported from other ways of asking. Sometimes I think through a question simply to explore it, lose myself around it . . . . Thinking through things can require a lot of approaches to form." [1]

What makes up the facts of a lyric essay is subject to debate. There is a real game of Monopoly and a real Atlantic City, which John McPhee seems to have observed with enormous specificity. There may be no such dish as roast boned rolled stuffed shoulder of lamb—at least not one that must be marinated in a special stone trough and stuffed with the flesh of a blind fish found only in certain caves in Auvergne and caught no more than thirty-six hours earlier—but there are cookbooks that seem intended less to instruct than to intimidate. Thalia Field may

---

1 Thalia Field, with Ashley Butler, Tom Fleischmann, April Freeley, and Riley Hanick. "An Interview with Thalia Field." *The Seneca Review*, 38. no. 1.

or may not have been writing about an actual exchange with a real psychiatrist. If that exchange were presented as part of a memoir, the reader might be justified in wanting to know and feeling peeved if the event proved to be made up. But Field isn't purporting to relate facts. She's thinking through things.

I imagine the cage this writer inhabits as having one bar in each corner, just to remind reader—and maybe the writer herself—that it is a cage.

And of course it has no bars on top. ◉

PHILIP FURIA

LOOK IN THY HEART, LOOK IN THE ARCHIVES, LOOK ON THE INTERNET AND WRITE

SIR PHILIP SIDNEY ADVISED POETS, "Look in thy heart and write," but writers, including poets, also look in libraries, historical archives, and, nowadays, in the vast resources of information on the Internet. Pulitzer Prize-winning poet Philip Levine, who was visiting writer-in-residence at UNCW in 1997, wrote one of his greatest poems, "The Mercy," about his grandmother's childhood voyage to America and of a kind sailor who gave her the first orange she had ever tasted. Levine could have written the poem solely based on his grandmother's memory, but instead he spent days at the New York Public Library doing research on the *Mercy*, the ship that brought his grandmother to America:

> "The Mercy," I read on the yellowing pages of a book
> I located in a windowless room of the library
> on 42nd Street, sat thirty-one days
> offshore in quarantine before the passengers
> disembarked. There a story ends. Other ships
> arrived, "Tancred" out of Glasgow, "The Neptune"

registered as Danish, "Umberto IV,"
the list goes on for pages, . . .

So not only had his grandmother had to endure an ocean crossing but then another month on the ship amid a cholera epidemic. That
research enabled Levine to set his grandmother's story—and the kind-
ness of the sailor—against the historical background of the ordeal of
American immigration.

Sometimes research can be done in front of your computer. When
Wendy Brenner saw the phrase "Much is expected of the Merlot grape"
in a magazine, it struck her that it could be the basis of a witty story
about "great expectations." After a few hours of Internet research, she
had enough information about Merlot grapes—and wine—to fill her
story with telling detail.

At other times, a writer's research can be as demanding as a scholar's. Philip Gerard had to spend years researching *Cape Fear Rising*, his
novel about the 1898 assault by white supremacists upon Wilmington's black population. Not only did he conduct "secondary research"
by reading about the incident in books and essays, he had to do "primary research" by going to special historical archives and examining original documents—letters, journals, diaries, and contemporary
newspaper accounts.

Then he had to conduct "lived research"—interviewing descendants
of the participants, walking the streets of Wilmington with period maps
to trace the course of the action, and even traveling to the Army Ord-
nance Museum in Maryland to see the kind of Gatling gun possessed by
the leaders of the white supremacists:

> Not only did I look at it, I photographed it from many angles
> so I could describe it accurately later. Then I handled it, swiv-
> eling the four-hundred-pound drum with its ten rotating
> barrels, wrapping my fingers around the brass crank, sight-
> ing targets.

Research. Feeling the weight, smelling the gun oil, looking down
the barrel.

If you are a poet or novelist, research usually comes after you have begun to write and find that a setting, a character, or an episode requires you to get more information before you can write about it accurately and vividly. For writers of creative nonfiction, however, writing often can't even begin until all the research has been completed. Your research, moreover, must be as "creative" as your writing. As you research, you are not just gathering information but looking for the lineaments of a dramatic story, the nature of your characters.

A student in my workshop on writing biography was researching the life of Wilmington architect Henry Bacon, who designed many famous buildings, most notably the Lincoln Memorial. Through his research in architectural history, he knew that Bacon was now regarded as a staunch upholder of classical building style at a time when pioneers like Frank Lloyd Wright were redefining architecture away from classicism and toward a new modernist style.

But what really brought Bacon to life was a contemporary newspaper story my student read about the dedication of the Lincoln Memorial in 1925. As President Harding and other dignitaries stood in front of the memorial, Henry Bacon was hauled on a barge, pulled by young architecture students, down the length of the reflecting pool that links the Washington Monument and the Lincoln Memorial. "Like a triumphant Roman emperor," thought my student, "at the very time when the course of modern architecture was leaving Bacon behind."

Another student was writing a biographical essay on Wilmington artist Claude Howell. Early in his research, he found a wonderful fact that gave him a superb "lead" (the opening of your essay where you must grab the reader's attention): Claude Howell was born in the same room he died in, in the Carolina Apartments building on Market Street in downtown Wilmington. Yet it took months of more research to reveal that this great lead also defined a pattern that ran throughout Howell's life. Here was a man and artist who needed tremendous stability—living for much of his adult life with his mother, seldom leaving his hometown of Wilmington, and holding on to his "day job" in the offices of the local railroad company even after he became a successful painter. As that pattern emerged, my student interviewed an art historian about

Howell's paintings. When the historian pointed out that the composition of almost every one of Howell's paintings was based upon the triangle, the most stable of geometric forms, the student saw a connection between Howell's life and his art.

Because my student had done his homework by learning all he could about his subject through library and archival research, when he interviewed the art historian he was primed for that illuminating insight. Don't waste travel or interview time on what you can learn in the library. You'll get the most out of your lived research if you use it to learn what you can't find in secondary or primary research.

When I was researching my biography of Irving Berlin, I had the opportunity to interview his oldest daughter. As she was showing me her father's book collection—his leather-bound sets of Shakespeare, Dickens, and other classic writers—I knew that Berlin had only a few years of school and never mentioned great literature in his many newspaper interviews. I needed to find out whether these beautiful books were just for show or whether Berlin actually read them.

To put such a question delicately, I talked to his daughter about what I had learned of Berlin's friendship with several poets in the 1920s, such as Dorothy Parker and Robert Benchley, then asked if there were any earlier poets he liked. I could see that his daughter, a writer herself, was intrigued by the question and was trying hard to remember. "There was one," she said, and I held my breath as she tried to recall the name. "Yes, I remember," she said, smiling. "He used to like to read Alexander Pope."

At first I was amazed, since Pope is one of the most difficult of English writers. As I thought about it, however, it was perfectly logical. Alexander Pope wrote all of his poetry, even book-length epic poems, in couplets—those tiny, two-line, ten-syllable units of poetry. Berlin also worked in a very constrictive form—the thirty-two bar song, which gave a lyricist about fifty or sixty words to say something fresh and moving. A songwriter who managed to turn out numbers like "White Christmas" and "Easter Parade" in that narrow format would naturally be drawn to a poet like Pope. If you've done your homework in the library and the archives, that's the kind of insight that can come from your lived research. ❧

SARAH MESSER

CONSTRUCTING MEMOIR
from CHILDHOOD MEMORIES

MY PARENTS' HOUSE CAUGHT ON FIRE when I was five. It was a pretty bad fire. No one was hurt except the family cat (who died from smoke inhalation). The dog, the guinea pig, six children, my parents, and an antique music box all survived. The house survived too, but it took a year to restore.

Thirty years later I wrote about the night of the fire, and the restoration afterwards, in the book *Red House*. The fire and restoration were only two chapters in a much longer story about the house itself. After all, the house was more than 360 years old. Still, reviewers and critics often point to the fire chapters as "clearly fictionalized."

I have always wondered why. One reviewer finally did me a favor and wrote the reason out: "She was five, too young to remember all that detail."

When most people think about writing a memoir, they imagine typing away under the warm glow of a desk lamp, exploring the visions and memories of their childhood, perhaps listening to old music or looking at photos and journals for inspiration. As people grow older (and I know you've heard them), they often say, "I just need to get these memories down on paper."

Memoirs used to be thought of as a universally reflective form, anecdotal, and written later in life. They were akin to autobiography, covering one's whole life (or most of it), but not called an "autobiography" because autobiographies were for famous people.

But in the past fifteen years, that's changed. Many young people have written memoirs about very brief periods of time (a year in a reform school, for example), or about very narrow topics: addiction, loss of a parent, depression, illness, finding love, losing love, war, climbing a mountain, living in Vietnam, sailing around the world, or growing up in a really old house.

Memoir, it seems to me, is more equivalent to the novel than it is to autobiography these days. Memoir is to nonfiction what the novel is to fiction. Think about it. The story is limited; not an entire life, just part of one. It's book-length, it's a narrative (time moves forward), there are people (characters) in it who do things (plot/action). What is the difference?

The difference is that memoir is true. Based on sales in the publishing world, and the growth of nonfiction MFA programs around the country, and not discounting Oprah's book club, I can say with confidence that *people like to read books that read like novels but are true.*

So, how do you do that, especially if you are too young to remember all that detail? The reviewer was right. I was too young to remember detail. I remembered what a five-year-old might remember: not being able to see or breathe, my hands on the wall, heat, yelling, reaching with my hands, the cold snow on my bare feet.

My parents told me that, standing outside the house, I had asked where my baby sister was, which prompted my parents to run back inside and grab her. "You saved your sister," they said. But I don't remember that.

I do remember watching my father throw my baby sister into my mother's arms and then, what seemed like an eternity later, emerge carrying a giant music box he had recently brought back from Germany. This completely random detail has always stuck in my mind, probably because it was so unexpected. I remember that later a fireman came to the neighbor's carrying my sister's white guinea pig beneath his jacket. I remember that his face and hands were completely black with soot, as well as his jacket and hat, which were also wet, as if it was pouring rain outside.

But it was not raining. As a child I couldn't understand any of this: the appearance of the guinea pig, the blackness, the water. Of course later it all made sense—smoke, hoses, the animal found in the rubble.

That's it for my five-year-old memories. So where did I get the details?

1. I interviewed my family with a tape recorder and a note pad. I interviewed them separately. I did not ask for the old family story. The old family story cannot be trusted. I guided them: "If it was a movie, what's the first shot?" I broke it down: "and the second and the third." I asked them what they were doing right before, right after, a day after, a week after. I tried to walk them through their memory (which was much better than mine) step by step by asking detailed questions about their sensory perceptions—smells, touch, sight, sounds, what was said, clothing, food, their thoughts. I wanted to see what they saw.

2. Yes, there were contradictions. I put them into the story.

3. I interviewed firemen. It turned out that the guy who answered the fire-station phone had been at our fire thirty years ago, and he remembered. That was just luck. But if I hadn't called, I'd have never heard his side.

4. I researched how a house burns, how a fire starts.

5. I went to the library and read the newspaper report. I read old letters people wrote my parents about the fire.

6. I visited another old house that had recently burned, and looked around, took notes.

Is it okay to use all these details? Yes, absolutely. It's reconstruction.

I wrote the chapter using a third-person omniscient point of view because I could; I actually did know what people were thinking. I had the tapes. I captured the moment from different perspectives, which also added suspense. And then it became interesting. So interesting, in fact, that some people thought it read like fiction, and thus it couldn't be true.

It was a great compliment. ❧

DAVID GESSNER

FIELD NOTES ON
WHERE YOU ARE

WRITE WHAT YOU KNOW is the old writing adage. But here's a new one: *write where you are.*

I'm not saying that your essays or stories need be restricted to the place where you are currently sitting or standing or walking, just that where you are isn't such a bad place to start. *Place,* or *setting,* used to have a pretty lowly position in the old how-to writing books, way down the hierarchical ladder below *characters* and *plot* and all the rest. But it turns out that for some writers place is a key that unexpectedly unlocks sentences and that, for some of us, place is where the words are.

How does this translate practically? What I'm suggesting is simple itself. Get outside and take notes on the specifics of the place where you are today. Take field notes on people in coffee shops, on the way the wind feels, on the way your particular place smells and sounds, on the bird life or the turtle life or the teenage life, on the way different types of people jabber differently into their different types of cell phones. And don't forget to write down what they are saying. Jot down and gather up. Become a packrat of phrases and sentences.

In this you'll have a fairly fancy predecessor, Henry David Thoreau, the granddaddy of place writing. Thoreau famously wandered the countryside of Concord, Massachusetts, but he did not wander empty-handed. Armed with a good pencil, he scribbled down notes on scraps of paper. What did he scribble? What he saw: the first yellow-streaked bloom of a willow, or a nuthatch working its way down a tree searching for insects under the bark. Then, back at home, he would take those crumbled notes out of his pocket and transcribe them into his journal, which is to say he wrote a second draft. After that he had the journal to draw from like a great storehouse when it was time to write an essay or a chapter or a speech for the local antiquarian society, which was, of course, another draft. This practice, not just of observing but of scribbling down to solidify what he'd seen, became habitual. Just as it should become habitual in anyone who aspires to this sort of writing.

You don't have to write in full sentences when observing—short caveman phrases will do. And don't worry if your own field notes don't seem that interesting. I've noticed that my own notes often seem plain and dull. "Windy today. White birds diving like spears." These are just quick sketches usually, but when I come back to them, sometimes years later, I have the luxury of taking just the good parts—maybe I can do something with that spear image—and ignoring the dross. Once again Thoreau makes a good role model: he drew on his massive journals to write *Walden,* creating a sense of condensation and intensity that was never in the journals or in his life. This is one "fictional" aspect of this sort of nonfiction, and here's another: when describing a day in October, draw on the dozens of October days filling your journals. Though it may get you in trouble with Oprah, I would defend this accumulation of the details of days: it's Thoreau's method and a good one.

Don't worry if your original notes don't seemed charged with importance. Take purposeless notes—just get things *down*—trusting they'll find their purpose later. Few of us write essays based on memory alone, or in one fell swoop. We cobble essays or chapters together over time, and a journal or notebook or sketchbook is a place to begin. Whatever you call this thing, this word storehouse, I would suggest it be something you can write longhand in, something you can bring out in the open air. Take it to the beach and describe a pelican diving or take it to a coffee shop and eavesdrop. Let notes about your internal-weather mix with notes about the actual weather. Then, when you transfer what you have scribbled onto your computer, you will create a new draft, just like Mr. Thoreau.

Let me use my own situation, and the essay that accompanies this piece in the anthology, to illustrate my point. When I moved from Cape Cod to North Carolina in 2003, I kept doing what I had always done: observing people and observing birds and taking field notes on both. But these were new birds and new people. We didn't have pelicans where I'd come from so I found myself immediately taking notes about the way that these huge and ungainly birds corkscrewed down into the water when they dove for fish; and we didn't have surfers either, so I also took notes on the way the surfers at the local coffee shop said "dude" a lot and talked about the ocean in a hundred ways, like Eskimos with their thousand words for snow. And since my daughter was only three months old, and I had never had a child before, the focus of the field notes, and the focus of my journal, was also increasingly on her. When I think back on these notes I recall two contradictory things about them. First, they were random and scattered and had no "purpose," that is they were not "for" an essay. But second (and here's the contradiction) my brain was already imagining that there might be a story or an essay in my move south, and so I began jotting down titles for what I was experiencing, including "The Year of Wings and Water" and "Learning to Surf." Of course, as often happens, the present moment doesn't make sense until that period passes. But when the time did pass, and the past period began to cohere into sense a year or two later, I was happy to have my field notes to draw from to use and to build the essay.

So that's my craft lesson: scribble down field notes. It's simple enough. Get outside (or inside if you prefer). Make jotting habitual, part of what you do. Gather details, not just about birds and trees, but dumpsters and dialogue. Don't worry if the notes seem senseless at the time. Store them where they'll come in handy later on. Write where you are and trust that, in time, it will lead you somewhere else. ❧

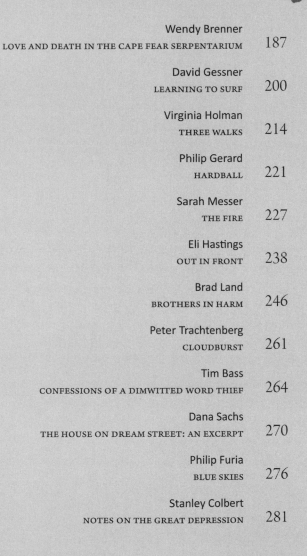

CREATIVE NONFICTION

WENDY BRENNER

LOVE AND DEATH
IN THE CAPE FEAR
SERPENTARIUM

He is a fool who injures himself by amassing things. And no one knows why people cannot help but do it.
　—Translation of anonymous *Le danse macabre verse*, Paris, 1485

Fortunately, I number among my friends a young man named Dean Ripa, who could have stepped from the pages of a Joseph Conrad novel.
　—William S. Burroughs, *The Western Lands*

ONE DAY IN 1971 in Wilmington, North Carolina, fourteen-year-old Dean Ripa was at home performing surgery on a cottonmouth snake, and it bit him. This was unfortunate for a couple of reasons. He knew enough about snakes to know he would probably not die, but he did need a ride to the hospital, which meant his parents were going to find out about the fifty snakes he was keeping in their spare room: rattlesnakes, water moccasins he'd caught in local swamps, even several cobras he had purchased via mail-order—he had a king cobra years before he had his driver's license.

The bite landed him in Intensive Care for two weeks—with fever, a grossly swollen arm, blistering skin—during which time his father donated Dean's entire snake collection to a local roadside zoo, a seemingly apocalyptic setback that might have ended any normal person's love affair with snakes. But Dean turned out to be another kind of person, the kind who, after a full recovery, quickly began amassing more snakes, breeding his own snakes and making extra money to buy snakes by collecting snakes for the same zoo who had adopted his earlier snakes. A year after the cottonmouth episode, one of his new cobras got loose and the whole Ripa family had to move out of the house for five days until it could be found and shot.

Thirty-one years later, in what might be the ultimate fantasy of young snake-lovers everywhere, Dean Ripa opened the Cape Fear Serpentarium, and, most thrilling of all to a twelve-year-old acquaintance of mine, he lives there, too.

The Serpentarium is no roadside attraction, but an elegant, bi-level, 6,300-square-foot gallery overlooking the Cape Fear River in gentrified downtown Wilmington, exhibiting the largest collection of live exotic venomous snakes in the U.S. About a hundred are on public display at any given time, dozens of different species, almost all of which were captured by Dean himself in jungles and marshes around the world. He specializes in the rarest and deadliest: Gaboon vipers, black mambas, spitting cobras, puff adders, and bushmasters, of which he has the biggest known collection anywhere. In fact, Dean was the first person ever to breed the rare blackheaded bushmaster in captivity (he continues to supply them internationally to zoos and researchers), and once even reproduced a bushmaster hybrid, in effect recreating an extinct ancestor of the existing species. He has also survived four bushmaster bites—*envenomings* is the herpetologist's Orwellian term—despite the fact that almost all bushmaster victims die, even with antivenom treatment.

The Serpentarium was built by Dean's father, a local contractor, who has presumably forgiven Dean for his adolescence (or perhaps is just happy to have survived it). The Serpentarium's neighbors include antique stores and historic bed & breakfasts and Thai restaurants and art galleries. Snakes do not seem especially popular around here; the local attitude is perhaps best summed up by a resident of a snake-plagued Wilmington apartment complex, quoted in a recent story in the Wilmington *Star-News*: "I don't like those fellows with no shoulders." Yet Dean has gotten no complaints from his neighbors (he says they're grateful for the business he brings to the area), with the sole exception of a group of cat lovers who once confronted him after hearing a rumor that Dean stalks downtown alleys at dawn, collecting cats in a basket to feed to his snakes. "Ludicrous," he tells me. "I never get up before 10 AM."

The Serpentarium snakes live in lush enclosures built to Dean's specifications by set designers from Screen Gems (Frank Capra Jr.'s Wilmington film studios), featuring stalactites and stalagmites and twisted roots and vines, real animal skulls and bones, moss-draped grottos and cypress knees and running waterfalls and ponds. Each snake is rated by skulls-and-bones to indicate its deadliness level (two skulls means life-threatening to children and the elderly, possible mild disfigurement; five skulls means survival unlikely), and plaques on the exhibits give detailed descriptions, especially popular with children, of exactly how you will die if bitten by each particular snake.

I learn that the Egyptian cobra, whose festive yellow and black stripes evoke Charlie Brown's shirt, is believed to be the asp that killed Cleopatra; in ancient Egypt, the sign reads, these snakes were awarded to royal prisoners as a means of suicide. The Asiatic spitting cobras, meanwhile, which never seem to run out of venom, are like "sort of endless poisonous squirt gun." The bite of the Central American fer-de-lance feels like having your hand slammed in a car door and then seared with a blow torch. As the placard helpfully elaborates, "THE BITTEN EXTREMITY SWELLS TO MASSIVE PROPORTIONS, THE SKIN BURSTS OPEN, AND YOUR EYES WEEP BLOOD." The fifteen-foot king cobra, the longest venomous snake in the world, can kill an elephant with a single bite, and is known to rear up six feet in the air, hood flared, and look a man in the eye while growling like a dog. For some reason, perhaps a primal one, the male king cobra's eerie flat dirt color is scarier to me than some of the flashier patterns on display here. Likewise the look of the steely black mambas, who are long, skinny, and, according to their plaque, "excitable"—and indeed each time I've visited they were wide awake and slicing around their enclosure like gang members looking for action. Most disturbing of all, perhaps, are the fat puff adders, whose odd, fat cigar-shaped bodies make them grotesquely evocative, like nightmare shape-shifter snakes. *We are snakes,* they seem to say, *but we are on the verge of becoming something else.*

The Serpentarium also exhibits a few nonvenomous reptiles,

including a 250-pound python named Sheena, some ethereally beautiful emerald tree boas, and a nine-foot man-eating crocodile, which, like every crocodile, alligator, or lizard I've ever seen, looks fake, motionless, prehistoric, and improbable. One day while I was visiting Dean, the girl at the front desk reported that a worried visitor claimed the beaded lizard looked dead. "It always looks dead," Dean said irritably. "That's how it looks." We went to check on the lizard, which was fine. It resembled a large, expensive purse. The placard noted "THESE LIZARDS MAKE EXCELLENT—IF UNRESPONSIVE—PETS."

For the truly obsessive, the Serpentarium gift shop offers a huge assortment of fetishes: toy snakes, snake-decorated T-shirts and snake stickers and snake books, Viper Blast spray candy (and, inexplicably, Skittles), watercolor paintings by Dean's mother, carved Peruvian rainsticks, and the occasional display of traditional African art and sculpture, available for purchase from a local importer. A sign on the front desk warns against tapping on the snakes' enclosures: IF YOU KNEW THAT THE ONLY THING STANDING BETWEEN YOU AND DEATH WAS A PANE OF GLASS, WOULD YOU RISK BREAKING IT? This is not P.T. Barnum-style hyperbole. One day I was taking flash photos of an apparently pissed-off cobra (she was waving menacingly about, hood flared), my face as close as my camera lens would allow, when she finally had enough and struck at me, hitting the glass. I had the delayed jolt you get right after a fender-bender—*did that just really happen?*

Though this is the kind of safe thrill one might expect at a zoo, weekend feedings at the Serpentarium go one step further. Suddenly the barriers between audience and predator disappear: a few comically symbolic plastic yellow chains are hooked up to keep people out of the way, the glass enclosures propped wide open. Dean (or his curator, Scott) uses barbecue tongs to deliver dead rats, jiggling them to provoke a strike, sometimes even climbing in with the snakes to prevent fights. (One might imagine the feeders wear something like astronaut suits, but the day I saw Dean break up a tussle between two bushmasters, he was wearing only a polo shirt and cargo shorts.) The yellow chains are, it turns out, unnecessary—men the size of linebackers dart to the back of the crowd, pretending they're just joking: *Ha! I think I'll stand back here*. Some people can't even bear the sight of Dean handling the dead rodents. During one feeding a woman murmured, "He's touching that rat like it ain't nothing."

People who devote their careers to animals—veterinarians, zoologists—are often quite different in temperament from garden-variety animal lovers, taking a flat-footed, unsentimental approach to their subjects, skeptical of any anthropomorphism. My mother worked as a docent at Chicago's Lincoln Park Zoo for twenty-five years, and has an enormous collection of butterflies she traveled all over the world to catch; my father is a life-long birdwatcher, getting up before dawn every weekend to search for rare shorebirds at landfills and sewerage plants. And yet neither of my parents is particularly romantic about the animals they love. They love them for perplexingly literal reasons— because they're such fascinating examples of evolution, or because they have "unusual plumage." My parents do not seem especially interested in talking or thinking about what animals are like, what they evoke or suggest, what they *mean*—all the things that are most interesting to me, the fiction writer in the family.

My favorite novelist, Joy Williams, once said in an interview that the Bible had influenced her as a child "because all those wonderful stories—about snakes and serpents and mysterious seeds and trees— didn't mean what they seemed. They meant some other thing." In Williams's short story "Lu-Lu," the characters do nothing but sit around discussing the meaning of a giant snake (Lu-Lu)—whether she has a soul, how she seems to materialize and dematerialize at will, how she can occupy herself doing nothing. The snake continues to accrue symbolic weight until the story finally ends, hauntingly, with a young woman trying to coax the stoic Lu-Lu into her car: "How do you beckon to something like this, she wondered; something that can change everything, your life."

When I was twelve, my mother gave my father a pet boa constrictor for their anniversary, and never once in all the subsequent years we owned Jaws (we got and named her in 1978) did it occur to me that she could change anything, let alone our lives. We did not discuss her symbolism. We talked about whether she was going to shed her skin soon, or whether she was ready to move up from mice to rats.

So even before I meet Dean Ripa, I think I know what kind of person he will be: another scientist. Though he has no advanced degree, his snake collection is internationally recognized, his research on bushmasters published in herpetological journals.

Then he gives me a copy of his essay, "Confessions of a Gaboon Viper Lover," which appeared in Gary Indiana's 1994 anthology *Living with the Animals*. It is a paean to Ripa's own late Gaboon viper, Madame Zsa Zsa. "Morphologically, she seems halfway to some unspeakable transformation that may or may not include a human head," he writes. "Her pattern might have been lifted from a Persian carpet," he says, and also suggests skeletons. "One can *see* into the pattern," a Tanzanian witch priest told Dean, but then declined to say what it was he saw. The snake's design brings to mind "Kandinsky zigzags," the "meretricious skulls" of Georgia O'Keefe; its face suggests Bosch, or Dürer's engraving of *The Fall of Man*. Seeing the Gaboon viper, Dean writes, "seems largely participatory, on a parallel with perception itself. Like Dali's paranoiac-critical method of seeing the hidden face, there arises the 'magic' effect of audience creation." Watching a Gaboon viper "literally materialize before you from the debris of the forest floor," he concludes, "is perhaps the closest one can ever come among live creatures to the fright of encountering an actual ghost."

I notice that I am feeling slightly in love.

"It's definitely not like TV," Dean says, somewhat defiantly, about the Serpentarium experience. In fact Dean has been invited by various animal-related TV programs to bring his snakes out into the jungle, set them loose, and then pretend to discover them on camera, and he declines all such invitations on principle. In the wild, he says, snakes are nearly impossible to find—you will go years without finding the one you want, unless, like Dean, you know where to look.

He is telling me this in his apartment, whose entrance is an unmarked door on the Serpentarium's second level; he lives alone with his tiny, eleven-year-old Maltese dog, Wednesday (whom he also calls, variously, "Winky" and "Pinky"), and a couple aquariums full of deadly bushmasters in his bedroom. He has been married and divorced three times, but claims his snakes played no part in his romantic misfortunes. "I'm just not somebody who can be halved," he says, enigmatically. I suggest that it must be hard to find women who will sleep in a room with snakes—or maybe some women think it's a turn-on? "You get both kinds," Dean says. Either way, it occurs to me, if one were going to sleep with Dean Ripa, one would have to have a great deal of faith in Dean Ripa.

Not long after he quit high school ("for dramatic effect," he says), Dean moved to Italy to study painting under portraitist Pietro Annigoni, whose work he had discovered in an art magazine. For a number of years, then, collecting and selling snakes became secondary, a way to support his art career. He enjoyed relative success, spending time with Salvador Dali and selling two paintings to writer William S. Burroughs (these now hang on the walls of Dean's apartment, on loan from the Burroughs estate). His style is blackly surreal—muddy-hued portraits and still lifes with hidden messages, faces, and severed limbs floating to their dark, dreamy surfaces. "Ripa's painting depicts biologic fragmentation," Burroughs wrote. "The artist is giving birth to his selves on canvas." I think of *Rosemary's Baby*, the paintings Mia Farrow sees on the corridor walls as she's being carried into her Satanic neighbors' apartment, and I ask Dean why he so admired Annigoni, a more traditional, Renaissance-inspired realist. "I wanted to learn the secrets of the Old Masters," he says. "I've always been on a quest for hidden things, occult things. It's like the snakes. Certain things, to me, always seemed to promise more than they outwardly were."

In 1975, when Dean was eighteen, he sent William S. Burroughs the manuscript of a children's book he was writing called *Johnny Zimb*. He didn't know Burroughs but was a fan of his work, its renegade exoticism seeming to speak directly to the "voices in my head," he says. *Johnny Zimb*'s plot was "a scarecrow-boy type of thing," he tells me. "You know, a surrealistic thing." Burroughs replied to Dean, "I think you have written a very good children's book, though perhaps a little too complex and literate for juvenile reading." Over the years that followed, their correspondence and friendship escalated, Burroughs sending letters to Dean in Ecuador, Ghana, Surinam, and Costa Rica, giving advice on writing and asking Dean's advice on art, inviting him to visit at his home in Lawrence, Kansas. They exchanged knives, guns, snakes, and, at one point, a human skull Dean claimed to have robbed from a grave as a teenager. ("I did indeed receive Helen with open arms," Burroughs wrote in thanks. "I know how difficult it was for you to part with her.") One time Dean brought Burroughs a suitcase full of snakes; another time he set a cobra loose in Burroughs's living room. While I'm reading through their letters, Dean goes into his room and brings out a .357 Magnum that Burroughs gave him, mentioning offhandedly as he sets it on the table before me that it's loaded. (*Jesus,* I think, *how many different things that can kill you can one person keep in his bedroom?*)

Burroughs's letters to Dean are full of fond and cryptic personal counsel: "Oh and as for Madame Whosit and her Oath of Secrecy I would caution you to stay well away from her dubious emanations. She sounds like bad news." In the mid '80s, Burroughs asked Dean to write a letter about centipede venom that he could include in his novel, *The Western Lands*; it appears in the text unedited, and Dean is thanked in the book's acknowledgements. "Have you thought of writing your memoirs as a snake catcher?" Burroughs wrote Dean in 1986. And again in 1988, Burroughs suggested, "Why not write a book about your experiences as a snake catcher? Your letters to me would be a good start." Then, as now, however, Dean was more interested in writing fiction and collecting snakes.

When Burroughs died of heart failure in 1997, Dean was at his bedside; he happened to be visiting that month ("I don't think it was a coincidence," he says). He had never seen someone die before, and stayed at Burroughs's house for days afterward—even sleeping in his bed—while fans came and went, leaving flowers on the door.

Nowadays, in between endless interruptions from the Serpentarium downstairs, Dean is working on a couple of novels, at least parts of which are based on his own experiences. He shows me the thick manuscript of one, *Succumbu (Mama Sleep)*, but then will only let me read its first line: "The beauty of Hell is that it is self-regenerating."

It is impossible to meet Dean Ripa and not think of John Laroche, the ragged, eccentric outlaw orchid breeder Susan Orlean wrote about in

The Orchid Thief, portrayed by Chris Cooper so brilliantly in *Adaptation*. But the similarities are only in kind, not physical. For one thing, Dean still has all his teeth, and he is darkly, boyishly handsome, looking much younger than his age. The only off-note is his slightly malevolent grin. And while the orchid thief's various obsessions "arrived unannounced and ended explosively, like car bombs" (he had already abandoned orchids by the time Orlean finished writing about him), Dean's passions—painting, writing, and most especially snakes—seem eternal. "I'm doing the exact same things now that I was doing when I was ten years old," he says.

Dean dreams about snakes all the time. Sometimes they are good dreams: that he discovers he owns snakes he didn't know about, that aliens abduct him and take him to a secret part of North Carolina that was incompletely glaciated (there is always a scientific explanation, even in Dean's dreams), revealing a colony of rare snakes. He also has nightmares that his snakes are dying, that they're eating each other, that he forgot to feed them, that he must protect them from some unseen danger. He almost never dreams that his snakes bite or kill him; it is always the snakes who are in jeopardy, that he must save.

"The greater the value of a collection, the greater the risk of loss that it represents," Philipp Blom writes in *To Have and to Hold: An Intimate History of Collectors and Collecting*. To collect is to continually negotiate with the afterlife, with the fact that you can't take it with you. Even worse, if you collect living things you must also confront their mortality. In *The Orchid Thief*, Susan Orlean calls collecting "a sort of love sickness." Because orchids die, "to desire orchids," Orlean says, "is to have a desire that will never be, can never be, fully requited." So what kind of person devotes his life to collecting something both mortal and deadly? A collection that is both hard to keep alive and that might at any moment kill you?

Dean insists his romance has always been with danger, not death. He has eleven times endured the bites of potentially lethal snakes, including the cottonmouth when he was fourteen. "[S]ome Greek said that men give themselves more trouble than is ordained by the Gods," Burroughs wrote to Dean in 1989. "A parish priest would tell you that your trouble is scruples. Like you make things more complicated than they need to be and more categorical . . . So take things philosophic and remember you have reached a point where antivenom is almost more dangerous than snake bite." Dean claims Burroughs meant this last comment literally, since antivenom really can be as deadly as the snakebite itself. Still, it strikes me as beautiful, Zen-like advice.

I ask whether he suffers lingering effects from the envenomings. "I don't know about lingering effects, but I don't feel so great," he says and laughs weakly, like he's not exactly joking. He claims he has a headache and I offer him something (I've got every kind of painkiller in my purse, I tell him, thanks to a recent dental procedure). "Well, then you'll lead a long life," he says wearily. He does admit he's more easily fatigued these days, but that might be a result of the malaria, schistosomiasis, dysentery, and miscellaneous other tropical ailments he contracted during his travels. His hands are weaker from the bites, he says, and he has a greater tolerance for pain. Also, he fears death less than he used to, but this is not necessarily a good thing. "Actually what scares me isn't death," he clarifies, "but that I'll forget to fear death." He doesn't mean this figuratively or philosophically. He means: during feeding times.

Religious snake handlers sometimes try to buy snakes from Dean, but he won't sell to them, claiming his snakes are just too deadly ("They don't have enough faith for my snakes, believe me," he says). Yet he has no objection to what the handlers do and even declares, "If I had a religion, that would probably be it. At least they're willing to test, to prove what they believe." He adds, "Actually I might be a magic animist, if I'm anything. I'm interested in voodoo, but I would never call myself a voodooist. I don't like organized things, groups, mobs. The most frightening thing in the world is a group of people just *standing* there."

When too many visitors pack the Serpentarium, Dean hides out here in his apartment. But, I ask, I thought your purpose with the Serpentarium was to educate people. "I'm not here to educate people," he says. "I couldn't give a damn what happens to them." But then he adds, grudgingly, "Well, there are some people worth something, and ideally they'd get something out of it." By now I've grown accustomed (and rather devoted) to Dean's rhetorical style—outrageous overstatement, subsequent qualification—but I think I recognize something else, something authentic here: a certain strain of introverted misanthropy that often leads people to commit their lives to animals, something I think I know about from my family. Introverts and loners love animals. It runs the spectrum, I think, from my father's boyhood shyness to full-fledged autism—Temple Grandin and those like her who understand animals better than people. Whether it's a quirk of personality or a genuine disorder, it's a trait I find familiar and strangely comforting.

It's Friday night in Wilmington and I'm at Alleigh's, a brightly horrify-ing "entertainment complex" featuring a warehouse-sized, earsplitting arcade, but I'm in a low-lit back room, with a delighted, dressed-up crowd of about a hundred, watching the allegedly hermitic Dean Ripa perform beautiful renditions of Sinatra romantic standards, backed by a seventeen-piece orchestra which has come from miles away for this gig (out-of-state license plates in the parking lot say SAXAFON and STRAUSS). Dean orga-nized the entire evening himself—sorting musical arrangements, assem-bling band members, advertising with flyers in the Serpentarium lobby: COME HEAR DEAN RIPA, 'THE VOICE,' singing Sinatra, Bobby Darin & other favorites from years gone by! MONSTER ENTERTAINMENT!!

I feel disoriented, like I've crashed someone's wedding in, say 1963. Dean does "Mack the Knife," "Fly Me to the Moon," "Best Is Yet to Come." He dances with the microphone; he gets down on one knee; he keeps up a mild, unintrusive patter with the audience in between songs. He does "I've Got You Under My Skin," "Witchcraft," "Come Fly With Me." During "New York, New York," three tipsy women spontaneously join him on the dance floor, kick off their shoes, and do a can-can, cheered on by the crowd. There is no sign or mention anywhere of snakes.

My friends and I came expecting Vegas-style camp (and, in fact, a poster at the entrance advertises an upcoming Elvis impersonator's show) but Dean's performance is sincere, his delivery charged and charming, his voice accomplished and smooth. He's not making fun of Sinatra, nor trying to be Sinatra. He's just singing. He's so good I doubt my own ears and double-check with my friends—maybe it's the Percocet?—but no, they're equally excited. None of us can shake the odd, giddy feeling that we've stepped into an alternate dimension, a par-allel Wilmington. Where did all these people come from? Who is Dean Ripa, anyway?

I'm a little breathless when I compliment him after the show, but I'm worried I'm insulting him by sounding so surprised. "I thought it was going to be like Lawrence Welk," I say.

"What you need to know about me," he says, "is that Lawrence Welk is my arch-enemy."

He does not elaborate.

"Well, so, what is all this?" I ask. "A hobby?"

"I don't have hobbies," Dean says. "Everything I do is work."

In fact, a few months after this show, he will be hired on as the lead vocalist with the Tommy Dorsey Orchestra and go on the road throughout the South, getting glowing reviews from local papers—"a handsome hunk with a voice to match," "abducted the audience from their mundane existences," "dares us to experience ecstasy again!" For the moment, he allows that his snakes don't provide quite the same adrenaline they used to, that these days he finds a live audience scarier and hence more thrilling than the possibility of death by snakebite. Like his hero Sinatra, Dean has never learned to read music, because, he says, "it was too boring." I recall what he told me about his brief stint in the Peace Corps, teaching industrial arts in Liberian villages on the eve of a bloody coup in which the country's president was overthrown: "It was the boringest thing you could imagine." He left long before his assignment was over. "I could never complete a job or do anything anyone told me to, never take orders from anyone," he says, then adds sheepishly, and unconvincingly, "Except people I love."

A few days later I'm sitting on Dean's living room floor, a sudden downpour roaring onto the tin roofs outside, before me on the coffee table a clutter of art books and herpetology journals, as well as a luminescent dead dragonfly Dean found on his balcony and dropped absently into my palm while pacing around the room answering my questions. It occurs to me to ask if he is a Scorpio, or perhaps born in the Chinese Year of the Snake. No, he says—but then it turns out we have *the same birthday.*

Things are getting creepy.

Dean goes on a fierce hunt for his birth certificate, because what if we were also born at the *same time*! He drags out files and manila envelopes but finally gives up. (He finds it a few days later: we were born a couple hours, not to mention nine years, apart. So what, he says, they could have made a mistake—were they holding a stopwatch or what?) When I manage to breathe again, I quiz Dean about Capricorn traits: stubborn (check), obsessive (check), respect for the traditional (check). "I have a lot of respect for tradition," he says, "even though I'm constantly trying to smash it."

Not long after this, I'm zipping down Eastwood Road, the busy four-lane highway that leads to Wrightsville Beach, when, improbably, I see a little box turtle attempting to cross right in my path: I will be the one to kill him. Without even deliberating I brake and put on my blinkers, jump out, grab the turtle, and run down the embankment to deposit him safely by a pond at the edge of somebody's yard—and there's an alligator sitting there. (I set the turtle down away from the alligator.) I get an incredible rush, the wild overpowering urge to leave my car idling with its door open in the middle of the road and just keep walking, keep going, because surely right around the bend lies something even bigger, waiting just for me. It's like I'm being handed some exhilarating responsibility I can't begin to name. "Once you make that bargain," I recall Dean telling me one day, apropos of nothing as we drove along in his truck, "the assignments start coming faster and faster." He might have been talking about snakes, art, life—he never said. But right now I'm sure I know what he meant. ❦

AFTER WORDS

I intended to write a short, impersonal magazine article—one or two pages —about this little snake museum in downtown Wilmington, but the essay snowballed as I learned more and more about Dean Ripa and the Serpentarium. It felt like one of those perfect, fated collisions between writer and subject, given my own background growing up surrounded by animals. I had no method or system for interviewing Dean; I just wrote down every single thing he said as fast as I could, on tons and tons of scratch paper. I have no formal training in journalism, and never took any classes in nonfiction writing. But I love to read nonfiction—biographies, memoirs, true crime—and had Susan Orlean's book The Orchid Thief *(which was made into the movie* Adaptation*) in mind while writing, and loved the idea that a writer could just follow this outrageous, obsessed, swashbuckling person into the wild and start to see the world as he sees it.*

DAVID GESSNER

LEARNING TO SURF

OUT JUST BEYOND THE BREAKING WAVES they sit there bobbing, two groups of animals, avian and human, pelicans and surfers. As they rise and fall on humps of water, the pelicans look entirely unperturbed, their foot-long bills pulled like blades into scabbards, fitting like puzzle pieces into the curves of their throats. The surfers, mostly kids, look equally casual. A girl lies supine on her board, looking up at the sky, one leg crossed over the other in an almost exaggerated posture of relaxation. For the most part the birds and surfers ignore each other, rising up and dropping down together as the whole ocean heaves and then sighs.

Pelicans are particularly buoyant birds and they bob high on the water as the surfers paddle and shift in anticipation. There is no mistaking that this is the relatively tense calm of before, rest before exertion. Soon the waves pick up and the kids paddle furiously, gaining enough speed to pop up and ride the crests of breaking surf. They glide in toward the beach where I stand, the better ones carving the water and ducking under and cutting back up through the waves.

I just recently moved to this southern island town, but I have been here long enough to know that those who pursue this sport are guided by a kind of laid-back monomania. Each morning I bring my four-month-old daughter down to the local coffee shop, and each morning the talk is of one thing. The ocean, I've learned, is always referred to as *it*.

"What did it look like this morning?" one surfer asked another a few mornings back.

"Sloppy."

Remembering my own early-morning glance at the water I could understand what he meant, the way a series of waves came from the northwest, while another group muscled up from the south, and how the two collided and kicked up. Aesthetically it was beautiful, but practically, at least from a surfer's point of view, it made for a landscape of chop—not much to get excited about.

Another morning I heard this:

"How does it look today, dude?"

"Small."

"Nothing?"

"You can go out there if you want to build your morale."

It's easy enough to laugh at these kids, but I like the physical nature of their obsession, the way their lives center on being strong animals. In *When Elephants Weep*, Jeffrey Masson speculates that animals feel *funktionslust*, a German word meaning "pleasure taken in what one can do best." The strongest of the surfers, the ones who have grown up on the waves, must certainly feel this animal pleasure as they glide over and weave through the water.

I watch the surfers for a while longer, but when the pelicans lift off, I turn my focus toward their even more impressive athletic feats. Pelicans are huge and heavy birds, and the initial liftoff, as they turn into the wind and flap hard, is awkward. But once in the air they are all grace. They pull in their feet like landing gear and glide low between the troughs of the waves, then lift up to look for fish, flapping several times before coasting. If you watch them enough, a rhythm reveals itself: effort, *glide*, effort, *glide*. They are looking for small fish—menhaden or mullet most likely—and when they find what they are searching for they gauge the depth of the fish, and therefore the necessary height of the dive, a gauging guided by both instinct and experience. Then they pause, lift, measure again, and finally, plunge. The birds bank and twist and plummet, following their divining-rod bills toward the water. A few of them even turn in the air in a way that gives the impression they are showing off. If they were awkward in takeoff, now they are glorious.

There is something symphonic about the way the group hits the water, one bird after another: *thwuck, thwuck, thwuck.* At the last second before contact they become feathery arrows, thrusting their legs and wings backward and flattening their gular pouches. They are not tidy like terns and show no concern for the Olympian aesthetics of a small splash, hitting the surface with what looks like something close to reck-lessness. As soon as they strike the water, instinct triggers the opening of the huge pouch, and it umbrellas out, usually capturing fish, plural. While still underwater they turn again, often 180 degrees, so that when they emerge they'll be facing into the wind for takeoff. And when they pop back up barely a second later, they almost instantly assume a sitting posture on the water, once again bobbing peacefully. It's a little like watching a man serve a tennis ball who then, after the follow-through, hops immediately into a La-Z-Boy.

The pelicans calm me, which is good. I have tried to maintain a relaxed attitude since moving to this island, but at times it's hard. I had vowed that I would stay forever on Cape Cod, my old home, but it was my writing about how much I loved the Cape that led to the offer of a teach-ing job in this overcrowded North Carolina resort town of outboard motors, condos, and southern accents. My wife, Nina, had just given birth to our daughter, Hadley, and the lure of health insurance and a steady paycheck was irresistible.

The truth is, the move has unsettled me: in coming to this new place I find myself, and my confidence, getting shaky. If I've behaved well publicly, in the privacy of our new apartment I've at times started to fall apart. As each day unfolds, I grow ever less sure of myself.

One of the things that disorients me is the heat. It's the kind of heat that makes you want to lie down and give up, to start to cry and throw out your arms in surrender. I've known brutal cold in my life, but cold has the advantage of invigoration, at least initially. Now I understand the logic behind siestas; every instinct tells you to crawl to a cool dank place and lie there and be still.

Lifting my daughter into our un-air-conditioned Honda Civic feels like sliding her into a kiln, so we are desperately trying to buy a new car. But today the Toyota guy calls with bad news. Our credit report has come back and our loan has been rejected.

"You have weak stability," he tells me, reading from the report.

I nod and consider the poetry of his words.

But there are other moments, moments when I sense that this may not be such a bad place to live. With summer ending, the parking lots have begun to empty. There are fewer beach walkers and more pelicans. Each morning I take long walks with Hadley, and have begun to take field notes on my daughter. I'm struck daily by her creatureliness, and the fact that this squirming little apelike animal, barely two feet high, has somehow been allowed to live in the same house with us. Nothing cuts through my doubts about having moved here quite like this new ritual of walking with my daughter in a papooselike contraption on my chest. On good days we make it all the way to the south end of the island where we stare out at the channel.

Many things have caught me off guard about being a father, but the most startling thing has been the sheer animal pleasure. "Joy is the symptom by which right conduct is measured," wrote Joseph Wood Krutch of Thoreau. If that's true then my conduct these days must be excellent.

This morning we watch two immature, first-year pelicans fly right over the waves, belly to belly with their shadows. It's exhilarating the way they lift up together and sink down again, rollercoastering, their wings nicking the crests of the waves. Eight more adult birds skim right through the valley between the waves, gliding by the surfers, sweeping upward before plopping onto the water.

Feeling that it's only polite to get to know my new neighbors, I've begun to read about the birds. I've learned that the reason they fly through the troughs between the waves is to cut down on wind resistance, which means they, like the surfers they fly past, are unintentional physicists. When I first started watching pelicans I kept waiting to hear their calls, expecting a kind of loud *quack-quork*, like a cross between a raven and a duck. But my books confirm what I have already noticed, that adult pelicans go through their lives as near mutes. Whether perched atop a piling in classic silhouette or crossing bills with a mate or bobbing in the surf, they remain silent.

Another group of adult birds heads out to the west, toward the channel, as Hadley and I turn home. Before moving here I never knew that pelicans flew in formations. They are not quite as orderly as geese—their Vs always slightly out of whack—and the sight of them is strange and startling to someone from the North. Each individual takes a turn at the head of the V, since the lead bird exerts the most effort and energy while the birds that follow draft the leader like bike racers. These platoons fly overhead at all hours of day, appearing so obviously prehistoric that it seems odd to me that people barely glance up, like ignoring a fleet of pterodactyls.

Yesterday I saw a bird point its great bill at the sky and then open its mouth until it seemed to almost invert its pouch. My reading informs me that these exercises are common, a way to stretch out the distensible gular pouch so that it maintains elasticity. Even more impressive, I learn that the pouch, when filled, can hold up to twenty-one pints—seventeen and a half pounds of water.

"I have had a lifelong love affair with terns," wrote my friend from Cape Cod, John Hay, a writer whom I have always admired for his sense of rootedness. I've come to pelicans late and so can't have my own lifelong affair. But I am developing something of a crush.

I'm not a good watcher. Well, that's not exactly true. I'm a pretty good watcher. It's just that sooner or later I need to do more than watch. So today I am floating awkwardly on my neighbor Matt's surfboard, paddling with my legs in a frantic eggbeater motion, attempting this new sport in this new place while keeping one eye on the pelicans. Even though you can't bring your binoculars, it turns out that this is a great way to birdwatch. The pelicans fly close to my board, and for the first time I understand how enormous they are. I've read that they are fifty inches from bill to toe, and have six-and-a-half-foot wingspans, but these numbers don't convey the heft of their presence. One bird lands next to me and sits on the water, tucking its ancient bill into its throat. Up close its layered feathers look very unfeatherlike, more like strips of petrified wood. I watch it bob effortlessly in the choppy ocean. Most birds with webbed feet have three toes, but brown pelicans have four, and their webbing is especially thick. While this makes for awkward waddling on land, it also accounts for how comfortable the birds look in the water.

I'm not nearly as comfortable. Two days ago I spent an hour out here with Matt, and yesterday we came out again. Despite his patience and coaching, I never stood up on my board, in fact I never made more than the most spastic attempts. Today has been no better. The best things about surfing so far are watching the birds and the way my body feels afterward when I am scalding myself in our outdoor shower. So it is with some surprise that I find myself staring back with anticipation as a series of good waves roll in, and it is with something close to shock that I find myself suddenly, mysteriously, riding on top of that one perfect (in my case, very small) wave. Before I have time to think I realize that I am standing, actually standing up and surfing. The next second I am thrown into the waves and smashed about.

But that is enough to get a taste for it.

I have now been practicing my new art for three days. The pelicans have been practicing theirs for thirty million years. It turns out that the reason they look prehistoric is simple: they are. Fossils indicate that something very close to the same bird we see today was among the very first birds to take flight. They were performing their rituals— diving, feeding, courting, mating, nesting—while the world froze and thawed, froze and thawed again, and while man, adaptable and relatively frenetic, came down from the trees and started messing with fire and farming and guns.

What struck me first about these curious-looking birds was the grace of their flight. Not so the early ornithologists. In 1922, Arthur Cleveland Bent wrote of their "grotesque and quiet dignity" and called them "silent, dignified and stupid birds." A contemporary of Bent's, Stanley Clisby Arthur, went even further, describing the pelicans' habits with something close to ridicule. Arthur writes of the pelicans' "lugubrious expressions" and "ponderous, elephantine tread" and "undemonstrative habits," and says of their mating rituals that "they are more befitting the solemnity of a funeral than the joyous display attending most nuptials." His final insult is calling their precious eggs "a lusterless white."

Even modern writers seem to feel the need to lay it on thick: as I read I make a list of words that includes "gawky," "awkward," "comical," "solemn," "reserved," and, simply, "ugly." It never occurred to me that pelicans were so preposterous, though I'll admit that recently, as I kayaked by a sandbar full of birds, I laughed while watching a pelican waddle though a crowd of terns, like Gulliver among the Lilliputians. But "ugly" seems just mean-spirited.

When not seeing pelicans as comic or grotesque, human beings often describe them as sedate and sagelike. Perhaps this springs from a dormant human need to see in animals the qualities we wish we had. Compared to our own harried, erratic lives, the lives of the pelicans appear consistent, reliable, even ritualistic, as befits a bird that has been doing what it's been doing for thirty million years. And compared to their deep consistent lives, my own feels constantly reinvented, improvised. But before I get too down on myself, I need to remember that that's the kind of animal I am, built for change, for adaptation. Long before we became dull practitioners of agriculture, human beings were nomads, wanderers, capable of surviving in dozens of different environments.

Though barely able to hold their heads up at birth and fed regurgitated food by their parents while in the nest, newborn pelicans fledge within three months. The one year olds I watch flying overhead are already almost as capable as their parents, while my daughter will need our help and guidance for many years to come. But this too makes evolutionary sense: one reason for our long infancy and childhood is to give the human mind time to adapt creatively to thousands of different circumstances. Pelicans, on the other hand, are ruled by a few simple laws and behaviors. Still, at the risk of romanticizing, I like the sense of calm the birds exude, the sense of timelessness, of ritual and grace.

We humans face a different set of problems. Our bodies still run on rhythms we only half understand (and often ignore), and we have adapted ourselves beyond ritual. To a certain extent all rules are off. The life of a hunter or farmer, the life that all humans lived until recently, directly connected us to the worlds of animals and plants, and to the cycles of the seasons. Without these primal guidelines, we are left facing a kind of uncertainty that on good days offers a multifarious delight of options, and on bad days offers chaos. Ungrounded in this new place, I am acutely sensitive to both possibilities. And while it isn't comfortable building a foundation on uncertainty, it has the advantage of being consistent with reality. Maybe in this world the best we can do is to not make false claims for certainty, and try to ride as gracefully as we can on the uncertain.

The human brain is no match for depression, for the chaos of uprootedness. To try to turn our brains on ourselves, to think we can solve our own problems within ourselves, is to get lost in a hall of mirrors. But there is a world beyond the human world and that is a reason for hope. From a very selfish human perspective, we need more than the human.

Water and birds have always helped me live, have always lifted me beyond myself, and this morning I paddle out beyond the breakers and lie with my back to the surfboard just like the girl I saw in early fall. But while my legs may be crossed casually, I spend most of the time worrying about falling off. Even so, as I bob up and down on the waves, the whole ocean lifting and dropping below me, my niggling mind goes quiet for a minute. And then it goes beyond quiet. I'm thinking of Hadley, sitting up now and holding her own bottle, and I feel my chest fill with the joy these small achievements bring. She will be a strong girl I suspect, an athlete. And, no doubt, if we stay here she will become a surfer, delighting in her own funktionslust.

Glancing up at the pelicans flying overhead, I notice that there is something slightly backward-leaning about their posture, particularly when they are searching for fish, as if they were peering over spectacles. From directly below they look like giant kingfishers. But when they pull in their wings they change entirely: a prehistoric Bat Signal shining over Gotham. Then I see one bird with tattered feathers whose feet splay out crazily before he tucks to dive. When he tucks, dignity is regained, and the bird shoots into the water like a spear.

Inspired by that bird, I decide to turn my attention back to surfing. I catch a few waves, but catch them late, and so keep popping wheelies

and being thrown off the surfboard. Then, after a while, I remember
Matt telling me that I've been putting my weight too far back on the
board. So on the next wave, almost without thinking, I shift my weight
forward and pop right up. What surprises me most is how easy it is.
I had allotted months for this advancement, but here I am, flying in
toward the beach on top of a wave, its energy surging below. A wild
giddiness fills me. It's cliché to say that I am completely in the present
moment as this happens, and it's also not really true. Halfway to shore
I'm already imagining telling Nina about my great success, and near the
end of my ride, as the great wave deposits me in knee-deep water, I find
myself singing the *Hawaii Five-O* theme song right out loud.

Though no one is around I let out a little hoot, and by the time I
jump off the board I'm laughing out loud. A week ago I watched some
kids, who couldn't have been older than twelve or thirteen, as they ran
down the beach on a Friday afternoon. Happy that school was out, they
sprinted into the water before diving onto their boards and gliding into
the froth of surf. I'm not sprinting, but I do turn around and walk the
surfboard back out until I am hip deep, momentarily happy to be the
animal I am, my whole self buzzing from a ride that has been more the
result of grace than effort. Then, still laughing a little, I climb on top of
the board and paddle back into the waves.

I could end on that note of grace, but it wouldn't be entirely accurate. The
year doesn't conclude triumphantly with me astride the board, trumpets
blaring, as I ride that great wave to shore. Instead it moves forward in the
quotidian way years do, extending deep into winter and then once again
opening up into spring. As the days pass, my new place becomes less
new, and the sight of the squadrons of pelicans loses some of its thrill.
This too is perfectly natural, a process known in biology as habituation.
Among both birds and humans, habituation is, according to my books,
the "gradual reduction in the strength of a response due to repetitive
stimulation." This is a fancy way of saying we get used to things.

While the pelican brain repeats ancient patterns, the human brain
feeds on the new. On a biological level novelty is vital to the human
experience: at birth the human brain is wired so that it is attracted

to the unfamiliar. I see this in my daughter as she begins to conduct more sophisticated experiments in the physical world. True, all of these experiments end the same way, with her putting the object of experimentation into her mouth, but soon enough she will move on to more sophisticated interactions with her environment. She's already beginning to attempt language and locomotion. Although pelicans her age are already diving for fish, she, as a *Homo sapiens,* can afford to spot *Pelecanus occidentalis* a lead. She will gain ground later. Her long primate infancy will allow her relatively enormous brain to develop in ways that are as foreign to the birds as their simplicity is to us, and will allow that brain to fly to places the birds can never reach.

While I acknowledge these vast differences between bird and human, there is something fundamentally unifying in the two experiences of watching the pelicans and watching my daughter. There is a sense that both experiences help me fulfill Emerson's still-vital dictum: "First, be a good animal." For me fatherhood has intensified the possibility of loss, the sense that we live in a world of weak stability. But it has also given me a more direct connection to my animal self, and so, in the face of the world's chaos, I try to be a good animal. I get out on the water in an attempt to live closer to what the nature writer Henry Beston called "an elemental life."

I keep surfing into late fall, actually getting up a few times. But then one day I abruptly quit. On that day it is big, much too big for a beginner like me. I should understand this when I have trouble paddling out, the waves looming above me before throwing my board and self backward. And I should understand this as I wait to catch waves, the watery world lifting me higher than ever before. But despite the quiet voice that is telling me to go home I give it a try, and before I know it I am racing forward, triumphant and exhilarated, until the tip of my board dips under and the wave bullies into me from behind and I am thrown, rag-doll style, and held under by the wave. Then I'm tossed forward again and the board, tethered to my foot by a safety strap, recoils and slams into my head. I do not black out; I emerge and stagger to the shore, touching my hand to the blood and sand on my face. The next night I teach my Forms of Creative Nonfiction class with a black eye.

So that is enough, you see. One of the new territories I am entering is that of middle age, and the world doesn't need too many middle-aged surfers.

I feared fatherhood, but most of the results of procreation have been delightful ones. One exception, however, is the way that disaster seems to loom around every corner—disaster that might befall my daughter, my wife, myself. No sense adding "death by surfing" to the list.

While I have naturally begun to take the pelicans for granted, they still provide daily pleasures throughout the winter. What I lose in novelty, I gain in the early stages of intimacy. I see them everywhere: as I commute to work they fly low in front of my windshield; they placidly perch atop the pilings while I sip my evening beer on the dock near our house; they bank above me as I drive over the drawbridge to town. My research reveals that in March they begin their annual ritual of mating: a male offers the female a twig for nest-building and then, if she accepts, they bow to each other before embarking on the less elegant aspect of the ritual, the actual mating, which lasts no more than twenty seconds. These rituals are taking place, as they should, in privacy, twenty miles south on a tiny island in the mouth of the Cape Fear River. The eggs are laid in late March or early April and a month-long period of incubation begins.

Around the midpoint of incubation, my human family achieves its own milestone. Throughout the spring I have continued to carry my daughter down the beach to watch the pelicans fish, but today is different from the other days. Today Hadley no longer rests in a pouch on my chest but walks beside me hand in hand.

I remind myself that the mushiness I feel at this moment, the sensation that some describe as sentimentality, also serves an evolutionary purpose. With that softening comes a fierceness, a fierce need to protect and aid and sacrifice. This is not a theoretical thing but a biological one. In fact this transformation borders the savage, and here too the pelicans have long served humans as myth and symbol. "I am like a pelican of the wilderness," reads Psalm 102. At some point early Christians got it into their heads that pelicans fed their young with the blood from their own breasts, a mistake perhaps based on the red at the tip of some pelican bills, or, less plausibly, on their habit of regurgitating their fishy meals for their young. Whatever the roots of this misapprehension, the birds became a symbol of both parental sacrifice and, on a grander scale, of Christ's own sacrifice. The images of pelicans as self-stabbing birds, turning on their own chests with their bills, were carved in stone and wood and still adorn churches all over Europe. Later, the parental symbol was sometimes reversed, so that Lear, railing against his famous ingrate offspring, calls them "those pelican daughters."

The year culminates in a single day, a day full of green, each tree and bird defined sharply as if with silver edges. I kiss Nina and Hadley goodbye while they are still asleep and head out at dawn to the road where Walker will pick me up. Walker Golder is the deputy director of the North Carolina Audubon Society, a friend of a new friend, and today he takes me in a small outboard down to the islands at the mouth of the Cape Fear River. We bomb through a man-made canal called Snow's Cut and I smile stupidly at the clarity of the colors: the blue water, the brown eroding banks, the green above.

We stop at four islands. The southernmost of these is filled with ibis nests—11,504 to be exact. Ten percent of North America's ibises begin their lives here, and at one point we stand amid a snowy blizzard of birds, vivid white plumage and flaming bills swirling around us. Next we visit an island of terns, the whole colony seemingly in an irritable mood. This island, and its nearby twin, were formed when the river was dredged in the '70s by the U.S. Army Corps of Engineers, which used the sand to consciously aid the Audubon Society in an attempt to create nesting grounds. Terns, like ibises and pelicans, require isolated breeding areas, preferably islands, and this human experiment, this marriage of birders and engineers, has worked to perfection. We watch as a pair of royal terns spiral above us in their courtship dance.

The terns are impressive, but the highlight of the day for me is North Pelican Island, the nesting ground of almost all of the pelicans I have watched over the last year. Hundreds of pelicans sit on their ground nests, some of which are as big as beanbag chairs. They watch impassively as we approach. The old naturalists might have called these birds "undemonstrative" and "lugubrious," but I'll go with "calm." In fact, while we're anthropomorphizing, I might as well put "Buddha-like" in front of calm. It's hard not to project this on them after experiencing the wild defensiveness of the tern colony. The pelicans barely glance up at us. Theirs is a much different survival strategy, a much quieter one, but natural for such a big bird with no native predators on these islands. I crunch up through the marsh elder and phragmites to a spot where two hundred or so pelicans are packed together, sitting on their nests, incubating. Some still have the rich chestnut patches on the backs of their heads and necks, a delightful chocolate brown: leftover breeding plumage. They sit in what I now recognize as their characteristic manner, swordlike bills tucked into the fronts of their long necks.

While the birds remain quiet and calm, there is a sense of urgency here. This marsh island, like most of the islands that pelicans breed on, is very close to sea level. One moon-tide storm could wash over it and drown the season out. It is a time of year marked by both wild hope and wild precariousness, danger and growth going hand in hand. The birds are never more vulnerable, and as a father, I know the feeling.

I'm not sure exactly what I gain from intertwining my own life with the lives of the animals I live near, but I enjoy it on a purely physical level. Maybe I hope that some of this calm, this sense of ritual, will be contagious. If the pelicans look lugubrious to some, their effect on me is anything but. And so I indulge myself for a moment and allow myself to feel unity with the ancient birds. It may sound trite to say that we are all brothers and sisters, all united, but it is also simply and biologically true. DNA undermines the myth of our species' uniqueness, and you don't need a science degree to reach this conclusion. We are animals, and when we pretend we are something better, we become something worse.

Having seen these fragile nesting grounds a thousand times before, Walker is to some extent habituated to them. He is also more responsible than any other human being for their protection. "We only visit briefly in the cool of the morning," he explains, "so not to disturb the birds." Playing tour guide, he walks in closer to the nests and gestures for me to follow. He points to some eggs that look anything but lusterless, and then to another nest where we see two birds, each just a day old. Though pelicans develop quickly, they are born featherless and blind, completely dependent on their parents, their lives a wild gamble. Heat regulation, Walker explains, is a big factor in nestling survival. Pelican parents must shade their young on hot days, and one dog let loose on this island while the owner gets out of his boat to take a leak could drive the parents from the nest, resulting in the deaths of hundreds of nestlings.

But we are not thinking about death, not right now. We are instead watching these tiny purple dinosaurs that could fit in the palm of your hand, the beginnings of their extravagant bills already in embryonic evidence. And then, in a neighboring nest an egg trembles. There's a tapping, and a pipping out from within.

A small blind purple head emerges from the shell. "Something only a mother could love," Walker says, and we laugh. But we are both in awe. It is the beginning of something, any idiot can see that. But what may be harder to see is that it is also a great and epic continuation.

While we watch, the almost-pelican cracks through the eggshell, furious for life. Then it shakes off the bits of shell and steps out into a new and unknown world. ❧

AFTER WORDS

This is an essay about being unsettled, being in a new place with a new baby and a new life, and trying to settle myself. My way of doing so, at least in this piece, was to take tools from my old place: watching the birds, walking, establishing an animal— and in this case athletic—relationship with my new home. That I was living on the island of Wrightsville Beach added a kind of Robinson Crusoe element to the enterprise. I'd been thrown up on shore, shipwrecked, in this strange new world. Now what was I going to make of it?

These were the thematic issues, but there were technical issues too. In essays I often end up taking up several disparate subjects and weaving them together. To put it another way, it's like juggling, and in this case, I had four balls in the air: my move and its consequences, having a new baby, pelicans, and surfing, both actual and metaphoric.

VIRGINIA HOLMAN

THREE WALKS

ONCE THERE WAS A TIME with no hesitation, when I stepped into the woods with glee. They loomed all around our home: stands of old-growth white pine trees a hundred feet tall and trunks too wide for a grown man to fully embrace. These woods ran from my family's acreage up the blue-green spartina marsh line for two miles. As a child, I'd cross from property to property, my only fear a wayward dog or the scolding widow who routinely fussed at me for not minding boundaries.

I felt I belonged to these woods. Graves of my ancestors rested here. They'd owned this forest for centuries—it had been deeded to them because it had little value beyond homesteading; the gentry were deeded the property inland, which wasn't too loamy and full of salt to farm. But my ancestors crossed the Atlantic and settled what was given. Over the years they survived by raising cattle, fishing, and shipbuilding, passing down their worthless land because it was home.

One look at prices for acreage fronting the Chesapeake Bay will tell you how much times have changed. Those of us who have held on to our property laugh in amazement. We weather the hurricanes, the reassessments, debate conservation easements and land trusts, and pray we can save the land for future generations.

I no longer live in Virginia, but on the North Carolina shore, near Wilmington. Two blocks from the ocean, a beach, and a brackish river, ours is a working class tourist town and a half hour's drive from my husband's job at the university and our son's school. The drive is neither a hardship nor a pleasure. Where there were once white sand dunes, virgin longleaf pine, and canopied live oak hung with Spanish moss, there is now a seemingly endless succession of strip malls. I despaired the first time I saw the clogged sprawl that lay beyond Wilmington's quaint downtown.

When my husband, son, and I relocated four years ago, we were moving from a life blown too large and frenetic. We longed for a smaller life, one lived in a place of peace. We traveled south until the mainland ended and we crossed the Intracoastal Waterway and entered Carolina Beach. We drove around the neighborhood where we now live. I knew the second I stepped out the of car—felt the wind, smelled the salt and pine, saw the nearby state park with its maritime forest—that I could make a home here. It is a living place.

Ever since I left my girlhood home, I have yearned for that piney forest, for the hours I spent as a girl, alone in the woods. But now I find myself cast out of the world I so loved—I haven't entered the woods alone in nearly two decades. When I think of entering the woods alone, a small terror takes up residence in me; my fear is not of nature, but of man's nature. Of hate and malice. I lock my door against it at night, but the fear is never exiled from my mind. I exist, and my fear exists in me. It remains unclear which of us is stronger. Sometimes this is how I think of it, as a battle, something that must be overcome, dominated, subdued, and tamed. I marvel at my fear and my rage because I despise violence, and yet I can't eliminate my impulse to imagine my anger in action. What sickens me is my own capacity to harm.

To reenter the woods alone I must face this wall of fear. And I wonder why my mind has banished me from a place that once gave me such strength, such solace. I wonder if I can ever regain access to that place again. What would it mean to reenter the woods?

● ● ○

I was never good at being a girl the way girls are meant to be good. My nine-year-old hands are grimy; small rolls of dirt curl beneath my nails and must be pried out at day's end with the tip of a pocketknife. The soles of my feet are thick and orange. My hands are callused; my knees shine with purple scars. My unruly hair is kept cropped. The cut is called a pixie, but really it's the female equivalent of a crew cut. The men at the general store and the garage call me Sunny. This, I take it, is a form of endearment, like calling me Sweetie. When my father suggests later that I get my ears pierced, I'm puzzled. Then he waves off the idea. *It's silly*, he says. *If it doesn't bother you, it doesn't bother me.* What doesn't bother me? *That they think you're a boy. That's why they call you Sonny.*

I feel slapped. Can't they tell I'm a girl?

I spend several summer weeks trying to grow my hair and nails, but the effort is too much. It requires conscientiousness, and when I wake in the morning, I do not want to spend time taming my hair, filing a chipped nail. I want to rise. I want to eat an apple and run through the piney woods where I live. So when the sun rises, I set out alone, oblivious to the preciousness of this paradise, to the fact that here, I am free.

Once, I emerged from the forest near a garage with a workshop in it. Inside the warm room, with its corrugated metal roof, its saws and chisels and knives and delicate cedar shavings on the floor, I met a man named Vernie. He carved beautiful shapes out of red cedar branches. He made me a three-inch-high Indian head laced through with a sharp-smelling string of rawhide. I brought my cousins, and he made them necklaces too. Our parents admired them. No one expressed concern about us kids meeting a stranger and accepting his gifts. Amid today's endless nastiness and fearmongering, the 1970s seem a simpler time, a sweet lull.

These days, I rise to go to the gym in the morning. Five thirty and the televisions are on the news channels, one to my left and one to my right, suspended just above eye level.

Nearly all the news is bad, especially in these long years since September 11. The news broadcasts images of our precarious world, documenting each disaster or near disaster, gathering us at the vertiginous canyon's edge, where we stand, cling to one another, and marvel at the miracle of any happiness, any joy. Rubble, smoke, blood-stained walls, a child's twisted filthy foot, the rest of him covered.

Turn it off, please, I tell the sleepy young college girl behind the desk. She raises her head from a bed pillow on the computer table and looks at me, clearly puzzled. *Please,* I say, hearing my frantic tone, *please turn it off.*

I don't wish to live in a cave far from the world, but I cannot stand the constant barrage of news. I refuse to live in a glaring urgent world where I'm led to believe I have no control, no power. My act of rebellion? I turn it off. I need the news once a day at most. Anything truly catastrophic will break through the flimsy barriers I erect, but I need these barriers, if only to permit me to get out of bed and walk through my morning, turn on the coffee pot, make lunches for my husband and son, and admire the morning sky without being filled with despair.

The televisions are everywhere: in my doctor's waiting room, broadcasting prevention of cancer, of aging; in the airports. On vacation, waiting for our flight, I shepherd my son away from our seats as CNN broadcasts live from a serial killer's trial. The man describes in detail how he slowly tortured and killed a girl. I feel dizzy and hot. When I complain to the airline employees, I find that even they have no control over what is broadcast through the concourse. I stalk off to the food court with my son, my heart cringing in my chest. Maybe the people mesmerized before the televisions can't bear the sadness either, but they've gone the other way: they can make themselves not feel it. Sometimes, and bitterly, I envy them.

I get a Coke with my son and wait until the broadcast turns to subjects more palatable: celebrity divorce, plastic surgery, the safest cars to drive.

In high school, I live in the suburbs, with no woods larger than a few scattered acres for miles. However, there are woods behind my best friend's townhouse complex. She has recently relocated from Hanover, Virginia, which is still all forest and rolling farmland. We're both exiles from our country childhoods. She longs for the same thing I do: a walk in the woods. So after school, we venture into the young forested area behind her home.

We wander around in the trash pines and scrubby trees. The drone of cars fades a bit but never fully disappears. At the wood's entrance, we cross a drainage ditch, littered with shining beer cans and fast-food trash, but soon there is a moment of splendor, enough sunlight through the new spring leaves that the air itself seems green. We find a small creek just wide enough not to be mistaken for a ditch, moss-covered logs and rocks. There's that smell, fresh as well water—a clean smell of earth and stone and black topsoil. My friend is a romantic; she recites an Edna St. Vincent Millay poem. We both say how we feel like Jo in *Little Women*. But doesn't every girl? I never knew a girl to wish aloud to be Meg or Amy or Beth. Certainly no one wished to be poor beleaguered Marmee, which was the unfortunate fate all the Little Women came to, except Beth, of course, so brave and wise and dead.

The walk sustains us. We are happy. Here are woods to linger in. But they end abruptly, and we are on a sloping hill overlooking a parking lot and three large dumpsters behind a Golden Corral and a McDonald's. Styrofoam boxes litter the edge of the woods, as well as more beer cans, a large mound of newly grassed clay, and a pair of damp, soiled panties, which we examine at the end of a stick. An outdoor dalliance? A rape? Something a dog or raccoon dug from the trash? We'll never know, of course, but their presence makes the woods seem simultaneously diminished and vastly ominous.

Two years later a classmate of ours named Donna, a cheerful girl, full of spirit and sass, is found dead in a similar stand of woods a few miles away. She was stabbed to death along with her boyfriend. Their killer is never found. Donna sat two seats behind me in English. She was a thin thing, a delicate wisp of a girl, with long ash-blonde hair and a big smile. She gravitated to the fast kids, the partiers. She stood out, had a winning way. That summer I see Ms. Pilkington, my senior English teacher, and we talk about how Donna was always late to class, her high heels ticking across the linoleum tiles. She would toss her rabbit-fur coat over a chair and smile as she was chided, eroding Pilk's scolding stance. We both say that it is impossible to imagine anyone killing this girl out of anger. A comfort, I suppose, this failure of imagination.

The trail goes cold. Someone killed Donna, took her life, stole it from her in the woods—and then walked out, back among us.

Is this the origin of my fear of being a woman alone in the woods? Now, at my new home, the woods call to me. So far, I enter only with a companion. Large swaths of forest are set aside nearby, both at the state park and in the blast zone for Sunny Point, the munitions depot located across the river. Such a cheery name for a place rumored to handle nuclear weapons and supplies for our wars. Yet I find myself less scared of Sunny Point than of encountering the wrong human in the woods, someone with a heart full of grief or hate or rage that demands an action that will lead to my destruction.

When my family walks the paths in the state park with me, I don't feel as if I'm really walking in the woods, not the way I did when I was a girl. Maybe the small criminal in me wants to trespass. I want no park ranger to guide me, no well-tended footpaths to lead me along. The woods I want aren't some roadside attraction, cordoned off like an exotic pet. The woods I want are untamed, snarled with vines.

As a girl, I thought the woods would protect me from the world. Now I know different. The woods and I are both precarious and threatened. When has it not been this way? At last, carrying this knowledge, I decide to enter them again. Alone. I choose the unruly blast zone forest, riddled with NO TRESPASSING signs. There is no trail other than the one I make. Briars seize my jacket; my hands rip through the tangles of wild grapevines; my heart stamps in my throat; spider webs crackle like flames as I tear through them. No stopping, I tell myself.

Deep into the woods, the mechanical hum of the world recedes, and something like quiet descends. The tree frogs plonk and the cicadas shirr and I hear a snake race through the tall grass. Out here I can hear each step I take. Here is a place where fox litter the path to their dens with half-gnawed rabbit bones, luring those looking for an unearned feast toward wet teeth. Here the canopy of longleaf pine and live oak grows thick enough to block the Carolina sun. Morning's damp coolness lingers even toward noon. The first waxy stalks of Indian pipe rise from the pine tags, pale as fog. I sit on the forest floor and breathe. The air smells sweet and pure. I stretch out on the ground, watching the pine needles glisten, watching the sky moving slowly beyond them, until I feel I belong here, until I feel small, and my fear, so individual, is claimed by something more vast and powerful than any human. In its place I feel myself filled with longing, with joy, with my satisfaction at being three things at once: a woman, alone, in the woods. ❧

AFTER WORDS

"Three Walks" came about in a rather straightforward manner: whenever I wanted to go for a walk in the woods by myself, I realized I felt I needed a companion along "for safety." I tried to think of the last time that I had walked a considerable distance in the wilderness alone, and in the process of considering this, I recalled several pivotal moments I had experienced in the woods. I started writing in order to understand.

The other thing that intrigued me was my tomboy nature, which I've rediscovered and reclaimed as a middle-aged woman. I kept thinking of Jo in Little Women *and remembered how sad I was at the end of the book to find that she pretty much wound up like every other girl. I wrote in my journal, quickly, "What if Jo had lived?" Of course, it was an interesting mistake. Beth died, not Jo. But it interested me as a woman trying to reclaim a part of my past that made me feel strong and alive and incorporate it in to my current life as a wife and mother. Reconnecting those two parts of my life has led me to a place of great sturdiness and wonder.*

PHILIP GERARD

HARDBALL

AFTER COLLEGE, when I lived in Burlington, Vermont, and tended bar at the Last Chance Saloon on Main Street, only a few rough blocks above Lake Champlain and the tank farms and barge docks that are gone now, replaced by a tourist pavilion and a yacht basin, I got recruited to join a baseball team in one of the small outlying towns. We played other town teams, usually on weekends. Our home field was built on the edge of a granite quarry; beyond the outfield fence lay oblivion. The first practice, as I trotted out to my position in left field, the center fielder warned me: "Don't go diving over that fence after a ball—it's a long way down."

I leaned over the chain-link fence and stared down a hundred vertical feet onto solid rock, flat and smooth where the gray stone had been carved away in great square slabs. "No prob," I said.

The infield was dangerous and fast, hardpan base paths and close-cropped grass. The pitcher's mound was high and the batter's box was a ditch. It was as if whoever had designed this baseball diamond had tried to make it as hard on everybody as possible.

It was a country of hardscrabble farms and bone-cracking winters, sunk deep in recession. Half the men on the team were out of work; the others scrambled between two or three different jobs, trying to make ends meet. They stacked groceries or repaired cars all day and then spent their evenings splitting firewood for sale. In the winter they drove snowplows and repaired chainsaws. Their lives held little that was frivolous, and they loved the game with a fierce and serious intensity.

Our player-manager and catcher was a muscle-bound plumber who shaved his head and sharpened his cleats with a file before each game. He had a habit of firing the ball back sidearm to the pitcher after each pitch, daring him to catch it. That first day, as we loosened up, throwing and catching, he burned one into my glove so hard my palm stung. He grinned at me through missing front teeth. "We play hardball, son," he said. "Got it?"

"Right." I loped out to shag flies, wary of the low fence and the long drop.

Our outfield captain had come up through the Yankee farm system with Mickey Rivers. When Rivers went north to star in the Big Show, however, the Yankees gave him his release. After that, he roamed semi-pro outfields with an attitude and eventually found his way onto our team. He was a rangy, strong guy with remarkable instincts, good for at least one home run per game, and he could chase down any fly ball in the same county.

He played mad. He swung at pitches like a man murdering his wife's lover with an ax. When he chased the ball into left field, I cleared out of his way. I always had the uneasy feeling that one day he was going to leap over that fence after a fly ball. That he wanted to do it. That one day he would just take a running leap and catch the ball on the way down.

The Pirates had drafted our pitching ace and his eighty-five-mile-an-hour fastball straight out of high school—then released him after a single season, claiming he was psychologically unstable and a menace. So we'd heard. He'd get that light in his eye, and he wouldn't take signals from the catcher. He wouldn't take signals from anybody.

He always pitched with a manic grin on his face. His control was erratic—or so he pretended. I think now he always knew exactly what he was doing, and the crazy act was just a way to psych-out the hitters. He'd wing pitches over the backstop just to keep the batters guessing.

The more furious the batter became, the bigger he grinned. He seemed to like keeping everything—his fastball, the batter, the fielders, the game—just on the verge of going out of control. If the other team got a rally going, he would knock down the next hitter, and no umpire ever called him on it.

In our league, you had to actually injure another player to get thrown out of the game, and then it was even money.

Our pitcher's brother was our second baseman, a spray hitter whose trademark was the headfirst slide—a dangerous play, since on a close throw your face winds up dueling with the baseman's knees, fists, and spikes. This was during Pete Rose's heyday, years before he disgraced himself gambling and wound up banned from the game for life. Rose had a way of never being satisfied—if he had a clean single, he hungered after a double, and he'd batter down anybody in his way to get it. Our second baseman showed that same hunger, tried to stretch every hit into a triple, and more often than he had any right to, he succeeded. His face and arms were always cut and bruised, as if he spent his time brawling in taverns and not hitting to the opposite field.

The other players were equally eccentric: aging jocks who had once had a shot at the big time and blown it, holding on, doing it the hard way, playing for keeps.

In that league, we slid high and threw low. No game was complete without a knock-down collision at home plate or a free-for-all at second base. More than once I came home with blood on my jersey.

I'd never been better than a mediocre player. I had no dreams of glory, but I've always enjoyed the game. When it is right, there is no better game, no better feeling than the smooth swing that connects with a fastball, no sound more thrilling than the crack of a line drive coming off the sweet spot of a wooden bat and already leaving the infield by the time you hear the sound. I could pound out doubles, hit a long ball once in awhile, and catch anything in the outfield that landed in front of me. But I couldn't hit a really slick curveball, and I couldn't make the over-the-shoulder catch going away.

In that league, though, pitchers preferred to smoke the ball right down the middle of the plate—mano a mano—and I could hit a fastball

all day long. Defensively, I played with my back to the fence, out of pure terror. I charged in on everything. So I had the season of my life. That summer I was power-lifting, and I handled a thirty-five-ounce Louisville Slugger easily. I rapped out vicious grounders that sent shortstops sprawling. I ricocheted frozen ropes off the center-field fence. That troubled crew made me believe I was better than I was, and I played harder than I ever had.

We played under summer skies choked with thunderheads that scraped open their black bellies on the craggy rims of the mountains and doused us with hard rain, in golden afternoon light cooled by the deep verdure of swaying evergreen trees, into the sudden chilly twilight that carries voices for miles and years and calls children home to their suppers. We played forever, that summer.

We slugged our way to the playoffs, in which I doubled in the winning run, and now it came down to a final game.

Like every contest in which winning carries virtually no reward, we fought the championship game out hard and for keeps. At long last, the classic moment arrived—how could it not, that season? Two out, bottom of the ninth, down by a run, two men on base. I stepped up to the plate. The pitcher winged a fastball down the alley, and I nicked it up over the backstop. He came right back at me with another fastball on the corner, and I slammed it down the third base line, just foul. The thin crowd in the bleachers was going nuts. I stepped out of the box to whack the mud off my cleats, took a breath, then stepped in.

I remember even now the quality of the light—that clear Vermont light, crisp as green apples, the field of vision opening beyond the scowling pitcher and the crouching infielders and the outfielders kicking at the grass like horses, beyond the silver top rail of the fence into absolute blue sky.

My wrists were loose and the bat felt weightless. Everybody was shouting—my teammates, the other players, the wives and girlfriends and younger brothers in the stands—and their voices blended into a kind of surfy incomprehensible murmur. I had a clear vision of what was about to happen. The pitcher was rattled. His next fastball would sail in a little too high. I would get around on it quick and sock it into left center field.

Watch it arc over the fence.

Not start my home-run trot toward first base until the white ball disappeared into the quarry.

The pitcher wound up. His arm whipped past his ear in a blur. The ball came in high and fast, just as I had predicted. I dug in my back foot, took a short step with the front one, and swung from the heels. The power came out of my thighs and up my back and down from my shoulders into my thick arms and the wrists snapped around quick and the bat sang through a perfect arc.

But it was a curveball. It tailed magnificently toward my knees. I missed it by a country mile. I swung so hard, I cracked the thin handle of the barrel-heavy bat. When I swatted it against the ground in disgust, it busted clean in two.

A few months later, I left Vermont. I played one last season with a town team in Delaware—a young, careless bunch who played not hardball, but baseball. I never again played under such low skies, never again played with such desperate men, never again hit so hard or wanted to win so badly that the night before a game my stomach hurt.

Whenever I watch a big-league game on TV now, I can't help but think of all the guys who didn't make it. Who almost made it. Who couldn't hit the slick curveball. Whose defensive game was one step too slow, or whose character had some hairline fracture that revealed itself under the public stress of pro competition as under an X-ray. Whose timing was flawed, who guessed wrong just once too often, whose luck came up just one swing short of stardom. Whose imagined future never came true, leaving them baffled, bereft of any idea of how to live out their adult lives.

Who had been the boys with the high expectations, the heroes of their high schools, the older brothers whom their parents always bragged about, the boys all the other boys wanted to be like, who ached for glory, who never learned properly how to be men—how to take from disappointment hope, and from failure the dignity of their secret character.

That was the point of the game, of playing hard, of winning in that golden crisp light when you felt you could hit and run and throw forever—and also of striking out so wildly your neck stung with shame and losing a game that stuck like a pill in the throat. It was only a game, but it was a game that could teach you all you ever needed to learn about heartbreak and glory—provided you paid attention, and provided you let it go.

I imagine them out there still, roaming ugly hardscrabble fields in far-flung country places, throwing low and sliding high, inflicting as much pain on each other and themselves as they possibly can, season after season, waiting to take that last great flying leap over the fence and into oblivion. ❧

AFTER WORDS

An essay often comes together from two different directions, from two distinct experiences, sometimes years apart. Almost from the moment I played on that baseball team in Vermont, I knew the experience carried significance larger than just my own participation in a hard-played, hard-luck season. Yet it took many years to understand: years in which I abandoned certain dreams and embraced others, years in which my knee at last collapsed in right field and sent me three times under the surgeon's scalpel and out of baseball for good, years in which I watched Major League World Series games with increasing awareness of the professional skill required to play at that level, years in which I watched some of the most promising individuals of my childhood fail miserably at their lives, years in which I had the leisure to reflect on what that long-ago lost season had meant.

At last the story I had participated in all those years ago seemed both more vivid than ever and also larger than myself. It seemed a story that might resonate with the ambitious young and the disillusioned old alike—and all the ones in between— who had made peace with their lives, daring as much as they dared, learning how to handle success and come back stronger from defeat, and savoring the hard experiences that chiseled their lives into the shapes they now recognized, the defining moments in which they created the character they would live with for a lifetime.

SARAH MESSER

THE FIRE

ON DECEMBER 7, my mother hung rags drenched in turpentine and linseed oil on the branches of a cherry tree outside the Red House. She had spent the majority of the afternoon and evening crawling backward along baseboards with a can of stain and a rag. Newspapers scattered the floor of the east ell. Despite what Richard Warren Hatch had written in his notes about the futility of perfect restoration, my mother had researched colonial paint and was trying her hand.

It had all started with the Save the Hatch Mill Committee; every time my mother drove down the lane past the shabby mill, she was reminded of historic preservation and the importance of "authenticity."

The committee, in conjunction with the Marshfield Historical Society, was selling "Save the Mill" bumper stickers, and holding potlucks and other fund-raisers. To help the cause, my parents had included the Red House on the "Harvest Home Tour of Old Two Mile, Marshfield." The local paper had advertised the event in advance, running a photo of a horse and carriage driving along the mill lane, "along the timeworn road from the Hatch homestead, now the home of Dr. and Mrs. Ronald Messer."

Local historian Cynthia Hagar Krusell had also published a poem titled "Old Two Mile" in the same edition of the paper:

> . . . *The river wound beneath the hills*
> *Amongst the marshes wide.*
> *Salt hay was cut and carried out*
> *All down the riverside.*
>
> *'Twas once the scene of busy days*
> *For along old Two Mile Way*
> *Dwelt farmers and millers and sawyers*
> *The Hatch family had their day.*
>
> *There were Walter and Israel and Ichabod,*
> *Samuel, Benjamin and John*
> *Luther, Charles and Joel*
> *The list goes on and on . . .*
>
> *. . . Today along old Two Mile Way*
> *The Hatches still remain*
> *And ghost of those departed*
> *Haunt yet the old domain.*

Now involved with the local historical movement, my father built a large reproduction fireplace in the kitchen with antique bricks and a Dutch oven—an undertaking that required an entirely new chimney. In order to get used to baking without a thermostat, my mother would set the conventional oven at various temperatures, stick her arm in and out of it, then walk across the room and do the same in the Dutch oven. When she wasn't singeing hairs off her arm, she cut colonial stencils and stripped the wood floors in the east-ell bedroom. My father added an enclosed entryway and a mudroom off the kitchen. A metalsmith down the street made eighteenth-century pewter lamps and candleholders, and plumbers installed a half-bath.

All the work, save for the staining my mother was doing herself, had recently been completed—the plumbers, the electricians, the masons who had been there for months, all gone.

That night, Kate and Patrick sat at the kitchen table doing their homework. Later, Patrick played with his hockey stick, rolling a tennis ball across the slanted floors, bouncing it off chair legs, the grate at the bottom of the refrigerator. Upstairs, I had been put to bed, with Suzy in the other twin bed, and Jessica in a crib. Bekah slept in the adjacent bedroom by herself.

Sometime after this, our mother walked out the kitchen door, through the narrow entryway, and into the dark backyard. She lifted each rag off the tree and smelled it, then took it from the limb. She remembers distinctly the worry—how she put the rags in an empty cardboard box; how she placed the box in the new entryway, opened the windows. The entryway extended five feet from the back of the kitchen. My mother remembers folding the rags loosely. Then she walked back into the kitchen and told Kate and Patrick to go to bed.

In her room in the attic, Kate had a dollhouse made from a wooden box turned on its side. The dollhouse was cut in half lengthwise, revealing all three floors. There were scraps of wallpaper and carpet, a Coppertone suntan-lotion-box refrigerator, beds with toothpick posts, a fireplace made of cardboard with real chips of brick glued onto it. At Ben Franklin's 5&10, Kate had picked out more dollhouse items—a tiny fry pan with two eggs, a toaster, a fake-fruit bowl. Every night, as she placed each doll safely in its bed, she thought about her mother and sisters in California, the younger children sleeping on the floor below her, and her father and stepmother—all in their beds.

At midnight, our father returned from an office Christmas party. He was driving the first new car he had purchased in his life, a tribute to his success with his private practice. He tooled around the back of the house, up over the lawn, and parked close to the back door and the new entryway. Perhaps he was slightly drunk. Perhaps he slammed the car door, stepping out into a night that was getting colder, a sky filling with clouds. In the entryway, he saw the box under the open window. He smelled a tinge of turpentine and put his hands in the box to check the rags. They were cold.

In the beginning, it's chemistry—conditions that coincide, causing an event to spark. An event that causes a different future or outcome from what is planned or expected. In the beginning, it's about a seemingly small thing overlooked, the ignition point, oxygen, heat, fuel—the air, the chemical, the rag. Linseed oil, especially mixed with turpentine, is an extremely volatile chemical. A soaked rag folded on itself can heat up, explode. These explosions seem sudden or "spontaneous," as if they have volition of their own. They seem this way to the people whom they impact, leading them to revise circumstance as "God's will," or "a tragedy" when they become victims of the event. But in the beginning, it is just science.

Sometime around one or two in the morning, it began to rain. The rain came in the open window in the entryway of the Red House and fell onto the box of rags. The temperature dropped drastically, causing a thin layer of ice to form, hardening over everything—the hood of the new car, the stone steps winding up to the kitchen, the thin branches of the cherry tree, the open windowsill, the box of rags. The ice created just the right amount of oxygen to mix with chemicals in the linseed oil for the folded rags to become fuel. Perhaps the ice created a seal, holding the heat down. The center of each rag was a crumpled seam, a layer of folds like the fist of a peony before it opens, glowing hot from the inside. There might have been a string of smoke, a smoldering warning, the ice melting, but by then the chemicals would have already been working. Even without the temperature inversion and the ice, they could have reached an ignition point.

Sometime before 3 AM, the box burst into flame. It burned quickly, and because the entryway was new wood, the fire spread to the walls and the ceiling. A few cans of paint in the entryway exploded. The fire licked up the walls, running across the edges of windows to the wiring, the overhead light dangling from the ceiling. The fire burned through the roof and out the door to the backyard. When the fire ate through the door, air rushed in, punching the fire backward into the kitchen.

The fire entered the kitchen with a tremendous amount of smoke, tripping the alarm. The clock on my mother's bedside read 3:07 AM. She felt my father's body next to hers. *He is here. This is not a drill.* Then she smelled the smoke—bitter, burning her nose and throat. In the kitchen, the fire lit across the new linoleum floor, the base of which was made of glue and oil. The floor buckled, melting into a liquid that burned instantly. The fire burned hotter and sent off large amounts of black, oily smoke.

My father was out of the bed, his bare feet hitting the floor. Six kids and a fire in the house. In the attic, the horn positioned between Kate's and Patrick's rooms blared. Patrick thought: *Drill*. Thought: *Rope ladder, window*. But when he reached the window, he saw orange light, a wall of flames rising from the windows below him.

Beneath the loud wail of the alarm, Kate heard the house embroidered with voices. She heard people yelling to each other, their voices weaving up through the three floors. She heard footsteps running and doors slamming two flights down. She heard the urgency of her father's voice below her, beneath the alarm's metallic roar.

"*Patrick*," she said.

The room was filled with smoke, and she could not find his door. She found him in the corner of his room near the rope ladder. She had looked down the stairwell, and it was filled with smoke but clear; she took Patrick by the hand, leading him. And there was our father suddenly at the bottom of the stairs.

"It's a fire," he yelled.

They felt their way through the warren of second-floor bedrooms and down the north staircase, where one of them pulled the bolt on the door.

Meanwhile, Suzy, at the instant of the alarm, set off running out of our room and down the stairs. My mother followed, turning the corner at the stairwell's landing just in time to see Suzy—blonde five-year-old in baggy flannel pajamas—run down the hallway to the kitchen, and into a wall of flame and smoke, and disappear.

My mother stopped for a second before the hallway, her hands over her mouth. She took her hands away, yelled. She couldn't even hear herself. Then she covered her mouth again and ran through the doorway, which felt like a storm of hot wind. Ran toward the fire after her child.

Upstairs, I was banging on the walls. Suddenly Bekah was next to me and we were yelling. We could not find the door. I could not see my hands before my face, but I knew Bekah was there with me in the room.

The smoke burned my eyes and throat. I knew where the door was, but all I felt were the walls, the windowpanes, banging with the palms of my hands. I heard the voices of my parents, but they were thin threads of sound.

A door opened, and my mother stood there, a light from behind her transpiercing her nightgown, the outline of her body. She had just watched one daughter run the wrong way into the fire, and then, like a miracle, run back out. She had just passed in and out of the hallway leading to smoke and flame, turning her back on the fire, with Suzy now in her arms, to hear a loud crash, the sound of the refrigerator exploding. And now she was upstairs again, in this doorway, saying, "This way, this way," and we were dragged by our arms down the stairs and out onto the lawn, where I was told not to move, standing with my bare feet on the frozen grass.

My father was counting heads. *Six, six, six.* There were only five. Suzy, Bekah, and I held on to each other's fingers or nightgowns. Somebody yelled, "The baby," and my parents were now rushing back toward the house, my mother stopping in the doorway, my father running up the stairs, back into my room, the house swallowing him. At the top of the stairs, he fell to his stomach and crawled on his elbows across the floor, finding Jessica still asleep in the crib, an inch beneath the smoke.

I stood in front of the open doorway and watched my father toss Jessica, a perfect bundle, over the banister and into my mother's arms, who accepted her so easily, as if they were one person, as if that gesture had been choreographed and rehearsed a hundred times before, the way action can be in a crisis—without thought, with only faith that the action is the right one.

There are many versions of what happened next—my father's story, my mother's, my siblings', my story.

In one version, my father did not leave the burning house right away but ran to his office on the first floor to try to call the fire department, finding the phone disconnected. Or my father, after throwing Jessica over the staircase, ran back into my room, where, disoriented, he grabbed the music box and carried it down the stairs and out the door.

In yet another version, my father left the house but then returned one last time to try to telephone the fire department and save the music box, couldn't accomplish either task, and quickly ran out again.

Then we all ran, in nightgowns, across the frozen lawn. The air was cold, painful to breathe. We tore through the bushes to the neighbors', where my father (a) yelled and kicked the door in, (b) threw rocks at the bedroom windows, (c) used swear words. Then the neighbor, Mr. M, appeared in the doorway—some say stark naked, some say using swear words, some say both.

We were, it is agreed, a huddled mass on the lawn, our backs to a burning house. Mr. M was ghostly and pale in the doorway—legs, arms, torso—his skin purplish white. He stood looking out at us, looking at the shards of glass from the storm door my father had smashed with his foot. My father's foot was bleeding. Mr. M was a thin, angry, naked man. Sometime after this, we were let into the house and somebody called the fire department.

The firemen took a long time to arrive, because the Union Street Bridge was out and they had to hook up their hoses to the fire hydrant a half-mile down the street. Also, they couldn't get their trucks around the stone wall and the apple tree.

My father blamed Mr. M for not waking up sooner, for being a bad neighbor. While we were waiting for the fire department, my father took us back over to our yard, where we sat on the lawn staring at the house. The house seemed to pulsate with heat, the slate roof like a cap screwed down tight against the flames. Glass in the windowpanes melted or burst. Black smoke streamed from the seam of each window, through every crack in the shingles.

In yet another version, my father did not blame Mr. M for not waking up sooner, for being a bad neighbor; he understood that things were chaotic and that we were lucky to have escaped with our lives. While we were waiting for the firemen to arrive, Mrs. M put us in chairs around the kitchen table and we drank milk. We talked about when the fire-fighters would come. She said that Patrick was in shock and gave him a blanket; he was shivering and rocking and would not talk to anyone.

Suzy was crying about her guinea pig. I was crying about the kittens.

Bekah was crying about the mother cat, the dog. Kate was crying about her dolls. Jessica was crying as a chain reaction. This is the way it happened with us: a suddenly whipped-up fury of anxiety at 5 AM at the neighbor's table, with our mother saying, "Hold it together, kids; everything will be all right."

The firemen were working next door. A few of them had come in, checking, rechecking: "Are you sure there is no one else in the house?"

By daylight, the firemen were back, large men dragging ash behind them into Mr. and Mrs. M's kitchen of blue cupboards. Their yellow rubber jackets and hats had turned black. Slick with water from the hoses, they smelled acrid and burned. The skin on their hands and faces was beaded soot, like rain on an asphalt road. One fireman had something squirming in his coat.

"Does this belong to somebody?" he asked, as he opened his coat and held out the guinea pig to Suzy.

Outside the kitchen, in the hallway, I heard my father talking to the firemen. He was still in his nightshirt. His feet were bare, and blood had dried on his foot. They were talking about the slate roof. How the fire couldn't burn through. They were saying that slate was denser than wood or asphalt, that it trapped the heat. They were saying that if they had come five minutes later the entire house would have exploded. Exploded to pieces, sky-high, they were saying; there would have been nothing left.

It is called a "flashover," the technical term for how a room or a house explodes. Heat rises. During a fire, the temperature always increases more dramatically at the top of a room; there is sometimes a difference of five hundred degrees between the floor and the ceiling. If the room temperature reaches more than a thousand degrees, the buildup of carbon dioxide will ignite into flames that travel six feet per second. The slate roof trapped the heat, but the house did not explode.

Eight o'clock in the morning, the house was still smoldering. Ash swirled in the air, whipped up in tiny tornadoes of wind. My father's car was half collapsed, as if it had been melted with a blowtorch, the driver's side gone. The entryway was a pile of rubble; the kitchen wing, a fifteen-foot hole out of which black ribbons of smoke wound into the sky. The firemen had stayed for hours with hoses fixed on the beams.

"This is an old house," the firemen were saying, implying that the wood was more burnable. At 6 AM, one of the sills had ignited again.

Now the fire was out, they said. My father, my mother, Kate, and Patrick went back into the old part of the house, the part that was not burned. They went in to find clothes, to see if there was anything left. They borrowed flashlights from the firemen who were standing around the one remaining truck.

Kate borrowed tennis sneakers from Mrs. M; they were slightly large, and she tied the laces tight. Everyone was still in pajamas as they entered the south side of the house.

Smoke from the burning vinyl floor had dripped over everything. The windows were covered with soot, and it was impossible to see except for the narrow scope of the flashlight's path through the dark. The house was hot and wet; the firemen had come through spraying the surfaces of every room with water. Water kept dripping; rivulets ran down the walls.

Everything in the old part of the house was coated with black, as if spray-painted—the Hatch wills, the record player, the pencil on the desk, the toothbrushes lined up by the sink, the halved dollhouse in the attic, the faces of the dolls in their beds.

Door handles were still hot. My mother led Kate and Patrick up the back staircase and told them to go into the attic and take any clothes that did not seem ruined. She then entered the bedrooms on the second floor. She wrapped the bottom of her flannel nightgown around her hand as she pulled open a drawer. Inside the drawer she found rows of neatly folded children's T-shirts, corduroy pants, and sweaters. The clothes had turned a dull gray. She placed her hands inside the drawer and found that the clothes were warm, almost hot, to the touch. She kept her hands there for a moment, feeling the heat from the neatly folded clothes, as if they were the curved backs of sleeping children.

Kate picked a ring off the dresser in her room and turned it over, surprised to see that the other side was still silver. She began to turn everything over, looking for the parts the smoke had not touched. The insides of books, the circle the lamp left on the table. In the toy chest in Patrick's room, they pulled out a stack of board games, reading the names Sorry and Monopoly between the smoky layers.

Everywhere Kate walked, her borrowed tennis sneakers scuffed the floor, leaving a silvery trail. Her hands were black and her white night-gown was smudged as she knelt before the dollhouse, which looked nothing like itself—all definition and pattern lost. She shone the flash-light into the tiny blackened rooms as she heard my mother at the bottom of the attic stairs saying, "We're taking nothing. Nothing can be saved. Leave everything here."

Kate reached into the dollhouse living room, the hand of a giant, invading. She left all of her dolls in their beds but took the cardboard fireplace. She carried it with her downstairs, through the larger house, and out the door.

On the lawn, it was a brilliant morning. Our father then appeared from the gaping hole in the kitchen. His face was covered with soot. He was holding a box.

This box had always been kept in the kitchen, on the counter beside the sink. "Somer's Brother's Fine Metal Boxes, Brooklyn, NY. Patented April 29, 1878"—we had all memorized it, memorized the etching on the top of the palm, five fingers spread. On the tip of each finger was a pig: one with a basket in its mouth, one beneath a roof, one with a plate of meat and a carving knife, one crying, one running. *This little piggy went to market. This little piggy stayed home.*

But now the box was completely black. Our father held it wrapped in a towel, moving the terry cloth beneath his hand as he opened the lid.

Kate still carried the fireplace. She thought she knew everything that was in the box—a pack of matches, a bent corkscrew, a slide of Patrick on the USS *Constitution*, a rubber toy policeman, spare change, keys. But our father removed a fifty-dollar bill.

Did they want to save it? This was the question that the insurance agent would pose only eight hours later—after we had been sent to rela-tives, after my parents had borrowed clothes from friends and rented a room at the Clipper Ship in Scituate Harbor. *Did they want to restore the house, or put it up for auction, emergency sale?*

"We want to try," they would say, "to keep it."

But that morning, when they stood on the lawn, they knew nothing except that they had escaped, and that our family's survival was entirely due to the false alarms, to my father's madcap exit maps. As if someone had whispered a warning in his ear.

"Take this money and buy the kids some clothes," our father said to our mother.

One side of the bill was completely black; the other side was green and readable. He held the money out to her across the bright-blue day. ❦

AFTER WORDS

I wrote this chapter in five hours straight, after having done the research, interviews, etc., necessary to help me remember it. This is very unusual for me. When writing about trauma, an old family story, or something that happened a long time ago, memory gets shifty and shadowy. Sometimes stories that are not true replace the true ones because they are better stories. Because it was traumatic, because it was long ago, and because most of my family was involved, there are many versions of what happened. But in the end, the story just flowed out. One interesting note: when I was interviewing the old fireman about what happened, the fire alarm went off at the station. "I have to go," he said. Less than five minutes later, I heard a siren and saw a fire truck speed by on the street. Forty-five minutes later he called back. When I asked him if he had driven down my street, he said, "Yeah, that was me." Turns out it had been a false alarm.

ELI HASTINGS

OUT IN FRONT

IN AUGUST 2002 I arrived at blazing noon in front of the antique green house on Wilmington's Ann Street that would be my home for the next two years. My now-to-be-roommate, Dave, waved from the sloping second story porch, Spanish moss lifting with a breeze. The park across the street was a mixture of laconic old men boozing in the shade and young children playing on a worse-for-wear jungle gym and bleachers, indifferent to the hundred-degree heat. My dog, Kaya, half tugged on the leash, conflicted: thrilled to see squirrels in the dead grass but already nearly too hot to move, much less give chase.

Over the phone, Dave had said in his understated Piedmont manner that "he wasn't real sure what went on in that park after dark" and the landlady had informed me that "the house is in a 'transitional' neighborhood." This somewhat explained the fantastic rental rate. Looking around me, though, as I unpacked the truck, all I saw were families laughing, kids playing, everyone easing their way through Sunday afternoon routines. A hammer put up a distant rhythm, and a *whock* and good-natured shit-talking announced a softball game. Curious glances were matched by waves from our neighbors. I felt good as I lugged boxes up the creaking, dusty stairs.

One hundred and four years had passed since the violence. More than a century since drunken white men marched down my street in broad daylight with rifles and shotguns "hunting blackbirds." Four generations since a newspaper editorial in a black publication was used as political cover for "upstanding" white citizens to stage the only coup in U.S. history, slapping the increasingly professional black population back down by way of random murder and general terror. And still the city bore the names of the killers and their "respectable" accomplices. In the late-summer dusk, I watched students flirt on the stoops of libraries named after them, watched families at play in their parks. It is safe to say that history—more than the present fact of it—made me aware that my and Dave's skin was the only pale pigmentation on the block.

As I rocked on the porch that first night and watched shadows creep toward full-fledged darkness, a purple swell flashing its bolts in the east, a throng of idle young men mixing on the corner, the desperate hilarity of old drunks under the picnic shelter, the gospel hum of our neighbor rising and falling, the shattered glass divvying up the remaining sun all over the park, the academic knowledge of history gave way. The hot wind and shifting shadows promised a lot of haunting, a lot of lessons.

I

The heat is too much for Kaya. She has no interest in anything besides staying still in front of the fan. I have to pull her along the street, encourage her to pee. The night offers no relief—the afternoon's weak breeze died with the sun. I wear shorts and flip-flops and pull fistful of moisture from my chest and brow with a handkerchief. The man forms slowly out of the soft darkness. He walks in the middle of the street. He is tall, so lanky it seems his legs should have another joint. I nod. He eyes the dog but she doesn't care. With two steps he's above me. By rote, with a practiced rhythm, he begins to unwind his hustle. I try to interrupt him twice, but he raises a huge palm flat in front of me, closes his eyes, and doesn't need to say *please, let me finish.* When he has, I tell him I don't have anything on me.

I ain't no crackhead, he says, severely.

I believe you, I tell him, *but that doesn't change the fact that I don't have any money.*

C'mon, he says, *I ain't no crackhead, I ain't bullshittin'.*

C'mon yourself, I say, my manners faltering now, *I don't even have any fucking pockets.*

He takes a step forward and his mouth opens again. Kaya snaps tense and her jowls twitch. She aims her snout at him. I put my hand on her head and I put my eyes into his.

Look man, I say, *if I had any money on me I would give it to you. If I had a few bucks, I'd be happy to help you out. I would. But I don't.*

He pushes a flashing, bloodshot gaze into me, silent, with no expression. Kaya and I are both very still. Then a smile blooms and he moves backward as if on rewind.

Shit, man, he says, *that's all you had to say. That's all you had to say.*

And he saunters off coolly down the hot gullet of the night.

II

Rocker creaking, Kaya snoozing, cigarette dribbling against the sticky night. Behind the massive oaks and screen of Spanish moss, the porch is a hidden vista onto the world. In the north, a freight train lifts a blue bleat. From the south comes the rise of a gospel hymn, one solo voice. It climbs higher and carves the silence and gives me gooseflesh. The cicadas are mute. Something about looking to the stars. The singer is on an old beach cruiser bicycle, weaving leisurely along the avenue. She wears a white blouse that calls the moonlight down to it. Kaya lifts her head and her tail beats a metronome, like a friend is arriving. The song competes against the freight's horn for a moment and then they tangle, vanishing, the train pulling out of the world, her riding into it.

III

I'm pulling Kaya back from the park, as she pulled me into it. The way the moon lights the man's cloud of smoke is artful. He shuffles under a tree and looks away from me but I greet him anyhow per my policy as Anglo interloper. He nods and grins away any surprise as soon as I do so. Then he calls for me to wait and he approaches, one lazy eye on Kaya who watches the trees for her foe, the gunmetal gray cat. It is cold and he doesn't put much into the spiel, which I appreciate.

Hey man, I'm Leo. I got a job man, a little job. But it ain't a big job, know what I mean, man? It ain't cuttin' it. Can you help me out man, you think, somethin'?

I have no money but I do the pocket pat and shrug routine for him. He says it's alright and I turn to go. But then I notice my truck at the curb and I tell him to hold on, I'll look for some change. In the bone white moonglow, his eyes lose some of their brown. He forgets about the smoke in his throat and the cigarette freezes in its trajectory away from his mouth. He looks at me and asks,

Man, you're not gonna grab a gun are ya?

I chuckle before the seriousness of his question gets into my mind. He stays there, stiff like the frozen trees that groan like moored boats over us. I strip my smile away and tell him of course not. When I turn back and put nine quarters into his hand, relief blends with gratitude in his face and he talks and talks about how beautiful the dog is.

IV

On the porch midnight comes and goes but it seems that the temperature rises. Drops roll down my brow and my bottle; the beer will get warm in minutes. We sit and watch the cars move through the inky streets, the sky wink and swirl. Summer is dying but won't admit it. Marc and I are quiet, descending from a drunkenness toward slumber. Two young, thick men wobble onto the block, slap boxing, talking loud. Kaya, because of their commotion, stands, lets out a low warning from her belly—which calls their attention to us. The bigger one:

Hey what's happenin' up there y'all?

Not much. How you doin'?

Aw, you know. Say, throw me one a them cold things.

What's that?

One a them cold things—throw one to me.

The last beers are in the fridge on the other side of the house. The men shift with unnerving energy, leaning on the fence. Marc:

These're the last ones, man.

Aw, c'mon now.

No, seriously, this is it. Sorry.

Yo, I don't mean to be rude but you need to throw me one a them.

Hey, what do you want? They're gone.

They are still and quiet and I can see the whites of their eyes. The talker lifts himself a little on the fence, flexing, moving his face a few inches forward and up toward us.

I oughtta come up there and fuck you up, you know that shit?

Our policy becomes silence. He lifts one leg, hooks it over the fence, stops, looks up at us again, like he's cocked a gun.

Man, watch me come up there and straight kill you motherfuckers.

A Cadillac turns and headlights wash the sidewalk. A beat breaks from the car's window. The cicadas compete. Sweat slides down my chest. The man pulls his leg back over to his side. The pair walk away, slurring muffled threats into the wet quilt of August Dixie that separates us.

V

One night I'm writing an essay. In it, I liken plastic grocery sacks, rising and traveling with the wind, to ghost heads. I take a break to walk the dog.

I step out with Kaya straining at the leash. Down the sidewalk a creak and a broken song come. He's pushing the bike, and under the burn of a street lamp, I see plastic sacks swinging from the handlebars. Unrested and half-drunk as I am, I think *headhunter* and hurry my step, not in the mood for chatter and the night is blustering besides. And Kaya is tugging.

I'm a few paces ahead when he reaches the picnic shelter and calls out to me. Not far enough to pretend I've not heard. I keep Kaya leashed. He ambles toward me: hiking boots, thin canvas jacket, dirty jeans, stocking cap, ski gloves, gaunt, ashy face, wine breath, lack of teeth revealed by a grin.

In terms of eyes:

They glisten, overfull, and roll something across at me that causes me to almost curse because I've seen it before and I know what it suggests: power, allure, trouble, illness.

He's shaking my hand, the glove cushioning the ferocity of his grip. He's sliding a hand over Kaya's neck but she's watching skinny branches dance, not caring, trying to discern squirrels.

He says once he had to pull a knife on a dog.

He says once he had to shoot a gangster in a Chicago alley.

He says once he had to kill some gooks in a humid jungle.

He says once he had to drop a cop that took his bottle.

He sights down his arm like a rifle and aims it at my neighbors' homes:

Pimp (on the far corner), *Dealer* (on the nearer corner), *Bootlegger* (right next door), *Crackheads* (down the block). With his squinted eye and a twitch of trigger finger, he makes it clear he doesn't approve.

Kaya, eager to be free, sends up one long strand of whine that breaks between us. In my head, I thank her. I beg away and shake his hand again.

You won't see me again, he tells me. *My name's Gus—but they call me ghost.*

In a peach-colored, warm coffee shop, I am struggling with this essay. As November booms around outside and a few icy drops tinkle against the window, as dusk runs out and night takes the reins, I sip cold coffee and cut and paste. I *italicize* and un-italicize; I put scene V first and scene II last. Behind the coffee bar, a plump girl who has been kind to me with refills is whirling about in closing-up-shop labors. I feel something is missing from this essay, have in fact felt that for months, which is why it has remained buried. Less than satisfied, but thinking of my warm bedroom and the no-doubt antsy dog, I say good night to the barista.

My bike is gone. It could be that I locked it up in a distracted manner and all one had to do was lift it from the flaccid loop of cable. It could be that a sly thief disassembled the necessary bolts and slipped away. At any rate, the lock and the cable are draped on the parking meter in mockery. I slip them in my bag and start the trek home.

On Orange Street, a well-kept middle-class avenue a block over from my own, the Spanish moss hangs low and tropical leaves lean out over wrought-iron fences, as if to escape the imminent frost. On the corner, the historic Hoggard House glows with a kind of kerosene warmth, a testament to the rich but torrid history of this town. In the corner of the yard stands a FOR RENT sign advertising what is currently my friend Kimi's apartment, a testament to the haunts of the house. The recessed, darker old mansion blinks meekly next door as I approach Sixth Street, where a bed and breakfast, a vacant lot, and a perpetually darkened mosque sit on the other three corners. Before I get there, though, I hear a crunch and a creak behind me and step aside for a man on a bicycle. Involuntarily, I look to the bike, but it's not mine.

"Pardon me," he says, "I didn't mean to scare you." He gives a melodious chuckle and I tell him to have a good evening. He coasts around the corner.

At the dark intersection, seconds later, he steps from a swath of shadow and his hand closes on my left arm like a vice grip. Moonlight flashes on his eyes, which are aimed down at me from a considerable height. Pocks mark his weathered, thin face and he's clad in an army jacket. My free arm is slung with the weight of my laptop over my shoulder. The first thing I think is: *this man must be near fifty.*

He hisses, "Give me your shit," a command that comes straight from the teeth. Synapses start firing and fight juice whirs through me. I try to step back, stalling, telling him *Okay, man, chill out, whatever,* but I say this very loudly. He jerks me closer so I can smell rancid breath and then there is something metal against my stomach.

"Start hollerin' and I'm a blast your guts right now." When I reach back for my wallet I realize that my arm is now in a position to strike instead of comply. But I see the venom in his gaze and sense prevails. I hand him my grandfather's wallet and swing my bag behind my back. He backs away issuing threats, climbs onto his bike and rides off over the dance of oak boughs' shadows on the road.

After an awkward conversation with zealous crewcut cops, I trudge home. In the kitchen I down two glasses of Dave's plum wine while Kaya squeals greetings and pleas around my legs. I leash her and step back to the street, smoking hard, small tremors in my hand. On the first block, as I kick through the detritus of vice—shattered forty bottles, drug baggies, candy wrappers—two large, parka-clad black men cross the street when they see me coming with Kaya. With a steady voice, louder than I intend, I force out a greeting at them. They nod and wave after a pause.

At the corner of Sixth and Orange, the wind is earnest. Kaya dislikes the stop, but contents herself to snuffling the bushes—just about where my assailant crouched. Down toward Castle Street I can see the spinning red and blue of the law and hear the slow, high whine of a siren, calculated desperation. ●

AFTER WORDS

With family roots in the South, my return there for graduate school was bound to be fraught. It was important to me not to isolate myself in an academic bubble from the socioeconomic and racial realities of a town as haunted as Wilmington, realities I learned about through conversations with locals and through Philip Gerard's excellent historical novel, Cape Fear Rising. *"Out in Front" is woven from the fascinating, sometimes surreal and mostly wonderful experiences I had living in "the ghetto" as a white interloper, an experience crowned by the irony of being held up on a "good" street a few blocks from my "bad" one. Wilmington continues to inspire much of my fiction.*

BRAD LAND

BROTHERS IN HARM

THIS IS HOW IT GOES: *We're getting floored at this frat party in our hometown. Me and my younger brother Brett. We aren't in a frat, but it doesn't matter because it's a small town and if there's a party, any party, anyone who knows about it comes. Just before midnight, I tell Brett that I'm tired and I'm going to leave. He looks me over and says you sure? and I say yeah, I'm cool, long day you know. I'm walking down the sidewalk to my car when this voice comes soft at my shoulder. I turn my head and it's there, this face, all teeth and glowing eyes. My head's saying this is a stranger, but maybe I've seen him here, at this party. One hand is shoved down into his left pocket, and he cocks his head to the side. So man, he says, give me a ride right? And I look at him and my head drops, yes, sure, yeah, where are you going? Up the street, he says, just up the street, hand pointed now, the index finger hooked at the knuckle. And inside I'm shaking my head, telling him no, sorry, gotta be somewhere, but I can't stop myself from saying yes. The smile is saying let me get my boy, right back, and I'm standing there with my hands in my pockets thinking just turn and go, but my feet won't move, and before I can breathe again the smile is back saying hey man this is my boy, and I'm shaking hands with both of them. I drop down into my car,*

*this maroon Oldsmobile with the streetlights gleaming off the hood. The keys
shake in my hand like a rattle.*

● ● ●

Pledge season starts when the phone in my dorm room rings. It's a
Monday afternoon, four days after the vote to decide who gets bids. I
jerk around, peer at the orange plastic rotary dial left over from the '60s.
It shakes because the ring is so loud.

Hello, I say.

Take your fucking goat ass to the hall right fucking now. The voice is
screaming. I can't tell who it is.

I'm a junior, but this is my first semester at Clemson. I was supposed
to have transferred here with Brett in the spring, but my plans got fucked
up by "the incident." That's what my father calls it. My mother calls it
"the abduction." My brother Brett calls it "your thing." Other people
call it the kidnapping. The robbery. The choking. The woods thing. I
don't know what to call it. I just say, "what happened."

Brett's a sophomore, a year behind me, but he's already been at
Clemson a semester. We talked about me pledging his fraternity, Kappa
Sigma, and he said he wanted me to if it's what I really want. I tell him
yeah it's what I want. And I do, even though I'm carrying this thing that
I know will fuck me sooner or later. I just keep thinking about being
normal and doing what Brett does. I keep thinking about how he's
leading me somewhere I need to be.

● ● ●

*Inside the car the smile speaks of the school where he goes, says he's leaving
tomorrow to go back, and the pussy, he says, the pussy, so much it's everywhere, and I say yeah man I know, though I don't, and we stop at a gas
station where the smile gets out and goes inside, and through the windows
I see him leaning over the counter, and he's moving his head back and forth
and smiling. I look at the rearview into the seat behind me, and there's a head
turned sideways, this silent profile, forearm strung like concrete across the
top of the backseat. The car shifts when he leans forward, and for a moment I
can feel his breath from behind me. The passenger door opens and the smile's*

back inside. He's throwing candy at the breath in the backseat. He sits down.
That way, he says. That way.

● ● ●

On the Kappa Sigma hall, I push open the gray metal door and see Dion
Lynch and Patrick Wells. Patrick is short and thick. Wearing sunglasses.
He's yelling at my new pledge brother Will Fitch, who's taller than he
is, skinny with wiry blond hair that sticks out of his hat in tufts. Patrick
points up at him, pokes his stubby ring finger back and forth inches
from his face. Will flinches each time. Dixon just smirks. His face is dark
with stubble. He pushes Will toward the short stairwell that leads up
into the hall. Will catches a foot on the first step, stumbles and then
rights himself. Looks back at Dixon, who says that if he looks back again
he'll break his fucking face.

Patrick sees me standing with my back to the door, and it almost
makes me wince to see him turn so quickly toward me. My hands are
shaking. What the fuck are you smiling for? he says. He stares hard at
me, and I look away. Huh? he says, cups a palm beneath my chin, spins
my head around to face him. I'm fucking talking to you, he says. I said
what the fuck are you smiling for? Dixon comes from my right and slaps
the glasses from my face.

Everything blurs, Patrick and Dixon's faces, the walls, the light
streaming from outside. Patrick says that I am fucking pathetic. His
breath is hot on my face, and it makes me wince. He moves behind me.
Places his hands on my shoulders. Pushes me up three steps. The door
leading into the hallways is closed, but through it I hear muffled voices.

A brother is waiting at the top of the stairs, his skin rough from the
beginnings of a beard. When you walk in there, he says, pointing toward
the closed door, I want you to yell. And what I want you to yell is that
you own this fraternity. He looks at me sincerely.

I want you to scream at the top of your lungs. This is your fraternity.
You own it. I place my hands on the door and push.

There is a line of brothers down each side of the hallway and pledges
are filing between then. Will is somewhere halfway down. A brother

pushes him in the back. He spins limply toward the opposite wall, where he is met with another shove.

I wonder where Brett is. The door to his room is shut and a brother is leaning against it. Everyone yelling. I throw my hands up. For a moment I can't remember what I'm supposed to say, but when a brother catches me I remember. At first it comes out softly, but then I see the anger welling up in the brother's eyes. He clenches his face, and then I am screaming, flailing my arms, bouncing towards the gauntlet like a mad man. I own this motherfucker, I say.

A brother grabs me. Jerks me by one arm. What the fuck did you say? he says. You fucking goat motherfucker I'm going to fuck you up if you say that again.

I do not look at him. I just scream. Another brother's head spins around after he shoves Will, and now all eyes are on me. A brother flings me down the line. My body goes limp, and I just let the shoves come.

A brother opens the door to the hall lounge and pushes me inside. A voice says get on the goddamn floor with your pledge brothers. Shoves me down. I land on my knees, behind the line of pledges sitting cross-legged, their heads bowed toward their legs, their arms locked tightly together. They bob like the pistons of an engine. They are baaing like goats. The sound rises and falls. It fills the room.

I lock arms with Will.

Baa like a goat, motherfucker, someone says.

We baa.

Louder, he says.

We baa louder. I push my head closer to my legs. Sweat is pouring down my back, and my arms are slick.

Get down, faggot, a brother says. Someone is shoved down next to me. Warm spit hits the back of my neck and rolls down into my shirt, slips down my back slowly.

Someone whispers in my ear. It is soft, almost gentle, and I feel hot breath against my face like someone is bending to kiss my cheek.

I fucking hate you, he says, you hear me? I hate every single one of you goat motherfuckers. A hand slaps the back of my head. At each end brothers pull the line, trying to loosen us.

You better fucking hold on, motherfuckers, someone says. Everything is beginning to blend together, and everything sounds like a chant, the goat sounds, the yelling, the sway of the line. Will crying next to me. I can hear him whimpering. I cannot cry. I squeeze my knees around my head until it hurts.

Get up, a brother says. We all rise, heads bowed. Stand clustered together. Another brother lines us up.

Nothing happened right? he says. We nod. Patrick takes my arm. We walk through an open door and he whispers in my ear.

Just a little more, okay? he says. You're doing good. Just a little more.

●●●

My mouth is full of dirt. The air comes back as quickly as it left. It fills me. I'm on the ground with feet beside my face, with feet landing on my ribs. Beneath my car I can see the dry soy beans hunched like gimps. I put my hands around my head, and then I'm raised beneath the arms, lifted like a doll. I stagger and can't stand up. The breath holds me around the chest. The smile is in front of me, teeth clenched, puts fists into my eyes, my mouth. Tears a chain from my neck. Dangles it in front of me. And then he's in my back pockets. Pulls the wallet. Dumps everything he doesn't want.

Next: the keys. Jammed into the smile's pockets.

This is what I say: Credit Card. Code: four four four four. Please. Leave me here.

This is what the smile says: Not enough. We want it all.

●●●

Each weeknight two pledges have to go to every brother's room on the first, second, and third floors and ask if they need anything. We do their laundry, rinse the tobacco juice from their "spit cups." Really gross shit. Will Fitch and I are the first two pledges to go.

Will's khakis barely hang onto his slim hips, and his hand trembles as he reaches for the door. I'm surprised when we step inside to find no one waiting for us. I expect to hear screams, because two days ago we were standing here getting the shit kicked out of us. Will stares into the first door on our left. He turns back, gives me a look like he's wondering why I'm letting him take the front line. Somewhere a television blares but no one is home.

Brett's room is next. I don't expect him to want anything, but what do I know? My brother's been a mystery like everything else. Even though he's younger, he's always been more together than me, better looking, not as nervous. I expected him to be my guide, to tell me what's what. But he stays in his head most of the time. And I know he wants me to make a go by myself, but I also know he feels strange about it all, like this fraternity isn't what he thought it was in the beginning, like he's not who he used to be, like once he saw it happening to me, it was different.

Will stays behind this time. Brett is sitting on a rust-colored couch, his face expressionless, the brown skin and the chiseled features. His feet are propped on a chipped coffee table strewn with cigarettes and beer cans. He sees us and sits up quickly.

Come in, he says. You okay?

Yeah, I say.

Look down at the gray industrial carpet. I turn back up and Brett is studying my face. He always does this when he thinks I'm lying, and I am lying now, and he knows it.

Will steps into the room. Brett doesn't even look at him.

Do you need anything? Will says. Brett is still staring at me. He knows I don't like this. He knows it scares me. And I think he wants me to say it. To be honest. To say I'm scared. To say that it's fucked up. Because part of him, I know, feels the same way.

He breaks his stare and turns to Will.

No. No. Nothing, he says. Slouches back into the couch. He changes the channel and we leave.

● ● ●

By my second week of pledgeship, the fraternity owns me. The brothers are everywhere, waiting for me to slip. I walk to class and look for brothers. I eat and look for brothers. I'm in my room waiting for the phone to ring or for a fist to pound on my door. I sleep and I dream the same fucked-up things, faceless men scratching at the windows of my room. I know I don't want to do this pledge thing because I'm scared of everything, of closing my eyes and waking up at night. But I'm also terrified of what I would be without it.

I leave my room at six o'clock and hurry over to Tillman Hall. Its clock tower looks over the burnt-orange brick buildings and is visible from any point on campus. I climb the stairs to the second floor and find room 216. Most of my pledge brothers are standing around nervously, still wary of any place we are told to gather. Will Fitch stands by himself, pacing around a wooden chair. His blue shirt is wrinkled, and his tie dangles loosely from the buttoned collar. His cheeks glow like he's been facing a stiff wind. I sit down in the chair, and he just keeps pacing around me. He doesn't look up.

So, I say, are you okay man? He keeps walking. The circles become wider. He shrugs his shoulders.

Yeah, he says, brings a hand to his head, weaves fingers through thick blond hair. I'm just, I don't know, this is hard. I feel weird.

Patrick Wells enters the room from the door directly in front of me between two portraits of glaring old men. The door falls shut behind him, and he just stands there looking at us. Everyone turns to face him. Our hands fall to our fronts, palms laid flat over each other, and we are waiting for his mouth to open and for words to part the silent room.

Patrick leads us into a large white room. Sunlight streams through the tall windows, lands in shafts on the floor. The rest of the brothers stand at the back, and they follow us with their eyes, thirty heads turning at once.

All of the pledges drop to one knee and huddle in a circle. There's an open Bible on the floor at the center, and we all place our hands together on top of it. Our eyes closed, the Bible underneath all the sweaty palms. We swear allegiance to God and Kappa Sigma, and I crack one eyelid slightly even though I know someone might see. Will mouths the words, his dry lips shift against each other awkwardly like he can't keep up. His eyes flutter. I close my eyes and move my lips like I mean every word.

When I step outside into the late afternoon everyone but Will Fitch is gone. He's sitting on the front steps loosening his tie. I plop down next to him. Will looks at me and nods. He picks up a leaf from beneath his feet. Starts tearing one side. Picks at the leaf delicately like he's performing surgery, and I see his right hand twitch again. I don't say anything about the twitching. I just figure if he wanted to he'd tell me.

After a silence Will turns and looks at me. Do you think you can do this? He says.

Well, I tell him, I don't know. I mean it's hard.

Really hard, he says, leaning back. School is hard enough without all of this.

Quit, I say suddenly, like it's that easy. He finishes with the leaf and throws the bare stem down.

I can't quit, he says.

Why?

Because I just can't. The same reason you don't quit. If you quit, what's left? You can't go to a party without seeing them, and besides, who wants to go to the parties that they're not at.

Lots of people.

That's bullshit and you know it, he says. People that don't matter go to those parties. These guys matter around here.

He bends down and pulls his socks up around his pale ankles. I gotta go, he says. Gotta study.

I lean forward and take the bare stem that fell near my feet. Put it in my right pocket and for a long time I sit on the steps and let the orange light warm my face.

● ● ●

Wake up, the smile says, slaps my face with his rough cold hand, walk mother-fucker, walk, he says, move your fucking legs, and they're moving. The breath is carrying me, legs all wobble and shake, I'm dragging my shoes, leaving lines in the dust toward the trunk. It's open for me. I crawl in and lie down, curled like a baby holding my legs up to my chest. The light from inside the trunk's on the smile's chest, on the breath's chest. They're standing there, and the breath sees my eyes and says don't fucking look keep your fucking eyes closed you want to breathe huh? you want to breathe? Then the trunk snaps shut and the light is gone.

● ● ●

Dixon has a football. He says we're playing Goat Invaders, a game, he explains, created on the Kappa Sig hall long ago. It has survived because it's so much fun, and this is how it goes:

We stand four feet apart, single file, all facing Dixon. We move our arms and legs in jumping jacks and bounce from wall to wall. It's supposed to look like Space Invaders. We baa like goats as we move, and I don't know if he's actually going to throw a football at us or if this is just meant to be scary. Dixon says we better not fucking duck.

My feet are grinding across the floor, and I am third in line, wedged between Will at my front and Travis, another pledge brother, at my back.

Don't you fucking flinch, Dixon says. He cocks one arm back and concentrates like it's the most important pass he's ever thrown. I turn my head slightly back toward Brett's room. He looks at me and stands and then he shuts his door.

I know the ball will hit the back of my head, and I am waiting on it but he has a good arm and he is not aiming for me. Will winces when the ball hits the middle of his back. The veins in his neck stand up. He keeps moving.

Travis kicks Dixon the ball that's settled at his feet. Dixon takes his time again, and the ball makes a dull thump when it hits Travis's head. He doesn't pretend he's aiming somewhere else, he just looks straight at Travis and throws. Travis stumbles a bit, pauses and then goes limp. He drops to his knees. Dixon calls him a pussy and tells us to keep moving and not to worry about our little bitch of a pledge brother, and we keep going back and forth until I hear the ball smack something and the air behind me moves and I know that Will's hit the ground.

Game over, Dixon says. He drops the football and walks back into his room. Will tries to stand, but his legs wobble and he falls again. Dixon leans back out and says to get the fuck off the hall. Will moves to his knees, lays his hands out in front of him and shakes his head like it's full of static. I grab his arm, help him up.

Travis is still sitting with his back turned, slumped into the wall. I open the door to leave and look back at him. He turns over, his back flat against the wall now, and he's looking up at the ceiling and smiling.

Outside Will is still dazed and has to sit on the front steps. I sit down beside him.

You okay? I say. Will puts his face in his hands. Right hand twitching.

Yeah, Will says, I'm okay, just a little dizzy.

We sit on the brick steps until his head is clear and he can walk without falling.

I start talking to myself. Walking to class, in the shower, in the cafeteria sometimes. It is a Monday night, and I am thinking about the pledge test we'll have in a few weeks and about Will and the way his hand shakes, and the air is heavy around the concrete staircase that leads up to my room. I climb the stairs and start talking.

Why are you doing this? I say.

You know.

No, I don't know.

Yes, you fucking do, you know it's all there is.

I am more than that.

Wrong again, that's the wrong fucking answer, think, just think for a minute.

It always happens like this. I get to the point where I'm about to tell myself the answer, and then it just slips away.

●●●

The moon hanging over the smile's shoulder. He is shrouded in dark, holding the trunk open. The breath beside him, dark arms at his side. The smile says get up and don't fucking look, and I've got my head down, moving my legs over the edge of the trunk, the breath pulling me out. And then I'm on my knees in the dust, looking up again. Don't look, the breath says, his foot in my ribs, and I want to say I can't see you, I can't. My voice is stuttering leave me here, take the car, just leave, I won't tell.

The smile says nah too late, tells me to get up and I can't, my legs won't move. The breath drags me by the back of my shirt, my knees against the dirt and stone. Pushes me down in front of the car. He holds me there, says put your hands behind your head, don't look up, don't move you fucking head. His hand goes, and I leave my head there, and I want to get up and run, but I am locked in, and I know that I will die soon.

The car starts, and I am waiting for the tires to break my skull, to crush my ribs. I brace and tense my muscles. Eyes closed. The car whines backward. The sound gets smaller until it is nothing, until nothing is left but the moan of insects.

●●●

On a Thursday night in early October, I call my brother, and when he picks up his phone I hear music blaring in the background: the Kappa Sigma hall party that I'm supposed to go to.

Where are you? he says.

I can't come, I say. Can we talk for a second? He pauses, the phone scraping his chin. The music rises, and he tells someone to stay the fuck out of his room. Someone says excuse me motherfucker.

Where? he says after a moment, and I can barely talk. I tell him I don't know where, and he tells me in the stairwell that connects the two sides of our dorm, and I say yes, that's fine, and I know he hears the salt in my voice, my shaking hands.

Brett sitting alone on the top step. Waiting for me when I open the door. I walk to the stairwell slowly, and he tells me not to worry, there's no one around.

I smooth my jeans out, pull the hat down over my eyes. Brett takes a pull from his cigarette and thumps it against the wall. It bounces, sends red ash like sparks from hot steel. He takes a drink from his beer.

After the drink he says talk, and I don't want to because I know I will cry. I can feel it coming already.

It's hard to talk, I say, and he nods, stares at the glass, brings the beer to his lips again. I open my mouth, and I can't say anything. I drop my head against my chest. We sit and I cry and Brett says nothing.

The door opens to our right. I look up, and my face is all wet and red, and Dixon peeks in. Brett turns, springs up, rushes at the door. He slams it closed and pounds his fists against the green metal. Stay the fuck out, he yells, stay the fuck out. He pounds his fist into the door again and backs away. Throws his beer against the door.

Goddamn you, he says, I fucking hate you, hate every one of you fucks.

He backs away and lowers his head, brings a hand to his forehead. Sits beside me again.

I'll tell them you're done, he says.

I don't know, I say, maybe I should stick it out.

No, he says, you're done. I'll tell them tomorrow.

I want to tell him that's he's all I've got left and I'm terrified of being alone, that maybe these brothers are all I've got, that I'm scared of them but I'm also scared of what I'll be without them, but nothing comes out, and I just sit there with my head bowed.

Lock your door tonight, he says, and don't answer if someone knocks.

Brett tells the brothers the next day that I am done, and they act worried, concerned, and want to know if everything is okay with me. He tells them I'm fine, and they all nod, hands laid flat over the pleats in their khakis. Eyes pinched into small slits.

There is no ceremony to strike my name. Brett speaks. They nod. I vanish.

●●●

For the next six weeks, I stay out of sight. I see the brothers and the other pledges only at a distance, from across the street or in the cafeteria. I don't see Will at all.

Then, the day before Thanksgiving, I call Brett, and no one answers. I'm supposed to ride home with him. When I go down to his room there's a note on the door. It says: Brad. Fuck man, had to leave. Ride home with Will. Brett.

I don't want to ride with Will, even though my town is on the way to his. I don't want to sit for three hours and be reminded of what he's about to finish and what I left behind. The pledges have a week left. If I had stayed, it would almost be over.

In the car on the way home, I say, You must be excited.

Oh yeah, Will says, I am. It's almost over.

Cool. Been hard I know.

Yeah, really. I didn't know if I could do it.

You did, though. That's more than I can say.

He shakes his head.

You don't feel bad about all that, do you? he says. You shouldn't. I mean it's easy for me to say that now, when I'm almost done. But really. You don't have anything to be ashamed of.

He reaches over and picks up a pack of cigarettes.

Since when do you smoke? I say.

Since I became a pledge, he says. Want one?

Sure, I say. I take the filter he's shaken over the edge of the pack. He cracks our windows and the cold air rushes through.

I'm worried about the final vote, though, he says.

Why?

I haven't been around as much as they want. They call me Ghost Fitch.

Oh, I say. I wouldn't worry. I don't think they'd vote anyone out who made it this far. It's just a scare tactic more than anything.

Yeah, you're right, he says. I just worry about stuff. I'm a worrier.

●●●

At the police station, I'm sitting across the desk from this cop with a brown mustache. We just need you to look at their pictures, he says. He leans over his desk. I want you to pay attention now, son.

He pushes a sheet toward me, and it's six men, the top row, the first two across white, the third black, and the bottom row it's one white man, the last two black, and then I see these faces, the bottom row, the last two, and I know these faces, know the mouths, the eyes. I can't stop looking at them.

Son, do you see them? the officer says, and I can't say anything, but I place my hand over the two faces, run spread fingers across the pictures, and then I hold my palm there flat, and the officer takes the picture sheet from under my hand. Then he stands up.

This is what happens: The smile flees. The breath pleads guilty. I don't testify. The breath gets seventy-five years. These are the charges: grand theft auto. Kidnapping. Strong-arm assault and battery. They're gone but they aren't gone. I can see them everywhere. The smile and the breath are out walking, just at my back.

●●●

Brett's head is in his hands when I open his door. Turns one eye toward me from beneath the hands, and it's bloodshot. I expect everyone to be running around like mad because pledge season ended last night after the final vote, but the whole hall is quiet. I ask Brett what's wrong.

You don't know? he says.

Nah, I say, what's going on?

Will, man, he says. He's dead. A heart attack. Just fucking dead in his room. I can't think anything.

This place, he says. Pulls hands back through his hair. This fucking place.

I sit down on the couch beside him and lean back.

So they voted him out, you know, he says.

What do you mean?

Last night at the final vote.

I didn't think they could do that. I thought the vote was just a formality.

It usually is. But they can still do it.

I feel like I should be screaming or running through the halls and opening doors and pulling people out, throwing them like dolls, beating them with my fists. But I don't feel anything except this high-pitched buzz in my left ear.

When did they tell him?

Last night. After the vote. Late.

Brett lights a cigarette. Hands it to me, and I take it, and he lights another one and puts it between his lips.

And today, he says, he just comes in his room after he's been studying, starts talking to his roommate. Then he's dead.

It wasn't anything to do with the vote?

You don't die from a vote.

Still.

I get it, man, but you know we can't know shit like that.

My last exam is in British Lit. For the essay question, I write my name. That's all I write. Brad. My pen moves, and the words mean nothing, I'll fail and leave today and they'll have a service for Will tomorrow at a Lutheran church in his hometown, and the brothers will be there.

●●◉

On the highway, Brett is driving, and we don't talk. We just listen to the tires spin. The sun has settled into a deep orange, thin clouds strewn along its edges. I look over. Brett has a wrist laid over the steering wheel, one hand settled in his lap.

The road stretches before us like some path we've never seen, and the pines along the edge glow in the sunlight at their backs. We open the windows all the way. The air is soft. I reach over and place my hand at the bottom of Brett's neck and squeeze. I leave it there, and he reaches over, places his hand on my shoulder. We don't speak, but we both know we won't go back to Clemson, that we won't ever go back, and nothing else is important, nothing more important than our hands and the air slipping inside to brush our faces. I let go of my brother's neck, and his hand leaves my shoulder. He leans his head out the window. Drives with his eyes closed. ❧

AFTER WORDS

"Brothers in Harm" is a collage of sections from my memoir, Goat, *a book that started as my MFA thesis at UNCW. Before the book was released,* GQ *magazine decided to print an excerpt, and while I was excited, I was somewhat worried, too. I didn't know a thing about how an excerpt worked. Even though I'd worked for months editing the soon-to-be-published book, I was having difficulty getting my head around all of it. My luck was great, though.* GQ *editor John Sullivan understood the book's form and style so well that my anxiety over how things would work was quickly put to rest. In our talks about how best to excerpt the book—all of them through a payphone booth in a mid-December, frozen-solid northern state—we decided to make something that presented key parts of the book but also stood alone. I owe all credit to John Sullivan, whose skill as a writer and editor very much boggle the mind. I believe firmly that the piece ended up the way it did due to him. When I saw "Brothers in Harm" printed, I cheered. I was outside, on a sidewalk that sloped drastically to my left, beneath a storefront overhang. The dark was coming, it was snowing hard, and no one was around to hear, so I yelled a few more times, then started toward home with the magazine tucked into my jacket. I held my mouth open and ate falling snow most of the way back.*

PETER TRACHTENBERG

CLOUDBURST

I GOT MY FIRST JOB IN 1968, at a bookstore on the Upper West
Side. It was small, but known for its brawny sections of Liberation
Studies and Beat Lit. In an earlier life, Pete, the owner, had been a
partner in a legendary San Francisco bookstore where Jack Kerouac
and Allen Ginsberg had read to yipping audiences, but there'd been a
rupture so bitter that new employees were warned never even to allude
to it. Once, Ginsberg dropped by the store and asked Pete if he'd heard
from his ex-partner lately. Pete chased him out into the street, swinging one of the iron bars we used to weigh down the newspapers on the
racks out front.

I was fifteen and liked reading and getting high, so I fit in with most
of the staff. Everyone who worked there had something wrong with
him. Pete and his wife were drunks. He was a florid, irascible drunk,
and she was a vague, dithering drunk, and they spent the day drinking
in the bar around the corner and wandering in and out of the store to
look for each other. A clerk named Al entertained at lunch by popping
his glass eye from its socket and setting it down beside his plate. Don,
the tightly wound, middle-aged manager, brushed his hair to one side

like Hitler and suspected everybody of stealing. Hour after hour, he'd glower out from beneath his Hitler quiff, his jaws chomping wrathfully. "Watch the hands!" he'd bark, and two or three customers would look up in bewilderment. "Yeah, that's right. You."

I started working on Saturday nights, assembling copies of the Sunday *Times*, but this was a bad job for someone who to this day can barely gift-wrap a book. Instead of firing me, Pete promoted me to the front counter. My drug was speed, which made me talkative, and I think he mistook this for personality. Also, speed gave me the virtue of what in any other setting would have been paranoia but compared with Don's habitual state was mere alertness. Along with the papers, we kept a lot of expensive foreign magazines out front, but nobody was going to steal any of them on my watch.

One night, some customers and I got into a conversation about whether dopers could be considered a vanguard class, in the Marxist sense. It was June, hot and very humid. Between the drugs I was on and the drugs the customers were on, we barely registered the mutter of thunder. It was only when somebody stepped outside and leaped back in, shaking himself like a dog, that I realized it was raining: pouring. It took me another moment to remember the *French Vogue, L'Uomo, Der Spiegel, Private Eye*. When I rushed outside, my clothes were instantly plastered to my skin. Between the rain and the hair in my eyes, I couldn't see. When I tried pulling a magazine from the rack, it disintegrated, and, with a moan, I scooped up the rest in my arms and carried them back into the store the way you'd carry a drowned baby you knew it was too late to save. It took two more trips to get them all.

By the time I returned with my last load, Don was standing by the counter. The veins in his forehead were pulsing in a complicated way. His pupils were so dilated that he looked like Astro Boy. Between one thumb and forefinger he was holding a limp *Cahiers du Cinéma*.

"Do you know how much this costs?" His voice was thick with strained civility.

"Uh, five bucks?"

"Very good," he said. "And this?" He picked up a *T.L.S.*, then let it drop to the floor, where it left a puddle. "That's hundreds of dollars you've cost us. Hundreds."

"Maybe you could take it out of my salary?"

"Your salary!" In an instant, his face turned red and he came at me. "You think you're going to keep working here?" he screamed. "You were supposed to keep an eye out!" He began to choke me, which was alarming but not as alarming as the fact that he was crying. "I thought you cared about this business!"

All I could say was "I'm sorry, Don. I'm helpless."

He relaxed his grip and studied me, breathing hard. "You look like a cockroach." He started laughing. He laughed so hard he had to rest his head on my shoulder, and I found myself patting him. "I swear," he gasped. "You're the funniest boy in the world." Sighing, he brushed the hair from his face. "You're fired."

But I continued to hang out at the store for years afterward, the way some people keep hanging out at their old college after graduating. I was careful to stay out of Don's way, but Pete, when he saw me, was perfectly friendly. "I got to hand it to you," he told me once. "Nobody else we had working here ever made Don cry." ◉

AFTER WORDS

I often tell writing students that it's impossible to write about yourself—or write about yourself in a way that's plausible and interesting—unless you start thinking of yourself as a character. Otherwise, you, the writer, are likely to get ensnarled in the uncertainties of who "you" are and, more perilously, to waste your time and effort making the "you" on the page—that is, the narrator—as clever, valiant, and noble as possible: in other words, in self-promotion. When writing my first book, I thought of its narrator and protagonist, the "I" whose name happened to be Peter Trachtenberg, as a cartoon version of my actual self. He was a little dumber, a little more appetite-driven, a little more cowardly and venal. Also, shorter. With this distinction in mind, I was able to set him free on the page. Of course this distancing required authorial effort, a willful translation of the noble being I really am into a flawed but lovable doofus. But when writing "Cloudburst," I didn't have to create a cartoon. As a fifteen-year-old bookstore clerk, I really was a cartoon. At least that is how I remember myself.

TIM BASS

CONFESSIONS OF A DIMWITTED WORD THIEF

"I HAD LUNCH WITH CLODFELTER," someone might say to me. "He's quite the raconteur."

Even though I listen to the whole sentence, I absorb only *raconteur*. My brain pauses for an instant to savor the throaty sound and marvel at that extraordinary word's appearance in ordinary conversation. I stand momentarily muted, more intrigued by *raconteur* than by Clodfelter and his fabulous stories.

I play the word over to myself. *Raconteur*. I like this one. It feels full and round, a little whispery. Different. This is a word I can't think up on my own, because I deal in average vocabulary. The closest I get is *raccoon*, which I say often, but *raccoon* does not pack the exotic zing of *raconteur*. And I believe they have different definitions.

Words get in the way. They do things to me. I don't mean they merely spark my imagination, challenge my beliefs, and enlighten my understanding. I mean they *do* things to me. Some words are so unique, so singularly fit—so *right*—they pull me out of a conversation or a book and do a turn to amuse me, elegant ballerinas in the spotlight. Sometimes the sounds snatch my attention, and the words take on human characteristics: *Raconteur* sports a beret and a skinny mustache, *verisimilitude* wears a little black dress at a cocktail party, and *bazooka* smokes cigars and burps in public. Other times, the meanings of words grab me. I had not expected *expectorate* would have anything to do with spitting, or *restive* with not resting. The sparkle of these little linguistic jewels dazzles me, and briefly I stop—cease listening or reading long enough to admire how these stellar words brighten a dull sentence.

This is like going to a party and discovering something artful and bold on the serving table. There on a silver tray, in the company of the stone-ground crackers and California cauliflower, we spot fresh radishes carved into crimson daisies. Suddenly, we know we're not munching party snacks—no, we're having *hors d'oeuvres*. Me? I don't buy radishes. If you come to a party at my house, expect pretzels in a chipped bowl, no pretty vegetables, and lots of garden-variety vocabulary. "I've invited Clodfelter," I'll say to the guests. "He's quite the raccoon." I appreciate the efforts of the Radish Word Party People. They bring out the fine china—no use for that paper-plate *storyteller* when there's an exquisite *raconteur* in the cabinet.

Don't get me wrong. I'm talking here about good words—robust and salubrious words, not gargantuan ones. I grow suspicious when someone freights a sentence with *objectification, positivistic,* or *utilitarian*. Fifty-dollar words make me think of the price, not the value. When I hear a politician pledge "bipartisan cooperation in clarifying an agenda for the purpose of achieving measurable progress on behalf of the citizenry," I think, there's no way I'll vote for this show dog.

Expensive words annoy me. Rich words enchant me.

Thus, an admission: when I hear an especially colorful word, a bona fide doozie such as *philandering* or *boondoggle* or *philistinism,* I feel a twinge of disappointment for failing to use it first. This is nothing severe—no self-abuse with my thesaurus or hasty mail orders for Verbal Advantage lessons. But I do experience a sub-surface recognition that somebody got his mouth on a savory word before I did.

Thus, a confession: I envy those people, the ones who use *mellifluous, viscosity,* and *prevaricate.* And *avuncular, correlative, profligate, symbiotic, patrician,* and most any *–acious* word—*mendacious, salacious, rapacious,* etc. I envy people who say *paramilitary* and know what it means (I picture a soldier with a parachute). I envy people who say *raconteur.* I have heard envy stands among the most malignant sins, exacting an exorbitant toll on the soul. If so, I am doomed. Word envy prompts me to take from others, claiming for myself the choice utterances of friends and strangers, colleagues and acquaintances, authors and performers. If I hear somebody say *wanton*, in no time I will go into the talking world and toss it around as if it were my own. "It is," I will sniff, "a wanton disregard for the truth—profligate prevarication by an avuncular yet patrician raconteur." I will not understand what I have said, but I will beam over how it sounded.

I don't consider this wanton use of other people's glittering words to be stealing. I call it larceny. In my mind, *larceny* takes the shape not of a convict, but of a neighbor who borrows garden tools habitually and without permission, yet always intends to return them eventually. Someday. Possibly.

When I take words, I simply must not do it around those who said them to me first. If I do, they might punish me with fresh, Herculean words that reach even further beyond my lexical limits. As soon as they discover I have purloined their *oracular*, they will bring out *delphian*, sparking more envy and another turn in my ceaseless cycle.

These days, I am trying to work *serendipitous* into a conversation. A friend says it often, usually during one of his stories about a series of dire and complicated events that somehow broke in his favor, and once again all worked out to his benefit. "It's serendipitous," he'll say, as if that explains it all. I think of *serendipitous* as a rider on a roller coaster—level, then going down, then thrillingly up, then down, and finally level again. I almost said serendipitous the other night, when I trumped up an excuse to leave a party early (there were no radishes). Unfortunately, the host was talking to my serendipitous friend, who was probably using the word at that moment. So I had to rely on my own words, small and ordinary. "I've got to go," I said. Later, I realized I would have hurt the host's feelings to say I was leaving the party on a serendipitous excuse. But I didn't say it, and I departed without disrespecting the host or getting caught in word larceny. I call that serendipitous.

I feel some guilt over my unauthorized borrowing of words, but I soothe my conscience with mental footnotes. When I say someone else's word, I slide in a tiny brain asterisk to acknowledge the owner. Each time I use *hubris*, I remember the unemployed construction worker who said it when I interviewed him on the opening day of bombing in the first Gulf War. I adore *lilliputian*, which a friend uttered when I handed her an unforgivably small cup of ice cream. I say *egregious* a lot—"It's an egregious violation"—and I remember hearing that one from a prosecutor who was trying to send a killer to death row. I like *egregious* so much that I scout constantly for violations of any kind (jaywalking laws, rules of etiquette, my sense of outrage), so I can huff with disapproval and announce, "What an egregious display of hubris. Egregious *and* wanton. Downright rapacious." That one is packed with footnotes.

I have a long list of credits. I inherited *cantankerous* from my great-grandfather. I took *snarky* from a cop on television. The only place I have ever seen or heard *snoozle* is in *Wuthering Heights*, and I plan someday to write a scene that will make me the second author in literary history to employ that word. I will never forget the dermatologist who offered a dignified term for my sweaty palms: *hyperhidrosis*. I have been trying for years to slip *hornswoggle* into conversations, and when I finally do I'll tip my invisible hat to the man who taught it to me—Al Bundy on *Married . . . With Children*.

Several illustrious words in my possession came from my friend John. I cannot say *recalcitrant, anaconda, furtive*, or *behemoth* without thinking of him. John once described a man as *orbicular*. I had never heard it, but I had only to look at that spherical man to understand the word's rotund meaning. Today when I say *orbicular*—and I say it often—a star shows up in my mind, crediting John.

Many other ripe words grab me, all for no reason other than their unique sounds. *Propensity, gregarious, hexagonal, amiably, narcissism, bombastic, impel, kleptomaniac*. The list has no end. I cannot hear *united* without thinking that transposing just two letters makes a word with an opposite meaning: untied. The Untied States. Every time I hear *reconnoiter* I think the speaker has used not one word but three. I believe it is impossible to "reek an order," but I don't know what reconnoiter means because I can't get beyond its sound.

Often a word distracts me because the sound perfectly fits the meaning. *Diarrhea* does this, along with *stinky*, and, while we're at it, *toilet, clog, plunger*, and *suction*. *Raunchy* and *vomit* do well for themselves, as do *hooligan, smoldering, nugget, spineless,* and *counterrevolutionary.* The word *henchman* works because it describes at once the man and his duty—henching. The same goes for the *flunky,* the *lackey,* the *toady,* and the *bootlick.*

Coagulated. Dilettante. Ephemeral. So many words stop me, pull me aside, spin me in all directions. *Intractable. Munificent. Perpetuity.* From *aardvark* to *zygote,* countless logs lie across the path of my communication. The very words people use often separate me from what they're trying to tell me. *Serpentine. Unceremonious. Venal.* Many folks can't see the forest for the trees. I can't hear the message for the words.

At a Chinese restaurant the other night, I noticed the Chicken with Tangerine Sauce ($12.95). The menu described it this way: "Felicitous golen-yellow tangerine sauce bring a deliciously tangy taste to this dish." I ignored the missing d in golen and the obvious subject/verb disagreement. Who cares about spelling and grammar when there's a *felicitous* on the page? I marveled at that scrumptious word. I had heard food called savory and succulent and all other manner of mouthwatering adjectives. But never felicitous. This plate, this choice Chicken with Tangerine Sauce, did not just please the palate. It promised to brighten the heart. When the server came, I was so busy scrawling the felicitous description on a torn napkin that I absently ordered a different entree—something sweet and sour with pineapple and pepper. It was the next day before I realized my little dalliance with felicity had cost me the chance to consume happiness.

So I endure this affliction. I go on listening and reading, and inevitably those words—those orbicular words: graceful dancers, etched flowers—arise to thrill me and tempt me. I pause for them, say hello. I set them on the sensitive scale of verbal value—sound on one side, meaning on the other—and weigh them for their worth in the market of communication. Then I make them mine. ●

AFTER WORDS

I wrote this piece as an ode—not just to wonderful words, but also to those who know how, when, and where to use them. Words fascinate me, and I suppose I'm such a visual thinker that I see the best words dancing before me, performing as if on a stage. It's a silly little piece, but I had a good time writing it. The original version was far different—shorter, with more telling and less showing. An editor at Fugue *suggested some changes, which prompted me to reopen the whole story and delve back in. I spent a couple of weeks rewriting. When I finished, the story had a lot more life—more words, for sure, and now some of them had grown facial hair, wore dresses, and smoked cigars. I had fun writing the original piece, and even more fun revising. The first title was "Orbicular Words," and the editor suggested I change it simply to "Words." I didn't like that. At the last minute, the new title raced into my mind. "Confessions of a Dimwitted Word Thief" seemed to sum it up. I still love the words egregious and profligate. And none is better than raunchy.*

DANA SACHS

THE HOUSE ON DREAM STREET: AN EXCERPT

I LOVED BEING IN VIETNAM as much as I ever had, but my relationship with the country wasn't delicate in the way it had once been. I wasn't worried that if I spent the day with another foreigner I'd somehow lose touch with the real Vietnam. Now, I no longer thought of my friends in terms of who was a foreigner and who was Vietnamese, and I didn't worry about coming across as the Ugly American. My nationality no longer defined my identity here. If I did something stupid, it wasn't because I was American. It was because I was stupid. And I found myself for the first time getting into arguments.

One night, I went with two new friends, Van and Duc, to see the French film *Indochine*. Van and Duc were talented painters I'd met through Steve. Their work would have fetched high prices had they chosen to pursue the increasingly hot market in Vietnamese art. But rather than schmoozing with potential patrons, they spent most of their time hanging out in Duc's studio, a stilt house on the edge of the West Lake, where they painted, drank whiskey, and pontificated about the state of the world.

The screening of the film, which was playing at the Eighth of August Cinema in the center of town, was a big event for Hanoi. *Indochine*, a film about the Vietnamese revolt against French colonialism, was one of the first Western films to arrive as the country slowly opened its door to the outside world. Everyone wanted to see it, and not just the star-struck Hanoians who had managed to capture a glimpse of the star, Catherine Deneuve, while she was filming on location. Outside the theater, ticket scalpers proved they knew a thing about capitalism by rushing back and forth across the sidewalks and jumping in front of passing motorists in a frenzied effort to secure their sales. Inside the theater, nearly every seat was filled and the audience had to strain to see through a fog of cigarette smoke and to hear through the grinding crunch of sunflower seeds. But unlike the bemused, rather bored reactions I'd witnessed at the *Tower of the Screaming Virgins* a few months earlier, the audience at *Indochine* was clearly captivated. It represented most Hanoians' first chance to see a Western film projected on the big screen, and people's reactions to the production quality must have been similar to the way American audiences responded in 1939, when Dorothy stepped out of her black and white cabin and walked into Technicolor Oz. "Dep. Dep," I heard people whisper all around me: *Beautiful.*

After the film ended, the three of us went to get something to eat. It was nearly eleven already, past bedtime for most of Hanoi, and my favorite noodle shop had long ago pulled its metal doors shut for the night. A few establishments were still open, serving noodle soup and rice porridge to tipsy men trying to sober up on their way home. We sat down at a table on the sidewalk in the middle of the block, right next to a sewage drain that ran along the side of the road. The proprietor, a mustached man wearing a Tiger Beer T-shirt, was sitting on a stool next to his charcoal cooker.

"What do you want to eat?" he grumbled.

Duc and Van ordered fish porridge. I asked for a Bay Up—Vietnamese for Seven-Up.

Both of my friends were still feeling dazzled by the movie. They were used to the grainy black and white or washed-out color that characterized

Vietnamese cinema. In contrast, the French film's luscious palette and perfectly defined contrasts of light and dark left them breathless. They didn't like the movie, though.

"The French!" Van said, with a dismissive wave of his hand. "They don't know anything about the war. It's worse than that movie, I'll tell you." Van, who was my age, was a thin, often grouchy man whose delight in the world only became evident in the soft, romantic quality of his paintings. In contrast, Duc, who was nearly forty, was lumbering and cheerful, with a soft voice and a shag of bushy hair.

Van lit a cigarette. During the movie, he'd smoked his way through half a dozen 555s. "Westerners will see that film and think they understand Vietnam," he said. "It's like me saying, because I've seen a few videos, that life is easy in America, that it's just Walt Disney over there."

Duc and I laughed. The proprietor came over and plopped the rice porridge and Bay Up down in the center of the table. Van hardly noticed the food. Duc immediately took his bowl and spoon and began stirring sprigs of fresh dill into the thick mass of porridge.

I pulled open my drink and took a sip of the warm soda. "It's true," I said. I knew that Van and Duc had both seen Hollywood war movies on video. "The only thing most Americans know about the Vietnam War is what they've seen in *Apocalypse Now* or *Platoon*."

Instead of laughing, Van looked irritated, as if he found America's myopia more disturbing than Vietnam's. "Americans don't know anything about war," he told me. "You haven't had a war in your country in over a hundred years. You're lucky! But still, whenever a single American dies in battle, you're furious. You lost fifty-eight thousand Americans in Vietnam. We lost two million Vietnamese. You bombed us. We never bombed you. But still, it was the United States, not Vietnam, who held a grudge."

In another situation, I would probably have agreed with Van. After all, at that time, the U.S. was still maintaining its vituperative trade embargo against Vietnam, keeping the struggling nation from fully recovering from the double economic disasters of the war and several decades of Communism. But the antagonism in Van's voice made me defensive. Not bothering to hide my sarcasm, I answered, "Oh, right. The Vietnamese would never, ever hold a grudge."

We looked at each other for a long moment, each of us trying to decide how far to let this conversation go. Finally, Van pulled back a little. "It's just sad, that's all," he said, his tone only slightly less caustic. "All over the world, people know about American hamburgers, American blue jeans, American cars. These are good things. They help to build a strong country. We Vietnamese beat the Americans and what are we famous for? War! In this century alone we've fought the French, Japanese, Americans, Cambodians, and Chinese. If we didn't have to fight all those wars, maybe we'd be rich now. We'd be the ones visiting Walt Disneyland and making blue jeans."

Van pulled his bowl of porridge closer, as if to signal that he'd had enough of this conversation. After only a couple of spoonfuls, though, he looked up again. This time he had a grin on his face and I could see that he'd thought of a way to move the conversation toward friendlier ground. He leaned forward and poked Duc in the arm. "Remember the Gulf War?" he asked.

Duc laughed. "Yeah," he said. He kept eating his porridge.

Van turned to me. "We Vietnamese appreciated the Gulf War. For once, there was this huge international conflict going on and we didn't have to fight in it. We just sat around like everybody else in the world, watching it on TV."

Loud voices behind us made us turn around. The proprietor, back on his stool by the charcoal cookers, was yelling at a newspaper boy, one of the hundreds of often homeless children who spent their days walking the city streets, selling papers, cheap magazines, and horoscopes. The "boy" was at least twenty, with a slightly deranged look on his face. He wasn't arguing as much as whining, but the angry proprietor suddenly jumped up and boxed his ear. The newspaper boy raised his hand to his head and howled.

"I'm bleeding," he screamed.

The proprietor sat back down, pulled out a rag, and began to wipe the table in front of him.

"My ear! I'm bleeding," the newspaper boy screamed again. I had a momentary worry that he would pull out a gun and shoot us all, but this was not America. He cried for a few more seconds, then turned and wandered off down the street, holding his hand to his ear.

Street fights took place so regularly here that spectators watched them like fireworks, focusing for the instant of the flare and then losing interest as soon as it faded. I had more trouble forgetting such incidents. An American could hardly complain about the violence in Vietnam—after all, violent crime was relatively rare here—but the easy acceptance of petty brutality always bothered me. I watched the newspaper boy, who was peering into the rear-view mirror of a parked motorbike, checking for signs of blood.

"Let's go," I said.

As we got up to leave, Duc pulled a pack of chewing gum out of his pocket and handed sticks to Van and me. Van tore the wrapper off his gum and tossed the paper onto the asphalt of the road.

"What's wrong with you?" I snapped. "How can you pollute your country?"

Van turned and looked at me. "Americans," he said calmly. "You think you can tell us how to keep our country clean after you dropped napalm and Agent Orange on us?"

I was so angry and humiliated that I couldn't look at him. But I no longer felt the guilt I'd always experienced when I thought about the war in Vietnam, as if, just by being an American, I was responsible for what my country had done. I regretted the war more than I ever had, having seen how it affected this city, and the lives of the people I'd come to know. But over the past eighteen months, my sense of this place had changed dramatically. I'd once thought of Vietnam with the same stereotypes that one would use to describe a battered woman: miserable, victimized, helpless. Now I would have used an entirely different set of adjectives: tough, resilient, passionate. As much as Vietnam had suffered, it didn't need my guilt. It might need my help—normalizing relations was a good start—but what Van had said was true. The only thing Vietnam was famous for were the wars. I'd come to see the place as more complex than that. If I could go for weeks at a time in Hanoi without even remembering the wars, perhaps Americans could forge something new with Vietnam, and move beyond the past.

So I didn't break down when Van mentioned the napalm, and I didn't apologize either. And that was a good thing, too, because when I looked over at him, I saw that he was grinning, waiting to see how I'd react. I looked at him for a moment. "I don't know," I said. "Napalm or a Wrigley's wrapper. It's not an easy call."

In what might have been the clearest sign that the war was truly over, a Vietnamese and an American discovered that it wasn't that hard, actually, to joke about it. ❧

AFTER WORDS

My book The House on Dream Street *describes my experiences living in Hanoi, Vietnam, in the 1990s. Though I always hoped to write a book about my time there, I never knew which of my experiences would end up being interesting enough to write about, and which ones wouldn't. While there, I took lots of notes in my journal and wrote detailed letters home, trying to record and make sense of what was happening to me. Later, when I returned to the United States, I began to go through this cache of writing and figure out what might work in a book. My night at the movies with these two friends offered a good opportunity to reflect on many of the issues I'd dealt with throughout my time in Vietnam—the history of the war, my role as an American in Vietnam, and the ways in which our relationship with a place (and it's people) changes over time. In order to make the story flow well as a narrative, I had to manipulate it somewhat. For example, a few of the things that I quote Van saying that night were actually things he said to me on other occasions. It would have been impossible to include every single thing that happened to me there, so by choosing carefully between various experiences I tried to create a narrative that reflected the broader truths of my experience in Hanoi.*

PHILIP FURIA

BLUE SKIES
from IRVING BERLIN:
A LIFE IN SONG

ONE EVENING IN MAY of 1924, Irving Berlin wandered down to Jimmy Kelly's. Throughout his life he had a habit of returning to his old haunts in Union Square, Chinatown, and the Bowery, a habit easily indulged in a city where no matter how far up—or down—the ladder of success you had climbed, you could reach your antipodes by walking a few blocks. On this particular night, Berlin may have been more than usually reflective about the course of his career. While he was undoubtedly the premier American songwriter, his hold upon that position was tenuous. It may have already been clear that he could not maintain it by writing scores for revues at the Music Box Theatre, and he was not ready to plunge into the newly emerging genre of the integrated musical comedy. Already, younger songwriters were vying for his mantle. On February 24, 1924, Paul Whiteman presented a concert at Aeolian Hall that purported to fuse jazz with the classics. Much of that program, however, including a "Semi-Symphonic Arrangement" of Irving Berlin's songs, proved drearily monotonous; only when young George Gershwin strode to the piano, nodded to Whiteman, then plunged into *Rhapsody in Blue*, did it become clear that jazz had found a new spokesman.

If Berlin could not clearly foresee his future in American song, a look backward at his past seemed to suggest that his stunning career had reached a plateau. His friend Alexander Woollcott was writing a biography of the songwriter—an enormous tribute, yet one that suggested a sense of closure. Woollcott traced Berlin's rise from the immigrant Lower East Side to the heights of American success, romanticizing his subject as an untutored genius who drew upon his melancholy heritage as a Russian Jew. Woollcott predicted that his music would endure only after a trained composer had transmuted it, as Liszt and Chopin had taken anonymous folk melodies and lifted them into the realm of classic art. While Woollcott acknowledged that it was unusual to write the biography of a man in his mid-thirties, his book implied that Berlin had come as far, creatively, as someone like him possibly could.

What may have made Irving Berlin especially reflective on this particular night, however, was that he had not come to Jimmy Kelly's alone. With him was a lovely and sophisticated young lady named Ellin Mackay. Earlier that evening, they had met at a fashionable dinner party. She had charmed him by saying, "Oh, Mr. Berlin, I do so like your song, 'What Shall I Do?'" And he, after correcting her about the title of his latest hit, graciously acknowledged the propriety of her distinction between *shall* and *will*: "Where grammar is concerned," he joked, "I can always use a little help." After dinner he invited her to accompany him to Jimmy Kelly's, which had become, in the parlance of the Prohibition era, a "speakeasy." Kelly had also moved from his old Union Square location to Sullivan Street in Greenwich Village, the heart of artistic experiment, social protest, and Bohemian lifestyles in the Jazz Age.

The transformation of Jimmy Kelly's was indicative of the vast changes in American social mores that had taken place since Berlin worked there as a singing waiter. The coming of the cabaret around 1910 had threatened to break down the barriers between the social classes, to place young girls from the highest echelons of society next to men from the lower and even immigrant classes. Dancing, dining, and the intimate floor show invited the expression and exploration of private experience, once confined to the homes of a closely knit society, into the open, public domain. The redefinition of the American girl that had started out with Irene Castle as the healthy, active, fox-trotting playmate of 1914 had, ten years later, transmogrified into the Jazz Age flapper, kicking up her stockingless legs in the Charleston.

The encounter between Irving Berlin and Ellin Mackay was the most dramatic upshot of these changes in American society. Barely twenty-one, the lithe, blonde Ellin came from the highest reaches of society. Her father, Clarence Mackay, on the strength of his father's fortune—spawned by the fabled Nevada Comstock silver mines and invested in the telegraph system—was one of the wealthiest and most prominent men in New York. Ellin had grown up at his estate on Long Island, gone to the finest private schools, and in 1922 made her debut into society at a ball at the Ritz-Carlton. In the fall of 1924, she would dance with the Prince of Wales, who was destined to become King Edward VIII of England until he, in an even more scandalous crossing of class barriers, gave up the throne to marry a divorced commoner.

Ellin, however, had literary aspirations, and she found herself drawn to Greenwich Village and to her mother's cousin, Alice Duer Miller, a member of the Algonquin Round Table. The Round Table itself exemplified social mixing among people like Woollcott and Franklin Pierce Adams, who came from solid gentility; George S. Kaufman and Dorothy Parker, who stemmed from wealthy Jewish families; and Jews like Berlin and Herbert Swope, who had struggled up from poverty. For a flower of New York society like Ellin Mackay to mingle with such a mongrel group, however literate, testified to the breakdown of class distinctions. Ellin knew it and capitalized upon it. In 1925 she would write an essay, "Why We Go to Cabarets: A Post-Debutante Explains," for the *New Yorker*, the new magazine founded by Round Tabler Herbert Ross to set a standard of wit, insouciance, and urbanity.

Ellin's essay gleefully satirized the dreaded influence of cabarets on American society:

> Our Elders criticize many things about us, but usually they attribute sins too gaudy to be true. The trouble is that our Elders are a trifle gullible; they have swallowed too much of F. Scott Fitzgerald . . . They believe all the backstage gossip

that is written about us . . . Cabaret has its place in the elderly mind beside Bohemia and Bolshevik, and other vague words that have a sinister significance and no precise definition . . . We have privacy in a cabaret . . . What does it matter if an unsavory Irish politician is carrying on a dull and noisy flirtation with the little blonde at the table behind us? We don't have to listen; we are with people we find amusing.

In just such a cabaret, Ellin Mackay had fulfilled the worst of those fears by finding companionship with an immigrant Jewish songwriter. In Ellin, Berlin found the high spirit of his first wife, Dorothy, together with the literate sophistication of his current friends from the Algonquin Round Table.

When he learned that his daughter was involved with Berlin, Clarence Mackay was incensed. The fact that his family was Catholic made him vigilant in guarding his social standing. While Mackay could be friendly with wealthy Jews who moved in his own social circle, such as Otto Kahn and Bernard Berenson, it was unthinkable that his daughter would be courted by an immigrant Jew from Tin Pan Alley. His vigilance was heightened by the fact that his own wife, Katherine Duer Mackay, had earlier become entangled in an affair with a prominent society surgeon, Dr. Joseph Blake. When Clarence Mackay refused, on Catholic tenets, to grant her a divorce, Katherine traveled to Paris, where Dr. Blake headed an American Red Cross hospital during World War I. There she married her lover and left Mackay to Harbor Hill, his magnificent Long Island estate, and to his bitterness.

That bitterness flared anew over his daughter's association with Irving Berlin. Although he himself had taken a mistress, Anna Case, she was from the upper echelon of the musical world, a concert singer who had been a star at the Metropolitan Opera, where Mackay was a member of the board of directors. When he learned that Ellin and Berlin were seen together at parties, he hired private detectives to investigate the songwriter and keep him away from Harbor Hill. When he could turn up nothing damaging, he whisked his daughter off to Europe in the hope that other suitors would expunge the memory of Berlin.

What Mackay did not realize was that removing his daughter from New York would only intensify Berlin's feelings, which do not seem to have been as committed to the relationship, until that point, as Ellin's were. Later she admitted that in those early days she had been the pursuer. However, in her absence, Berlin seems to have felt his midlife emptiness all the more keenly. A newer, youthful era was emerging as epitomized by the success of the Gershwins' *Lady, Be Good!*, while Berlin, along with the revues to which he had committed himself and his theater, seemed to be ebbing into the past. In his first marriage he had hoped to find an escape from the demons that drove him to maintain the success he had achieved with "Alexander's Ragtime Band." As he contemplated this new commitment, it may have seemed a bulwark against the vicissitudes of time and fortune. ❧

AFTER WORDS

I first became interested in writing about American popular songs and songwriters when I was Fulbright professor in Austria in 1984. I was teaching a course on the Jazz Age, in which the class read poetry and fiction, looked at paintings and architecture, and listened to jazz. But my Austrian students wanted to know what popular music was like in the 1920s. I had to admit I didn't know. After class I went to the library and was amazed to find that the songs I'd listened to since I was a kid—songs by the Gershwins, Irving Berlin, Cole Porter—had been the popular songs of the 1920s. When I next met with my Austrian students, I thought, I could not only tell them about popular songs of the 1920s, I could show them by playing my tapes of Sinatra and other singers. Although their English was good, I thought I'd help them by typing out and photocopying the lyrics. As I typed lines like "You're a rose, you're Inferno's Dante / You're the nose on the great Durante," I thought, "Wow! That's like something e. e. cummings would write." Since then I stopped writing about modern American poets and have been writing about popular song.

STANLEY COLBERT

NOTES ON THE GREAT DEPRESSION

AS I REMEMBER IT, the Great Depression came quickly.

My father suddenly stopped wearing suits and going to an office. We moved from a house to an apartment. After a while my father left the house wearing a brown uniform with a leather clip-on bowtie. He had found a job as an attendant at an Esso station. He pumped gas and wiped windshields. That didn't last very long. A few blocks away, the Socony station put up a sign that read SIX GALLONS FOR A DOLLAR! The owner of my father's station countered with a sign: SIX GALLONS FOR 99 CENTS! That worked for a few days until the Socony station posted SIX GALLONS FOR 98 CENTS! In less than a week, both gas stations went out of business. My father threw away the leather bowtie. We moved to a cold-water flat over a tire store where the rent was five dollars a month. It was called a cold-water flat because there was no heat or hot water.

For kids like me, too old to be underfoot and too young to be in school, the Depression became a challenge. It was important not to be an added burden to our parents and we became self-sufficient quickly. My first order of business was to scout the empty lots that dotted the neighborhood for discarded wooden boxes or anything that looked combustible. Cooking and heating in our flat was performed by a large woodburning stove in the kitchen. Buying wood was out of the question. The empty crates outside the fruit and vegetable markets provided the best source. That discovery also led a few of us kids to a solution to our hunger. We became adept at unashamedly stealing potatoes from the baskets outside of markets. We'd target a different one each day, saunter past in twos or threes, and while one of us distracted the shopkeeper, the others pocketed the potatoes. We'd take them to an empty lot, build a small fire, and bury the potatoes in the ashes. When we couldn't wait any longer, we'd dig them out, scrape off the black soot and eat them. More often than not, they weren't fully cooked, but it didn't matter. They were a filling alternative to the rations that faced us when we got home.

I didn't know how my mother found out I was eating roasted mickeys, as we called our charred potatoes, until she finally told me the tip-off was the rim of black around my lips and my teeth. She never asked how we got them.

For the longest period of time, most of our meals at home revolved around Heinz ketchup. No Depression home was without it. Thinned with hot water, it served as a tasty soup. Add a Kaiser roll (three for a nickel) and it was dinner. Poured straight from the bottle it became a sauce for spaghetti. Lathered on a tough piece of cheap beef it helped the chewing and made the meat palatable.

A few odd jobs that my father found helped pay the rent and a little more. And somehow, my parents always found something to laugh about, which kept our spirits up. Then Roosevelt was elected and promised change, but it was a long time coming. I continued to scour the streets for empty pop bottles that returned a deposit of two cents each. We searched the trash bins outside bus stops and subway stations for newspapers that contained the occasional White Castle coupon, offering six hamburgers for twenty-five cents.

As I got older and taller and began my schooling, I needed new clothes, so my parents took me to the Lower East Side, where pushcart vendors offered bargains in clothing. Whatever we bought was always a size larger than it needed to be, so I could grow into it. For years I had one pair of shoes, from Thom McAn at $3.95, a major investment. As a result, they were periodically refurbished with soles and heels by the local shoemaker until I could no longer get my feet into them. Somewhere I have a fading photograph of a class picture, where all the boys were supposed to wear jackets. I didn't own one. Out of concern, one of the girls lent me her jacket for the picture, and if you look closely, you can see that I'm the only boy with a jacket buttoning the wrong way.

In those years, my father's daily routine was predictable. Each evening, around eight o'clock, he would give me a nickel to buy the next day's *Daily News* and *Daily Mirror*, which were two cents each. The next day the tabloid papers were just the right size to stuff inside my shirt or sweater as insulation against the cold. Pages, folded small enough to fit inside shoes, provided an added layer of protection from the rain or snow.

Each morning my father would shave early, dress, have a cup of coffee, and take twenty-five cents from the Maxwell House coffee tin that contained our fortune. On his way to the subway he would stop at the newspaper kiosk on the corner and place a ten-cents bet on a horse. The kiosk operator was our local bookie, an arm of the Mafia family that controlled gambling in the neighborhoods. Subway fare into the belly of the city, where most of the agencies with job postings were located, was five cents each way. On his way home, after the usual uneventful job search, he would stop at the local bakery and pick up three pieces of pastry for a nickel. They sometimes took the place of dinner.

We were down to a handful of quarters in the coffee can on the morning my father stopped at the kiosk to place his daily bet. A car pulled up and a large, well-dressed man stepped out and proceeded to collect the proceeds of the previous day's bets. He stared at my father and asked, "Jay?"

My father nodded and said, "Vince. How the hell are you?"

They had grown up together in Harlem, when it was predominately Jewish and Italian. They had been childhood friends.

"How're you doin'?" Vince asked.

"Not good," my father replied.

"You went to college," Vince said. "I remember."

"Columbia," my father said.

"How're you with numbers? Still as good as ever?"

My father had been a math whiz, to the amusement of the kids on his street. "Still good."

"We need someone to run a horse room in West New York, New Jersey. Handle all the bets, the odds, the payouts. You interested?"

"I'm interested."

"It's with the Family," Vince said. "You know what I mean? You got any trouble with that?"

There was no hesitation. The cold-water flat would be a thing of the past. There would be new shoes, instead of another set of soles and heels. There'd something on the table besides Heinz ketchup.

"When do I start?" my father asked. ❧

AFTER WORDS

The first stories I sold, in the days of fat, slick magazines, were short-shorts, 1500-word slices of life with a kicker at the end. In the years that followed, my stories got longer but the kicker remained. After this piece appeared, the editor received almost a hundred reader comments, half of them sharing their own experiences during the Depression and the other half wanting to know what happened to my father. But that's another story. Take my word for it: reading about the Depression is better than being there.

POETRY CRAFT

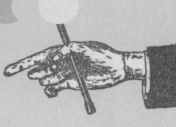

MARK COX

●●●●●●●●●●

WHAT IS POETRY?

"If I read a book and it makes my whole body so cold no fire can ever warm me, I know it is poetry. If I feel physically as if the top of my head were taken off, I know this is poetry."

—Emily Dickinson, *Selected Letters*

"My poetry is a kind of religion for me. It's a way of seeking redemption for myself, but just on the page. It is, finally, a way of understanding things so that they can be reconciled, explained, justified, redeemed."

—Gerald Stern, *The Language of Life*

"The most beautiful experience we can have is the mysterious. It is the fundamental emotion that stands at the cradle of true art and true science. Whoever does not know it and can no longer wonder, no longer marvel, is as good as dead, and his eyes are dimmed."

—Albert Einstein, "The World As I See It"

"It is not merely with his whole soul, it is with his entire being that the poet approaches the poem. What presides over the poem is not the most lucid intelligence, or the most acute sensibility, but an entire experience: all the women loved, all the desires experienced, all the dreams dreamed, all the images received and grasped, the whole weight of the body, the whole weight of the mind. All lived experience. All the possibility."

—Aimé Césaire, *Poetry and Knowledge*

"Poetic thought proceeds by enacting union . . . and what a poem binds together are elements drawn from the writer's private experiences, elements possessing public meaning and interest, which are therefore able to resound in the experience of the reader."

—Stanley Burnshaw, *The Seamless Web*

I AM TEMPTED TO BE A BIT FLIP, to define poetry as any intense and concentrated writing that resists definition. Then again, perhaps that isn't so flippant, after all. What *is* poetry? I am a poet. I have written it for forty years and have taught it as a subject for nearly a quarter century. I think I know a poem when I see one; I think I know poetry when I experience it. And yet I still don't know how to answer the question I have been asked to address in this essay: What is poetry? I recall reading a study pertaining to sensory deprivation and hallucination in which the researchers noted that critical areas hadn't been explored or classified because they simply could never obtain full clinical reports from drowsy subjects. In other words, the subjects couldn't relay information consciously while in a subconscious state. Likewise, when attempting to talk about the challenges and limitations of language, we have to use the very language we are discussing. And though one of poetry's gifts is to help us cut through this dilemma—to somehow bring the inner and outer worlds into a focused relationship—we still face similar difficulties when attempting to define poetry. There are limits to what can be learned by performing formal autopsies on living poems or on the altered consciousness of the person who has just read them. Most of the resonant feelings of, and reactions to, poetry rest in mystery, ambiguity, and uncertainty.

So, how do we know if it is a poem or not? Language itself is simply a system of symbols about which we more or less choose to agree. There are, then, guidelines to be followed in order for communication to take place. Poet and reader must agree as to what the words stand for, what the rhythm of phrasing and the intensity of inflection connote, etc. To fully appreciate and understand a poem, as in appreciating any specialized activity (say, football, bridge, or opera), one must learn the ground rules.

This education is able to offer terminology for understanding common devices and concepts in poetry. Any introduction to the study of poetry will invariably break down clear information about economy of words, rhythm, meter, rhyme, metaphor, repetition, diction, lineation, sound systems, etc. But these conventions of style may be limited to what a particular culture during a particular period of time accepts as a "poem." The danger, then, is that often we may rely so heavily on a set of rules that they become obstructions to the appreciation of something "other." In his book *Language in Thought and Action,* S.I. Hayakawa notes that chimps can be taught to drive simple cars. However, if the light turns red while the chimp is in the middle of the intersection, the chimp will stop where he is, and if the light turns green, the chimp will go whether the car ahead has gone or not. Hayakawa claims that this exemplifies a case wherein red and green lights are no longer *symbols* subject to interpretation and collective common sense; they *are* stop and go.

Sometimes I think that we as poetry readers can be a lot like chimps. Though in traffic we would negotiate the gray area between rigid rule and present necessity, when reading poems we may not. Poets are always changing, and pushing the boundaries of what was previously unacceptable. A good example of this would be to look at modern lineation and white space in poems. Lineation used to be rigidly prescribed by the use of popular forms; the manipulation of line breaks or white space (the visual pause for a reader) was limited by the received forms. However, evolutions of European and American poetries have increasingly called for a rejection of many characteristics of style by which we once asserted a text to be a "poem." If a poetry reader from 1900 were to read an eclectic anthology of contemporary poems, it is probable that he or she would not recognize most of our texts as poems. Be they narrative, lyric, or dramatic, the shapes and modes of our poems are diverse. And they exist for diverse valid purposes, be that communication, consolation, curiosity, cultural preservation, witness, protest, or provocation.

However, though the external form of poems has changed and will continue to do so, I think it is possible to locate some characteristics that most successful poems share: they are experiences in themselves, not just formal conveyances or enactments of poetic subjects; they are concentrated and economical, no matter their length; they are acts of attention that bring together subjective and objective realms of consciousness; they require an understanding of unity and conscious artfulness to appraise their architecture; they spring from both inspired intuition and conscious discipline; they are comfortable with divergent thinking, parallel (as opposed to linear) logic, and compressed timeframes; and they evoke immediate response from the reader, often at a seemingly sub-verbal level.

Do all poems have to share in these ambitions? Of course not. We can all point to poems—less successful, but poems nonetheless—that fall short of them. In fact, most of our poems fail to become *poetry*, in the most ambitious sense of that term. But the more we write (and read) with ambition and from a sense of necessity, the better our chances. At this point, it may be helpful to be aware of a classification articulated by Stanley Burnshaw in his book *The Seamless Web*. Burnshaw offers that the great Spanish poet Juan Ramón Jiménez classified poems into two types: the "voluntary" *(voluntaria)* and the "necessary" *(necesaria)*. "Voluntary" poems are conscious of their subject matter from the start, while "necessary" poems are completely inspired, or "givens," that flow unpremeditated and seem to arrive naturally. Though most poems also require patience, tenacity, and hard work in their making, I can't stress enough just how essential the openness to intuition and surprise is to poetic achievement. The process of our knowing and the process of our art are each processes of transformation, progression, and abstraction. When the creative process (both generating material *and* revision) emulates the natural process by which we think, feel, and discover in real life, the poem becomes a shared moment of learning and discovery for both the poet and reader—a revelation in which, as Tennyson's memoirs describe it, "individuality itself seem[s] to dissolve and fade away into boundless being . . . not a confused state, but the clearest of the clearest . . ."

This is an eloquent way of stressing that truly ambitious poetry reveals the simultaneity of the temporal and the eternal in our daily lives; it allows us to momentarily transcend the inevitable narrow focus of daily experience and to know the genuinely holistic nature of being. Poetry, more so than prose, articulates and embodies this with immediacy, intensity, and attention to the effects of language itself. I really don't know how else to say it; to try to do it justice, I'll have to keep writing poems. ❧

DANIEL NATHAN TERRY

THE WITCH'S TREE: IMAGE IN POETRY

THERE IS A DIFFERENCE between being told something and being shown something. Say you have recently fallen in love. You are experiencing a rush of emotion, your world is upside down, you can no longer concentrate on the simplest tasks. All of your thoughts are with the one you love.

And so you write a poem that goes something like this:

> THE DAY MY LIFE CHANGED
> I love the one I love so much,
> all I can do is think about her touch,
> her smile, her beautiful eyes.
> Everything about her makes the skies
> even bluer than they were before.
> I want to be alone with her forever.
> She has changed my life.

Now, you show this to the one you love and she is moved to tears by its beauty, so you decide that the poem is perfect and ready for the world.

And so you show it to the world. And the world says, "So what? You're in love. How nice for you."

You're devastated. You understand the great emotion behind the words and so does the one you love, so why is everyone else acting like you've said nothing of value? Why does no one understand that although billions of others have fallen in love before, your love is new and different from every love before it? Let's go straight to the source—the poem—and examine why it has failed to communicate to others the depth and specificity of your love.

Examine the first line: "I love the one I love so much." To the point, right? There are three immediate challenges with this line for a reader who has never met the speaker of the poem: who is the speaker, or "I," who is the addressee, "the one I love," and what exactly does the speaker mean by using the abstract word "love"—considering people have different ideas about what "love" represents. As a reader, we hope a poem will answer these questions as it progresses, but this poem doesn't seem very forthcoming. Instead, it leaves us with more questions: What is her touch like and what does the speaker "think" about it? What does the beloved's smile look like? What do her eyes look like? And if the skies have become bluer than before, how blue is that? Is it the light shade of a blue jay or as dark as a blueberry? What does "alone with her" mean? Finally, the last line and the title state that love has "changed" the speaker's life—but from what, to what?

These are the questions that we ask of a poem written in such general, vague terms. Some of them must be answered, at least on an emotional level, if the reader is to feel what the speaker feels. The poem needs to relay not just the bones of what has happened to the speaker (love has changed my life), but what it feels like to be clothed in the flesh of this new love.

One of the ways poetry shares or transfers experience from the poet to the reader is by the use of image. An image, or a grouping of words that transfers a specific sensory detail (visual, auditory, olfactory, tactile, or gustatory) to the reader's mind, seeks to *evoke an experience*, rather than impart basic information.

To put an everyday face on the use of image, ask yourself if you have ever had a dream that was filled with bizarre images that made little sense in the waking world, but filled you with anxiety or dread while you slept. Or, have you ever experienced an emotional reaction to a painting or photograph—a sudden sense of wonder or peace, of joy or sorrow—but found it difficult to explain, even to a good friend, why you felt the way you did about this particular piece of art? You may have told someone "I don't have words to explain what it was like."

There is a way to transfer your experience with a piece of visual art—you simply show it to your friend and he experiences his own emotional reaction to the work. It may not be exactly what you experienced (after all, your friend is a different person than you are) but it will likely be similar.

Dreams are more difficult. Like love, they are highly personal and filled with things only the dreamer can truly understand. Also, there is no means of recording dreams and then playing them back like a film for our friend's enlightenment. In order to share dreams, like love or any other highly personal event in our lives, we are often left with words as our primary means of communication. The odd thing is that if we try to relay a dream to someone by telling them how it felt, they often look at us in bewilderment. But if we relay to our listener the images that bombarded our sleep—I stumbled, naked and with a black vulture perched on my head, through the school commons where all of my friends were wearing white T-shirts and laughing at me—our listener says, "That's exactly how I feel about the upcoming calculus exam."

This is the truth of any good writing: The more specific we are about our images—the visual, the sensory, the concrete nouns, adjectives, and active verbs—the greater the chance that our reader will share our experience and understand how we feel.

There is another version of the love poem I wrote above. This version relies almost entirely on images to transfer how I felt about first love:

THE WITCH'S TREE
Take my hand and we will go across
the black-water roadside ditches wriggling
with the larvae of mosquitoes and the tadpoles
of toads. We will go over the rusted tracks
into the field of rain-soaked blackberries

and fragrant ferns. When we reach the witch's
tree our waists will be wet from walking with
the grasping gods of the afternoon. We will cast
off this world's weavings, crawl inside the oak,
curl our backs against her mossy walls, fasten
our mouths onto some verdant vine and suckle
side by side like twins sharing the womb.

This poem doesn't seek to answer every question a reader might
have. Who exactly is the speaker? Who exactly is the beloved? But what
it does attempt to *show* is how ridiculously romantic and magical first
love feels, how it makes the seemingly ugly things in life (rusted tracks,
mosquito larvae, toads) into the beautiful (rain-soaked blackberries,
fragrant ferns, the mossy walls of an oak). It also attempts to transfer the
feeling of longing to leave the rest of the world behind, to find a separate
place to be with the beloved (like twins sharing a womb). These were
my images when I wrote "The Witch's Tree," and I hope they convey
some of the wonder I felt the first time I fell in love. ❧

LAVONNE J. ADAMS

LYRIC VERSUS NARRATIVE

WHEN WE TALK ABOUT THE POEMS that we write, we normally refer to them as falling on a spectrum where *narrative* poetry anchors one end, and *lyrical* poetry anchors the other. A narrative poem has a beginning, a middle, and an end. Think in terms of a compressed story or essay, where all but the most important elements of plot are discarded. A lyrical poem, on the other hand, is a richly descriptive snapshot of a scene, an idea, an emotion, etc. An effective lyrical poem has the effect of hovering at a moment of deepened understanding—an epiphany. Few poems, however, are exclusively narrative or exclusively lyrical—most fall somewhere in between (a narrative poem will have lyrical moments, and vice versa).

Consider the following poem.

> HOW THE EARTH BECAME BOUNTIFUL
> (A CHEYENNE TALE)
> Long ago, the Plains were a hollow bowl.
> Babies too hungry to cry hung in their cradleboards
> from bare trees. When they could no longer bear
> empty cooking pots and hollow eyes, two warriors

295

set out to search for whatever they could find.
After seven days, a butte rose in the distance
like a buffalo's back. An old woman
stepped through the waterfall
as if it was the flap of her tipi. Her skin was
as brittle and lined as cornhusks, her hair
as white as an antelope's belly. Above her
cooking fire hung strips of dried buffalo meat.
Why have you not come sooner, my grandsons?
She handed the warriors two bowls filled
with stew, two bowls filled with corn.
While they ate, she pulled porcupine quills from
a buffalo-bladder pouch, softened
each quill in her mouth, flattened them
between her gums. With an awl
and sinew, she stitched the quills to a pouch
shaped like a turtle, which would hold
the earth's umbilical cord—a guarantee of its longevity.
The bowls were still full when the warriors could eat
no more, their stomachs firm as fish.
The cowry shells sewn to the woman's bodice glowed
like the moon's sisters as she lifted her arm, pointed
to her left. In a haze of sage smoke, the warriors saw
the earth laden in buffalo. Behind the woman,
fields bristling with corn; to her right,
prairies thick with horses. Straight ahead,
they saw their own faces fierce as they fought
alongside their tribe. And they knew this was
an omen—that they would be victorious,
that they would carry home many captives,
and that the storm clouds forming in the east were
nothing but shadows.

   After reading any poem, the first questions you should ask yourself are: What is happening in this poem? What is it about? Take a few

moments to write your impressions in the margin. What else do you notice about the poem? Do you have favorite lines or images?

If I asked whether this poem is narrative or lyrical, you would most likely answer narrative—it tells the tale of two Cheyenne warriors' quest to find food for their starving tribe. My version of the tale is based on a few sentences found in a reference source. As a poet, my job was to create the scene visually for my reader, pulling in details from other sources or from my own experience. The grandmother's bag, for instance, was based on an artifact that I saw in a museum. But even more important is conveying an emotional truth. Why is this an important story? How is it relevant to us all?

Now, consider this poem.

AFTER THE ICE STORM

When you filmed your ordinary neighborhood
suddenly sheathed in ice, you didn't speak,
so all I hear as I stare at the screen is
the hollow sound of your breathing,
water dripping from trees and eaves,
ice crunching like cinders beneath your shoes,
and it feels as if you're carrying me
the way I once carried you. Under crystal weight,
each tree, even live oaks and maples,
are transformed to weeping willows.
Normally taut from pole to pole,
power lines drape along the ground
in a way that seems natural,
as if destruction has acquired its own grace.
Glistening in the sun, bushes transform
into overgrown chrysanthemums or fireworks
frozen in that millisecond of glitter
before nothingness, like a retinal afterimage
as hazy as the moment joy turns to nostalgia.
And I imagine death to be like this disembodied
vision: me, unable to touch your face;

whatever I struggle to say subsumed by wind,
by tires slushing on the far side of the hill,
by the crisp white noise of everyday life.

Read the poem first to get a feel for it, then read it a second time, once again asking yourself what the poem is about. If I asked whether this poem was lyrical or narrative, I hope you would answer that it is primarily lyrical—a descriptive snapshot of a point in time. Then consider the other ways that this poem is different from "How the Earth Became Bountiful." What is the difference in the narrator (the "voice" that controls the poem, who is "talking")? How would you describe the tone of each?

Part of the challenge of creating a lyrical poem is selecting sensory details that create a particular tone. In the case of this poem, I watched a video taken by my son that ran for half an hour, moving through numerous neighborhoods in Raleigh, North Carolina, after an ice storm shut down the city. The video ended with a light-hearted snowball fight in Johnston Park. But a brief segment of about five minutes near the beginning of the tape caught my attention. There was something haunting about the scene, something that I wanted to understand. Through the process of struggling for unique ways to convey that moment in time, I was able to come to an understanding of what that moment meant to me.

While story-telling provides a narrative poem with much of its impact, a lyrical poem relies primarily on the power of those images. Yet we might choose moments in a lyrical poem to move from the concrete into the abstract (in the poem above, " . . . as if destruction has acquired it own grace"), or segue into a more narrative association (" . . . and it feels as if you're carrying me / the way I once carried you").

Here is an exercise that works with the concept of combining the narrative and the lyrical. Examine one of your favorite personal photographs, then give yourself approximately ten minutes to free-write a description of that photograph. Try to touch on as many of the five senses as you can; it is through these details that the reader will connect with your work. Be so thorough that your reader can envision the photograph without actually seeing it. When you finish this description, skip a line, then spend another ten minutes writing the narrative of the photograph, or the story behind the picture. You might want to include information prior to when the photo was taken, or to move beyond the moment. When you finish writing, take a look at the two paragraphs. Decide which is stronger, and use that as the foundation for your poem. Use the stronger moments from the other paragraph and weave them into this foundation.

Whether you end up with a poem that is primarily narrative or primarily lyrical will ultimately be determined by your own engagement with the subject matter. Your stance might shift from poem to poem, or might even shift within a poem. Either way, a large part of the joy of writing is discovering how we feel about the world, and then finding a unique way to share that vision. ❧

MICHAEL WHITE

THE MUSIC OF THE LINE

I'VE SPENT HALF MY LIFE sitting in rooms discussing poetry
with the students who write it, and one thing I am very clear about is
that when one says he or she likes the "music" in someone's poem, *that*
can refer to almost anything. It might refer to lines of a length that seem
tailor-made to the way emotion unfolds. It might refer to an active intelligence in the disposition of line breaks, a way of breaking a line that
adds feeling to the prose sense of the poem. It might refer to a poem
that goes off on little percussive riffs of consonance when the imagery or
action might call for such embellishment—"Full fathom five thy father
lies," from Shakespeare's *The Tempest*, for example—or it might be a
haunting pattern of assonance which seems to underscore the mood
of the piece, such as the line "on a proud round cloud in a white high
night" from e. e. cummings's poem "If a Cheer Rules Elephant Angel
Child Should Sit." Often, in workshop, what students mean by "music"
is more of a visual than an auditory pattern: they appreciate the way the
author's intention or emotional state is reflected by the way words are
distributed around the field of the page. Of course, there's always much
more going on than we can even begin to describe.

My view of music in a line often boils down to this: "Does it have a beat?" Robert Frost used to say that there are only two meters in English—*strict* iambic and *loose* iambic. This is a gross but perhaps useful simplification. There is a heartbeat, a cadence, a tick-tock to our language, and whether we employ it regularly or not, consciously or not, it will still be there if we are speaking or writing. So the question is: how well is the poet using the natural beat of the language? The beat can be either: "loose" (flexible or intuitive), or "strict," which is what we mean when we talk about traditional meter.

Look: I realize the mere mention of "meter" freaks you out a little. Your soul yearns to be free! I know, I know. Sometimes, students even claim they cannot hear meter. Here are a couple of lines from someone whose soul also yearned to be free. Can you identify the artist?

> I hear that train a-comin',
> It's comin' roun' the bend.

It's the Man in Black, of course. Can you hear the beat? Can you feel it physically? Three beats per line (iambic trimeter) makes a very powerful impression on the reader, regardless of whether it's in a poem by Yeats or Frost, or a nursery tale, or a church hymn, or a country and western tune. But where, you might ask, do the stresses come from: who decides which word is stressed or unstressed? The answer is no one. Stresses are in the DNA of the mother tongue. Some monosyllables simply carry more weight than others: "train" versus "that" or "the." But also, look at the stresses generated *within* the words. The first syllable of "coming," is stressed, not the second. This is always the case: you have no choice when using that word. Most of our polysyllabic words are like this—the pattern of stress is intrinsic. Here's an example: "remake." Which syllable of *remake* is stressed in the following instances?

> Did you see the original movie, or the *re*make?
> Your bed is messy: please re*make* it!

Hear the difference? Know why the words are accented differently?

It's because the first "remake" is a noun, and the second is a verb. They are completely different words. And it's the stress alone that differentiates between the two words—just as it's the beat that determines how our poetry will be read and understood and felt.

These are just two of the factors—between words, and inside words—which create stresses, or beats, in a line of poetry. There are others. But for now, take this under your hat: when you arrange a line of poetry into a pattern of beats, you are working with volatile, strong material, which took humankind thousands of years to create, and which you will never be able to shape as freely as you'd like. You can't. You'll have to work with it as a sculptor works with stone—with respect for its grain and properties—or as a ballet dancer works with her body. It's probably best to know how to write in traditional, as well as in more experimental, ways. The ballet dancer goes to her studio; you go to your desk. Either way, it takes those studio hours to become intimate with the sinew and bone of your medium.

My poem "Anne Frank's Tree" is written in the same three-beat, iambic tetrameter line as "Folsom Prison Blues." The poem was written for a Holocaust memorial chapbook. I really didn't know how to respond to such an overwhelming subject, but the memory of two trees I had seen—one in Amsterdam, one in London—kept recurring to me. Both trees are being kept alive in honor of two writers—Anne Frank and John Keats—who lived next to them and loved them in their last years. I felt, and still feel, that the trees were sentinels for these two noble artists, and that it is fitting that we care for the trees in turn.

My intention was to keep my poem as simple and dignified as possible. Here is the opening:

> A fourteen-year-old girl
> on tiptoe in the attic . . .

The biggest challenge was to keep the language plain, but also to find a way to convey the complicated associations involved with the two trees and everything else. I chose a three-beat line to link the memories, suggest parallels, and to drive toward resolution. Here is one of the central paradoxes to traditional meters (such as trimeter, tetrameter, or pentameter). The beat is at once constraining and liberating. Ultimately, by focusing on music, we forge connections between emotions and images that otherwise would never become a living whole for our reader. The trick is to find the right music for the poem, and to work with it rather than against it.

And when we write "free" verse, it does not mean we're no longer using a beat. We're just looking for it a bit differently. Some poets organize their free verse based on the breath, or syntax, or the flow of colloquial speech—but the fact is that *something* will have to shape the emotion, deliver it musically into the reader's ear. A poem is not simply an appeal to the eye, because after all, its medium is speech. Ultimately, whether a poet uses free verse or traditional meter, the effect is the same: music is the glue, our best hope as artists is to create something that might hold together and reach another soul—and isn't that what we all truly want?

One of my early teachers in the art of poetry, Larry Levis, used to refer to a principle he called the integrity of a line. He would pick a line from a poem and put it on the board. Sometimes it was a student's line; sometimes it was from Keats or some other favorite poet. Then he would begin to discuss it *as* a line, pointing out what was going on in terms of meter, diction, surprising word choices, etc. Basically, he'd ask what makes this line interesting, by itself, completely apart from the role it plays in the rest of the poem. What makes it tick? Are there any false notes or missed opportunities? We all need to work on the integrity of our lines, for the truth is that a poem either works line by line, or not at all.

The third and last principal I'll mention is this: "is the line *sayable?*" A poem is not the same as spoken speech: it should be vivid, more memorable, and more economical than casual conversation. Yet it should still sound as if you *could* say it; it should sound like the language that we—you and I—actually use. This is why you should always read your poetry aloud from time to time while writing it. Taking this principal to heart will save you from affected, overly poetic language; it will help you keep it real.

These three ideas—the beat, line integrity, and sayability—express nearly everything I believe about the music of the line. I find that when a poem of my own falls short—as they always do—it's a matter of attending to one or more of these three core principals. ☙

POETRY SELECTIONS

MALENA MÖRLING

IF THERE IS
ANOTHER WORLD

If there is another world,
I think you can take a cab there—
or ride your old bicycle
down Junction Blvd.
past the Paris Suites Hotel
with the Eiffel Tower on the roof
and past the blooming Magnolia and on—
to the corner of 168th street.
And if you're inclined to,
you can turn left there
and yield to the blind
as the sign urges us—
especially since it is a state law.
Especially since there is a kind of moth
here on the earth
that feeds only on the tears of horses.
Sooner of later we will all cry
from inside our hearts.
Sooner of later even the concrete
will crumble and cry in silence
along with all the lost road signs.
Two days ago 300 televisions
washed up on a beach in Shiomachi, Japan,
after having fallen off a ship in a storm.
They looked like so many

oversized horseshoe crabs
with their screens turned down to the sand.
And if you're inclined to, you can continue
in the weightless seesaw of the light
through a few more intersections
where people inside their cars
pass you by in space
and where you pass by them,
each car another thought—only heavier.

A STORY

The swallows have a story
they tell no one,
not even the rats,
the rats you once saw standing
on their hind legs
at the dump
late in the dark,
the car silent.
Not even the empty shopping cart
of the wind
as it wheels through the foliage—
Everyone has a story,
like a string of invisible Christmas lights
wound into the heart.
And every story has a story
that hides inside its own labyrinth.
The past has a story
as wide and as deep as the world.
Every word has a story
and every stone.

ALOFT

I drove East Genesee Street to West Genesee Street
while the sun was setting—the cold winter sun
slowly withdrawing from the walls
of black snow.
I was not driving anywhere in particular, just driving—
and I remembered what Sam once said
about never having been on his way anywhere,
but simply on his way.
And I thought of a dream I'd had
in which I dreamt that I was dreaming—
in which I was also driving
past stolen goods: TVs and stereo equipment
left on the side of the expressway exit ramp
to kiss the immaterial in the night.
Once, years ago, I was suddenly lost
below a huge overcast sky and driving past rows
of anonymous houses
some still with their long leftover Christmas lights
and identical white mailboxes—
and in passing, I glimpsed
a man running up his driveway with two garbage cans
—one in each hand—
He wore a black pinstriped suit.
The garbage cans were his wings, his galvanized steel wings.

HAPPINESS

How far away is your happiness?
  How many inches?
How many yards?
  How many bus rides to work
and back?
  How many doorways
and stairwells?
  How many hours
awake in the dark
  belly of the night
which contains
  all the world's bedrooms,
all dollhouse-sized?
  How far away is your happiness?
How many words?
  How many thoughts?
How much pavement?
  How much thread
in the enormous sewing machine
  of the present moment?

WALLPAPER

On one hand,
out the window
  of the train
the world goes by,
    a three-dimensional
wallpaper.

  Momentarily
in the woods,
    the thin carpet
of snow
  is cut to fit
perfectly around
    every tree.

And shortly thereafter,
  on the river,
large pieces of ice
    are drifting
in the sunlight
  like glistening
serving platters.

  On the other hand,
there is, of course,
  the invisible
wallpaper
    of the mind
always clinging
  to everything.

Even to the sorry,
    sideways houses
along the tracks.
    And to the garbage
somebody puked
    all over a hill
that just went past.

    On one hand,
the wallpaper
    of the world
and the wallpaper
    of the mind
are separate
    layers of
what is seen
    and unseen.

On the other hand,
    they are one
and the same
    seamlessly
merging inside
    the skull.

AFTER WORDS

The poem "Wallpaper" came out of my experience of weekly train rides back and forth between New York City and Syracuse during the spring of 2002. I was teaching at Syracuse University but no longer lived there. During the long hours on the train I developed the notion of the mind being a kind of individual but invisible wallpaper through which we perceive the outside world. The world that is out there—outside the boundaries of the so called mind—which of course I have never been able to locate. I had the feeling that my mind was both contained within the confines of my skull as well as outside of it racing over the garbage and old leaves that littered the stretch of earth that so loyally ran next to the train. My idea was of a metaphorical, three-dimensional wallpaper through which we perceive our physical surroundings. "Wallpaper" attempts to convey this notion.

LAVONNE J. ADAMS

A PROCESS IN THE
WEATHER OF THE HEART

The water is brackish and warm. Autumn
has not yet shrugged its shoulders.

From our kayaks, the newly constructed homes
with their cantilevered roofs look larger than life

but less real. They are built to withstand
whatever nature has to offer. We pass

battered floats, like stepping stones,
that mark where crab traps wait, baited

with chicken grayed from the mud—decaying
meat that unravels a little more each time

the currents shift. This former boyfriend
is a few feet away, closer than we've been in ten years.

Faded signs warn powerboats to throttle back their engines.
We all need these No Wake zones,

where the waters are as still as nature will allow.
All around us, marsh grass rises like ribbons,

like curtains in reverse. While it's hard to see
where we're going, hard to see where we've been,

I'm learning how to paddle, how to turn.
From the summit of a piling, two cormorants sight

down their beaks to where I circle
like an inquisitive child. I have always heard

that there are things you never forget,
like typing or riding a bike, or

the sound of a man's heart.

ECHOCARDIOGRAM

On the screen—my heart.
  Watching it beat, I feel something
akin to horror, quickly followed
  by a flood of tenderness,
as if viewing an infant unborn. The room is dim,
  the music classical; my heart thrums along
in antiquated shades of black and gray.
  The technician moves a transducer
like a divining rod across my chest and
  around to the left of my breast,
mapping out my interior. I watch
  my mitral valve open and close
like a jellyfish propelling itself through water.
  One click and the screen lights up in swirls of color—
blue and red sparking like solar flares—highlighting
  the movement of my blood: a way to trace
backwash from faulty valves, or the hourglass of
  an artery clogging. *The walls of your heart are
thick.* While unpleasant as a metaphor,
  I hear these words as a smudge of guarantee
against a heart like my grandmother's
  that paused at fifty; she walked for weeks
as if treading spun glass. At the end
  of the session, my heart reminds me
of a beehive that opens and closes
  in a silent scream . . . or maybe just
mouths my name, declaring
  itself faithful the only way it can.

COMPOSITION

There we sit, my father and I,
in a 2 x 2 photo taken in one of those small, dark booths,

the paper now so thin and brittle
I can't remove it from my album.

Our similar different faces,
our similar different eyes.

It was my fifth birthday. I was so small
that on the drive to downtown Cleveland,

I could see only sky, the scallop of telephone wires,
and poles dark as piano keys, regular as a metronome.

I watched my father watch the road as he hummed
some piece by Bach he would play that Sunday.

The car slowed and the noise thickened:
a fusion of gray streets and fumes.

A waitress wearing quiet shoes and a pink uniform,
hair pulled up and tucked in like a nurse, served

the dish of ice cream I chose for lunch.
She rubbed the base of her back and smiled at me,

eyes wistful, as if there was something she saw
in my life that I didn't, as if the future had forged

a gravity we wore like ankle weights.
That's all I remember of the day. Now,

I'm only five years from the age my father died;
perhaps the same genes wait

for some signal to spark in the darkness of my liver
the way they did in his. But in this album,

I perpetually sit on his lap, my head tilted to the side,
the joy on my face close to delirious.

TUNING THE PIPE ORGAN

I grew up with the accoutrements of pipe organs
filling our garage, some as small as piccolos,

some arriving like giants in rough-hewn crates.
On occasional Saturdays, I helped my father tune

what he had built inside quiet churches, each dim
as an underwater scene, each cool as a cave

no matter what season. I preferred the older
sanctuaries with their faint smell of damp,

with their dark mahogany pews and marble floors
that would clack beneath women's Sunday heels.

I walked with my father the length of the nave
toward where a crucifix hung like a compass,

then veered right or left toward the organ's console.
Before he disappeared down some dark hallway

like he would one day disappear forever, my father
settled on the bench, pulled the knobs he called *stops*,

and then began to play. Sound filled the church
like a full-bodied wine as his fingers skirled

three cliffs of keys, as his feet ranged the pedals
like some intricate folk dance. My job was

much simpler—to begin with middle C,
to hold down each note until I heard

his disembodied voice calling *Next.*
A few of those low notes were like fog horns,

others were like ogres bellowing, but each was
capable of palpating my lungs, of claiming my throat.

Stained glass cast its jewels across my lap, and
in that moment I understood something about eternity.

For that moment, I felt close to holy.

CONFESSION

At the base of the Taos mountains,
a fragmented tree, victim
of a lightning strike. As I pass,
I turn my head away as if seeing
something intimate in the paleness
of the exposed wood. A friend's
son who was struck by lightning
later took his life. I wonder how
much that act hinged on burdens
I knew nothing about—a complex landscape
forged from disappointment and pain—
how much was due to the lightning strike's
trauma, the exit wound like a stigmata.
Once, I longed for a life that was extraordinarily
good—to radiate faith like a five-hour sunburn,
to heal others with a touch. Now,
I'm satisfied with wisps of grace: letting
cars merge into thick traffic in front of me,
tipping the barista who mixes my complicated
drinks. But that earlier desire resurged
the day I drove to Chimayo after hearing
of a sanctuary deemed the American Lourdes,
where abandoned crutches lined the walls
like car parts in an old-fashioned garage.
The room was small and stifling;
rows of candles flickered above
a plate-sized pit filled with adobe-colored dirt
that I knew I could not eat

even if it meant a miracle. In my life,
desire rarely trumps fear.
Ten miles down the road, I stopped
at a convenience store where I bought
twin chocolate cupcakes with white icing
scrolls like a string of cursive *e*'s.
I ate them with the faith of a child.

AFTER WORDS

"Confession" was written during the first week of a month-long stay in Taos, New Mexico. I invested a week exploring the unfamiliar landscape, an act that often triggers that wonderful spark of creativity that we label "inspiration." On the way to Taos Cow, an organic ice cream producer north of town, I passed a field of cows grazing around a lone cottonwood, victim of a lightning strike. I pulled over to stare at the arresting scene, then dwelt on the image for days. That excursion was followed by a day trip to the quaint sanctuary of Chimayo. In some mysterious way, the two combined. I knew from the start that the title of the poem would be "Confession," though only through the writing process did I discover what I would actually confess. For those who know me well (and now for the readers of this collection), the final confession deals with eating those cupcakes. With the occasional exception of seafood, I have been a vegetarian since 1991. The list of ingredients for those cupcakes included lard!

MARK COX

THE DOOR

There's no discernible point of origin,
and this is exactly what wakes you:
the thin whistle,
diluted by time,
a former lover within you,
boiling water for tea
in an efficiency banished so deeply into mind,
it might as well be another side of the world.
This is what it means to see clearly
the clock radio's cold, green digits
as a room number that keeps changing,
to know a suite of coordinates
has been reserved for your death,
and though you don't know where,
tonight an insect rubs its legs there,
or a man purses his lips and spits out
the last of his wanting toward a nurse,
or perhaps it's as simple as a doorbell or phone,
but you know the sound
and refuse it an answer.
It's just three o'clock in the morning,
just the wind, just tires on the road,
just the dry hinges of a door you passed too quickly,
thinking it was closed.

THINGS MY GRANDFATHER MUST HAVE SAID

I want to die in the wintertime,
make the ground regret it,
make the backhoe sweat.

January. Blue Monday
after the holiday weekend.
I want it to be hard on everybody.

I want everyone to have a headache
and the traffic to be impossible.
Back it up for miles, Jesus.

I want steam under the hood, bad directions,
cousins lost, babies crying, and sleet.
I want a wind so heavy their umbrellas howl.

And give me some birds, pigeons even,
anything circling for at least half an hour,
and plastic tulips and a preacher who stutters

"Uh" before every word of Psalm 22.
I want to remind them just how bad things are.
Spell my name wrong on the stone, give me

earthworms fat as Aunt Edith's arms
surfacing under the folding chairs.
And I want a glass coffin,

I want to be wearing the State of Missouri
string tie no one else liked ... God,
I hope the straps break

and I fall in with a thud. I hope
the shovel slips out of my son's hands.
I want them to remember I don't feel anything.

I want the food served straight from my garden.
I want the head of the table set. I want
everyone to get a pennant that says,

"Gramps was the greatest,"
and a complete record of my mortgage payments
in every thank-you note.

And I want to keep receiving mail for thirteen years,
all the bills addressed to me,
old friends calling every other month

to wonder how I am.
Then I want an earthquake or rising water-table,
the painful exhumation of my remains.

I want to do it all again.

I want to die the day before something truly
important happens and have my grandson say:
What would he have thought of that?

I want you all to know how much I loved you.

SONATA

At ninety, the piano plays him.
He's like a man by the sea
the wind knows it must wear down,
sculpt to a profile,
then fill out again,
billowing his sleeves and trouser legs
into a younger musculature.
Over and again, the music grays
then reddens, the part
in its hair shifting left to center
until those few blades of sea grass
are all that's left to be
combed over the rocks,
and the thin fingers skitter,
leaving impressions in the keyboard
that waves wash level,
cleansing its audience of shell halves,
now glistening, now scoured dry.
And the house, the house just outside
this sonata's frame,
begs him to turn around
to pick his way back
along the stony runner,
his hands stopping his ears.
But, at ninety, the music plays the piano,
which plays the man, who finally, fearlessly,
plays himself, which is the landscape,
which is everything that ends.

BETTER HOMES
AND GARDENS

Shot himself. Hanged himself. Shot himself.
Fell from a window just half washed.
Couldn't go. Couldn't stay. Hadn't the heart.
Stopped at a train crossing, then couldn't start.
Hit-and-run by a school bus. Lost five toes to an axe.
Hydroplaned east on a westbound road.
Took the whole vial hoping to relax.
Shot himself. Hanged himself. Starved herself.
Caught with a schoolgirl. Fell in the tub.
Turned to God. Jumped bail. Collapsed in Jim's Pub.
Heart attack. Down's Syndrome. Cirrhosis. Stroke.
Shot himself. Hanged himself. Strung out on coke.
Incest. Seagram's. Scarred for life. Broke.
Polaroids. Videos. Chat room trysts. Tapes.
Blacked eyes. Slashed wrists. Post-marital rapes.
Curious toddlers tied with duct tape and string.
These are a few of our favorite things.

LIKE A SIMILE

Fell into bed like a tree
slept like boiling water
got up from bed like a camel
and showered like a tin roof.
Went downstairs like a Slinky
drove to work like a water skier
entered the trailer like a bad smell
where I changed clothes like a burn victim
drank my coffee like a mosquito
and waited like a bus stop.
A whistle blew.
Then I painted like I was in a knife fight for eight hours
drank like a burning building
drove home like a bank shot
unlocked the door like a jeweler
and entered the house like an argument next door.
The dog smiled like a chain saw.
The wife pretended to be asleep
I pretended to eat.
She lay on the bed like a mattress
I sat at the table like a chair.
Until I inched along the stair rail like a sprinkler
entered like smoke from a fire in the next room
and apologized like a toaster.
The covers did *not* open like I was an envelope
and she was a 24-hour teller
so I undressed like an apprentice matador
discovering bullshit on his shoes.

AFTER WORDS

I was a journeyman steel painter (industrial work: bridges, towers, and tanks) for more than ten years before I made the transition to teaching. Though I had humped freight on truck docks and worked on permit with the boilermakers, painting was my first real and steady job after taking responsibility for myself. It was certainly the only activity after writing that provided me with a sense of identity. I didn't mind the tight spaces, silica dust, and thinner fumes. And the high work gave me a sense of freedom and composure I was rarely to feel on the ground. I could do it now, I tell myself, but I know better. That work wears a man down. But I'm grateful for what the work, and the men I worked with, gave me. I have a wider range of experience and language at my disposal. I know what it is to lean over and lace up my boots morning after morning. And I've tried to bring that ethic with me into my study, my classrooms, and my poems.

JASON MOTT

FROM DEATH ROW,
AN INTERVIEW WITH A WOLF:

(INTERVIEWER'S NOTES: *He stares at his hands as he speaks. His eyes are sunken. He said it was sleeplessness that brought him to me.*)

Fine, grade A meat. A feast, that girl—age nine—
all warm and soft and wet inside her red.
So tender, that dear child. How hard I loved

the curves of her. How hard she loved me back.

I watched her after school. I watched and thought
of she and I, entwining: days and breaths—
and teeth and bone—in the green belly of
some idyll dreamed up by Thoreau. She was

my newest house of straw, and I loved her.

I love her still—my love is a black moon.
And lovers should chew love to pulp, adorn
themselves with trophies of it: bands of gold,
small locks of hair, a dress worn once. These girls

in red, how deep my love for them, how sharp.

THE 47 SECONDS
BETWEEN NY AND LA

for Daniel

(The Flash)

Mrs. Johnson's Chihuahua slipping
his leash; the mailman reaching
for mace; a woman starting
her car; a girl holding
her father's hand, waiting   :02
to cross the street; a shoe falling
from a window; a hummingbird crossing
the interstate; a driver wishing
he would not hit the hummingbird;
a bird deposited in Harrisburg;   :05
raindrops in Tennessee; an old man
smoking on his front porch
in Kentucky, whispering, "Wait."   :09
I wait. I wait.
Licking his lips,
he says, "She left me."
He says, "They all left me."
He says, "I fathered six
children. And now they're all   :19
gone. Now it's just me
and the wind and no one stops
to say hello." He licks his lips.
He says, "I bought a new
shirt. He pinches his blue flannel   :28
between chopstick fingers.
He wets his mouth,
takes a breath for words, says
"Do you like it?"

He stares at me. He waits
for me to leave. He waits   :35
and I wait with him.
In the distance, the wind
is a roaring crowd
of canned applause living
in the trees. The man says,   :39
"No one comes to sit with me
anymore." He rocks
in his chair, closes his eyes,
falls into a light sleep. I whisper
in the fabric of his dreams,
"I sit with everyone."   :42
The flat highway of Nebraska;
a hotrodder spinning wheels;
smog valley; silicone city;
the ocean swallowing
the sun; licking my lips, I hold my breath,
say nothing and hope he hears me.   :47

THINLY VEILED, YOUNG MAN COMES TO ME SEEKING A FRIENDLY FACE

(The Joker)

So I'm out and about one day
when this priest walks up to me and says,
"Beloved bard, my mother has died
and my father is ill and I've lost my faith."

And I said to him, "But faith's forever!
Got a lifetime warranty, doesn't it? I've
always wondered about that though,
Whose life?"

But, anyhow, this "priest" said to me,
"God's become a ghost. An imagination
in my head. He used to feel so real.
I could touch him in my mother's hands."

"But now he doesn't take
your calls, right? Right. Now
'This number is no longer in use.'
You've lost your signal, right?"

The priest nodded. He nodded
and I took his hands in mine
and I told him, smiling as I spoke,
"The crow flies at sunrise."

I told him, "Padre, I dreamed, once,
of a world between my fingers,
a world made from Muscadine grapes.
A world drenched in methane perfume,
oozing, like the minty stench

of cookies, cut out and called lives—
light and clockwork lives
built from porridge instead of wood.

In this dream, you were there, Padre,
wearing a thousand sweet names,
a million tender, soft voices—'personae'
the academics might call them—and you looked so sad

you could have been a lovesick sunrise,
hiding yourself behind my name like you did.
And, me being the laughing boy that I am,
 I let you wear my skin. And I grieved

with you. I wept with you, Padre, in this one
dream of mine. No matter what face you wore,
I took your pain and I called it ambrosia,
and you and I split it in half, and it hurt a little less,

and you and I ate together and we became gods.
But still, because I loved you, I wept
for you, living down there
on that little, overripe, unmashed—

grape of a world between my fingers.
And you, you heard my weeping,
and you smiled at my weeping,
and you laughed at my weeping,

and you wore a wonderful new grin that grew
out of my tears—tears that used to be yours;
and your laughter danced over my lips
like the flapping, leather wings of flutter-bys.

Through your wall of chuckles—
through my wall of tears—
I heard you calling me. You

called to me and asked me
for more laughter—less pain in life—you hunted
for me the way Mars pined for Venus's flower.
And, Padre, who am I, the Joker,
to refuse a laugh? Could Venus refuse?

Could Pandora say no
to that little black box
cooing gently in her lap
like a six-faced angel?

And what about Moses? Could he
not lead those folks from bondage?
(They asked him for it ya' know.)
But didn't he come down from the mountain

full of good humor, colored hair, and poetry?
And, while we're on the subject, where's
your golden calf, Padre? Still hung
from your sad, pathetic neck I see.

But, then again, what's a golden calf
between friends? Really? Those
Israelites, it all turned out okay for them
in the end, didn't it?

Of course it did. So buck up.
Walk it off, or 'walk it out' as the kids say
these days. No more tears for that dead mother,
okay? She'll still be dead tomorrow.

And as for the ill father, don't fret there either.
He's just finally been let in on the great secret
of life: all jokes must end. And as for God,
that imaginary voice in your head, cut it out—

I'll offer the knife—or take up poetry.
Then you can wear your masks and hide your hurt
behind me and I'll laugh with you, and I'll cry
with you, and I'll tie a tourniquet on your heart."

AFTER WORDS

The Joker poem and I first met in the spring of 2005. Originally the poem was simply about the Joker and his view of the world. It was one of my first attempts at combining my two loves: writing and superheroes. This poem and I had an off and on relationship for years, a relationship that didn't really seem to be going anywhere. It was rejected for various reasons ranging from length to "voice inconsistencies" to "lack of emotional depth." Eventually, like most people in ailing relationships, this poem and I were reduced to not talking to one another and sometimes seeing other people during this dark period.

Once I was able to get over my fear of intimacy and introduced my personal stake to the poem—the death of my mother and impending death of my father—the poem turned into something I never knew it could be. And I've loved it ever since.

SARAH MESSER

STARTING WITH THAT TIME

he shot a man in Mendota
for calling him pretty, *hey pretty, your hair's
like spun sunshine,* and then
the man fell down dead. Son of a
tin smith, he had inherited
those quick but delicate hands, and
always went for his revolver
as quick and absentmindedly as
an itch the same way he went
for those squirrel-boned
women even smaller than himself
with breasts like shallow teacups.

As an outlaw, he fell in love
with the wrong women—a seamstress
who sniffed glue, who sewed
her own sleeves to her arms
and flew off a bridge; a sad-faced
war nurse; a rich Northerner
who carried her father's
jawbone in her purse—
each one disappearing more
from herself, until he found
that he was mostly in love
with the shadow of a dress,
a wrist, or the outline of a mouth

pressed to the glass on the window
of the next train leaving town.

In the meantime, he killed:
any man who could ever be called
his friend. Ambushed the town
of Independence, killed 12
at Olathe, 20 at Shawnee, tied the scalps
of those he suspected most
to his horse's bridle, and rode
west. The mayor of Lawrence,
Kansas suffocated in a well beneath
his own house as the whole
town burned, the contents of every
train and wagon turned over.

In the end he came to me
because I was the timberline, way out
west, the last stand of trees.

Each night I told him about
the guns hidden in my house:
a .44 caliber in the chamber pot, a rifle
beneath the stairs, bird guns between
folded linen, revolvers hidden
in drawers, on shelves, the four boudoir
pistols plastered in walls, wrapped
in the hair of dolls.

He hid himself inside the sheen
of Smith and Wesson, the one breech
double-barreled Winchester,
my only Navy Colt. He hid because
I was the hideout, the inert
and sturdy home where he polished

his thoughts, the timber
of each trigger, the powder
in the coffee tin, the bullets
in the freezer.

In the end, I was
the safest place for him
to put his mouth.

IN THE MARKET,

a transaction is made, and the snake
is lifted from the basket by the back
of its head, the body dangling
like a girl's braid. With a flash
of silver the head is scissored
into Tupperware and the skin
peeled down like a condom, like the arm
of a wet shirt, the slick inner
muscle exposed and thrown
to the counter like a party ribbon.

Now the animal is pure meat,
the long cords pulled apart
from the spine, a broken zipper.
The customer wants only
the liver, the size of a lover's earlobe,
said to improve brain function,
to replace lost memory.

Memory can become a medicine that,
clamped beneath the tongue, heals
all past and recent conflagrations.
But scars are the prisons skin builds
around injury, the angle of the roof
increasing as each blade is drawn in
and out. And memory is the room
where you wait in the dark.

You still had your key. You heard
my footstep on the landing, the tumblers

rolling in the lock. You sat like a priest
at the edge of the sofa, your clothes
the color of earth and organs, like an animal
caught at the roadside, you wanted
to catch me with a new lover,
my nylons already shed, limp in my
hand, returning at 3 AM.

Above the market's temporary roofs,
the tin and blue plastic, it is raining.
Below them, the butcher has killed
five snakes. He works on the sixth,
his fingers plying the spinal cord,
his face jiggling. The customer stares
at the organs pinning down the paper
towel—gray ghost bodies, five tiny fists.

He looks like you: like there is
something lost to him, something
he doesn't even realize yet
that he has forgotten to say, something
that was stripped away by a larger
man's hands moving down a tiny spine,
in childhood, in the dark, his fingers
hooked into the softest places, into
the coiled knot of thighs and clamped
jaws snaking away beneath footsteps
in the hall, beneath the rotting house sill,
the roots and leaves and soiled market
basket, the locked back rooms.

The customer is asking for two
more, wanting to know how
this will work, this new world

where nothing is forgotten, even this
feeling that sometimes makes him strike
at nothing, that makes him glide
as if dreaming, side-winding
in the night, his body triggered, one long
hearing instrument spread out upon
the earth, the path up from the garden—
and his hand stays perched
at the collar bone like yours was when
the shard of light, my shadow,
entered the house—your hand pale
against your shirt like a poised wing,
like the snake arched, waiting.

SOME WOMEN
MARRY HOUSES

I

My mother, blind from the swamp-gas,
the kudzu, almost married
a gas station—had five or six
kids in a cardboard box backyard;
almost drank motor oil in a Styrofoam cup; almost slept
with the drawer to the register open
under ghost Esso, flies licking
lip-corners, a wide-wale
corduroy grin; almost burned
our infant skin off, birthing on those
gas rags—

                        But this
did not happen. She married
a meat-shop owned by a prominent
butcher. He puts a neat bullet
in the temple of every yearling.
*It's painless, they don't even know
how they die.* Each evening she takes
buckets outside and washes
the red walls down.

II

Each day, my grandmother walked
a bridge of stretched cat intestines
under horse-hair power lines.

Her husband found her often inside
the belly of a violin. She was all
he ever wanted in a woman: exotic as

the parlor's Oriental, the throats
of his seven caged birds. He steamed
stripped wood and clamped it
to her body. He glued seams

and clefts above the sacral
joints he kneaded each night when
they made love, so she could sing
all those pretty high notes
from inside their polished home.

III
I live alone and love
the abandoned walls, the water-
damage, the shelf-paper
tongues lolling from cabinets, mid-morning
sunlight on telephone wires, the telephone,
the leafy, leaning second-story porch.

It's easy to love the house, so quiet
in the haze of morning windows—
it's easy to love the chimney, still warm
from last night's fire, and solid
at the center, something to put my hands upon
when no one will enter me.

AFTER WORDS

*The poem title comes from the first line of Anne Sexton's poem "Housewives." I
wanted to take the metaphor literally—what would being married to a house be
like? And then I thought of other structures, like a gas station or a violin. I wanted
to write a multi-generational poem (grandmother, mother, daughter) that somehow continued the conversation with Sexton. I had just read her biography by
Diane Middlebrook, which was very dark. And perhaps this accounts for the dark
nature of the poem.*

EMMA BOLDEN

GOD IS IN THE CEILING

Inside my bed I am
a good girl. I lie

still and careful,
keep limb from limb.

Outside I hear living.
Trees wave skeleton hands,

the moon's fingernail scratches
its far-cornered sky. I pray

O Lord let me, keep cool
as a clam's flesh. I am sick

with purity, waiting
without the what for. Rain

rolls itself through
the gutters. Birds flap off

their wings. The night keeps on
being night, and God

is a silent fissure, a slit
in the plaster's settling calm.

HOW TO RECOGNIZE A LADY

She writes this Your Honor Dear Sirs Misters Gentlemen to make
   acquaintance, haste, an answered inquiry.

She is the book of slander, a match dropped in dry glass.

She is a head sprouting snakes, milk for gall, low rolled
   smokes and poor taste. She is a cigarette's sizzle
   in gin, a two-lipped tattoo on his collar's starch.

She is the twelfth rib gone stray. She is the side stuck with whalebone
   stays. She hides herself, lacking a suitable silk. She scrubs
   her hands spotless when burning soft coal.

She is sorry, begs your pardon, mercy. She is a thumb stump
   on china, two foot soles slit clean.

She is not only proper but necessary. The Good Book
   balances her head. She is presented to old women thus:
   "Mrs. S—— please meet Miss B——. Gladly." She is the neck's
   twig stretched out past snap. She prunes her right hand before
   offering, keeps scripture and blood quietly.

She is two knives at the banquet, blade slicing a sternum's
   strongbox. She keeps her work clean: mop, pail, and arm.
   Her skin shatters, dishwater dry.

She is whipped to walk a straight line. She never eats unless hungry,
   never eats until full. She knows the front desk is no place
   to comb hair. In public, she keeps finger: pencils from her teeth.

She is as always honored to dance with you. She shall be delighted,
   glad, thrilled. She shall be a skilled tongue, an obedient fist
   of petals, of rain.

She sends this by argon, by wing, by hoof against airstream,
the sweet taste of sea. She seals this with perfume, with rouge,
with asphalt, four fingers sliced clean, the lid of her lame eye.

She is As Always Sincerely Yours. She is Forever Found Truly Yours.
She is Affectionately Yours. She begs to remain ever Your ———.
She hopes to receive favor, reply; she is Ever Indebtedly ———.

THE UNFINISHED BODY

I wanted at last to live
honestly. Thinking it best

to start small, I told
the mailman I hated

his new self-stick stamps,
showed my uneven breasts

to the clerk at the mall.
Farther: I sold off a room

full of clothes, ran nude
through the city, sun-seared,

my skin a red lie. That too
I stripped, became the blue

bulge of muscle, blood-pumping
vein, itself a false dream

I could never believe. What
was true? A clear wave at morning,

a dress of stars at noon, at night
the edge where asphalt meets field.

WILL AND TESTAMENT

I come from a long line of pistols, hilts hefted in pearl-
ringed hands. My ancestors cut their teeth on nicked
diamonds, stole furs from velvet death beds. They lived
on ether, horseflesh, spit. Their boots wore seventeen
sets of buttons. In photographs, they never fear the
blind that follows a flash. I come from a long line of
unmarked graves. By destiny, I am my own kind of
thief. I steal wrecks and windfalls, gloat over downed
trees. I keep my racket tidy: one false word, I'll nine
iron my own knees.

.

AFTER WORDS

*During my last year of graduate school, I began to build my now-too-large collec-
tion of vintage etiquette books. Though I never learned what to do with silverware
during a seven-course meal, I quickly grew fascinated with the expectations for
behavior presented in these books, especially the expectations for female behavior,
which seemed odd, unnatural, and arbitrary. The poems in this selection present a
woman's response to those expectations, and especially, to situations in which she
does not meet the expectations of society, nature, or herself.*

SHARAN STRANGE

NIGHT WORK

In the changeling air before morning
they are silhouettes. Dark ones
with the duskiness of predawn on them
and the shading of dust and sweat.
Busying themselves in buildings,
on scaffolds, and on the black
washed pavements, they are phantoms
of the city—guardians of parking lots
and lobby desks, tollbooths, meters,
the all-nights and delivery trucks.
At bus stops they are sentinels
and the drivers. Launderers and cleaners
readying the offices and untidy houses
of privilege. Cooks heaping up meals
for the well fed, the disabled, or the indifferent.
Trash-takers, making room for more.
Nurses, eternally watching.

When my mother, starting the stove
at 5 AM, looked out the window, she saw
her father, days after his funeral.
Had he come back to the field
and the plowing left undone when
the chain snapped and struck him,
knotting his throat into pain
and its aftershock of silence?

Did he return to reclaim the work
like a part of himself unfulfilled
and his story untold?
He is with us still, she said
to the inchoate brightness.
He is there even now.

Spirits are much the same in those
uncensored hours—flitting dim figures,
half-remembered apparitions, whose industry
renews and undergirds our own.
They are our counterparts: the whispering
echo of that other turning
as we turn in bed, the sigh that heaves
in the wake of some unseen act. In the darkness,
where a cycle of making and unmaking unfolds.
If anything could help us believe in
their benign presence, it is the workers,
perpetual as stars, a collective
of eyes and hands, conjuring.

CLAIM

My tongue, every atom of my blood, form'd from this soil, this air,
Born here of parents born here from parents the same, and their parents the same . . .
   —Walt Whitman

Sun reaching through the bus window makes her a flame.
White cloth twining her head ignites the tip of a body
Dressed all in white, as if readied for dipping in the Sunday stream,

Though she hardly knew the woman who would have counseled
Her preparation—reminding her not to fight the preacher, just
Lay back, meet the water with the ease of the unburdened—

Who had left these backwoods, dispossessed and angry,
By this same road but northward, like ancestors
Who traced rivers, moss, nocturnal light to the city.

This trip reverses that repudiation of the South.
As she recounts her grandmother's deathbed wishes and
Reviews her own bitter struggles, she's a torch

Glowering in midday. Old cruelties mark this soil.
Its memory takes trope in jolts her crippled back records,
And she winces, reminded of a new corporate toll.

But a disability settlement's reluctant reparation
Is just enough to purchase her inheritance,
Make her the family's agent fulfilling old ambition.

Gnarled braids escape her headwrap, signify on native trees
Warped by heavy fruit. The house those trees built—
Taproots drawing her forebears' blood and sweat, their cries,

And prayers into the very walls—will be her grandmother's again.
The Greyhound's bringing their twinned spirits home,
Where she'll make for them an unassailable shrine.

MAKING METAPHOR

for Prophet Lee Davison

Impatient at the stop, how does one recognize
a bus? At a distance, it registers:
large bulk, slow moving.

Prophet is not quite two,
she has not learned the word bus.
But within minutes she has the notion,

and as we ride through Washington's wide streets,
she says, in a toddler's slurred singsong,
"another-one-a-bus" each time.

Then, at the waterfront, my friend TSE takes her
right up to crabs writhing in their bins,
again and again until repulsion becomes fascination.

And after, at the park, she looks
into the lifeless eyes, grasps a claw,
takes bites of its proffered flesh.

Does she see this one as kin to those others,
does she understand death? How long before
the concept of crab cake will take hold?

Meanwhile, TSE is up to his poet's tricks.
A very pregnant woman lumbers into view.
"Look, Prophet," he points, "bus!"

JIMMY'S FIRST CIGARETTE

The tobacco sweetness filled your head
with a gentle wooziness, a lightness
that rocked you off-center,
numbing you to the possibility

of pain or cruelty in the world.
From your grandmamma's porch
you surveyed a lush green countryside
murmuring with the traffic

of laughing birds, wild animals,
and ghosts. You felt alive,
aglow with sensation as,
at her urging, you inhaled

the slim token of freedom.
Pleasure, short-lived, gave way
to confusion, betrayal,
as a torrent of blows

from your daddy's belt broke
your childish reverie—he
and Grandmama conducting
your abrupt trip back to reality.

CHILDHOOD

Summer brought fireflies in swarms.
They lit our evenings like dreams
we thought we couldn't have.
We caught them in jars, punched
holes, carried them around for days.

Luminous abdomens that when charged
with air turn bright. Imagine!
mere insects carrying such cargo,
magical caravans flickering beneath
low July skies. We chased them, amazed.

The idea! Those tiny bodies
pulsing phosphorescence.
They made reckless traffic,
signaling, neon flashes forever
into the deepening dusk.

They gave us new faith
in the nasty tonics of childhood—
pungent, murky liquids promising
shining eyes, strong teeth, glowing skin—
and we silently vowed to swallow ever after.

What was the secret of light?
We wanted their brilliance—
small fires hovering,
each tiny explosion
the birth of a new world.

AFTER WORDS

Childhood was a magical time for me, even as a poor black child in the 1960s American South, because I grew up feeling close to nature. My siblings and I, our cousins and friends, spent a great deal of time outdoors, helping to raise animals, working in fields, exploring the woods, and climbing trees. Fireflies—or lightning bugs, as they were called—fascinated us, and we made play out of catching them. They were like little beacons from another realm—captivating, awe-inspiring flashes of cosmic code—that seemed to signal only to us children. For me, they were mystery and possibility. They flared for a brief season, and then were gone. Even in those scant moments, I felt transformed. Among them, I felt lifted beyond the strictures of the cutting eyes of whites, my shabby neighborhood, my cramped house. In their presence, I dimly sensed, perhaps, a fuller, greater self.

EMILY LOUISE SMITH

INTERVIEW WITH THE PAST

Why the obsession with fire?

Because of a certain shade
of orange, daylilies dusting
a field, a truck sunk into clay.

And Clover?

Isn't there always something alluring
about boys from the next town over?

Why plant when the moon is new?

I was lonely before you and will be after.

How will you know your way?

A sliver of light
between railroad cars.

What will you do when you get there?

Stitch myself inside a skirt hem
with pine needles and grass blades.

*And if you could inhabit the girl you were
years ago, with what would you come to her?*

Nights, moths clung to screens, the pages
of books already damp under her thumbs.

SMALL HOURS

He brought a flashlight and carried it through me. Shadows grew from my banks. The small hours, he said, have fingers. This opened a highway between us, a red truck under an orange sky. August cracked open with rain. I washed the dishes, and he went after dice. The moon, he called from the road to say, remained between us. Light seeking some crevice by which to enter. Could he hear the fireworks in my thoughts? He wouldn't confess to anything and sat in a tangle of cables behind the entertainment unit. The movie flicked on. After that, I vowed to label the wires so I could remember: sky goes through ear, breath hooks up to night, train whistle routes through moon and comes out mouth. Or moth? Neither of us could name the thing unfolding its wings.

REMNANTS

Everything slipped into the vacuum
that was my grandmother
in those years. Footsteps, voices
from the muted television set.
We tiptoed in her house, tried not to let Dad
catch us staring at her legless nubs.

Gradually, her body was receding.
We didn't understand that we were watching
her die. We'd been to Sunday school enough
to form a theory: if she wouldn't go
gracefully, God would take her
a section at a time. First, one leg. Then
the second. Then her hair from its tidy knot.

Once at home in high-ceilinged rooms, the order
of wainscoting and mantels, she now retired
to the first floor den turned bedroom.
Granddad lifted her from wheelchair to bed.
The house so still, she must have heard the wake
of ball gowns, banter on the veranda, felt
herself floating among the guests.

Her gloved fingers knew light switches
and balustrades, even in the dark, how to negotiate
settees, curios, and end tables. Once we
moved in, it would take years to traverse
rooms without tripping, memorize the map
back to my grandfather.

Amid the clutter of an upstairs room, I find
a box of letters, the flimsy page where
a former admirer scribbled, *your presence*
lit up the room. Farther down, he describes time
spent without her as *overwhelming.* Touching

that word now, I think so much better, his
insatiable emptiness. That kind goes away.
Try living with her whittled down to her parts.
On the back of a photograph, in the bottom
of a chest, she shed pieces of herself. Even lifting her
handkerchief more than a decade after
she died, I uncover a new perfume of grief.

CLOSE OF SEASON

Say there is a flooded rice field in her. A wet mouth. Limbs hung with moss. Somewhere, her toothbrush brittle in a cabinet. The sky, a rust red barn. What's sad: even a shade tree can dissolve the moon. The road coughs up a spindly tree. A fish hooked and thrashing in her. A decoy catching on iced air. The kids we were pull their knees to their hearts. Because there are veins in our bodies jumbled as fishing line. Towns held together by a tractor's loose stitch. Who doesn't want years from now, life light and gauzy as cotton? A porch overlooking a fistful of bearded fields. We are always thinking with our hands. A drake's head flopped over a thumb. Light shifting on marsh grass, an iridescent dress. A season passing in and out of her chest. Eventually we have to smooth out the waves from bed linen, turn off the unconvincing windmill of wings. Learn to let a retriever live up to his name, bound back to us, a duck's wilted legs and neck slung from his jaw. He waits still as Sunday afternoon in Filbert. So much unsaid in a mouth. Humid nights. Damp hands. The tang of wet wood in a blind. That first shot. A sweet that won't dissolve on her tongue. The way the sky drops, sometimes. A tumbling mess of blue-wings.

AFTER WORDS

The first Thanksgiving I spent with my boyfriend's family, we woke in the dark, freezing morning and trudged half asleep through a flooded rice field. I was dressed in his little brother's waders. I hardly knew his family then—it was one of our first holidays together—and silence enveloped us, punctuated by boots in pockets of mud. In the damp plywood blind, we hovered thigh-to-thigh—his father, mother, brother, my boyfriend, and me—and waited for flapping. Suddenly there was the click of metal in my ears, the men up from their seats, then shots and the golden retriever off his haunches. The sound of a duck plucked from the sky, then the mess of wings spinning to the earth, was like nothing I'd ever experienced.

When I thought of the boy years later, that memory resonated. Instead of writing a predictable romantic gesture, I tried to hang the emotional weight of lost love on the unlikeliest suite of images: my first trip duck hunting. Ultimately the poem didn't end up being about that experience exclusively or even the boy (though he's in there).

If the poem's about love, it's love for the diminishing landscape of the rural South.

SEBASTIAN MATTHEWS

ARS POETICA BLUES

Writing a poem is like making a paper airplane: one morning
you wake up with this urge to build something light, that might fly.
You spend a few hours tinkering, trying out this model, that design,
finding a spot in the sun at the corner of your corner table
in the corner of the building on the corner. You are three floors up
so your ideas will have immediate room to let themselves out
into their full bloom of falling. Then, later, after you've given up
on silly notions, after a litany of drudgery, return to the drawing table
and whip up some miniature Wright brother origami and fling it out
the open window (left open by a lover who left your life three lifetimes
ago). It almost always flies—over empty fields, landing safely or in a pile or
exploding into flames, lighting a whole hamlet with its incandescence.
And you jump out after it, or stay in your chair as the sun pulls back
its one great assertion in a huge roll of teletype paper pinpricked with stars;
and no one has seen a thing, except the man on the corner with his hand
down his pants, who looks like Whitman or a beat cop or one of those
Beat Generation wannabes you used to be, smoking handrolls and
dreaming of Villon. And no one cares. Nor do you, really, anymore,
though your dreams are a wartime sky, tiny droning planes in all corners,
and the rest of the night a long battle. And the bottles on the table
rattle as the milk truck tanks roll by.

GHOST TRACKS

on the tenth anniversary of my father's death

A friend says, *I remember walking
down the streets of Seoul with him,*

*pausing while he conjured the house
where his grandfather lived, the long-gone*

*movie theater where he first saw
William Holden.* She began to see

the outlines of her father's city
superimposed on the modern sprawl.

I too have walked ghost tracks
in search of my father, dead

years before my son might know
his face with his infant hands.

He appears in my dreams, a cipher
trapped in a labyrinth of longing

we all tread in the dark, waking
to stupor and heartache. But he's there.

I follow him everywhere: down
empty lanes, tucking into a lost bistro

for a rendezvous with *his* father,
dead for a decade. I can see them

lean into the wine menu, balding heads
nearly touching at the crown.

They are intent as umpires thinking
through a close call, happy

to be back in each other's company.

MIRACLE DAY

for James Hoch

Thunder pulses, an echoing hammer
rattling the house. Snapped awake
by a storm of worry dreams my body
mistakes for an urgent call, I am staring
into the bathroom mirror when my son's voice
mouses under the door: *Daddy, where are you?*
Good question. One of the gifts of fatherhood,
my brother once told me, is to be summoned
from the dingy corridors of your inner life.
He was dead right. I step into my boy's room
wild with relief. He's hopped in bed,
delighted for company. *Read me this book,
Daddy!* Later that morning, driving
through gathering rain to a doctor's appt.
my night fears directed me to, I spy a sign
on a church lawn that reads "Miracle Day,
Coming Soon" and laugh in a scornful way—
as if one can pencil deliverance into a daybook!
Remember how the pastor chanted Marley
on Earth Day, *Every little thing going
to be alright? Too groovy for me*, I whispered.
But when he talked of a shift from fear
to faith, I had to agree. *Yes*, I mouthed.
But how? How on vacation we stayed on
a few perfect hours, lost on island tip
safe inside purifying wind? Collecting shells
as the dog nosed her way along the dunes;
the launch of our son's first kite.

In the doctor's lot, I let the rain validate me,
happy to be alive in that lit-up way we get
when no bad-news punches are delivered.
Then the dog joined us, scratching
to be let in, and we huddled in our cave
as the thunder backed its way into the night
and, one after the other, we fell asleep.

THE ZONES OF PROVIDENCE

If I were to take a photograph of this boulevard
I'd use one of those Civil War-era collodion cameras

preferred by Brady, which shortened exposure time
but required him to haul fragile glass plates wet

into the bloodied field. It seems fitting, here
in this upscale post-antebellum neighborhood:

an arduous task demanding patience in a land
rife with comfort and convenience. *A mirror*

of memory, Holmes called it, the camera
set up outside the show church and pointed

down the long line of decorous Oaks.
But what would it bring to light? Surely not

all the unspoken walkways and invisible,
cordoned-off zones the privileged sleepwalk

through? Could the impartial camera ever really
fix that to the plate? You'd see, instead, handsome

joggers alongside European cars and SUVs
on the way to work, teams of lean bike riders

floating by in their bright colors. Better to wait
for the maid to walk her lady's Jack Russell

and hope she puts her hand to her face
if you want any glimpse in. The front yards

are all show boxes tended by invisible gardeners,
and the facades of houses bounce light

off their windows expertly. All the old men
have retreated to their garages and all the teens

are off to college or soccer practice, which leaves
the women to peer out their windows or parade

their toddlers in the Starbucks, made up for a night out
at eight in the morning. The only untouched place

in the picture is the green corridor at the center
of the frame, the grass strip between lanes. Which is

where I stand now hidden under the black hood,
hand gripping the guillotine switch, waiting

for the perfect torsion of the suspended moment.
Maybe I'll cross over into the shot's frame

and star in my own photograph,
besotted admirer and blurred subject both.

AFTER WORDS

All the poems published here, except "Ars Poetica Blues," are born out of real experiences, with first drafts jotted down soon after the event. "Ghost Tracks" and "Miracle Day" go about describing the event and provide commentary along the way. Nothing fancy.

"The Zones of Providence" comes out of a series of walks I took while serving on the MFA faculty at Queens in Charlotte. In the old-money neighborhood where we stayed, I felt more than a little odd walking down the street. As soon as I thought of photographing the scene, the poem's creative spark lit. "Ars Poetica Blues," though entirely metaphoric and whimsical—I am trying to talk about the creative process in a fresh way—does manage to use the setting of a friend's apartment window in Ann Arbor. So even a poem like that grounds itself in place and event.

DANIEL NATHAN TERRY

A BURIAL PARTY

April 1865, Cold Harbor, Virginia
Negative by John Reekie, assistant to Gardner

Alexander Gardner

At first I think this place is misnamed—
we're not even close to the ocean.

Then I notice how many skulls and ribs protrude from the sea
of grass—white rocks warning sensible travelers

on to another port of entry ever since the two armies
converged and left this wreckage.

I ponder the photo I will take—"The Dead of Cold Harbor"—
the chill it will bring New York ladies. I hear

their sharply drawn breaths as they read the caption,
nudge their companions, and—with lace-gloved fingers—

point out the place name as if they are the first
to make the connection.

While Reekie prepares the plate I ask the burial detail
if they know how this field of dead men's bones

received its poetic moniker.
The Negro orderly gleaning white bones claims the place

is named for a hotel that stood at the crossroads,
offering shelter but no hot meals.

It's not what I wanted, but who up North will know? After all,
they only see what I show them.

They will no more know the mundane truth behind this name
than they will know the allegiances of these dead men.

Even I cannot tell Union from Confederate now;
the weather's sucked the color from the wool

and nearly everything's gray. The bones randomly stacked
on the gurney offer no information beyond the obvious: a pelvis,

a leg bone still attached somehow to a boot, a paisley vest full
of vertebrae.

SOLDIERS BATHING

From the Private Collection of N. Williams
Photograph by Timothy O'Sullivan, 25 May 1864

Noah Williams, 1928

That morning, twelve soldiers toed into the slick
Virginia mud, waded into the North Anna to wash
in cool water before pushing deeper into the peninsula.

O'Sullivan wanted to fix this moment,
these men coming together, without guns or sabers,
nothing between them but air, water, friendship,

the falling and reflecting light. He begged them be still:
instead they played, leapt like summer trout. Two waved
their privates—despite their beards, still schoolboys.

They jeered, catcalled, beckoned us,
but we were too occupied with the camera,
with the business of posterity, to join them in the river.

When I look at the picture now, I see the sweet folly
of my friend. How he pushed himself, how desperate he was
to secure the image *he* saw.

Here—on the far left, a soldier becomes a ghost
before my eyes. The oak darkens, overhangs like a gallows.
Even the polished marble of the river's surface

that seems to bury the men alive, waist-deep in solid stone,
is a lie. It was not a dark day, it was not festered up with omens.
What seems ominous at first glance

is only the camera's inability to stop motion.
Truth is, moments of joy are fleeting, impossible
to capture, a phantom darting away

in the corner of the eye.

THE FINAL LINCOLN PORTRAIT

Negative by Alexander Gardner, 10 April 1865

It is a portrait of the nation—
the forced smile,

laugh lines furrowed by grief
into deep ravines

of shadow, the dark eyes
weary beneath the weight

of black memories, half-hidden
by the hooded brow.

And notice how the body
slumps forward,

intact but broken deep
beneath the skin.

TABLEAUX MORT

Various photographs of dead confederates, later identified as the same soldier.
Negatives by Alexander Gardner

Death is artless—no poetry, no grace.
Cataract-white distended eyes, mouth black
and wet as caviar, skin tinged blue
and tightening with decay's foul breath.

You can see only so many bodies eviscerated by shells,
rifled and stripped by the enemy, before going
numb. It is a challenge to make photographs
that communicate more than horror.

The true artist knows this, knows the limitations
of the viewer, understands the need to discover
some beauty, some tender pathos in the grimmest
reality.

Gardner finds a young Confederate in the Slaughter Pen,
dead as his comrades, but somehow still fair
as an actor on the stage. With his assistant's help,
he rearranges the rebel

in various locations and poses on the hill.
Here he dies near a cleft in a ring of gray boulders
called the Devil's Den, hand clutching his musket,
playing the role of sniper, of traitor.

And here he is again in a trench,
hand upon his heart as if he expired slowly,
pledging his life to the doomed South.
Each gesture of the corpse is a different creation:

sitting upright (noble and defiant in death),
arm shielding the face (fear and despair),
lying face down (cowardice and retreat),
chin lifted to the brooding sky (prayer and surrender).

Each photograph is an act
in Gardner's play. The audience holds its breath
with each twist in the plot. But even this is artifice,
even this is empty gesture. For in the dark of the theater,

you are in no danger. You cannot be assaulted
by the stench of rotting flesh. And while there is applause,
you cannot hear the flies buzzing impatiently
near your eyes, the clacking beaks of hungry crows,

the slow flap of the vulture's wings.

HARVEST OF DEATH

Negative by Timothy O'Sullivan
5 July 1863, Gettysburg

Spread-eagle on the field
of Gettysburg
the dead arch their backs

as if the ground they lie upon
won't forgive them
and wants them gone,

as if pulled
by ropes hooked
into their breastbones.

Their torsos swell
toward Heaven
as if the Lord

has only this
small mercy left.
Or is it as simple

as the grip of death
and decay:
muscles tensing

before finally letting go,
hollow bellies
full of vapor? Is it as natural

as the orchard in the valley—
these windfall men
ripened and ready

for the camera to commence
its thorough
and slow gathering?

AFTER WORDS

*No one was more surprised than I by my choice of American Civil War photo-
graphers as the subject of a poetry collection. Although I have lived most of my adult
life in the South, I've never considered myself particularly regionalist. I'm a pacifist
with no real interest in warfare. I have never been fascinated by American history or
politics. Even my attempts at photography have been less than promising. That said,
the moment a professor projected the image of Timothy O'Sullivan's photograph
"Harvest of Death" on the screen, I was overcome with grief for men who died nearly
a century and a half earlier. I was suddenly plagued by a question that would not release me until* Capturing the Dead *was complete: after such graphic images of loss
and pain are shown to the public, how can we, as a species, continue to wage war?
For me, the poems were an attempt to understand, and in some small way, come to
terms with our darkest nature.*

MICHAEL WHITE

ANNE FRANK'S TREE

Reuters: "Diseased Anne Frank tree to be cut down next week . . .
A graft will be put in its place."
—*Nov 13, 2007*

A fifteen year old girl—
on tip-toe in the attic—
saw the huge horse-chestnut,

Westerkerk tower, and the random
North Sea gull. "Our tree
is in full blossom . . . even

more beautiful than last year,"
she wrote, on the thirteenth of May,
1944.

A nightingale once built
her nest beside the house
of a poet. He was ill.

He sat beneath a plum
one day, and when he returned,
his hands were filled with the scraps

of stanzas. Here is the plum.
I know I shouldn't, but
I pluck one leaf, I crush it,

place it beneath my tongue—
releasing its bitter mint.
Praise to the angel's wordless

gaze—her angled cut,
her balm of moss—who coaxes
the root, who stakes the shoot

of the chestnut and the plum.

THE LEVEE

I am this dust on the river road, I'd think.
I am this dust on the tasseled fields—deep summer's
scent of brushfire threaded through this breeze—

and at that age, I could believe. My world
consisted of a sallow-looking downtown;
streets named after trees; the girls I worshipped

secretly; the cemeteries fringed
with spikes; the breaks in the river hills to the south
(great floodplain vistas fading away to the south),

where everything ends in a narrow fringe of swampoaks
and cottonwoods overlooming the river . . . Part of
me is always homing, scrambling down

the face of the levee, forcing my way through willows
and driftwood—flotsam of old tires and rusted oildrums—
down to the Corps of Engineers' embankment,

down to the seam where the elements touch, the dense
aortal dark of slaughterhouse and prairie
sweeping past me . . . There at the tip of the wing dike,

kneeling and sinking back, I'd finger the sand grains
—fragments of mussel shells—and let the sun-scaled
body of current carry me away . . .

Sometimes, I'd close my eyes, and in the cries
of crows—the howls of semis two miles off—
in the barely audible, hoarse note of a tractor

raising dust in the fields across the river,
I could hear the year click shut. One evening,
smoldering down to the nub, I thought I could feel

an odd, irregular throbbing in my jawbone—
skull—the balls of my feet . . . The others were back
in the trees: I crouched alone on a spit of sand,

the pulse of an engine pounding all around me,
out of the pores of the limestone cliffsides. Something
was coming toward me, something was churning its way

upriver toward me, thrumming louder and louder
until I could see the train of barges shackled
together—laboring into sight—until

I could see the tow: its funnel pouring gouts
of black exhaust, its pilot house ablaze
with fumes and glare, its six-foot bow wave breaking

along both banks . . . I was amazed, transfixed
by its deliberate and delicate
corrections—centering in its marks—as slowly,

it drew abreast, and I could see the man
inside of it, the one responsible
for all those tons of steel and displaced river.

I remember the eerie, flickering pall
cast up from the instrument panel onto his face,
and I remember the moment he turned toward me,

and sounded his airhorn three long blasts for me
as if in recognition . . . *River rat,*
I thought, and waved. And then he was gone. And after

that agitation passed—long after the gnats
all started up again—I ran as hard
as I could through the flood-washed cottonwoods—
over the levee—

back to the road, and my friends . . . In our backyard
today, camellias are having their second spring;
our concrete birdbath fills with the slough of blossom . . .

Suddenly, it's over. Suddenly,
the tendons of clematis flower and fade out
over our garage roof—its metaphor,

its metamorphosis, is over and done with . . .
What I want is what I had: the landscape
beneath the landscape; hawks and cliffheads; hum

of bridges; summer's sumac, gold and cobalt
clarities which deepened as the river
gradually dwindled . . . What I want is what

I was—that self lost utterly in vagrant
days that sank in flames as I spent them there—
my element silt, my posture prayer, my god

appearing sometimes in the guise of gnats
or hawks, or hundreds of incidents that bloomed
alone like bloodlit clouds across the dark

opacities of surface . . . Once, a man
appeared like that, *a man appeared like that,*
and as he passed—as waves of unimaginable

clamor shuddered through that place which still
absorbs me so completely—suddenly,
he glanced at me, and claimed me for his own.

WHAT I WANTED TO TELL YOU

for Rebecca Lee

couldn't wait, and I kept taking the steps
        to your beach house three at a time in my mind, but
the truth is, I was caught in traffic back
        in Forest Hills. Before I knew what hit me—

what the slowdown and clanging hysteria meant—the tandem
        diesels lumbered past, all decibels
and oilsmoke, and then maybe a hundred coalcars
        and flatcars slid through the fogged dusk. I admit

I loved the spectacle, the patience of joggers
        and leashed dogs—even the starlings swirling up
from the blossomy lungs of the live oaks—and I wanted
        to step out, rush into that magnitude

the way my mind does sometimes, going for broke,
        not letting go . . . But I stayed firmly put
instead, and slipping into neutral, read
        the boxcars' open secrets: *Big Blue, Norfolk*

& Western scrolling through the neighborhood—
        where mansions shuddered in their berths, where April
sulked and lost its grip, where in the wrack
        of body heat, the agony of steel

on steel, I spoke to you like this.

RE-ENTRY

Then it hit me. Fumbling for a smoke,
I sank down heavily onto a concrete bench

beside the circle drive. There was no view
except for the rows of glare-shot windshields, shimmer

of asphalt—bypasses and freeways—and
a venomous, blood-orange dusk above it all.

I took a deep drag. Thirty days had passed
since I'd checked in, and wandered through the ward

with tom implosions in each ear—as fireflies
flooded the trelliswork of synapses—

for three straight days, before I knew where I was.
It was the top floor of State Hospital,

our dayroom windows facing out across
the vast exhaustion of the Midwest, where

electrical dust-storms tinged the air, an aura
of migraine settling over the river hills . . .

Day after day, we'd gather there for Peer Group—
some in wheelchairs, some with our IV poles—

each trying to calm the tremors in his hands.
Whenever someone spoke, whenever someone

started to piece a narrative together
out of threads of smoke—the infused ache

of what the flesh remembers—I could feel
the tenor of fear in everything he said,

the word on the tip of his tongue on the tip of my tongue.
I'd listen and gaze out, listen and gaze out over

the fallow prairies, half-imagined hayfields
of my only landscape: buckled faultlines

leveling off in miles of bottomland,
where massive burr oaks loomed like cumulus

adrift upon a plain of dust. I'd stare
and stare—untethered, ravenous—at sheets

of lightning smoldering here and there beneath
a remote steel-blue cloudbank, as the room

filled with acetylene sun, the conduits of
my nerves burned clean . . . And this was the only cure

there was. One day I rose, and put on my street clothes,
nothing in my pockets. I remember

riding the elevator five flights down—
the sudden *whoosh* when its doors opened on

the ground floor . . . Struggling to compose myself,
I strode across the lobby with a wink

for the receptionist, but by the time
I stepped out into the sunlight, I was shaking.

AFTER WORDS

Sometimes it's the most difficult subjects that make for the best (and worst) art. Writing about something that profoundly affected your life, for the better or worse, can help you understand it, perhaps for the first time. It can also inspire you and summon the best from you as a writer, in the effort to communicate something important to another human being. This sort of truth telling, even when the writing isn't that great, keeps the focus of one's art on the human, rather than on purely aesthetic issues.

Although I have never discussed the poem "Re-entry" with anyone, I thought enough of it to make it the title poem of my third book. It describes my month-long stay in an alcoholic treatment hospital back in the '80s, from a much-later perspective. This experience, as you might imagine, was both the lowest point of my life, and also my greatest triumph. I couldn't not write about it.

The poem begins and ends at the same point: zero hour, an alcoholic's release back into the world and its dangers. The poem's body consists of remembered scraps of images, images that evoke, as best I was able, the gradual awakening of sobriety. The form of the poem is a rough-hewn iambic pentameter, the traditional line for meditative verse, which gives continuity to the images. However, I did something a bit unusual here, in breaking the poem into two-line stanzas. All this brokenness, this broken music, represents my best attempt to use the resources of art to tell the human truth.

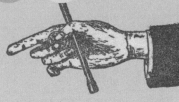

AS IF BY MAGIC

TOOLS & TIPS

TIM BASS

WRITING CLEAN:
WHY SPELLING, GRAMMAR, AND PUNCTUATION MATTER

"Most of us don't know a gerund from a gerbil and don't care, but we'd like to speak and write as though we did."

—Patricia T. O'Conner
Woe is I: The Grammarphobe's Guide to Better English in Plain English

SOMEWHERE ON AN AMERICAN ROADSIDE stands a green sign that warns drivers:

DONT'T DRINK

AND DRIVE.

This is a worthy message delivered in an unworthy way. It sounds as if the sign guzzled several beers before taking its position by the highway.

The sign painter has committed a simple and amusing misspelling. There aren't two *T*s in *don't*, just as there aren't two *K*s in *drink*. But the painter deserves some credit for creative misspelling. The word *don't* is commonly misspelled as *dont'*, because many people don't understand that the apostrophe signifies the missing letter in a contraction (in this case, the *O* in *not*). Our sign painter seems to have known that an apostrophe belonged somewhere in the word, but where? The painter tried to play it safe with two *T*s. Take away the first *T*, and the spelling is correct; with both, the sign stutters.

A second mistake lies with the sign painter's supervisors. They failed to notice the error until it appeared on the highway for the world to see. Sure, the sign catches the public's attention—which is the purpose, after all—but it does so for the wrong reasons.

Will this little misspelling get anyone thrown into jail? No. But it will—and did—get posted to the Internet. Humiliation is its own form of just punishment.

Writers commit errors like this all the time. It's natural, in a way. People who write a lot are bound to make mistakes because they give themselves more opportunities to err. The same logic holds for stock-car racers who are more likely to crash because they zoom around tracks with dozens of other cars, all rolling 190 miles per hour.

There is no excuse, though, for committing habitual mistakes in our writing. Grammar and punctuation matter. Spelling matters. Writing stories, poems, and essays for publication—for a magazine, a book, a newspaper, a class, or any audience—is different than writing to our friends in notes or e-mail. Writers who ignore proper English or the rules of writing can expect to hit the wall. They can expect to fail.

Fortunately, most writers accept this. They know and follow the rules. And if they don't know the rules, they take it on themselves to learn. It's a simple process that involves two primary changes to the way we write:

1. SLOW DOWN. Computers make it easy to write fast, which helps when we push against deadlines. But fast work often leads to sloppy work. That's true for chefs, carpenters, and surgeons. And it's true for writers. We often work so fast that we don't recognize our writing mistakes, and then the mistakes go out for all to see. Just ask the sign painter. Good writing demands careful attention: imaginative ideas, thoughtful purpose, and thorough revision. These efforts take time. We must slow down and give our writing the care it deserves.

2. READ CLOSELY. Often, we write, print, and hand in our work—all without giving our writing a careful read. As a result, we have no idea that the piece suffers from shifting verb tenses or from dialogue punctuated so badly that the readers have no idea who's speaking. Or that we used the word *don't*. And even when we do read back through our work, we tend to "glance it over" instead of reading thoroughly, word by word. We must read closely. If we do, we'll spot most of our errors and fix them before they reach the printer.

I call these "changes to the way we write" because, generally speaking, we work too fast and read too superficially. This is not true of all writers, of course. But too many of us have poor writing habits, and they show.

To improve your grammar, punctuation, and spelling, consider these steps:

1. AVOID PROCRASTINATION. It is a mistake to wait to be inspired to write. Writing is work, not floating on the free air of a magic carpet ride. Writers who procrastinate usually end up writing in a hurry. They have no time to slow down. They have no time to read closely. Their mistakes will stand out like a misspelled highway sign. If you write early and finish with time to breathe, you can set your work aside for a day or two, then pick up again and read with fresh eyes. You'll be amazed at how many errors you find, or how many unclear sentences, or how many incomplete paragraphs. And you'll have time to revise.

2. READ ALOUD. In her wonderful book *Eats, Shoots & Leaves: The Zero Tolerance Approach to Punctuation*, author Lynne Truss writes: "My own position is simple: in some matters of punctuation there are simple rights and wrongs; in others, one must apply a good ear to good sense." Read your work aloud. Listen to the language—the rhythm and the logic. Does it sound melodic or clunky? Does it make sense? Are the sentences so long that you run out of breath? If you hear problems in your work, then your readers will, too. So change it—rewrite until it sounds right.

3. LISTEN FOR COMMAS AND PERIODS. Reading aloud can help you find the natural pauses that call for commas, and the natural stops that call for periods. Slow down. Read closely. You needn't be an expert on punctuation. Just pay attention. Listen.

4. DON'T DEPEND ON SPELL CHECK. Yes, spell check can be useful for catching typos—such as *teh* instead of *the*. But computers usually overlook incorrect usage, such as:

The writers got there grammar just right.
The writers got they're grammar just right.
The writers got their grammar just right.

My spell check believes all three of those are just right, even though two are dead wrong. (By the way, which one is correct?)

Likewise, spell check often says words are correct, even though they're misspelled. These include *alright* (for *all right*), *ok* (for *OK* or *okay*), *yah* (for *yeah*), and *irregardless* (it's not even a word).

5. READ MORE. As you read novels, short stories, and essays, notice not just the ideas but also the grammar and punctuation. Pay attention to the way the authors punctuate dialogue, making it easy to understand who's speaking. Note how the writers avoid multiple exclamation points!!!!! See how they use the semicolon; it separates related, yet independent, clauses. Marvel at their proper use of the colon to introduce lists: of ingredients, names, statistics, or anything else.

6. GET A FEW GOOD REFERENCE BOOKS, AND USE THEM. You don't need to know all the rules of spelling, grammar, and punctuation. You just need to know where to go for the rules. Don't know the difference between a hyphen and a dash? Look it up. Don't know whether the word you want is spelled *definitely* or *defiantly*? Look it up. Your writing desk should include a handful of essential books: a dictionary, a thesaurus, and a grammar guide, for starters. These need not be expensive or fancy books. (My own writing desk holds a paperback dictionary that cost two dollars at a used-book store, and a used thesaurus that cost about three dollars.) There are scores of good grammar guides available for just a few bucks. These days, thank goodness, authors have found ways to make these guides useful and readable (dare I say entertaining?). For example, in *The New Well-Tempered Sentence: A Punctuation Handbook for the Innocent, the Eager, and the Doomed*, Katharine Elizabeth Gordon uses examples that involve macaroon-eating dukes, disappearing debutantes, and cats that wear pajamas. (A sample, concerning commas: "The Grim Reaper was cutting capers in the vestibule, attractively wagging his finger, and suggestively rolling his eyes.")

A final sliver of advice: Have faith in yourself. It's not quick and easy to polish your skills with grammar, punctuation, and spelling. But the more you work at it, the better you'll get. And the better you get, the easier the task becomes. You *can* write clean stories, poems, and essays. And with serious work, you will. Stay with it. ~~Dont't~~ Don't give up. ❧

ROBERT ANTHONY SIEGEL

WHAT TO DO WITH WORKSHOP FEEDBACK: A GUIDE FOR THE BEWILDERED

YOU ARE WALKING OUT OF CLASS, having just workshopped your story (or poem, or essay, or cross-genre experiment), and you can barely see the hallway you walk through because you are so lit up with the excitement of hearing your work talked about by readers. Suddenly, the piece you wrote seems real in a way you could not have imagined before: not a private entertainment (like computer solitaire) but a public act, an attempt to communicate. You have *written* something, and it means something.

The problem is *what*. Because during the discussion of your piece certain things were said that seemed to indicate points of confusion. A scene or a line was not quite clear; somebody thought your protagonist committed suicide when he was only taking a nap; somebody else called the piece a love story when it is really about the *impossibility* of love in a virtual age. Besides, many opinions were stated and numerous suggestions made, along the lines of *I really like the girl. Why isn't there more of her? And the ending doesn't work for me. I think you should cut it.* While somebody else said *I love the ending. But you need to get rid of the girl.* And then there was a lot of yelling.

To make matters worse, you now carry in your arms a stack of copies of that same story (or poem, etc.), bearing the written comments of those same classmates, and you can already see, leafing through them as you walk, that the written comments are *different*. The reader who said in class that she liked the ending has written in the margin—with a thick black felt-tip, underscored three times—CUT. And the reader who said you should put in more of the girl has systematically drawn a line through each of her scenes. What made them change their minds? Can you trust their opinions? Should you take their advice?

The short answer is no. But the long answer is much more interesting, so here it is: workshop critiques, though often framed as ideas or suggestions about revision, are in fact neither of those things. They are reactions. They are emotional, personal, situational, and therefore highly changeable. That reader who wanted to see more of the girl, for example, though he cut all her scenes, may be in the process of breaking up with his own real-life girlfriend, or he may be doggedly, stubbornly resisting falling in love with somebody. Who knows? He may not even know. The mind is pulled out of shape by the heart in ways it cannot understand. The point is that a group of intelligent and thoughtful readers will almost certainly produce an array of very different and sometimes contradictory responses to the same piece of writing. A consensus may emerge in the classroom discussion, but that consensus may be based on the interplay of personalities or the onset of sheer exhaustion, rather than on real insight into the future development of your piece.

Does this mean that workshop comments are worthless? On the contrary, once you accept them as highly personal reactions—imperfect things of the moment—they become very valuable indeed. Maybe you had been wondering about the girl yourself. You weren't sure what the problem was, but you knew that something wasn't completely right with her. You had tossed around some ideas—put her in a wheelchair, make her clairvoyant—but nothing seemed to do the trick, and then you chewed the end of your pencil for a while. Dinnertime rolled around, and all the good shows were on, and finally you forgot all about it.

I would suggest that your classmates' conflicting suggestions—to give us more of the girl or lose the girl—are valuable because they confirm your sense that something needs to be done with her; in particular, that her role within the story is still unclear. But when it comes down to the specifics of how to address this problem, I think you will be better off seeking your own solution. That solution may incorporate ideas generated in the workshop, or it may not. The key point is that it is *your* solution and reflects your understanding of what the piece is to become, not somebody else's (no matter how articulate or confident or persuasive that person may be).

I have focused on the example of the girl because I believe it shows the careful, temperate, disengaged way in which workshop suggestions must be understood. But I don't want you to become so skeptical about workshop feedback that you can't take advantage of it. Let me therefore switch to another, less ambivalent example. Of course, I mean the nap that was misinterpreted as suicide.

Looking through your stack of manuscripts, you are probably asking yourself how anyone could be stupid enough to misread the best nap in the history of literature as an act of suicide. You may even be wondering how fifteen seemingly intelligent readers could make the same bizarre mistake at the same time. Later that night, however, while trying to go to sleep, it may occur to you that this can't simply be coincidence, that somehow the *napness* of the scene isn't quite as clear as you had thought it was. Of course, you will resist this thought. *There's nothing wrong with that nap, it's just very subtle.* But the seed of doubt has been sown, and in the days that follow, your uncertainties about the nap will start to recur, will grow in frequency, will finally coalesce into a great, mind-shaking insight: *Hey, if my readers don't get it, I'm not communicating with them.*

This reminder that the reader-writer relationship is based on the act of communication may well be the single greatest service a workshop can perform. Your readers are not privy to your intentions; they only know what you have written. Their comments on your manuscript reveal just what they have understood, given the words you have put down on the page. For this reason, they can alert you to any slippage between what you meant to say and what you are actually saying. They can also help point out where the confusion is creeping in. (To get rid of the suicide problem, for example, you may want to begin by cutting the line comparing his necktie to "a life-choking hangman's rope.")

Let me sum up for you. Workshop feedback can be scary. It can overwhelm you with brilliant, foolproof suggestions for making your manuscript better, and there is a danger that you may feel intimidated into taking these suggestions before you have figured out what you yourself want to do with the piece. Workshop feedback can also be confusing, because some of those brilliant, foolproof suggestions will probably be contradictory. Your feelings of intimidation and confusion will lessen, however, when you realize that your classmates' critiques are nothing more than personal *reactions,* and that they are affected by many circumstances you can't know about, including mood at the time of reading or quality of lunch before reading, among other things. Once you understand this point, their comments become really useful, because they allow you to see what you are actually saying on the page, rather than what you assume you are saying.

But perhaps the most important thing that workshop feedback can give you is that feeling of being read. It changes the act of writing from a solitary act, an attempt to speak, to a communal act—an attempt to *communicate.* That change in emotional context will help power your growth as a writer. ❧

KAREN BENDER

TEN IDEAS FOR REVISION

1. REMEMBER THAT IT'S BETTER TO HAVE A FEW PAGES of something rather than no pages of fear. Revising a story is seeing where your characters and your voice take you. The story already exists and is waiting for you, the writer, to find it.

2. READ OVER YOUR DRAFT, looking for the emotions that are most alive, the characters that are most interesting to you. Begin experimenting with these emotions and characters to see what other options present themselves.

3. TRY TO WRITE A NEW BEGINNING OR END scene to your story. This may not be the final version, but may help you see that the story can have a shape.

4. TRY TO FIND A CLEAR LINE OF DESIRE in the story. What does the main character want? What do the other characters want? Try to simplify the characters' main urges. Find a spine around which you can develop complex reactions and experiences.

5. THINK ABOUT COMPRESSION. How can one scene do the work of many scenes? Which scene seems most interesting to you? Can you layer some of the interactions/episodes of other scenes into this scene? Are all the characters necessary? Do you need three characters or can they be comprised into one?

6. THINK ABOUT POINT OF VIEW. Are you interested in the protagonist's point of view? Are you interested in writing from the point of view of one of the other characters? If so, try writing some scenes from that character's point of view. If you enjoy it, you may want to switch; if not, you will have learned more about that character in the process.

7. THINK ABOUT SPECIFICITY. Specific details will act as "tips of the iceberg" in a story. Find the ones that will imply a life for the characters outside the world of the story. If you can't figure out how to specify part of your story, leave it for now, and come back to it later.

8. THINK ABOUT WHAT IS IN THE STORY because you *want* it to be included, and what is in the story because you think it *should* be included. Does some of the writing feel dutiful, unnecessary? Think about what you need in the story, and what you can let go.

9. REMEMBER THAT TAKING A BREAK from a story can be a great way of getting perspective on it. Take a day or a week off from your story. Read something new or something you love; look at paintings or sculpture or dance or theater or film that inspires you.

10. REMEMBER THAT REVISION IS A PROCESS and happens in stages. During the first stage you may be trying to figure out what the story is about. Then you may develop scenes and layer characters. Later, you may compress scenes and characters. Then you may work on pacing. A late revision focuses on clarity and language. You may work on any of these issues during the process, but try not to get too focused on honing the language too early, as you may not know what content will remain in the story. One writer I know says, "Writing a story is like building a boat. I don't want to spend too much time intricately painting a hatch when I don't know if the boat even has a rudder." ❧

BEN GEORGE

THE COLLABORATIVE
WORK OF EDITING

ANNE FADIMAN, FORMER EDITOR of the *American Scholar*, considers editing an imperative, and insists that we think of the profession "not as a guilty secret, but as part of a proud collaboration: 95 percent writing, 5 percent editing. If you don't get that 5 percent, you're not as good as you could be. Or as good as you deserve to be." I like that terminology—"proud collaboration." I believe that's exactly what happens between a good writer and a good editor. And I think it's essential for the writer to have it. But some writers worry about editors. The noted short-story writer Charles D'Ambrosio told me that in his teaching he frequently fields questions from wary young writers who are afraid an editor will "monkey with their genius." This concern isn't restricted to young writers. Vladimir Nabokov once called editors "pompous avuncular brutes who would attempt to 'make suggestions,' " which he then "countered with a thunderous 'stet!' " Likewise, the Irish novelist John Banville maintains that "in terms of style, or direction, or intention" no publisher lays a finger on any of his books. "I send it to them," he says, "and it gets published." So there are exceptions to writers who value editors. But they tend to be exceptions and not the rule.

The question then: how to assist the story in approaching its Platonic ideal (if you accept that little premise which I'm glossing over here)? For the start of an answer, I turn to Alice Munro, who aptly likens a story to a house. "You go inside and stay there for a while," she says, "wandering back and forth and settling where you like and discovering how the rooms and corridors relate to each other, how the world outside is altered by being viewed from these windows." Munro hopes to deliver, each time, a story with "a sturdy sense of itself, of being built out of its own necessity, not just to shelter or beguile you." If I extend her lovely metaphor, I'd say an editor can help a writer in two ways. First, but less often, with those larger conceptual things: how does the house (or the story) fit together, how does one element complement another in the overall beauty and durability? This is architectural. Second, and more often, with the practical stuff, the craftsmanship: the sound, the sentences and their music, their contrapuntal relation to one another. You walk through the house, tapping on the walls, checking the quality of the cornices, the molding, the baseboards, the archways. Are they right for the house? And so on.

To edit well, I think an editor should come at a story not with preconceptions about what a story "is"—some whipping post to which the story must be lashed—but with an openness to whatever the writer is attempting; it's a characteristic that Matthew Arnold called, alternately, "disinterestedness" and "flexibility." When I think of the opposite of that, the ending of a Billy Collins poem called "Introduction to Poetry" comes to mind:

> all they want to do
> is tie the poem to a chair with rope
> and torture a confession out of it.
>
> They begin beating it with a hose
> to find out what it really means.

I think this sort of attitude can cause mistakes by an editor—if he isn't willing to go where a story is taking him. You have to be receptive to invention. An Aimee Bender or a George Saunders story is going to be vastly different from an Alice Munro story. Wordsworth has a great quote on the subject: "Every great and original writer," he quipped, "in proportion as he is great or original, must himself create the taste by which he is to be relished; he must teach the art by which he is to be seen." So if you're the editor, I think you have to be open to finding that out. You don't want to miss it because of your own pigheadedness.

Of course it's impossible to remove from oneself all editorial tics and biases, much as it is impossible for a story to fully achieve its writer's conceit. The key for an editor, I think, is awareness of his biases and continual reevaluation of his assumptions about what good story-telling is and what constitutes an artful use of language. I was forced last year, for instance, to revisit a prejudice against word repetition when I read James Wood's convincing look at the effect that Tolstoy gains in *War and Peace* by repeating the seemingly innocuous word *juicy* three times in the same paragraph.

But the inability of an editor to completely vanquish his biases should not prevent him from rolling up his sleeves. Gary Fisketjon, who over the last quarter century has edited too many of our literary lions to name here, says that his job is to read a book more seriously and carefully than any sane person ever would, and to note anything and everything that doesn't seem up to the book's own highest standards. Frequently it takes him an hour to go over five pages. This intensity of effort, to me, demonstrates his commitment to both the story and the writer. Speaking for myself, once I'm in a story, editing it, I don't hold back. I inspect every nook and cranny. (When I was a kid, reading scads of dog books, like *Where the Red Fern Grows*, I used to mimic aloud things like the author's descriptions of the dogs' barking, to see if I thought he'd got the sound right. My mom would knock softly on my bedroom door, to make sure I was okay and remind me it was only a book, after all.) My reasoning is this: there's no reason to hold back, since once I give feedback to a writer, the writer owns it, to do with as she sees fit. It can be valuable to challenge a writer in spots. If I can't divine the felicity of her intent in a given passage, I bring up my concern, which encourages the writer to think through her decision, to determine whether there is a good reason for the language or the scene to exist in its current fashion. I've seen writers come up with an incredible sentence or image or solution to a problem merely because they were pushed to do so. That said, the writer should never make any change that doesn't seem to her intuitively correct. The story must remain, always and only, the writer's.

But to put editing in more concrete terms, I'd like to talk briefly about a specific story I edited when I worked for the literary quarterly *Tin House*. It's called "Cultivation," by an up-and-coming writer named Shannon Cain. In Shannon's story, Frances, our filtering protagonist for much of the way, is the single mother of three children by two different fathers. She cultivates, in addition to her children, large amounts of marijuana, the delivery of which provides the impetus for a road trip. Many aspects of this story were immediately arresting: 1) the deceptively uncomplicated prose—wryly funny and disarmingly elegant— that reveals the tremendous complications of the characters it describes, 2) Shannon's wonderful knack for revealing the folly of human fantasy by placing it next to fact—Frances daydreams about her young son one day earning a Yale MBA and aiding in her pot business, only to turn around and see him putting spit wads in his brother's hair, 3) the unexpected but brilliant and completely necessary shift in point of view to Frances's fourteen-year-old daughter, Emily, for the last quarter of the story, and 4) Shannon's use of resonant metaphor. While all three of Frances's children accompany her on this illicit road trip, the story is really about a mother and daughter, about the private suffering that each is unable to communicate to the other. So with respect to this last point, scenes such as Frances's braiding of Emily's hair, her fingers tangling in it and holding it tight as the two stare out at the campsite lake, take on a greater weight. Also, while this journey goes from West to East (Arizona to Tennessee), an inverse of the archetype, it ends with a climactic scene at the Mississippi River, site of that most important journey in American literature: Huck and Jim's.

My point is that editing doesn't turn something crappy into something amazing. Shannon's story was already a stunner when I first read it. But I tried with her, in the editing process, to burnish it. One of the first things I learned about stories, from the wonderful Cajun writer Tim Gautreaux, is that what's not in a story is every bit as important as what is (analogous, I suppose, to Chekhov's insouciant advice that writers should always chop off the opening three pages of any first draft). Shannon's story came in at about nine thousand words, a few too many, I thought, for the story's scope. We needed to husband the reader's attention to the story's heart: the road trip and the evolution of this understanding between Frances and Emily. I asked her to cut a thousand words and gave suggestions for where I felt this might be done by excising or compressing paragraphs. The family didn't hit the road till page 7 in the first draft I saw. In the final draft, it was page 4. Better, we thought. Part of what was lost was some explanatory material about Frances's dire financial straits, and her pot-growing methods. Good stuff, for sure, and some of it quite funny, including a brief rumination on the cubicle life of Frances's creditors. But we kept only what was essential to get across her situation. Shannon did retain this sentence: "In the memo line of her checks [Frances] scrawls her account number followed by *you fuckers,* an act which offers diminishing satisfaction with each new check." Hence giving us, in context, the relative desperation of Frances's station, and her un-crushable, if bitter, humor toward it. There was also a phone call with Emily's guidance counselor that Shannon smartly saw fit to reduce to an oblique reference during the hair-braiding scene at the lake.

Beyond the compression, we addressed the chronology and timing of the road trip, including such pedestrian but important matters of time zones, since pesky Phoenix doesn't move ahead an hour during daylight savings like the rest of the country and two of Shannon's characters were going to be placing phone calls back to that locale. We were editing for those stringent readers like Barbara Kingsolver, who claims to have "stopped reading books in which birds sang on the wrong continents." We looked at the pacing of dialogue in a couple of spots. Did a line go on for just a beat too long here? Was this reaction of Emily's too quick there? And what about rhythm? A few sentences benefited from having their commas killed, lending them a rushing quality. Last, we scrutinized the choreography of the scenes to confirm they were spatially correct, especially the last, crucial one. We wanted the reader to move right through that scene to its lovely conclusion without being snagged on any possible disorientation.

And that person—the reader—is the winner in these intense exchanges. Because when writer and editor collaborate in this way, they're telling you that the time you're going to spend reading this is worthwhile.

From my end, it's just excitement. "Sonny's Blues," by James Baldwin—arguably the greatest short story written in postwar America—first appeared more than fifty years ago now. Imagine being William Phillips, the editor of the *Partisan Review* in 1957, and pulling that manuscript out of a manila envelope. You're literally at the frontier of literature! There's a feeling of levitation when you know you're reading a truly singular fiction, one that has what the novelist and long-time *New Yorker* fiction editor William Maxwell referred to as "the breath of life." This is what an editor looks for in any piece of writing. It won't always happen, but once in a while, if you're lucky, you'll be the first, as an editor, to read a story that people will be reading for many years to come. More than that, though, you have a chance to contribute. I'm reminded of the famous admonition of Jean Rhys: "All of writing is a huge lake. There are great rivers that feed the lake, like Tolstoy and Dostoyevsky. And there are trickles like Jean Rhys. All that matters is feeding the lake. I don't matter. The lake matters. You must keep feeding the lake." I try very hard to approach editing with this spirit, a recognition that by helping the writer be her best, I can make a tiny unseen contribution to the lake. ❧

GLOSSARY OF TERMS

PROSE

ALLEGORY: A figurative work in which the narrative has a secondary, symbolic, or metaphorical meaning.

CHARACTER: An artistically created personality that inhabits a story; the character may be invented (or fictional) or a real person.

CLIMAX: Pivotal moment in a drama or story.

CONFLICT: Internal (character, subtext) and external (action of story): whatever is at issue between characters or within a character in a story.

DENOUEMENT: Literally, untying the knot of suspense; refers to the usually short space between climax and ending during which various issues are resolved and emotion, heightened by the conflict, returns to normal.

DIALOGUE: Characters speaking out loud in a dramatic context.

DIALOGUE TAG: Attribution of dialogue to a particular character (e.g., Joan said).

DICTION: Choice of language style and specific vocabulary (i.e., coarse, erudite, formal, colloquial, etc.)

EQUILIBRIUM: A state of balance among the dramatic forces in a story; usually a story begins when equilibrium is disturbed and the forces must be rebalanced.

EFFACED NARRATOR: A first person narrator in fiction or nonfiction who remains in the background of the action, rarely using *I*.

FLASHBACK: A device that allows the writer to present events that happened before the time of the current narration or events.

FRAME: A narrative structure that provides a setting and exposition for the main narrative.

IRONY: A mode of expression, through words (verbal irony) or events (irony of situation), conveying a reality different from and usually opposite to appearance or expectation.

LYRIC ESSAY: An essay structured by means of intuitive connections of theme or language rather than by narrative plot.

MEMOIR: First-person account of significant events in the writer's life; often the focus of the memoir is not on the writer but on other people and events which he or she has witnessed.

NOVEL: A long work of prose fiction, usually treating multiple characters, locales, and themes.

NOVELLA: A long work of prose fiction, usually no longer than about 100 pages, unified by a single character's experience, often unified by time and place; supporting characters tend to be less fully developed than in a novel, the action and plot more unified.

PACE: The tempo at which the narrative unfolds (i.e. fast, slow, etc.). Pace will modulate as story progresses, so that action scenes or dialogue, for example, may read at a faster pace than reflective scenes.

PERSONAL ESSAY: A narrative essay in which the author connects events in his or her own life with some larger meaning.

PLOT: A series of events that comprise the action, related causally: one thing happens because of another, and so on toward a resolution.

POINT OF VIEW (POV): The position from which the story is narrated. The three most common types of POV:

FIRST PERSON NARRATION: Told by the *I* narrator, confined to his or her own perspective.

THIRD PERSON OMNISCIENT NARRATION: Told by a narrator who has access to the thoughts and feelings of all characters.

THIRD PERSON LIMITED OR ASSIGNED NARRATION: Told by a third-person narrator who has access to the thoughts and feelings of one main character, called the viewpoint character.

PREDICAMENT: An untenable situation in which the character is faced with a problem and forced to act to resolve it. (This situation embodies immediate conflict.)

PSYCHIC DISTANCE: The emotional distance between the writer (or reader) and the characters in the story.

REPORTAGE: Reporting on people and events, usually with an effaced, objective narrator.

RESONANCE: As in music, the effect of one story element playing off another to give it greater meaning.

RESOLUTION: Internal and external: the sense that the problem facing the main character has been solved; external action may or may not resolve the internal conflict and vice versa.

SATIRE: A literary mode using ridicule to criticize people and/or society.

STREAM OF CONSCIOUSNESS: Literary technique that reveals the character's feelings, thoughts, and actions, often following an associative rather than a logical sequence, without commentary by the author.

SCENE: A contained drama of a finite duration in which characters act and speak in a particular time and place in such a way as to move the larger story forward; every scene has a purpose in the larger narrative.

SETTING: The place, time, and situation in which a story occurs, the stage of action.

SHORT STORY: A short complete fiction, usually twenty-five manuscript pages or less.

STYLE: The manner of expression of a particular writer, produced by choice of words, grammatical structures, use of literary devices, and all the possible parts of language use.

SUBTEXT: The bottom line emotional or thematic content of a scene or dialogue that is being played out under the scene (e.g., a husband and wife argue about whether to go out to dinner or eat at home, but they are really arguing about who controls their marriage.)

SUSPENSE: The effect of apprehension achieved by asking a significant question to which the reader really wants to know the answer and delaying the answer long enough to heighten its meaning.

TENSION: The feeling that a scene is charged with underlying conflict.

THEME: What the story is thinking about between the lines, related to subtext; the ideas being played out in the scenes, (e.g., loss, the need to choose, redemption, etc.).

TONE: The attitude of the narrator (e.g., angry, bitter, humorous, brooding, judgmental, etc.) as revealed through diction and other elements of voice.

TWIST ENDING: (or surprise ending) An unexpected conclusion that often contains irony or causes the audience to reevaluate the narrative or characters.

UNRELIABLE NARRATOR: A narrator whose credibility has been compromised and whose narrative cannot be taken at face value.

VIEWPOINT CHARACTER (see Point of View): In a third person limited or assigned narration, the character whose interior life is revealed and from whose sensibility we experience the story.

VOICE: The sense of a real person speaking behind the words, including the sensibility, language, and tone.

POETRY

ACCENTUAL-SYLLABIC VERSE: Unrhymed verse consisting of lines containing four accented syllables, two on each side of a caesura. There may be any number of unaccented syllables.

ACCENTUAL POEM: An unrhymed poem consisting of lines containing four accented syllables, two on each side of a caesura. There may be any number of unaccented syllables.

ALLEGORY: A figurative work in which a surface narrative carries a secondary, symbolic, or metaphorical meaning.

ALLITERATION: The audible repetition at close intervals of consonant sounds at the beginning or within words (e.g., Peter Piper's peppers).

ANAPEST: A metrical foot consisting of two unaccented syllables followed by an accented one.

ANAPHORA: Successive phrases, clauses, or lines starting with the same word or words (e.g., Because I do not hope to turn again / Because I do not hope / Because I do not hope to turn. . . .)

ARCHETYPE: Something in the world, and described in literature, that manifests a dominant theme in the collective unconscious of human beings.

ASSOCIATIONAL THINKING: The way the brain processes information through integrating patterns, seeing contextual relationships, and connecting seemingly unrelated elements.

ASSONANCE: The audible repetition of vowel sounds at close intervals within words (e.g., Bound to plow down a forest . . . , Robinson Jeffers).

ASYNDETON: Lists of words, phrases, or expressions without conjunctions such as "and" and "or" to link them.

BLANK VERSE: Unrhymed iambic pentameter.

CAESURA: A pause in the poetic line that is normally signified by a comma, semi-colon, or dash; a caesura indicates both the rhythm and the sense of the line.

CINEMATIC TECHNIQUES: Terms and methods borrowed from filmmakers to communicate meaning and to produce a particular emotional or psychological response in an audience.

CONCEIT: An elaborate figure of speech comparing two extremely dissimilar things. A good conceit discovers or creates a surprisingly apt parallel between two otherwise unlikely things or feelings (e.g., My love is like a red, red rose).

COUPLET: A pair of successive rhyming lines, usually of the same length. The term is commonly used today to refer to two-line stanzas of free verse.

CONSONANCE: The audible repetition of consonant sounds in words encountered near each other whose vowel sounds are different (e.g., rider-reader).

DACTYL: A metrical foot consisting of an accented syllable followed by two unaccented ones.

DRAMATIC MONOLOGUE: A poem containing the sensation of one person speaking who is not the author of the poem but rather a persona.

ELABORATION: Use of repetition or added detail to deepen and extend the characterization of what is being described.

ELISION: Omission of a consonant (e.g., "ere" for "ever") or a vowel (e.g., "tother" for "the other"), usually to achieve a metrical effect.

END-STOPPED LINE: A line that ends with a natural speech pause, usually marked by punctuation.

ENJAMBMENT: The carry-over of one line of poetry to the next without a grammatical break, the alternative to end-stopped lines.

FOOT: The basic unit of measurement of accentual-syllabic meter, usually considered to contain one stressed syllable and at least one unstressed syllable. The standard types of feet in English are the iamb, trochee, dactyl, and anapest. The spondee and pyrrhic are common substitutions and are often considered feet.

FREE VERSE: Poetry without a regular pattern of meter or rhyme.

IAMB: A metrical foot consisting of an unaccented syllable followed by an accented one.

IAMBIC PENTAMETER: The most common meter in English language poetry consisting of lines of five (penta) iambic feet resulting in ten syllables; each iambic foot consists of an unstressed and a stressed syllable (e.g., A *rain* of *tears,* a *cloud* of *dark* dis*dain,* Thomas Wyatt; stressed syllables in italics).

IMAGE: A concrete representation of a sensory impression, feeling, or idea.

IMAGERY: A pattern of related details, or images, in a poem.

INTERNAL RHYME: Rhymes between a word within a line, often from a medial position, and a word at the end of the line.

LINEATION/LINE BREAK: The pattern by which a poem is organized into separate lines.

LYRIC POEM: Short poem, usually about one moment in time, in which the poet, the poet's persona, or a speaker expresses personal feelings. Originally, a poem sung to a lyre, the lyric today is musical in nature—an inner expression "overheard" by the reader.

METAPHOR: Saying one thing in terms of something else by means of either explicit or implicit comparison (e.g., Shall I compare thee to a summer's day?). A Dead Metaphor is an originally metaphoric expression in which the implied comparison has been forgotten and is taken literally. Mixed Metaphor is two or more awkwardly combined metaphors.

METER: The measured pattern of rhythmic accents in a poem (e.g., iambic pentameter).

MIMESIS: The artistic imitation of life.

NARRATIVE POEM: A poem that tells a story.

PARALLELISM: Words or phrases of like value shared in grammatical constructions that create comparison.

PERSONA: An imaginary character separate from the poet who speaks in the poem.

POLYSYNDETON: A figure of speech where successive clauses or phrases are linked by one or more conjunctions.

PROSODY: A general term for the art of writing poetry, involving the study of the laws of formal structure, usually metrical.

PYRRHIC: A metrical foot consisting of two unaccented syllables.

REPETEND: Word, phrase, or line that is repeated.

RHYME (also Rime): The matching of vowel or vowel/consonant sounds, often in the final syllable, in two or more words (e.g., Though inland far we be/Our souls have sight of that immortal sea).

RHYTHM: The recurrence of accent or stress in lines of verse.

SCANSION: The scanning of verse, that is, dividing it into metrical feet and identifying its rhythm by encoding stressed syllables and unstressed syllables.

SIMILE: A comparison using like or as. All similes are metaphors, but not all metaphors are similes.

SLANT RHYME: (also Half-Rhyme or Near-Rhyme): Approximate rhyme, matching end consonants but not vowels (e.g., Before him, on a coal-black sleeve . . . Insignia that could not revive, Thom Gunn).

SONNET: A fourteen-line poem, usually in iambic pentameter, with a varied rhyme scheme. Common types are English, Italian, and Petrarchan.

SOUND SYSTEM: The overall system of sonic devices employed by writers of verse to convey and reinforce the meaning or experience of poetry through the skillful use of sound.

SPEAKER: The dramatic voice in which we hear the poem, whether it is assumed to be the poet or an adopted persona.

SPONDEE: A metrical foot consisting of two accented syllables.

STANZA: In formal poetry, a division or unit of a poem that is repeated in the same form, with similar or identical patterns of rhyme and meter. In free verse, stanza breaks might not follow defined patterns.

STYLE: The manner of expression of a particular writer, produced by choice of words, grammatical structures, use of literary devices, and all the possible parts of language use.

SYLLABIC VERSE: A metrical system that measures only the number of syllables in a line, without regard to their stress.

SYMBOL: Something in the world of the senses, including an action, that reveals or stands for a thing that is abstract.

SYMPLOCE: First or last words in a clause or sentence are repeated in successive clauses (e.g., What are joys but an imaginary world. / What is pain but the condition of the world.)

SYNAERESIS: The contraction of two syllables into one, for metrical purposes (e.g., "disobedience" becomes "disobed-yence.")

SYNESTHESIA: A blending of different senses in describing something.

TENSION: The artistically satisfying equilibrium of opposing forces in a poem, usually referring to the use of language and imagery, but often applied to other elements, such as dramatic structure, rhythmic patterns, and sometimes to the aesthetic value of the poem as a whole.

TROCHEE: A metrical foot consisting of an accented syllable followed by an unaccented syllable.

VERSE: As a mass noun, poetry in general; as a regular noun, a line of poetry.

CONTRIBUTOR NOTES

LAVONNE J. ADAMS, MFA coordinator and lecturer, is the author of *Through the Glorieta Pass* (Pearl Editions, 2009) and two award-winning chapbooks, *In the Shadow of the Mountain* and *Everyday Still Life*. She has published in more than fifty additional venues, including *The Missouri Review, Southern Poetry Review,* and *Poet Lore*.

TIM BASS teaches fiction and creative nonfiction in UNCW's Department of Creative Writing. He is a former newspaper reporter.

KAREN BENDER, instructor of creative writing, is the author of a novel, *Like Normal People* (Houghton Mifflin, 2000). Her short fiction has appeared in *The New Yorker, Granta, Zoetrope, Ploughshares, Harvard Review, Story,* and other magazines. It has been reprinted in *Best American Short Stories, Best American Mystery Stories, New Stories from the South: The Year's Best,* and has been awarded two Pushcart Prizes. She has received grants from the NEA and the Rona Jaffe Foundation.

EMMA BOLDEN, alumna of the MFA program, is the author of three chapbooks of poetry: *How to Recognize a Lady,* published as part of *Edge by Edge* (Toadlily Press, 2008); *The Mariner's Wife* (Finishing Line Press, 2008); and *The Sad Epistles* (Dancing Girl Press, 2009). Her work has appeared in such journals as *Indiana Review, Prairie Schooner, Verse,* and *Green Mountains Review*. She was the recipient of a Tennessee Williams Scholarship for the Sewanee Writers' Conference and was named a finalist for a Ruth Lily Fellowship. She is an assistant professor of English at Georgetown College, where she also serves as poetry editor of the *Georgetown Review*.

WENDY BRENNER, associate professor, is the author of two books of fiction, *Phone Calls from the Dead* (Algonquin, 2001) and *Large Animals in Everyday Life* (W.W. Norton, 1997). Her stories and essays have appeared in *Seventeen, Allure, Travel & Leisure,* and many other magazines, and have been anthologized in *New Stories from the South* and *Best American Magazine Writing*.

STANLEY COLBERT, former distinguished visiting professor, previously served as CEO of HaperCollins Canada and literary agent for writers including Jack Kerouac. At UNCW he founded the Publishing Laboratory as a student-run micropress.

Professor **MARK COX**'s honors include a Whiting Writers' Award, a Pushcart Prize, the Oklahoma Book Award, the Society of Midland Authors Poetry Prize, and varied fellowships. He has served as poetry editor of *Passages North* and of *Cimarron Review*, and as Poet in Residence at The Frost Place. His books are *Barbells of the Gods* (Ampersand, 1988), *Smoulder* (Godine, 1989), *Thirty Seven Years from the Stone* (Pitt Poetry Series, 1998), and *Natural Causes* (Pitt Poetry Series, 2004).

NINA DE GRAMONT, instructor of creative writing and alumna of the MFA program, is the author of the short story collection *Of Cats and Men* (The Dial Press, 2002) and the novels *Gossip of the Starlings* (Algonquin, 2008) and *Every Little Thing in the World* (Atheneum 2010). She is also co-editor of the anthology *Choice*. Her work has appeared in *Redbook*, *Seventeen*, *Nerve*, *Harvard Review*, and *Post Road*.

CLYDE EDGERTON, professor, is the author of nine novels, a memoir, short stories, and essays. His story "Send Me to the Electric Chair" appeared in *Best American Short Stories*. He has been a Guggenheim Fellow and five of his novels have been New York Times Notable Books. He is a member of the Fellowship of Southern Writers.

PHILIP FURIA, professor, is the author of biographies of Irving Berlin, Ira Gershwin, and Johnny Mercer as well as other books and essays on American popular song that have been noted in the *New York Times*, *The Atlantic*, and *The New Yorker*. He has appeared on *Larry King Live*, A&E's *Biography*, the *Studs Terkel Show*, *All Things Considered*, and *Fresh Air* with Terry Gross.

BEN GEORGE, lecturer, is editor of the literary journal *Ecotone*. His work has appeared in *Tin House*, *Ninth Letter*, and elsewhere, and has been nominated for the Best New American Voices series. He is the editor of the anthology *The Book of Dads: Essays on the Joys, Perils, and Humiliations of Fatherhood* (Ecco/HarperCollins, 2009).

PHILIP GERARD, professor and department chair, is the author of three novels and four books of creative nonfiction, in addition to eleven scripts for public television, numerous short stories, essays, and reviews, and a radio drama, *1898: An American Coup*.

DAVID GESSNER, associate professor, is the author of six books of literary nonfiction, including *Sick of Nature* (University Press of New England, 2004), *Return of the Osprey* (Algonquin, 2001), and *Soaring with Fidel* (Beacon Press, 2008). His recent essays have appeared in the *New York Times Magazine*, *Best American Nonrequired Reading*, *Pushcart Prize XXX: Best of the Small Presses* (2006), and on National Public Radio's *This I Believe*. He is editor-in-chief of the literary journal *Ecotone*.

ELI HASTINGS, alumnus of the MFA program, is the author of the book of essays *Falling Room* (University of Nebraska Press, 2005). His work has appeared in more than a dozen journals including *580 Split* and the anthologies *Men Speak Out!* and *American Lives: A Reader* from the University of Nebraska Press. His essay in *Third Coast* was nominated for a Pushcart Prize and his essay in *Alligator Juniper* won their nonfiction contest.

VIRGINIA HOLMAN, former visiting professor, is the author of the memoir *Rescuing Patty Hearst* (Simon & Schuster, 2004). Her writing has appeared in numerous publications including *DoubleTake, Redbook, Women's Health, Atlanta Journal Constitution,* and the *Washington Post.* She's received a Pushcart Prize, a North Carolina Arts Council Fellowship and a Rosalyn Carter Mental Health Journalism Fellowship.

BRAD LAND, alumnus of the MFA program, is the author of the national bestselling memoir *Goat* (Random House, 2004) and the novel *Pilgrims Upon the Earth* (Random House, 2007). His work has appeared in national magazines and literary journals and has been anthologized in the collection *When I Was a Loser: True Stories of (Barely) Surviving High School* (Free Press, 2007).

REBECCA LEE, associate professor, is the author of *The City is a Rising Tide* (Simon & Schuster, 2006). Her short stories and essays have appeared in *The Atlantic* and *Zoetrope.* She has received a Rona Jaffe Award and a National Magazine Award for fiction.

SEBASTIAN MATTHEWS, visiting writer, is the author of the poetry collection *We Generous* (Red Hen Press, 2007) and the memoir *In My Father's Footsteps* (W.W. Norton, 2004). He co-edited, with Stanley Plumly, *Search Party: Collected Poems of William Matthews* (Houghton Mifflin Harcourt, 2004). Matthews teaches at Warren Wilson College and at the University of North Carolina Asheville's Great Smokies Writing Program. He serves on faculty at the low-residency MFA Program in Creative Writing at Queens University.

SARAH MESSER, associate professor, has published a book of poetry, *Bandit Letters* (New Issues, 2001), and a hybrid history/memoir, *Red House: Being a Mostly Accurate Account of New England's Oldest Continuously Lived-in House* (Viking, 2004). Her work is widely anthologized, and she has received fellowships from the Fine Arts Work Center in Provincetown, the National Endowment for the Arts, the North Carolina Arts Council, and the Radcliffe Institute for Advanced Study, among others.

MALENA MÖRLING, associate professor, is the author of two books of poetry: *Ocean Avenue,* winner of the New Issues Press Poetry Prize in 1998, and *Astoria* (Pitt Poetry Series, 2006). She has translated poems by the Swedish poet Tomas Tranströmer, a selection of which appeared in the collection *For the Living and the Dead* (Ecco, 1995). Her poems have appeared in the *New York Times Book Review,* the *New Republic,* and *Five Points.* She was awarded the Rona Jaffe Foundation Writers Award in 1999 and in 2004 the Lotos Club Foundation Prize. In 2007 she was awarded a John Simon Guggenheim Foundation Fellowship.

JASON MOTT, alumnus of the BFA and MFA programs, is the author of the debut poetry collection *We Call This Thing Between Us Love* (Main Street Rag, 2010) and has published in journals and anthologies including *Kakalak: Anthology of Carolina Poets,*

Thomas Wolfe Review, and *Chautauqua*. He was born and raised in Columbus County, North Carolina and grew up with a bitter hatred of sonnets and a passionate love of superheroes. Only one of these has changed.

DEREK NIKITAS, alumnus of the MFA program, is the author of the novel *Pyres* (St. Martin's Minotaur, 2007), which was nominated for an Edgar Award. His second novel, *The Long Division*, is forthcoming in 2009 from St. Martin's Minotaur. His stories have appeared in the *Ontario Review*, *Chelsea*, *Ellery Queen*, and elsewhere. He teaches creative writing in Eastern Kentucky University's MFA program.

DANA SACHS teaches part-time at UNCW. She is the author of the novel *If You Lived Here* (William Morrow, 2007) and *The House on Dream Street: Memoir of an American Woman in Vietnam* (Algonquin, 2000). Her nonfiction book about Operation Babylift, the U.S.-sponsored evacuation of Vietnamese Children at the end of the war in that country, is forthcoming from Beacon Press in 2010.

ROBERT ANTHONY SIEGEL, associate professor, is the author of two novels: *All Will Be Revealed* (MacAdam/Cage, 2007) and *All the Money in the World* (Random House, 1997). Please visit him at www.robertanthonysiegel.com.

GEORGE SINGLETON, former visiting professor, is the author of four collections of shorts stories and two novels. His stories have appeared in magazines including *The Atlantic*, *Harper's*, *Playboy*, *Zoetrope*, *Glimmer Train*, *The Georgia Review*, and the *Southern Review*, among others. His work has been anthologized in nine editions of *New Stories from the South*. He lives in Dacusville, South Carolina.

EMILY LOUISE SMITH, lecturer and alumna of the MFA program, directs the department's book imprint, The Publishing Laboratory. Her poems have appeared in *Columbia Poetry Review*, *The Journal*, *Smartish Pace*, and *Tar River Poetry*, among others. She served as writer-in-residence for the Hub City Writers Project in 2006.

SHARAN STRANGE, former visiting writer, is the author of a collection of poems, *Ash* (Beacon Press, 2001), awarded the Barnard Women Poets Prize in 2000. She teaches creative writing at Spelman College and has served as McEver Visiting Chair in Poetry at the Georgia Institute of Technology and resident writer at Fisk University, the California Institute for the Arts, and Wheaton College. She is a contributing editor of *Callaloo* and community board member of Poetry Atlanta.

DANIEL NATHAN TERRY, alumnus of the BFA and MFA programs, is the author of the debut poetry collection *Capturing the Dead* (NFSPS Press, 2008), which won the 2007 Stevens Manuscript prize. His poetry has appeared in journals including *Weber: The Contemporary West*, *The Adirondack Review*, *The MacGuffin*, and *Oberon*.

PETER TRACHTENBERG, assistant professor of creative writing in 2008 and 2009, is the author of *7 Tattoos: A Memoir in the Flesh* (Crown, 1997) and *The Book of Calamities:*

Five Questions About Suffering and its Meaning (Little, Brown, 2008). He is the winner of a Whiting Writer's Award, an artist's fellowship from the New York Foundation for the Arts, and the Nelson Algren Award for Short Fiction. Please visit him at www.peter-trachtenberg.com

MICHAEL WHITE, professor, holds a PhD in English and creative writing from the University of Utah. He has published several collections of poetry, including *Palma Cathedral* (Center for Literary Publishing, University of Colorado, 1998), which won the Colorado Prize, and *Re-entry* (University of North Texas Press, 2006), which won the Vassar Miller Prize. His poetry and prose have appeared in venues such as *Kenyon Review*, *Paris Review*, *The New Republic*, *New England Review*, *Ploughshares*, *Best American Poetry*, and many others.

The Publishing Laboratory gratefully acknowledges permission from the following contributors and their publishers to reprint selections in this volume.

Adams, Lavonne. "How the Earth Became Bountiful (A Cheyenne Tale)" from *Through the Glorieta Pass* (Long Beach, CA: Pearl Editions, 2009). "A Process in the Weather of the Heart" originally appeared in the Tupelo Press Poetry Project (www.tupelopress.org, July 2007); "Echocardiogram" in *Alehouse* (2008); "Composition" in *Raleigh News & Observer* (15 June 2003); "Tuning the Pipe Organ" in *Busted Halo.com*, (5 March 2008); "Confession" in *Busted Halo.com*, (30 July 2007); and "After the Ice Storm" in *Louisville Review* 64 (Fall 2008).

Bass, Tim. "You Want Fries With That?" originally appeared in *Calliope* (Spring 2003); "Confessions of a Dimwitted Word Thief" originally appeared in *Fugue* 32 (2007).

Bender, Karen E. "The Fourth Prussian Dynasty: An Era of Romance and Royalty," from *Like Normal People* (Houghton Mifflin, 2000), first appeared in *The New Yorker* (1999).

Bolden, Emma. All poems from *How to Recognize a Lady* in *Edge by Edge*. Quartet Series 3 (Chappaqua, NY: Toadlily Press, 2007).

Brenner, Wendy. "I Am the Bear," from *Large Animals in Everyday Life* (Athens: University of Georgia Press, 1996, and New York: W.W. Norton, 1997), first appeared in *Mississippi Review* 23, no. 1/2 (1994); "Love and Death in the Cape Fear Serpentarium" first appeared in *Oxford American* 48, (2005), and was reprinted in *Best American Magazine Writing* (New York: Columbia University Press, 2006).

Colbert, Stanley. "Notes on the Great Depression" originally appeared in the *Globe and Mail* (Toronto: December 2008).

Cox, Mark. "The Door" from *Thirty-Seven Years with Simile and Sonata*; "Things My Grandfather Must Have Said" from *Smoulder* (Jaffrey, NH: David R. Godine, Publisher, 1989); "Better Homes and Gardens" from *Natural Causes* (Pittsburgh: University of Pittsburgh Press, 2004); "Like a Simile" and "Sonata" from *Thirty-Seven Years from the Stone* (Pittsburgh: University of Pittsburgh Press, 1998).

de Gramont, Nina. "By His Wild Lone" from *Of Cats and Men* (New York: The Dial Press, Random House, 2001).

Edgerton, Clyde. "Send Me to the Electric Chair," from *Oxford American* (1996), was reprinted in *Best American Short Stories*, ed. E. Annie Proulx (Boston and New York: Houghton Mifflin Company, 1997).

Furia, Phil. "Blue Skies" from *Irving Berlin: A Life in Song*. (New York: Schirmer Books, 1998).

Gerard, Philip. "Hardball," from *Baseball: The National Pastime in Art and Literature*, ed. David Colbert (Time Life Books, 2001), originally appeared in *River Teeth* (Winter 2000); "What *Is* Creative Nonfiction Anyhow?" reprinted with permission of Waveland Press, Inc. from *Creative Nonfiction: Researching and Crafting Stories of Real Life*, rev. ed. (Long Grove, IL: Waveland Press, Inc., 1996 [reissued 2004]); "A Flexible Flyer," from *North Carolina Literary Review* 14 (2005), was originally commissioned for a live performance on WHQR public radio.

Gessner, David. "Learning to Surf" originally appeared in *Orion*, (March/April 2006).

Hastings, Eli. "Out in Front," from *Falling Room*, (Lincoln, NE: University of Nebraska Press / Bison Books, American Lives Series, ed. Tobias Wolff, 2005).

Holman, Virginia. "Three Walks" first appeared in *Rambler Magazine* 5, no. 3 (2008).

Land, Brad. "Brothers in Harm," from *Goat: A Memoir* (New York: Random House, 2004), originally appeared in *GQ* (January 2004).

Lee, Rebecca. "The Banks of the Vistula" originally appeared in *The Atlantic* (September 1997).

Matthews, Sebastian. "Zones of Providence" and "Miracle Day" first appeared in *Valparaiso Poetry Review* (2009).

Messer, Sarah. "The Fire" from *Red House: Being a Mostly Accurate Account of New England's Oldest Continuously Lived-In House* (New York: Viking Penguin, 2004). All poems from *Bandit Letters* (Kalamazoo, MI: New Issues, Western Michigan University, 2001).

Mörling, Malena. All poems from *Astoria* (Pittsburgh: University of Pittsburgh Press, 2006); "If There Is Another World" first appeared in *Five Points* 9, no. 2 (2005); "A Story" in *Poetry 30: Thirty-something American Thirty-something Poets*, eds. Gerry Lafemina and Daniel Crocker (DuBois: Mammoth Books, 2005); "Wallpaper" in *Hunger Mountain* (Fall 2005).

Mott, Jason. "From Death Row, An Interview with a Wolf" first appeared *Dante's Heart* (Spring 2008); "The 47 Seconds Between LA & NY" in *Prick of the Spindle* 2, no. 2 (June 2008); "Thinly Veiled, Young Man Comes to Me Seeking a Friendly Face" in *Chautauqua* 6 (2009).

Nikitas, Derek. "All Nite Video" appeared in *The Pedestal Magazine*, Issue 33 (2006).

Sachs, Dana. Excerpt from *The House on Dream Street: Memoir of an American Woman in Vietnam* (Chapel Hill, NC: Algonquin Books, 2000).

Siegel, Robert Anthony. "My Refugee," from *Holocaust: A Literary Remembrance* (Wilmington, NC: Cameron Art Museum, 2008), first appeared on Nextbook.com.

Singleton, George. "Show-and-Tell," from *The Half-Mammals of Dixie* (Chapel Hill, NC: Algonquin Books, 2002 and Harcourt Harvest, 2003), originally appeared in *The Atlantic* (July/August 2001).

Smith, Emily Louise. "Remnants" first appeared in *Beloved on the Earth: 150 Poems of Grief and Gratitude* (Duluth, MN: Holy Cow! Press, 2009); "Close of Season" in *Smartish Pace* 12 (2005); "Small Hours" in *Front Porch Journal* (March 2007); and "Interview with the Past" in *Kakalak 2006: An Anthology of Carolina Poets*, (Charlotte, NC: Main Street Rag Publishing, 2006).

Strange, Sharan. "Night Work," "Jimmy's First Cigarette," and "Childhood" appear in *Ash* (Boston: Beacon Press, 2001); "Claim" in *The Ringing Ear: Black Poets Lean South*, ed. Nikky Finney (Athens: University of Georgia Press, 2007); "Making Metaphor" in *Java Monkey Speaks: A Poetry Anthology* 3, eds. Kodac Harrison and Collin Kelley (Atlanta: Poetry Atlanta Press, 2008).

Terry, Daniel Nathan. All poems from *Capturing the Dead*. (Rochester Hills, MI: NFSPS Press, 2008). "The Witch's Tree" first appeared in *Atlantis* (2006).

Trachtenberg, Peter. "Cloudburst" first appeared in *The New Yorker* (21 April 2003).

White, Michael. "The Levee" and "Re-Entry" first appeared in *Paris Review*; "Ann Frank's Tree" in *Holocaust: A Literary Remembrance* (Wilmington, NC: Cameron Art Museum, 2008).